SQL Server Advanced Troubleshooting and Performance Tuning
Best Practices and Techniques

Dmitri Korotkevich

Beijing · Boston · Farnham · Sebastopol · Tokyo

SQL Server Advanced Troubleshooting and Performance Tuning

by Dmitri Korotkevitch

Published by O'Reilly Media, Inc., 1005 Gravenstein Highway North, Sebastopol, CA 95472.

O'Reilly books may be purchased for educational, business, or sales promotional use. Online editions are also available for most titles (*http://oreilly.com*). For more information, contact our corporate/institutional sales department: 800-998-9938 or *corporate@oreilly.com*.

Acquisitions Editor: Andy Kwan	**Indexer:** Potomac Indexing, LLC
Development Editor: Sarah Grey	**Interior Designer:** David Futato
Production Editor: Beth Kelly	**Cover Designer:** Karen Montgomery
Copyeditor: Audrey Doyle	**Illustrator:** Kate Dullea
Proofreader: Piper Editorial Consulting, LLC	

May 2022:   First Edition

Revision History for the First Edition

2022-05-13:   First Release

See *http://oreilly.com/catalog/errata.csp?isbn=9781098101923* for release details.

978-1-098-10192-3

[LSI]

Table of Contents

Preface

It's been a few years since I published my last book. Many things have changed since then. Several SQL Server versions have been released. The product has become more mature, offering cross-OS support and true cloud-friendly capabilities. Nevertheless, I did not think it was the right time to publish the new edition of *Pro SQL Server Internals* (Apress).

There were a couple reasons for that. As great as the new features were, they did not change the way the product works *fundamentally*. Most of the content from my old books could be applied to SQL Server 2017, SQL Server 2019, and even upcoming SQL Server 2022 releases. More importantly, I wanted to write the book in a different way.

Perhaps, I need to elaborate. As some of you may know, I've been delivering SQL Server courses for many years, and I considered my books as supplementary materials for them. In fact, I started to write because I wanted to present the content in a more structured, non–Power Point format. I am glad that my readers liked it and found the books especially useful.

All my courses focused on SQL Server Internals. I've always believed that any professional needs to know their tools to be successful. I taught my audience how SQL Server works, helping them to use this knowledge and build efficient systems. Over time, however, I found that troubleshooting and performance tuning became the most popular topic in my classes—people like when I start with the *problem* and then explain *why* it occurs.

As I changed the way I teach, I also decided to change the way I write. Now, 18 months later, you look at the result of that decision. Personally, I like the outcome. It is still about SQL Server Internals, although, it is concise and more practical than any of my previous works. It would give you enough knowledge to detect and address key system issues, reducing the information overload. It will also point you in the right direction if you'd like to learn more.

This book describes the methodology used by many high-end SQL Server consultants. You'll learn how to collect and analyze the data, detecting bottlenecks and inefficiencies. More importantly, I'll show you how to look at the system *holistically* and avoid tunnel vision.

The content is not SQL Server–version specific. With a few exceptions, it would apply to all versions from SQL Server 2005 to soon-to-be-released SQL Server 2022 and beyond. It also works for managed SQL Server services running in the cloud.

Who This Book Is For

When people ask me about the target audience of my books, I always say that I write for *database professionals*. I purposefully use that term—I believe that the line that separates database administrators, database developers, and even application developers is quite thin. It is impossible to be successful in IT nowadays if you limit yourself and don't expand your area of expertise and responsibilities.

It is especially important with the DevOps culture. The teams become the owners of their destinies, developing and maintaining solutions on their own. It becomes common for developers to troubleshoot performance issues that may be caused by the infrastructure or inefficient database code.

In the end, if you work with SQL Server in any role—on-premises and in the cloud—this book is for you. I hope that you'll find useful information regardless of what your job title is.

Thank you again for your trust in me and I hope you will enjoy reading it as much as I did while writing it for you!

Overview of the Chapters

This book consists of 16 chapters structured in the following way:

- Chapter 1, "SQL Server Setup and Configuration", provides several guidelines and best practices on how to choose the hardware and configure SQL Server instances.

- Chapter 2, "SQL Server Execution Model and Wait Statistics", discusses a vital SQL Server component—SQLOS—and introduces you to the common troubleshooting technique called Wait Statistics. This chapter is the cornerstone for the book content.

- Chapter 3, "Disk Subsystem Performance", gives you an overview of how SQL Server works with I/O subsystem and shows you how to analyze and troubleshoot its performance.

- Chapter 4, "Inefficient Queries", talks about a few methods that allow you to detect nonoptimized queries and choose targets for further query tuning.

- Chapter 5, "Data Storage and Query Tuning", explains how SQL Server works with data in the database, and shares the set of query tuning tips and techniques.

- Chapter 6, "CPU Load", discusses most common causes that lead to high CPU load and the ways to mitigate CPU bottlenecks.

- Chapter 7, "Memory Issues", covers memory configuration in SQL Server and shows you how to analyze memory usage and address memory-related issues.

- Chapter 8, "Locking, Blocking, and Concurrency", talks about SQL Server's concurrency model and how to remediate blocking and deadlocks in the system.

- Chapter 9, "tempdb Usage and Performance", discusses tempdb utilization, and configuration best practices. It also provides a few guidelines on the optimal usage of temporary objects and shows how to mitigate common tempdb bottlenecks.

- Chapter 10, "Latches", talks about latches in SQL Server. It covers several cases when they may become the problem and the ways to address that.

- Chapter 11, "Transaction Log", provides an overview of how SQL Server works with a transaction log and explains how to deal with common bottlenecks and error conditions.

- Chapter 12, "AlwaysOn Availability Groups", covers the most frequently used SQL Server High Availability technology and common issues you may encounter in that setup.

- Chapter 13, "Other Notable Wait Types", discusses several common wait types that have not been covered in other chapters.

- Chapter 14, "Database Schema and Index Analysis", gives you a few tips on how to detect inefficiencies in database design and also evaluate usage and health of the indexes.

- Chapter 15, "SQL Server in Virtualized Environments", talks about configuration best practices and troubleshooting of virtualized SQL Server instances.

- Chapter 16, "SQL Server in the Cloud", discusses how to configure and use SQL Server in cloud VMs. It also provides an overview of managed SQL Server services available in Microsoft Azure, Amazon AWS, and Google GCP.

Each chapter will end with a "Troubleshooting Checklist" that covers the most important troubleshooting steps for the topic covered in the chapter.

Finally, use Appendix A, "Wait Types", as the reference for common wait types and troubleshooting techniques when you encounter them during the analysis.

Conventions Used in This Book

The following typographical conventions are used in this book:

Italic

>Indicates new terms, URLs, email addresses, filenames, and file extensions.

`Constant width`

>Used for program listings, as well as within paragraphs to refer to program elements such as variable or function names, databases, data types, environment variables, statements, and keywords.

`Constant width bold`

>Shows commands or other text that should be typed literally by the user.

`Constant width italic`

>Shows text that should be replaced with user-supplied values or by values determined by context.

 This element signifies a tip or suggestion.

 This element signifies a general note.

 This element indicates a warning or caution.

Using Code Examples

Supplemental material (code examples, exercises, etc.) is available for download at *https://github.com/aboutsqlserver/code*.

The `Troubleshooting Scripts` folder provides the set of Azure Data Studio[1] note-books with troubleshooting and diagnostics scripts I used in the book. You can also find example scripts and applications in the `Companion Materials (Books)` folder.

Unless noted, the scripts would work in all SQL Server versions starting with SQL Server 2005. Although, some dynamic management view columns may be unsupported in the old versions and you'd need to comment them.

I am planning to maintain and expand the diagnostics scripts library—check the repo for updates in the future.

If you have a technical question or a problem using the code examples, please send email to *bookquestions@oreilly.com*.

This book is here to help you get your job done. In general, if example code is offered with this book, you may use it in your programs and documentation. You do not need to contact us for permission unless you're reproducing a significant portion of the code. For example, writing a program that uses several chunks of code from this book does not require permission. Selling or distributing examples from O'Reilly books does require permission. Answering a question by citing this book and quoting example code does not require permission. Incorporating a significant amount of example code from this book into your product's documentation does require permission.

We appreciate, but generally do not require, attribution. An attribution usually includes the title, author, publisher, and ISBN. For example: "*SQL Server Advanced Troubleshooting and Performance Tuning* by Dmitri Korotkevitch (O'Reilly). Copyright 2022 Dmitri Korotkevitch, 978-1-098-10192-3."

If you feel your use of code examples falls outside fair use or the permission given above, feel free to contact us at *permissions@oreilly.com*.

O'Reilly Online Learning

 For more than 40 years, *O'Reilly Media* has provided technology and business training, knowledge, and insight to help companies succeed.

Our unique network of experts and innovators share their knowledge and expertise through books, articles, and our online learning platform. O'Reilly's online learning platform gives you on-demand access to live training courses, in-depth learning

---

1 You can download Azure Data Studio from the Microsoft website (*https://oreil.ly/zwwCf*).

paths, interactive coding environments, and a vast collection of text and video from O'Reilly and 200+ other publishers. For more information, visit *https://oreilly.com*.

How to Contact Us

Please address comments and questions concerning this book to the publisher:

O'Reilly Media, Inc.
1005 Gravenstein Highway North
Sebastopol, CA 95472
800-998-9938 (in the United States or Canada)
707-829-0515 (international or local)
707-829-0104 (fax)

We have a web page for this book, where we list errata, examples, and any additional information. You can access this page at *https://oreil.ly/sql-server-advanced*.

Email *bookquestions@oreilly.com* to comment or ask technical questions about this book.

For news and information about our books and courses, visit *https://oreilly.com*.

Find us on LinkedIn: *https://linkedin.com/company/oreilly-media*

Follow us on Twitter: *https://twitter.com/oreillymedia*

Watch us on YouTube: *https://youtube.com/oreillymedia*

How to Contact the Author

You can email me at *dk@aboutsqlserver.com* if you have any questions about the book or SQL Server in general. I am always happy to help any way I can.

You can also visit my blog at *https://aboutsqlserver.com*. Now that the book is published, I promise to blog more!

Acknowledgments

First and as always, I'd like to thank my family for their continuous help and support. Writing gives me the perfect excuse to avoid daily chores. I still don't understand why I can get away with it!

Next, I am enormously grateful to Erland Sommarskog, Thomas Grohser and Uwe Ricken who did a great job reviewing the manuscript. Their contributions dramatically improved the content, shaping it in its final form.

Erland Sommarskog (*https://www.sommarskog.se*) has worked with SQL Server for thirty years, and been a Microsoft Data Platform MVP since 2001. He works as an independent consultant in Stockholm, Sweden. He is passionate about sharing his knowledge and experience with the community. When he isn't playing with SQL Server, he plays bridge and enjoys traveling.

Thomas Grohser has been an IT professional for over 35 years and a Microsoft Data Platform MVP for 12 years. He has been using SQL Server since 1994 and specializes in architecture and implementation of highly secure, available, recoverable, and performing databases and their underlying infrastructure. In his spare time, Thomas loves to share the knowledge he gained over the decades with the SQL Server and data platform community by speaking at user groups and conferences all around the world.

Uwe Ricken is a Microsoft Data Platform MVP and Microsoft Certified Master (SQL Server 2008) based in Frankfurt, Germany. Uwe has worked with SQL Server since 2007, specializing in database internals, indexing, and database architecture and development. He regularly speaks at various SQL Server conferences and events, and blogs at *http://www.sqlmaster.de*.

Thank you very much, Erland, Thomas and Uwe! I truly enjoyed the ride!

Huge thanks to my colleague—Andre Fiano—one of the most knowledgeable infrastructure engineers I ever met. I learnt quite a few things from Andre over time, and he also helped me to prepare a few demos used in this book.

And, of course, I'd like to thank entire O'Reilly team and especially Sarah Grey, Elizabeth Kelly, Kate Dullea, Kristen Brown, and Audrey Doyle. Thank you for keeping my English sounding plausible and for making the impression that I can draw diagrams!

This book is about SQL Server, and I want to thank the Microsoft engineering team for their hard work on the product. I am very anxious to see how it would evolve in the future.

Last but not least, I'd like to thank all my #SQLFamily friends for all your support and encouragements! It is a pleasure to write to such a wonderful audience!

Thank you, all!

CHAPTER 1

SQL Server Setup and Configuration

Database servers never live in a vacuum. They belong to an ecosystem of one or more applications used by customers. Application databases are hosted on one or more instances of SQL Server, and these instances, in turn, run on physical or virtual hardware. The data is stored on disks that are usually shared with other customers and database systems. Finally, all components use a network for communication and storage.

The complexity and internal dependencies of database ecosystems make troubleshooting a very challenging task. From the customers' standpoint, most problems present themselves as general performance issues: applications might feel slow and unresponsive, database queries might time out, or applications might not connect to the database. The root cause of the issues could be anywhere. Hardware could be malfunctioning or incorrectly configured; the database might have inefficient schema, indexing, or code; SQL Server could be overloaded; client applications could have bugs or design issues. This means you'll need to take a holistic view of your entire system in order to identify and fix problems.

This book is about troubleshooting SQL Server issues. However, you should always start the troubleshooting process by analyzing your application's ecosystem and SQL Server environment. This chapter will give you a set of guidelines on how to perform that validation and detect the most common inefficiencies in SQL Server configurations.

First, I'll discuss the hardware and operating system setup. Next, I'll talk about SQL Server and database configuration. I'll also touch on the topics of SQL Server consolidation and the overhead that monitoring can introduce into the system.

Hardware and Operating System Considerations

In most cases, troubleshooting and performance tuning processes happen in production systems that host a lot of data and work under heavy loads. You have to deal with the issues and tune the live systems. Nevertheless, it is impossible to completely avoid a discussion about hardware provisioning, especially because after troubleshooting you may find that your servers cannot keep up with the load and need to be upgraded.

I am not going to recommend particular vendors, parts, or model numbers; computer hardware improves quickly and any such specific advice would be obsolete by the time this book is published. Instead, I'll focus on common-sense considerations with long-term relevance.

CPU

The license cost of a commercial database engine is, by far, the most expensive part in the system. SQL Server is no exception: you could build a decent server for less than the retail price of four cores in SQL Server Enterprise Edition. You should buy the most powerful CPU your budget allows, especially if you are using a non-Enterprise Edition of SQL Server, which limits the number of cores you can utilize.

Pay attention to the CPU model. Each new generation of CPU will introduce performance improvements over the previous generations. You may get performance improvements of 10% to 15% just by choosing newer CPUs, even when both generations of CPU have the same clock speed.

In some cases, when licensing cost is not an issue, you may need to choose between slower CPUs with more cores and faster CPUs with fewer cores. In that case, the choice greatly depends on system workload. In general, Online Transactional Processing (OLTP) systems, and especially In-Memory OLTP, would benefit from the higher, single-core performance. A data warehouse and analytical workload, on the other hand, may run better with a higher degree of parallelism and more cores.

Memory

There is a joke in the SQL Server community that goes like this:

> Q. *How much memory does SQL Server usually need?*
> A. *More.*

This joke has merits. SQL Server benefits from a large amount of memory, which allows it to cache more data. This, in turn, will reduce the amount of disk input/output (I/O) activity and improve SQL Server's performance. Therefore, adding more memory to the server may be the cheapest and fastest way to address some performance issues.

For example, suppose the system suffers from nonoptimized queries. You could reduce the impact of these queries by adding memory and eliminating the physical disk reads they introduce. This, obviously, does not solve the root cause of the problem. It is also dangerous, because as the data grows, it eventually may not fit into the cache. However, in some cases it may be acceptable as a temporary Band-Aid solution.

The Enterprise Edition of SQL Server does not limit the amount of memory it can utilize. Non-Enterprise editions have limitations. In terms of memory utilization, the Standard Edition of SQL Server 2014 and later can use up to 128 GB of RAM for the buffer pool, 32 GB of RAM per database for In-Memory OLTP data, and 32 GB of RAM for storing columnstore index segments. Web Edition memory usage is limited to half of what the Standard Edition provides. Factor those limits into your analysis when you are provisioning or upgrading non-Enterprise Edition instances of SQL Server. Don't forget to allocate some additional memory to other SQL Server components, such as the plan cache and lock manager.

In the end, add as much memory as you can afford. It is cheap nowadays. There is no need to over-allocate memory if your databases are small, but think about future data growth.

Disk Subsystem

A healthy, fast disk subsystem is essential for good SQL Server performance. SQL Server is a very I/O-intensive application—it is constantly reading from and writing data to disk.

There are many options for architecting the disk subsystem for SQL Server installations. The key is to build it in a way that provides low latency for I/O requests. For critical tier-1 systems, I recommend not exceeding 3 to 5 milliseconds (ms) of latency for data file reads and writes, and 1 ms to 2 ms of latency for transaction log writes. Fortunately, those numbers are now easily achieved with flash-based storage.

There's a catch, though: when you troubleshoot I/O performance in SQL Server, you need to analyze the latency metrics *within* SQL Server rather than on the storage level. It is common to see significantly higher numbers in SQL Server rather than in storage key performance indicators (KPIs), due to the queueing that may occur with I/O-intensive workloads. (Chapter 3 will discuss how to capture and analyze I/O performance data.)

If your storage subsystem provides multiple performance tiers, I recommend putting the tempdb database on the fastest drive, followed by transaction log and data files. The tempdb database is the shared resource on the server, and it is essential that it has good I/O throughput.

The writes to transaction log files are synchronous. It is critical to have low write latency for those files. The writes to the transaction log are also sequential; however, remember that placing multiple log and/or data files on the same drive will lead to random I/O across multiple databases.

As a best practice, I'd put data and log files on the different physical drives for maintainability and recoverability reasons. You need to look at the underlying storage configuration, though. In some cases, when disk arrays do not have enough spindles, splitting them across multiple LUNs may degrade disk array performance.

In my systems, I do not split clustered and nonclustered indexes across multiple filegroups by placing them on different drives. It rarely improves I/O performance unless you can completely separate storage paths across the filegroups. On the other hand, this configuration can significantly complicate disaster recovery.

Finally, remember that some SQL Server technologies benefit from good sequential I/O performance. For example, In-Memory OLTP does not use random I/O at all, and the performance of sequential reads usually becomes the limiting factor for database startup and recovery. Data warehouse scans would also benefit from sequential I/O performance when B-Tree and columnstore indexes are not heavily fragmented. The difference between sequential and random I/O performance is not very significant with flash-based storage; however, it may be a big factor with magnetic drives.

Network

SQL Server communicates with clients and other servers via the network. Obviously, it needs to provide enough bandwidth to support that communication. There are a couple of items I want to mention in this regard.

First, you need to analyze the entire network topology when you troubleshoot network-related performance. Remember that a network's throughput will be limited to the speed of its slowest component. For example, you may have a 10 Gbps uplink from the server; however, if you have a 1 Gbps switch in the network path, that would become the limiting factor. This is especially critical for network-based storage: make sure the I/O path to disks is as efficient as possible.

Second, it is a common practice to build a separate network for the cluster heartbeat in AlwaysOn Failover Clusters and AlwaysOn Availability Groups. In some cases, you may also consider building a separate network for all Availability Group traffic. This is a good approach that improves cluster reliability in simple configurations, when all cluster nodes belong to the same subnet and may utilize Layer 2 routing. However, in complex multisubnet setups, multiple networks may lead to routing issues. Be careful with such setups and make sure to properly utilize networks in cross-node communication, especially in virtual environments, which I will discuss in Chapter 15.

Virtualization adds another layer of complexity here. Consider a situation where you have a virtualized SQL Server cluster with nodes running on different hosts. You would need to check that the hosts can separate and route the traffic in the cluster network separately from the client traffic. Serving all vLan traffic through the single physical network card would defeat the purpose of a heartbeat network.

Operating Systems and Applications

As a general rule, I suggest using the most recent version of an operating system that supports your version of SQL Server. Make sure both the OS and SQL Server are patched, and implement a process to do patching regularly.

If you are using an old version of SQL Server (prior to 2016), use the 64-bit variant. In most cases, the 64-bit version outperforms the 32-bit version and scales better with the hardware.

Since SQL Server 2017, it's been possible to use Linux to host the database server. From a performance standpoint, Windows and Linux versions of SQL Server are very similar. The choice of operating system depends on the enterprise ecosystem and on what your team is more comfortable supporting. Keep in mind that Linux-based deployments may require a slightly different High Availability (HA) strategy compared to a Windows setup. For example, you may have to rely on Pacemaker instead of Windows Server Failover Cluster (WSFC) for automatic failovers.

Use a dedicated SQL Server host when possible. Remember that it's easier and cheaper to scale application servers—don't waste valuable resources on the database host!

On the same note, do not run nonessential processes on the server. I see database engineers running SQL Server Management Studio (SSMS) in remote desktop sessions all the time. It is always better to work remotely and not consume server resources.

Finally, if you are required to run antivirus software on the server, exclude any database folders from the scan.

Virtualization and Clouds

Modern IT infrastructure depends heavily on virtualization, which provides additional flexibility, simplifies management, and reduces hardware costs. As a result, more often than not you'll have to work with virtualized SQL Server infrastructure.

There is nothing wrong with that. Properly implemented virtualization gives you many benefits, with acceptable performance overhead. It adds another layer of HA with VMware vSphere vMotion or Hyper-V Live Migration. It allows you to seamlessly upgrade the hardware and simplifies database management. Unless yours is the edge case where you need to squeeze the most from the hardware, I suggest virtualizing your SQL Server ecosystem.

 The overhead from virtualization increases on large servers with many CPUs. However, it still may be acceptable in many cases.

Virtualization, however, adds another layer of complexity during troubleshooting. You need to pay attention to the host's health and load in addition to guest virtual machine (VM) metrics. To make matters worse, the performance impact of an overloaded host might not be clearly visible in standard performance metrics in a guest OS.

I will discuss several approaches to troubleshooting the virtualization layer in Chapter 15; however, you can start by working with infrastructure engineers to confirm that the host is not over-provisioned. Pay attention to the number of physical CPUs and allocated vCPUs on the host along with physical and allocated memory. Mission-critical SQL Server VMs should have resources reserved for them to avoid a performance impact.

Aside from the virtualization layer, troubleshooting virtualized SQL Server instances is the same as troubleshooting physical ones. The same applies to cloud installations when SQL Server is running within VMs. After all, the cloud is just a different datacenter managed by an external provider.

Configuring Your SQL Server

The default configuration for the SQL Server setup process is relatively decent and may be suited to light and even moderate workloads. There are several things you need to validate and tune, however.

SQL Server Version and Patching Level

SELECT @@VERSION is the first statement I run during SQL Server system health checks. There are two reasons for this. First, it gives me a glimpse of the system's patching strategy so that I can potentially suggest some improvements. Second, it helps me identify possible known issues that may exist in the system.

The latter reason is very important. Many times, customers have asked me to troubleshoot problems that had already been resolved in service packs and cumulative updates. Always look at the release notes to see if any of the issues mentioned look familiar; your problem may have already been fixed.

You might consider upgrading to the newest version of SQL Server when possible. Each version introduces performance, functional, and scalability enhancements. This is especially true if you move to SQL Server 2016 or later from older versions. SQL Server 2016 was a milestone release that included many performance enhancements. In my experience, upgrading from SQL Server 2012 to 2016 or later can improve performance by 20% to 40% without any additional steps.

It is also worth noting that starting with SQL Server 2016 SP1, many former Enterprise Edition–only features became available in the lower-end editions of the product. Some of them, like data compression, allow SQL Server to cache more data in the buffer pool and improve system performance.

Obviously, you need to test the system prior to upgrading—there is always the chance for regressions. The risk is usually small with minor patches; however, it increases with the major upgrades. You can mitigate some risks with several database options, as you will see later in this chapter.

Instant File Initialization

Every time SQL Server grows data and transaction log files—either automatically or as part of the ALTER DATABASE command—it fills the newly allocated part of the file with zeros. This process blocks all sessions that are trying to write to the corresponding file and, in the case of the transaction log, stops generating any log records. It may also generate a spike in I/O write workload.

That behavior cannot be changed for transaction log files; SQL Server always zeros them out. However, you can disable it for data files by enabling *instant file initialization (IFI)*. This speeds up data file growth and reduces the time required to create or restore databases.

You can enable IFI by giving the SA_MANAGE_VOLUME_NAME permission, also known as the *Perform Volume Maintenance Task*, to the SQL Server startup account. This can be done in the *Local Security Policy* management application (*secpol.msc*). You will need to restart SQL Server for the change to take effect.

In SQL Server 2016 and later, you can also grant this permission as part of the SQL Server setup process, as shown in Figure 1-1.

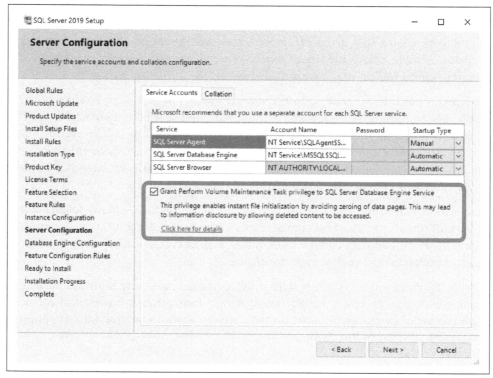

Figure 1-1. Enabling IFI during SQL Server setup

You can check whether IFI is enabled by examining the instant_file_initia lization_enabled column in the sys.dm_server_services dynamic management view (*https://oreil.ly/58Vd7*) (DMV). This column is available in SQL Server 2012 SP4, SQL Server 2016 SP1, and later. In older versions, you can run the code shown in Listing 1-1.

Listing 1-1. Checking if instant file initialization is enabled in old SQL Server versions

```
DBCC TRACEON(3004,3605,-1);
GO
CREATE DATABASE Dummy;
GO
EXEC sp_readerrorlog 0,1,N'Dummy';
GO
DROP DATABASE Dummy;
GO
DBCC TRACEOFF(3004,3605,-1);
GO
```

If IFI is not enabled, the SQL Server log will indicate that SQL Server is zeroing out the *.mdf* data file in addition to zeroing out the log *.ldf* file, as shown in Figure 1-2. When IFI is enabled, it will only show zeroing out of the log *.ldf* file.

	LogDate	ProcessInfo	Text
104	2020-10-26 15:57:45.370	spid32s	A connection timeout has occurred while attempting to establish a connection to availa…
105	2020-10-26 15:58:35.510	spid51	DBCC TRACEON 3004, server process ID (SPID) 51. This is an informational message only;…
106	2020-10-26 15:58:35.510	spid51	DBCC TRACEON 3605, server process ID (SPID) 51. This is an informational message only;…
107	2020-10-26 15:58:35.520	spid51	Zeroing C:\DB\Dummy.mdf from page 0 to 1024 (0x0 to 0x800000)
108	2020-10-26 15:58:35.530	spid51	Zeroing completed on C:\DB\Dummy.mdf (elapsed = 2 ms)
109	2020-10-26 15:58:35.530	spid51	Zeroing C:\DB\Dummy_log.ldf from page 0 to 1024 (0x0 to 0x800000)
110	2020-10-26 15:58:35.540	spid51	Zeroing completed on C:\DB\Dummy_log.ldf (elapsed = 2 ms)
111	2020-10-26 15:58:35.550	spid51	Starting up database 'Dummy'.

Figure 1-2. Checking if instant file initialization is enabled

There is a small security risk associated with this setting. When IFI is enabled, database administrators may see some data from previously deleted files in the OS by looking at newly allocated data pages in the database. This is acceptable in most systems; if so, enable it.

tempdb Configuration

The tempdb is the system database used to store temporary objects created by users and by SQL Server internally. This is a very active database and it often becomes a source of contention in the system. I will discuss how to troubleshoot tempdb-related issues in Chapter 9; in this chapter, I'll focus on configuration.

As already mentioned, you need to place tempdb on the fastest drive in the system. Generally speaking, this drive does not need to be redundant nor persistent—the database is re-created at SQL Server startup, and local SSD disk or cloud ephemeral storage would work fine. Remember, however, that SQL Server will go down if tempdb is unavailable, so factor that into your design.

If you are using a non-Enterprise Edition of SQL Server and the server has more memory than SQL Server can consume, you can put tempdb on the RAM drive. Don't do this with SQL Server Enterprise Edition, though—you'll usually achieve better performance by using that memory for the buffer pool.

 Pre-allocate tempdb files to the maximum size of the RAM drive and create additional small data and log files on disk to avoid running out of space. SQL Server will not use small on-disk files until RAM drive files are full.

The tempdb database should always have multiple data files. Unfortunately, the default configuration created at SQL Server setup is not optimal, especially in the old versions of the product. I will discuss how to fine-tune the number of data files in tempdb in Chapter 9, but you can use the following as a rule of thumb in the initial configuration:

- If the server has eight or fewer CPU cores, create the same number of data files.
- If the server has more than eight CPU cores, use either eight data files or one-fourth the number of cores, whichever is greater, rounding up in batches of four files. For example, use 8 data files in the 24-core server and 12 data files in the 40-core server.

Finally, make sure all tempdb data files have the same initial size and auto-growth parameters specified in megabytes (MB) rather than in percentages. This will allow SQL Server to better balance usage of the data files, reducing possible contention in the system.

Trace Flags

SQL Server uses trace flags to enable or change the behavior of some product features. Although Microsoft has introduced more and more database and server configuration options in new versions of SQL Server, trace flags are still widely used. You will need to check any trace flags that are present in the system; you may also need to enable some of them.

You can get the list of enabled trace flags by running the DBCC TRACESTATUS command. You can enable them in SQL Server Configuration Manager and/or by using the -T SQL Server startup option.

Let's look at some common trace flags:

T1118

This trace flag prevents usage of mixed extents (*https://oreil.ly/CnPxm*) in SQL Server. This will help improve `tempdb` throughput in SQL Server 2014 and earlier versions by reducing the number of changes and, therefore, contention in `tempdb` system catalogs. This trace flag is not required in SQL Server 2016 and later, where `tempdb` does not use mixed extents by default.

T1117

With this trace flag, SQL Server auto-grows all data files in the filegroup when one of the files is out of space. It provides more balanced I/O distribution across data files. You should enable this trace flag to improve `tempdb` throughput in old versions of SQL Server; however, check if any users' databases have filegroups with multiple unevenly sized data files. As with `T1118`, this trace flag is not required in SQL Server 2016 and later, where `tempdb` auto-grows all data files by default.

T2371

By default, SQL Server automatically updates statistics only after 20% of the data in the index has been changed. This means that with large tables, statistics are rarely updated automatically. The `T2371` trace flag changes this behavior, making the statistics update threshold dynamic—the larger the table is, the lower the percentage of changes required to trigger the update. Starting with SQL Server 2016, you can also control this behavior via database compatibility level. Nevertheless, I still recommend enabling this trace flag unless all databases on the server have a compatibility level of 130 or above.

T3226

With this trace flag, SQL Server does not write information about successful database backups to the error log. This may help reduce the size of the logs, making them more manageable.

T1222

This trace flag writes deadlock graphs to the SQL Server error log. This flag is benign; however, it makes SQL Server logs harder to read and parse. It is also redundant—you can get a deadlock graph from a `System_Health` Extended Event session when needed. I usually remove this trace flag when I see it.

T4199

This trace flag and the `QUERY_OPTIMIZER_HOTFIXES` database option (in SQL Server 2016 and later) control the behavior of Query Optimizer hotfixes. When this trace flag is enabled, the hotfixes introduced in service packs and cumulative updates will be used. This may help address some Query Optimizer bugs and improve query performance; however, it also increases the risk of plan regressions after patching. I usually do not enable this trace flag in production systems unless it is possible to perform thorough regression testing of the system before patching.

T7412

This trace flag enables lightweight execution profiling of the infrastructure in SQL Server 2016 and 2017. This allows you to collect execution plans and many execution metrics for the queries in the system, with little CPU overhead. I will discuss it in more detail in Chapter 5.

To summarize, in SQL Server 2014 and earlier, enable T1118, T2371, and potentially, T1117. In SQL Server 2016 and later, enable T2371 unless all databases have a compatibility level of 130 or above. After that, look at all other trace flags in the system and understand what they are doing. Some trace flags may be inadvertently installed by third-party tools and can negatively affect server performance.

Server Options

SQL Server provides many configuration settings. I'll cover many of them in depth later in the book; however, there are a few settings worth mentioning here.

Optimize for Ad-hoc Workloads

The first configuration setting I'll discuss is *Optimize for Ad-hoc Workloads*. This configuration option controls how SQL Server caches the execution plans of ad-hoc (nonparameterized) queries. When this setting is disabled (by default), SQL Server caches the full execution plans of those statements, which may significantly increase plan cache memory usage. When this setting is enabled, SQL Server starts by caching the small structure (just a few hundred bytes), called the *plan stub*, replacing it with the full execution plan if an ad-hoc query is executed the second time.

In the majority of cases, ad-hoc statements are not executed repeatedly, and it is beneficial to enable the Optimize for Ad-hoc Workloads setting in every system. It could significantly reduce plan cache memory usage at the cost of infrequent additional recompilations of ad-hoc queries. Obviously, this setting would not affect the caching behavior of parameterized queries and T-SQL database code.

 Starting with SQL Server 2019 and in the Azure SQL Database, you can control the behavior of the Optimize for Ad-hoc Workloads setting at the database level using the OPTIMIZE_FOR_AD_HOC_WORK LOADS database scoped configuration.

Max Server Memory

The second important setting is *Max Server Memory*, which controls how much memory SQL Server can consume. Database engineers love to debate how to properly configure this setting, and there are different approaches to calculate the proper value for it. Many engineers even suggest leaving the default value in place and allowing SQL Server to manage it automatically. In my opinion, it is best to fine-tune this setting, but it's important to do so correctly (Chapter 7 will discuss the details). An incorrect setting will impact SQL Server performance more than if you leave the default value in place.

One particular issue I often encounter during system health checks is severe under-provisioning of this setting. Sometimes people forget to change it after hardware or VM upgrades; other times, it's incorrectly calculated in nondedicated environments, where SQL Server is sharing the server with other applications. In both cases, you can get immediate improvements by increasing the *Max Server Memory* setting or even reconfiguring it to the default value until you perform a full analysis later.

Affinity mask

You need to check SQL Server affinity and, potentially, set an affinity mask if SQL Server is running on hardware with multiple non-uniform memory access (NUMA) nodes. In modern hardware, each physical CPU usually becomes a separate NUMA node. If you restrict SQL Server from using some of the physical cores, you need to balance SQL Server CPUs (or schedulers; see Chapter 2) evenly across NUMAs.

For example, if you are running SQL Server on a server with two 18-core Xeon processors and limiting SQL Server to 24 cores, you need to set the affinity mask to utilize 12 cores from each physical CPU. This will give you better performance than having SQL Server use 18 cores from the first processor and 6 cores from the second.

Listing 1-2 shows how to analyze the distribution of SQL Server schedulers (CPUs) between NUMA nodes. Look at the count of schedulers for each `parent_node_id` column in the output.

Listing 1-2. Checking the distribution of NUMA node schedulers (CPUs)

```
SELECT
  parent_node_id
  ,COUNT(*) as [Schedulers]
  ,SUM(current_tasks_count) as [Current]
  ,SUM(runnable_tasks_count) as [Runnable]
FROM sys.dm_os_schedulers
WHERE status = 'VISIBLE ONLINE'
GROUP BY parent_node_id;
```

Parallelism

It is important to check parallelism settings in the system. Default settings, like MAXDOP = 0 and Cost Threshold for Parallelism = 5, do not work well in modern systems. As with Max Server Memory, it is better to fine-tune the settings based on the system workload (Chapter 6 will discuss this in detail). However, my rule of thumb for generic settings is as follows:

- Set MAXDOP to one-fourth the number of available CPUs in OLTP and one-half those in data warehouse systems. In very large OLTP servers, keep MAXDOP at 16 or below. Do not exceed the number of schedulers in the NUMA node.

- Set Cost Threshold for Parallelism to 50.

Starting with SQL Server 2016 and in the Azure SQL Server Database, you can set MAXDOP on the database level using the command ALTER DATABASE SCOPED CONFIGU RATION SET MAXDOP. This is useful when the instance hosts databases that handle different workloads.

Configuration settings

As with trace flags, analyze other changes in configuration settings that have been applied on the server. You can examine current configuration options using the sys.configurations view (*https://oreil.ly/nsLMW*). Unfortunately, SQL Server does not provide a list of default configuration values to compare, so you need to hardcode it, as shown in Listing 1-3. I am including just a few configuration settings to save space, but you can download the full version of the script from this book's companion materials.

Listing 1-3. Detecting changes in server configuration settings

```
DECLARE
    @defaults TABLE
    (
        name SYSNAME NOT NULL PRIMARY KEY,
        def_value SQL_VARIANT NOT NULL
    )

INSERT INTO @defaults(name,def_value)
VALUES('backup compression default',0);
INSERT INTO @defaults(name,def_value)
VALUES('cost threshold for parallelism',5);
INSERT INTO @defaults(name,def_value)
VALUES('max degree of parallelism',0);
INSERT INTO @defaults(name,def_value)
VALUES('max server memory (MB)',2147483647);
INSERT INTO @defaults(name,def_value)
VALUES('optimize for ad hoc workloads',0);
```

```
/* Other settings are omitted in the book */
SELECT
    c.name, c.description, c.value_in_use, c.value
    ,d.def_value, c.is_dynamic, c.is_advanced
FROM
    sys.configurations c JOIN @defaults d ON
        c.name = d.name
WHERE
    c.value_in_use <> d.def_value OR
    c.value <> d.def_value
ORDER BY
    c.name;
```

Figure 1-3 shows sample output of the preceding code. The discrepancy between the `value` and `value_in_use` columns indicates pending configuration changes that require a restart to take effect. The `is_dynamic` column shows if the configuration option can be modified without a restart.

	name	description	value_in_use	value	def_value	is_dynamic	is_advanced
1	max degree of parallelism	maximum degree of paralle...	1	1	0	1	1
2	optimize for ad hoc workloads	When this option is set, ...	1	1	0	1	1

Figure 1-3. Nondefault server configuration options

Configuring Your Databases

As the next step, you'll need to validate several database settings and configuration options. Let's look at them.

Database Settings

SQL Server allows you to change multiple database settings, tuning its behavior to meet system workload and other requirements. I'll cover many of them later in the book; however, there are a few settings I would like to discuss here.

The first one is *Auto Shrink*. When this option is enabled, SQL Server periodically shrinks the database and releases unused free space from the files to the OS. While this looks appealing and promises to reduce disk space utilization, it may introduce issues.

The database shrink process works on the physical level. It locates empty space in the beginning of the file and moves allocated extents from the end of the file to the empty space, without taking extent ownership into consideration. This introduces noticeable load and leads to serious index fragmentation. What's more, in many cases it's useless: the database files simply expand again as the data grows. It's always better to manage file space manually and disable Auto Shrink.

Another database option, *Auto Close*, controls how SQL Server caches data from the database. When Auto Close is enabled, SQL Server removes data pages from the buffer pool and execution plans from the plan cache when the database does not have any active connections. This will lead to a performance impact with the new sessions when data needs to be cached and queries need to be compiled again.

With very few exceptions, you should disable Auto Close. One such exception may be an instance that hosts a large number of rarely accessed databases. Even then, I would consider keeping this option disabled and allowing SQL Server to retire cached data in the normal way.

Make sure the *Page Verify* option is set to CHECKSUM. This will detect consistency errors more efficiently and helps resolve database corruption cases.

Pay attention to the *database recovery model*. If the databases are using the SIMPLE recovery mode, it would be impossible to recover past the last FULL database backup in the event of a disaster. If you find the database in this mode, immediately discuss it with the stakeholders, making sure they understand the risk of data loss.

Database Compatibility Level controls SQL Server's compatibility and behavior on the database level. For example, if you are running SQL Server 2019 and have a database with a compatibility level of 130 (SQL Server 2016), SQL Server will behave as if the database is running on SQL Server 2016. Keeping the databases on the lower compatibility levels simplifies SQL Server upgrades by reducing possible regressions; however, it also blocks you from getting some new features and enhancements.

As a general rule, run databases on the latest compatibility level that matches the SQL Server version. Be careful when you change it: as with any version change, this may lead to regressions. Test the system before the change and make sure you can roll back the change if needed, especially if the database has a compatibility level of 110 (SQL Server 2012) or below. Increasing the compatibility level to 120 (SQL Server 2014) or above will enable a new cardinality estimation model and may significantly change execution plans for the queries. Test the system thoroughly to understand the impact of the change.

You can force SQL Server to use legacy cardinality estimation models with the new database compatibility levels by setting the LEGACY_CARDINALITY_ESTIMATION database option to ON in SQL Server 2016 and later, or by enabling the server-level trace flag T9481 in SQL Server 2014. This approach will allow you to perform upgrade or compatibility level changes in phases, reducing the impact to the system. (Chapter 5 will cover cardinality estimation in more detail and discuss how to reduce risks during SQL Server upgrades and database compatibility level changes.)

Transaction Log Settings

SQL Server uses write-ahead logging, persisting information about all database changes in a transaction log. SQL Server works with transaction logs sequentially, in merry-go-round fashion. In most cases, you won't need multiple log files in the system—they make database administration more complicated and rarely improve performance.

Internally, SQL Server splits transaction logs into chunks called Virtual Log Files (VLFs) and manages them as single units. For example, SQL Server cannot truncate and reuse a VLF if it contains just a single active log record. Pay attention to the number of VLFs in the database. Too few very large VLFs will make log management and truncation suboptimal. Too many small VLFs will degrade the performance of transaction log operations. Try not to exceed several hundred VLFs in production systems.

The number of VLFs SQL Server adds when it grows a log depends on the SQL Server version and the size of the growth. In most cases, it creates 8 VLFs when the growth size is between 64 MB and 1 GB, or 16 VLFs with growth that exceeds 1 GB. Do not use percent-based auto-growth configuration, because it generates lots of unevenly sized VLFs. Instead, change the log auto-growth setting to grow the file in chunks. I usually use chunks of 1,024 MB, which generates 128 MB VLFs, unless I need a very large transaction log.

You can count the VLFs in the database with the `sys.dm_db_log_info` DMV in SQL Server 2016 and later. In older versions of SQL Server, you can obtain that information by running `DBCC LOGINFO`. If the transaction log isn't configured well, consider rebuilding it. You can do this by shrinking the log to the minimal size and growing it in chunks of 1,024 MB to 4,096 MB.

Do not auto-shrink transaction log files. They will grow again and affect performance when SQL Server zeroes out the file. It is better to pre-allocate the space and manage log file size manually. Do not restrict the maximum size and auto-growth, though—you want logs to grow automatically in case of emergencies. (Chapter 11 will provide more details on how to troubleshoot transaction log issues.)

Data Files and Filegroups

By default, SQL Server creates new databases using the single-file PRIMARY filegroup and one transaction log file. Unfortunately, this configuration is suboptimal from performance, database management, and HA standpoints.

SQL Server tracks space usage in the data files through system pages called *allocation maps*. In systems with highly volatile data, allocation maps can be a source of contention: SQL Server serializes access to them during their modifications (more about this in Chapter 10). Each data file has its own set of allocation map pages, and you can reduce contention by creating multiple files in the filegroup with the active modifiable data.

Ensure that data is evenly distributed across multiple data files in the same filegroup. SQL Server uses an algorithm called *Proportional Fill*, which writes most of the data to the file that has the most free space available. Evenly sized data files will help balance those writes, reducing allocation map contention. Make sure all data files in the filegroup have the same size and auto-growth parameters, specified in megabytes.

You may also want to enable the AUTOGROW_ALL_FILES filegroup option (available in SQL Server 2016 and later), which triggers auto-growth for all files in the filegroup simultaneously. You can use trace flag T1117 for this in prior versions of SQL Server, but remember that this flag is set on the server level and will affect all databases and filegroups in the system.

It is often impractical or impossible to change the layout of existing databases. However, you may need to create new filegroups and move data around during performance tuning. Here are a few suggestions for doing this efficiently:

- Create multiple data files in filegroups with volatile data. I usually start with four files and increase the number if I see latching issues (see Chapter 10). Make sure all data files have the same size and auto-growth parameters specified in megabytes; enable the AUTOGROW_ALL_FILES option. For filegroups with read-only data, one data file is usually enough.

- Do not spread clustered indexes, nonclustered indexes, or large object (LOB) data across multiple filegroups. This rarely helps with performance and may introduce issues in cases of database corruption.

- Place related entities (e.g., Orders and OrderLineItems) in the same filegroup. This will simplify database management and disaster recovery.

- Keep the PRIMARY filegroup empty if possible.

Figure 1-4 shows an example of a database layout for a hypothetical eCommerce system. The data is partitioned and spread across multiple filegroups with the goal of minimizing downtime and utilizing partial database availability in case of disaster.[1] It will also allow you to improve the backup strategy by implementing partial database backups and excluding read-only data from full backups.

---

1 For a deep dive into data partitioning and disaster recovery strategies, please see my book *Pro SQL Server Internals, Second Edition* (Apress, 2016).

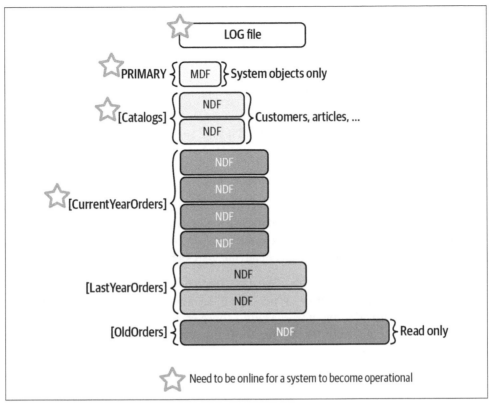

Figure 1-4. Database layout for an eCommerce system

Analyzing the SQL Server Error Log

The SQL Server Error Log is another place I usually check at the beginning of troubleshooting. I like to see any errors it has, which can point to some areas that require follow-up. For example, errors 823 and 824 can indicate issues with disk subsystem and/or database corruption.

You can read the content of the error log in SSMS. You can also get it programmatically using the xp_readerrorlog system stored procedure. The challenge here is the amount of data in the log: the noise from the information messages may hide useful data.

The code in Listing 1-4 helps you address that problem. It allows you to filter out unnecessary noise and focus on the error messages. You can control the behavior of the code with the following variables:

@StartDate *and* @EndDate
    Define the time for analysis.

@NumErrorLogs
    Specifies the number of log files to read if SQL Server rolls them over.

@ExcludeLogonErrors
    Omits logon auditing messages.

@ShowSurroundingEvents *and* @ExcludeLogonSurroundingEvents
    Allow you to retrieve the information messages around the error entries from the log. The time window for those messages is controlled by the @Surrounding EventsBeforeSeconds and @SurroundingEventsAfterSeconds variables.

The script produces two outputs. The first one shows the entries from the error log that include the word *error*. When the @ShowSurroundingEvents parameter is enabled, it also provides log entries around those error lines. You can exclude some log entries that contain the word *error* from the output by inserting them into the @ErrorsToIgnore table.

Listing 1-4. Analyzing the SQL Server error log

```
IF OBJECT_ID('tempdb..#Logs',N'U') IS NOT NULL DROP TABLE #Logs;
IF OBJECT_ID('tempdb..#Errors',N'U') IS NOT NULL DROP TABLE #Errors;
GO

CREATE TABLE #Errors
(
  LogNum INT NULL,
  LogDate DATETIME NULL,
  ID INT NOT NULL identity(1,1),
  ProcessInfo VARCHAR(50) NULL,
  [Text] NVARCHAR(MAX) NULL,
  PRIMARY KEY(ID)
);

CREATE TABLE #Logs
(
  [LogDate] DATETIME NULL,
  ProcessInfo VARCHAR(50) NULL,
  [Text] NVARCHAR(MAX) NULL
);

DECLARE
  @StartDate DATETIME = DATEADD(DAY,-7,GETDATE())
```

```
    ,@EndDate DATETIME = GETDATE()
    ,@NumErrorLogs INT = 1
    ,@ExcludeLogonErrors BIT = 1
    ,@ShowSurroundingEvents BIT = 1
    ,@ExcludeLogonSurroundingEvents BIT = 1
    ,@SurroundingEventsBeforeSecond INT = 5
    ,@SurroundingEventsAfterSecond INT = 5
    ,@LogNum INT = 0;

DECLARE
  @ErrorsToIgnore TABLE
  (
    ErrorText NVARCHAR(1024) NOT NULL
  );

INSERT INTO @ErrorsToIgnore(ErrorText)
VALUES
  (N'Registry startup parameters:%'),
  (N'Logging SQL Server messages in file%'),
  (N'CHECKDB for database%finished without errors%');

WHILE (@LogNum <= @NumErrorLogs)
BEGIN
  INSERT INTO #Errors(LogDate,ProcessInfo,Text)
    EXEC [master].[dbo].[xp_readerrorlog]
      @LogNum, 1, N'error', NULL, @StartDate, @EndDate, N'desc';
  IF @@ROWCOUNT > 0
    UPDATE #Errors SET LogNum = @LogNum WHERE LogNum IS NULL;
  SET @LogNum += 1;
END;

IF @ExcludeLogonErrors = 1
  DELETE FROM #Errors WHERE ProcessInfo = 'Logon';

DELETE FROM e
FROM #Errors e
WHERE EXISTS
(
  SELECT *
  FROM @ErrorsToIgnore i
  WHERE e.Text LIKE i.ErrorText
);

-- Errors only
SELECT * FROM #Errors ORDER BY LogDate DESC;

IF @@ROWCOUNT > 0 AND @ShowSurroundingEvents = 1
BEGIN
  DECLARE
    @LogDate DATETIME
    ,@ID INT = 0
```

```
WHILE 1 = 1
BEGIN
  SELECT TOP 1 @LogNum = LogNum, @LogDate = LogDate, @ID = ID
  FROM #Errors
  WHERE ID > @ID
  ORDER BY ID;

  IF @@ROWCOUNT = 0
    BREAK;

  SELECT
    @StartDate = DATEADD(SECOND, -@SurroundingEventsBeforeSecond, @LogDate)
    ,@EndDate = DATEADD(SECONd, @SurroundingEventsAfterSecond, @LogDate);

  INSERT INTO #Logs(LogDate,ProcessInfo,Text)
    EXEC [master].[dbo].[xp_readerrorlog]
      @LogNum, 1, NULL, NULL, @StartDate, @EndDate;
END;

IF @ExcludeLogonSurroundingEvents = 1
  DELETE FROM #Logs WHERE ProcessInfo = 'Logon';

DELETE FROM e
FROM #Logs e
WHERE EXISTS
(
  SELECT *
  FROM @ErrorsToIgnore i
  WHERE e.Text LIKE i.ErrorText
);

SELECT * FROM #Logs ORDER BY LogDate DESC;
END
```

I am not going to show the full list of possible errors here; it may be excessive and, in many cases, is system specific. But you need to analyze any suspicious data from the output and understand its possible impact on the system.

Finally, I suggest setting up alerts for high-severity errors in SQL Server Agent, if this has not already been done. You can read the Microsoft documentation (*https:// oreil.ly/AntEt*) on how to do that.

Consolidating Instances and Databases

You can't talk about SQL Server troubleshooting without discussing consolidation of database and SQL Server instances. While consolidating often reduces hardware and licensing costs, it doesn't come for free; you need to analyze its possible negative impact on current or future system performance.

There is no universal consolidation strategy that can be used with every project. You should analyze the amount of data, the load, the hardware configuration, and your business and security requirements when making this decision. However, as a general rule, avoid consolidating OLTP and data warehouse/reporting databases on the same server when they are working under a heavy load (or, if they are consolidated, consider splitting them). Data warehouse queries usually process large amounts of data, which leads to heavy I/O activity and flushes the content of the buffer pool. Taken together, this negatively affects the performance of other systems.

In addition, analyze your security requirements when consolidating databases. Some security features, such as Audit, affect the entire server and add performance overhead for all databases on the server. Transparent Data Encryption (TDE) is another example: even though TDE is a database-level feature, SQL Server encrypts tempdb when either of the databases on the server has TDE enabled. This leads to performance overhead for all other systems.

As a general rule, do not keep databases with different security requirements on the same instance of SQL Server. Look at the trends and spikes in metrics and separate databases from each other when needed. (I will provide code to help you analyze CPU, I/O, and memory usage on a per-database basis later in the book.)

I suggest utilizing virtualization and consolidating multiple VMs on one or a few hosts, instead of putting multiple independent and active databases on a single SQL Server instance. This will give you much better flexibility, manageability, and isolation between the systems, especially if multiple SQL Server instances are running on the same server. It is much easier to manage their resource consumption when you virtualize them.

Observer Effect

The production deployment of every serious SQL Server system requires implementing a monitoring strategy. This may include third-party monitoring tools, code built based on standard SQL Server technologies, or both.

A good monitoring strategy is essential for SQL Server production support. It helps you be more proactive and reduces incident detection and recovery times. Unfortunately, it does not come for free—every type of monitoring adds overhead to the system. In some cases, this overhead may be negligible and acceptable; in others it may significantly affect server performance.

During my career as an SQL Server consultant, I've seen many cases of inefficient monitoring. For example, one client was using a tool that provided information about index fragmentation by calling the `sys.dm_db_index_physical_stats` function, in `DETAILED` mode, every four hours for every index in the database. This introduced huge spikes in I/O and cleared the buffer pool, leading to a noticeable performance hit. Another client used a tool that constantly polled various DMVs, adding significant CPU load to the server.

Fortunately, in many cases, you will be able to see those queries and evaluate their impact during system troubleshooting. However, this is not always the case with other technologies; an example is with monitoring based on Extended Events (xEvents). While Extended Events is a great technology that allows you to troubleshoot complex problems in SQL Server, it is not the best choice as a profiling tool. Some events are heavy and may introduce large overhead in busy environments.

Let's look at an example that creates an xEvents session that captures queries running in the system, as shown in Listing 1-5.

Listing 1-5. Creating an xEvents session to capture queries in the system

```
CREATE EVENT SESSION CaptureQueries ON SERVER
ADD EVENT sqlserver.rpc_completed
(
  SET collect_statement=(1)
  ACTION
  (
    sqlos.task_time
    ,sqlserver.client_app_name
    ,sqlserver.client_hostname
    ,sqlserver.database_name
    ,sqlserver.nt_username
    ,sqlserver.sql_text
  )
),
ADD EVENT sqlserver.sql_batch_completed
(
  ACTION
  (
    sqlos.task_time
    ,sqlserver.client_app_name
    ,sqlserver.client_hostname
    ,sqlserver.database_name
    ,sqlserver.nt_username
    ,sqlserver.sql_text
  )
),
ADD EVENT sqlserver.sql_statement_completed
ADD TARGET package0.event_file
(SET FILENAME=N'C:\PerfLogs\LongSql.xel',MAX_FILE_SIZE=(200))
WITH
(
  MAX_MEMORY =4096 KB
  ,EVENT_RETENTION_MODE=ALLOW_SINGLE_EVENT_LOSS
  ,MAX_DISPATCH_LATENCY=5 SECONDS
);
```

Next, deploy it to a server that operates under a heavy load with a large number of concurrent requests. Measure the throughput in the system, with and without the xEvents session running. Obviously, be careful—and don't run it on the production server!

Figure 1-5 illustrates the CPU load and number of batch requests per second in both scenarios on one of my servers. As you can see, enabling the xEvents session decreased throughput by about 20%. To make matters worse, it would be very hard to detect the existence of that session on the server.

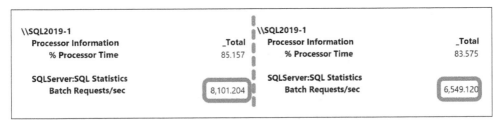

Figure 1-5. Server throughput with and without an active xEvents session

Obviously, the degree of impact would depend on the system's workload. In either case, check for any unnecessary monitoring or data collection tools when you do the troubleshooting.

The bottom line: evaluate the monitoring strategy and estimate its overhead as part of your analysis, especially when the server hosts multiple databases. For example, xEvents works at the server level. While you can filter the events based on the `database_id` field, the filtering occurs *after* an event has been fired. This can affect all databases on the server.

Summary

System troubleshooting is a holistic process that requires you to analyze your entire ecosystem. You need to look at the hardware, OS, and virtualization layers, and at the SQL Server and database configurations, and adjust them as needed.

SQL Server provides many settings that you can use to fine-tune the installation to the system workload. There are also best practices that apply to most systems, including enabling the IFI and Optimize for Ad-Hoc Workloads settings, increasing the number of files in `tempdb`, turning on some trace flags, disabling Auto Shrink, and setting up correct auto-growth parameters for database files.

In the next chapter, I'll talk about one of the most important components in SQL Server—SQLOS—and a troubleshooting technique called Wait Statistics.

Troubleshooting Checklist

- ☐ Perform a high-level analysis of the hardware, network, and disk subsystem.
- ☐ Discuss host configuration and load in virtualized environments with infrastructure engineers.
- ☐ Check OS and SQL Server versions, editions, and patching levels.
- ☐ Check if instant file initialization is enabled.
- ☐ Analyze trace flags.
- ☐ Enable Optimize for Ad-Hoc Workloads.
- ☐ Check memory and parallelism settings on the server.
- ☐ Look at `tempdb` settings (including number of files); check for trace flag T1118, and potentially T1117, in SQL Server versions prior to 2016.
- ☐ Disable Auto Shrink for databases.
- ☐ Validate data and transaction log file settings.
- ☐ Check the number of VLFs in the transaction log files.
- ☐ Check errors in the SQL Server log.
- ☐ Check for unnecessary monitoring in the system.

CHAPTER 2

SQL Server Execution Model and Wait Statistics

It is impossible to troubleshoot SQL Server instances without understanding its execution model. You need to know how SQL Server runs tasks and manages resources if you want to detect bottlenecks in the system. I will cover those topics in this chapter.

First, the chapter will describe SQL Server's architecture and major components. Next, it will discuss SQL Server's execution model and introduce you to the popular troubleshooting technique called Wait Statistics. It will also cover several dynamic management views commonly used during troubleshooting. Finally, it will provide you with an overview of Resource Governor, which you can configure to segregate different workloads in the system.

SQL Server: High-Level Architecture

As you know, SQL Server is a very complex product that consists of dozens of components and subsystems. It is impossible to cover all of them here, but in this section, you'll get a high-level overview. For the sake of understanding, I'll divide these components and subsystems into several categories, as shown in Figure 2-1. Let's talk about them.

The *Protocol layer* handles communication between SQL Server and client applications. It uses an internal format called *Tabular Data Stream* (TDS) to transmit data using network protocols such as TCP/IP or Named Pipes. If a client application and SQL Server are running on the same machine, you can use another protocol called *Shared Memory*.

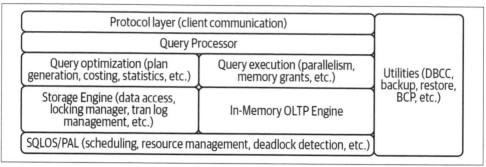

Protocol layer (client communication)	Utilities (DBCC, backup, restore, BCP, etc.)
Query Processor	
Query optimization (plan generation, costing, statistics, etc.) / Query execution (parallelism, memory grants, etc.)	
Storage Engine (data access, locking manager, tran log management, etc.) / In-Memory OLTP Engine	
SQLOS/PAL (scheduling, resource management, deadlock detection, etc.)	

Figure 2-1. Major SQL Server components

 It is worth checking what protocols are enabled when you trouble-shoot client connectivity issues. Some SQL Server editions—for example, Express and Developer—disable TCP/IP and Name Pipes by default. They do not accept remote client connections until you enable network protocols in the SQL Server Configuration Manager utility.

The *Query Processor layer* is responsible for query optimization and execution. It parses, optimizes, and manages compiled plans for the queries, and orchestrates all aspects of query execution.

The *Storage Engine* is responsible for data access and management in SQL Server. It works with the data on disk, manages transaction logs, and handles transactions, locking, and concurrency along with a few other functions.

The *In-Memory OLTP Engine* supports In-Memory OLTP in SQL Server. It works with memory-optimized tables and is responsible for data management and access to those tables, native compilation, data persistence, and all other aspects of the technology.

There are layers of abstraction between the components. For example, *Query Interop* (not shown in Figure 2-1) allows the Query Processor to work with row-based and memory-optimized tables, transparently routing requests either to storage or to In-Memory OLTP engines.

The most critical abstraction layer is *SQL Server Operating System* (SQLOS), which isolates other SQL Server components from the operating systems and deals with scheduling, resource management and monitoring, exception handling, and many other aspects of SQL Server behavior. For example, when any SQL Server component needs to allocate memory, it does not call OS API functions directly: it requests memory from SQLOS. This allows SQL Server granular control over execution and internal resource usage without relying on the OS.

Finally, since the introduction of Linux support in SQL Server 2017, there is another component called *Platform Abstraction Layer* (PAL), which serves as a proxy between SQLOS and operating systems. Except for a few performance-critical use cases, SQLOS does not call the OS API directly, relying instead on PAL. This architecture allows SQL Server's code to remain almost identical in Windows and Linux, which significantly speeds up development and product improvements.

From a troubleshooting standpoint, you'll see very little difference between SQL Server on Windows and on Linux. Obviously, you'll use different techniques when analyzing the SQL Server ecosystem and OS configuration. However, both platforms behave the same when you start to analyze issues *inside* SQL Server, so I am not going to differentiate between them in this book.

Let's look at SQLOS in more detail.

SQLOS and the Execution Model

Database servers are expected to handle a large number of user requests, and SQL Server is no exception. On a very high level, SQL Server assigns those requests to separate threads, executing the requests simultaneously. Except in cases when the server is idle, the number of active threads exceeds the number of CPUs in the system, and efficient scheduling is the key to good server performance.

Early versions of SQL Server relied on Windows scheduling. Unfortunately, Windows (and Linux) are general-purpose OSes, which means they use *preemptive scheduling*. They allocate a time interval, or *time quantum*, to a thread to run, then switch to other threads when it expires. This is an expensive operation that requires switching between user and kernel modes, negatively affecting system performance.

In SQL Server 7.0, Microsoft introduced the first version of User Mode Scheduler (UMS), which is a thin layer between Windows and SQL Server that was primarily responsible for scheduling. It used *cooperative scheduling*, with SQL Server threads coded to voluntarily yield every 4 ms, allowing other threads to execute. This approach significantly reduced expensive context switching in the system.

 Some SQL Server processes, such as extended stored procedures, CLR routines, external languages, and a few others, may still run in preemptive scheduling mode.

Microsoft continued to make improvements in UMS in SQL Server 2000, and in SQL Server 2005 redesigned it to the much more robust SQLOS. In later versions of SQL Server, SQLOS is responsible for scheduling, memory and I/O management, exception handling, CLR and external language hosting, and quite a few other functions.

When you start an SQL Server process, SQLOS creates a set of schedulers that manage workload across CPUs. The number of schedulers matches the number of logical CPUs in the system, with an additional scheduler created for a Dedicated Admin Connection (DAC). For example, if you have two quad-core physical CPUs with hyper-threading enabled, SQL Server will create 17 schedulers in the system. For practical purposes, you can think of the schedulers as the CPUs; I will use those terms interchangeably throughout the book.

 The DAC is your *last-resort* troubleshooting connection. It allows you to access SQL Server if it becomes unresponsive and does not accept normal connections. I will talk more about this in Chapter 13.

Each scheduler will be in an ONLINE or OFFLINE state, depending on its affinity mask setting and core-based licensing model. The schedulers usually do not migrate between CPUs; however, migration is possible, especially under heavy load. Nevertheless, in most cases this behavior does not affect the troubleshooting process.

The schedulers are responsible for managing the set of worker threads, sometimes called *workers*. The maximum number of workers in a system is specified by the *Max Worker Thread* configuration option. The default value of zero indicates that SQL Server calculates the maximum number of worker threads based on the number of schedulers in the system. In most cases, you do not need to change this default value—in fact, don't change it unless you know *exactly* what you are doing.

Each time there is a task to execute, it is assigned to an idle worker. When there are no idle workers, the scheduler creates a new one. It also destroys idle workers after 15 minutes of inactivity or in case of memory pressure. Each worker uses 512 KB of RAM in 32-bit and 2 MB of RAM in 64-bit SQL Server for the thread stack. You can think of *workers* as being the logical representation of OS threads and *tasks* as the unit of work those threads handle.

Workers do not move between schedulers; tasks do not move between workers. SQLOS, however, can create child tasks and assign them to different workers; for example, in the case of parallel execution plans. This may explain situations when some schedulers are running under heavier loads than others—some workers could end up with more expensive tasks from time to time.

By default, SQL Server assigns tasks to workers going through NUMA nodes in round-robin fashion, without considering the number of schedulers in the NUMA nodes. Uneven distribution of schedulers across NUMA nodes will lead to unbalanced work distribution between schedulers. (I will show you an example of this condition in Chapter 15.)

In most cases, we focus on tasks during troubleshooting. There is an exception, however: when a task is in the PENDING state, which means it is waiting for an available worker after the task has been created. This is completely normal, and workers are usually assigned to tasks very quickly. However, it can also indicate a very dangerous condition when the system does not have enough workers to handle the requests. I will discuss how to detect and address this issue in Chapter 13.

Besides PENDING, a task may be in five other possible states:

RUNNING
> The task is currently executing on the scheduler.

RUNNABLE
> The task is waiting for the scheduler to be executed.

SUSPENDED
> The task is waiting for an external event or resource.

SPINLOOP
> The task is processing a spinlock. *Spinlocks* are synchronization objects that protect some internal objects. SQL Server may use them when it expects access to the object will be granted very quickly, avoiding context switching for the workers.

DONE
> The task is complete.

The first three states are the most important and common. Each scheduler has, at most, one task in the RUNNING state. In addition, it has two different queues—one for RUNNABLE tasks and one for SUSPENDED tasks. When the RUNNING task needs some resources—a data page from a disk, for example—it submits an I/O request and changes the state to SUSPENDED. It stays in the SUSPENDED queue until the request is fulfilled and the page has been read. After that, when it is ready to resume execution, the task is moved to the RUNNABLE queue.

Perhaps the closest real-life analogy to this process is a grocery store checkout line. Think of cashiers as schedulers and customers as tasks in the RUNNABLE queue. A customer who is currently checking out is similar to a task in the RUNNING state.

If an item is missing a UPC code, a cashier sends a store worker to do a price check. The cashier suspends the checkout process for the current customer, asking them to step aside (to the SUSPENDED queue). When the worker comes back with the price information, the customer moves to the end of the checkout line (the end of the RUNNABLE queue).

Of course, SQL Server's execution is much more efficient than a real-life store, where customers must wait patiently in line for the price check to complete. (A customer at the end of the RUNNABLE queue would probably wish for such efficiency!)

Wait Statistics

With the exception of initialization and cleanup, a task spends its time switching between RUNNING, SUSPENDED, and RUNNABLE states, as shown in Figure 2-2. The total execution time will include time in the RUNNING state, when the task is actually executed; time in the RUNNABLE state, when the task is waiting for the scheduler (CPU) to execute; and time in the SUSPENDED state, when the task is waiting for resources.

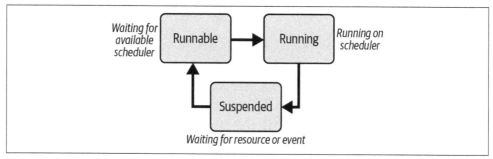

Figure 2-2. Task lifecycle

In a nutshell, the goal of any performance tuning process is to improve system throughput by reducing query execution times. You can achieve this by reducing the time that query tasks spend in any of those states.

You can decrease query RUNNING time by upgrading your hardware and moving to faster CPUs or by reducing the amount of work tasks must perform with query optimization. You can shrink RUNNABLE time by adding more CPU resources or reducing the load on the system. However, in most cases, you will get the most benefit by focusing on the time that tasks spend in SUSPENDED state while waiting for resources.

SQL Server tracks the cumulative time tasks spend in SUSPENDED state for different types of waits. You can see this data through the sys.dm_os_wait_stats view (*https://oreil.ly/Nh4s2*) to get a quick sense of the main bottlenecks in your system and further fine-tune your troubleshooting strategy.

The code in Listing 2-1 shows the wait types that take the most time in your system. (It filters out some benign wait types, mainly related to internal SQL Server processes that spend most of the time waiting.) The data is collected from the time of the last SQL Server restart, or since you last cleared it with the DBCC SQLPERF('sys.dm_os_wait_stats', CLEAR) command. Each new SQL Server version introduces new wait types. Some are useful for troubleshooting; others are benign and will need to be filtered out.[1]

Listing 2-1. Getting top wait types in the system (SQL Server 2012 and later)

```
;WITH Waits
AS
(
  SELECT
    wait_type, wait_time_ms, waiting_tasks_count,signal_wait_time_ms
    ,wait_time_ms - signal_wait_time_ms AS resource_wait_time_ms
    ,100. * wait_time_ms / SUM(wait_time_ms) OVER() AS Pct
    ,100. * SUM(wait_time_ms) OVER(ORDER BY wait_time_ms DESC) /
        NULLIF(SUM(wait_time_ms) OVER(), 0) AS RunningPct
    ,ROW_NUMBER() OVER(ORDER BY wait_time_ms DESC) AS RowNum
  FROM sys.dm_os_wait_stats WITH (NOLOCK)
  WHERE
    wait_type NOT IN /* Filtering out nonessential system waits */
    (N'BROKER_EVENTHANDLER',N'BROKER_RECEIVE_WAITFOR',N'BROKER_TASK_STOP'
    ,N'BROKER_TO_FLUSH',N'BROKER_TRANSMITTER',N'CHECKPOINT_QUEUE',N'CHKPT'
    ,N'CLR_SEMAPHORE',N'CLR_AUTO_EVENT',N'CLR_MANUAL_EVENT'
    ,N'DBMIRROR_DBM_EVENT',N'DBMIRROR_EVENTS_QUEUE',N'DBMIRROR_WORKER_QUEUE'
    ,N'DBMIRRORING_CMD',N'DIRTY_PAGE_POLL',N'DISPATCHER_QUEUE_SEMAPHORE'
    ,N'EXECSYNC',N'FSAGENT',N'FT_IFTS_SCHEDULER_IDLE_WAIT',N'FT_IFTSHC_MUTEX'
    ,N'HADR_CLUSAPI_CALL',N'HADR_FILESTREAM_IOMGR_IOCOMPLETION'
    ,N'HADR_LOGCAPTURE_WAIT',N'HADR_NOTIFICATION_DEQUEUE'
    ,N'HADR_TIMER_TASK',N'HADR_WORK_QUEUE',N'KSOURCE_WAKEUP',N'LAZYWRITER_SLEEP'
    ,N'LOGMGR_QUEUE',N'ONDEMAND_TASK_QUEUE'
    ,N'PARALLEL_REDO_WORKER_WAIT_WORK',N'PARALLEL_REDO_DRAIN_WORKER'
    ,N'PARALLEL_REDO_LOG_CACHE',N'PARALLEL_REDO_TRAN_LIST'
    ,N'PARALLEL_REDO_WORKER_SYNC',N'PREEMPTIVE_SP_SERVER_DIAGNOSTICS'
    ,N'PREEMPTIVE_OS_LIBRARYOPS',N'PREEMPTIVE_OS_COMOPS', N'PREEMPTIVE_OS_PIPEOPS'
    ,N'PREEMPTIVE_OS_GENERICOPS',N'PREEMPTIVE_OS_VERIFYTRUST'
    ,N'PREEMPTIVE_OS_FILEOPS',N'PREEMPTIVE_OS_DEVICEOPS'
    ,N'PREEMPTIVE_OS_QUERYREGISTRY',N'PREEMPTIVE_XE_CALLBACKEXECUTE'
    ,N'PREEMPTIVE_XE_DISPATCHER',N'PREEMPTIVE_XE_GETTARGETSTATE'
    ,N'PREEMPTIVE_XE_SESSIONCOMMIT',N'PREEMPTIVE_XE_TARGETINIT'
    ,N'PREEMPTIVE_XE_TARGETFINALIZE',N'PWAIT_ALL_COMPONENTS_INITIALIZED'
    ,N'PWAIT_DIRECTLOGCONSUMER_GETNEXT',N'PWAIT_EXTENSIBILITY_CLEANUP_TASK'
    ,N'QDS_PERSIST_TASK_MAIN_LOOP_SLEEP',N'QDS_ASYNC_QUEUE'
    ,N'QDS_CLEANUP_STALE_QUERIES_TASK_MAIN_LOOP_SLEEP'
    ,N'REQUEST_FOR_DEADLOCK_SEARCH',N'RESOURCE_QUEUE',N'SERVER_IDLE_CHECK'
    ,N'SLEEP_BPOOL_FLUSH',N'SLEEP_DBSTARTUP',N'SLEEP_DCOMSTARTUP'
    ,N'SLEEP_MASTERDBREADY',N'SLEEP_MASTERMDREADY',N'SLEEP_MASTERUPGRADED'
    ,N'SLEEP_MSDBSTARTUP',N'SLEEP_SYSTEMTASK',N'SLEEP_TASK'
    ,N'SLEEP_TEMPDBSTARTUP',N'SNI_HTTP_ACCEPT',N'SOS_WORK_DISPATCHER'
    ,N'SP_SERVER_DIAGNOSTICS_SLEEP',N'SQLTRACE_BUFFER_FLUSH'
```

---

1 The code in Listing 2-1 is good for versions up to SQL Server 2019. To exclude other wait types in future versions, see Microsoft's documentation (*https://oreil.ly/O4tzq*).

```
    ,N'SQLTRACE_INCREMENTAL_FLUSH_SLEEP',N'SQLTRACE_WAIT_ENTRIES'
    ,N'STARTUP_DEPENDENCY_MANAGER',N'WAIT_FOR_RESULTS'
    ,N'WAITFOR',N'WAITFOR_TASKSHUTDOWN',N'WAIT_XTP_HOST_WAIT'
    ,N'WAIT_XTP_OFFLINE_CKPT_NEW_LOG',N'WAIT_XTP_CKPT_CLOSE',N'WAIT_XTP_RECOVERY'
    ,N'XE_BUFFERMGR_ALLPROCESSED_EVENT',N'XE_DISPATCHER_JOIN',N'XE_DISPATCHER_WAIT'
    ,N'XE_LIVE_TARGET_TVF',N'XE_TIMER_EVENT')
)
SELECT
  w1.wait_type AS [Wait Type]
  ,w1.waiting_tasks_count AS [Wait Count]
  ,CONVERT(DECIMAL(12,3), w1.wait_time_ms / 1000.0) AS [Wait Time]
  ,CONVERT(DECIMAL(12,1), w1.wait_time_ms / w1.waiting_tasks_count)
      AS [Avg Wait Time]
  ,CONVERT(DECIMAL(12,3), w1.signal_wait_time_ms / 1000.0)
      AS [Signal Wait Time]
  ,CONVERT(DECIMAL(12,1), w1.signal_wait_time_ms / w1.waiting_tasks_count)
      AS [Avg Signal Wait Time]
  ,CONVERT(DECIMAL(12,3), w1.resource_wait_time_ms / 1000.0)
      AS [Resource Wait Time]
  ,CONVERT(DECIMAL(12,1), w1.resource_wait_time_ms / w1.waiting_tasks_count)
      AS [Avg Resource Wait Time]
  ,CONVERT(DECIMAL(6,3), w1.Pct)
      AS [Percent]
  ,CONVERT(DECIMAL(6,3), w1.RunningPct)
      AS [Running Percent]
FROM
    Waits w1
WHERE
    w1.RunningPct <= 99 OR w1.RowNum = 1
ORDER BY
    w1. RunningPct
OPTION (RECOMPILE, MAXDOP 1);
```

Figure 2-3 shows the output of this code from one of the production servers, early in the troubleshooting process. I can immediately see that the majority of the waits in the system relate to blocking (LCK*) and I/O (PAGEIOLATCH*). This makes it much easier to decide where to focus my troubleshooting efforts.

This troubleshooting approach is called *Wait Statistics Analysis*. It's one of the most frequently used troubleshooting and performance tuning techniques in SQL Server. Figure 2-4 illustrates a typical troubleshooting cycle using Wait Statistics Analysis.

First, you identify the main bottleneck in the system by analyzing the top waits. Next, you confirm that this is the main bottleneck using other tools and techniques and pinpoint the root cause of the problem. Finally, you fix the problem and repeat the cycle.

#	Wait Type	Wait Count	Wait Time	Avg Wait Time	Signal Wait Time	Avg Signal Wait Time	Resource Wait Time	Avg Resource Wait Time	Percent	Running Percent
1	LCK_M_U	538312358	2952904.553	5.0	278904.170	1.0	2674000.376	4.0	58.316	58.316
2	PAGEIOLATCH_SH	132056495	730022.059	5.0	17938.737	0.0	712083.322	5.0	14.417	72.733
3	LCK_M_S	196405075	379378.938	1.0	24706.314	0.0	354672.624	1.0	7.492	80.226
4	ASYNC_NETWORK_IO	36665258	254793.758	6.0	100063.339	2.0	154730.419	4.0	5.032	85.258
5	LOGBUFFER	11718571	165042.270	14.0	18931.562	1.0	146110.708	12.0	3.259	88.517
6	PAGEIOLATCH_EX	153474407	133057.566	0.0	3225.941	0.0	129831.625	0.0	2.628	91.145
7	LCK_M_IX	496185	98525.504	198.0	139.082	0.0	98386.422	198.0	1.946	93.091
8	IO_COMPLETION	93217317	81833.420	0.0	3505.294	0.0	78328.126	0.0	1.616	94.707
9	LATCH_EX	49863173	65876.146	1.0	10921.396	0.0	54954.750	1.0	1.301	96.008
10	ASYNC_IO_COMPLETION	57845	56036.933	968.0	22.078	0.0	56014.855	968.0	1.107	97.114
11	LCK_M_IS	57448	31694.644	551.0	9.403	0.0	31685.241	551.0	0.626	97.740
12	LCK_M_SCH_M	2228	31016.126	13921.0	0.918	0.0	31015.208	13920.0	0.613	98.353
13	WRITELOG	1969821	26014.687	13.0	715.277	0.0	25299.410	12.0	0.514	98.867
14	OLEDB	3041936	14911.992	4.0	6058.799	1.0	8853.193	2.0	0.294	99.161

Figure 2-3. Example of `sys.dm_os_wait_stats` *output*

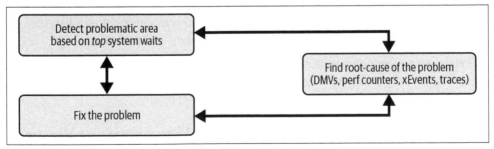

Figure 2-4. Typical Wait Statistics Analysis troubleshooting cycle

This process may never end. While there are always opportunities to make things better, at some point further improvements become impractical. Remember the Pareto Principle—you will get 80% of improvements by spending 20% of your time—and don't waste time on nonessential tuning.

This looks very easy in theory; unfortunately, it is more complicated in real life. Many issues are related to each other, which can hide the real causes of bottlenecks. To choose a very common example: excessive disk waits are often triggered not by bad I/O performance, but by poorly optimized queries that constantly flush the buffer pool and overload the disk subsystem.

Figure 2-5 shows some of the high-level dependencies you might run into. This diagram is by no means exhaustive, but it illustrates the danger of tunnel vision during troubleshooting.

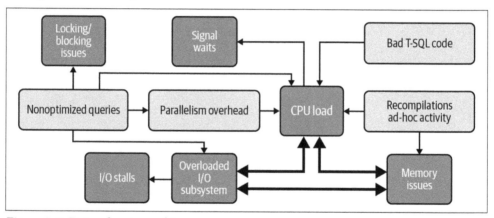

Figure 2-5. Dependencies and issues

I considered listing the most common waits and possible root causes, but I don't want you to chase symptoms rather than causes. Instead of jumping right to a list, read the book first so you can understand the possible dependencies involved.

I'll start going through specific issues and troubleshooting techniques in upcoming chapters, but for now, let's cover important dynamic management views in SQL Server related to SQLOS and the SQL Server execution model.

Execution Model–Related Dynamic Management Views

SQL Server comes with a very large number of dynamic management views. For details on all of them, consult the Microsoft documentation (*https://oreil.ly/TqA24*). Here, I will focus on just a small subset that I regularly use during troubleshooting. We will look at many others later in the book.

sys.dm_os_wait_stats

As you saw earlier, the `sys.dm_os_wait_stats` view (*https://oreil.ly/offh8*) provides information about waits in the system. It tells you how many times the wait occurs (`waiting_task_count`) along with cumulative times for resource waits (`resource _wait_time_ms`) and signal waits (`signal_wait_time_ms`). The resource wait time indicates how long a task was in the SUSPENDED queue as it waited for the resource. The signal wait time indicates how long the CPU was in the RUNNABLE queue after the resource wait time was over.

For example, let's say a task is requested to read a data page from disk. The I/O request might take 6 ms; then, the task might wait another millisecond to resume the execution. If you view the wait data for this, you'll see 6 ms of resource waits, 1 ms of signal waits, and 7 ms of total wait time.

Listing 2-2 shows how to compare cumulative signal and resource waits in the system.

Listing 2-2. Signal versus resource waits

```
SELECT
    SUM(signal_wait_time_ms) AS [Signal Wait Time (ms)]
    ,CONVERT(DECIMAL(7,4), 100.0 * SUM (signal_wait_time_ms) /
        SUM(wait_time_ms)) AS [% Signal waits]
    ,SUM(wait_time_ms - signal_wait_time_ms) AS [Resource Wait Time (ms)]
    ,CONVERT (DECIMAL(7,4), 100.0 * sum(wait_time_ms - signal_wait_time_ms) /
        SUM(wait_time_ms)) AS [% Resource waits]
FROM
    sys.dm_os_wait_stats WITH (NOLOCK);
```

In most cases, signal waits should not exceed 10% to 15% of the total wait time. A higher number may indicate a CPU bottleneck, with tasks spending a lot of time in the RUNNABLE queue. Do not jump to the conclusion that you need to add more CPUs, though—it may be entirely possible to address the problem with performance tuning.

Pay attention to how often waits occur. Sometimes you'll see waits with a low `waiting_task_count` and high total wait time. Depending on the situation, you may or may not want to analyze these tasks, especially during the initial phase of troubleshooting. Such waits are often triggered by production incidents or other atypical conditions.

Finally, make sure you are working with representative data. As I mentioned, statistics are collected from the time of the last SQL Server restart, and the workload on the server may change over time.

I usually ask customers to clear the waits a few days before starting troubleshooting. It's safe to use the `DBCC SQLPERF('sys.dm_os_wait_stats', CLEAR)` command in production, but it may affect data collection in some third-party monitoring tools.

As another option, you can collect two separate snapshots of wait statistics and calculate the delta between them. I am including the script to do that in this book's companion materials.

sys.dm_exec_session_wait_stats

Starting with SQL Server 2016, you can look at waits on the session level, using the `sys.dm_exec_session_wait_stats` view (*https://oreil.ly/iZ9uJ*). This is extremely useful when you need to troubleshoot the performance of long-running queries or slow stored procedures in the system. This view will show you the waits that occurred during execution and will help you pinpoint bottlenecks and areas to research.

The columns and data in this view are similar to those in `sys.dm_os_wait_stats`; you can easily adjust scripts to work in both scenarios. Remember that data in `sys.dm_exec_session_wait_stats` clears when a session opens and when the pooled connection resets.

You may notice that the data is not always updated for currently running statements. You need to wait until a query completes for the data to become available.

sys.dm_os_waiting_tasks

The `sys.dm_os_waiting_tasks` view (*https://oreil.ly/KgfXc*) shows a list of tasks that are *currently* waiting in the SUSPENDED queue. This view is handy when the server is overloaded or unresponsive and you want to understand why sessions were suspended. It is also very helpful when you troubleshoot concurrency issues and active blocking in the system, because it shows the session ID of the blocker for the task (more on this in Chapter 8).

The most useful columns in this view are as follows:

`session_id`
ID of the waiting session.

`wait_type`
Type of wait the session is waiting for.

`wait_duration_ms`
The duration of the wait.

`blocking_session_id`
> The session blocking the current task. As I mentioned, this column is extremely useful when you troubleshoot active blocking in the system.

`resource_address`
> Information on the resource the task is waiting for.

You may have more than one row per session in the output when you deal with parallel execution plans.

sys.dm_exec_requests

The `sys.dm_exec_requests` view (*https://oreil.ly/wJJe2*) provides detailed information on each request that is executing on the server. This gives you a great at-a-glance snapshot of what is happening now and allows you to pinpoint most CPU- or I/O-intensive queries *currently* running in the system.

This view will return information for both user and system sessions. You can filter out most system sessions by using the `WHERE session_id > 50` predicate, although you may have some system sessions with an id greater than 50 nowadays. You can also filter out system processes by joining the data with the `sys.dm_exec_sessions` view and using the `is_user_process` column there.

The most useful columns in this view are as follows:

`session_id`
> The ID for the session. Unlike with `sys.dm_os_waiting_tasks`, you get a single row in the output per session, unless you are using Multiple Active Result Sets (MARS) in your system.

`start_time`
> The time when the request started.

`total_elapsed_time`
> The request's duration.

`status`
> The current request status (RUNNING, RUNNABLE, SUSPENDED, SLEEPING). A SLEEPING status indicates an idle connection.

`wait_type`, `wait_time`, `wait_resource`, `blocking_session_id`
> Appear if the request is currently suspended. Like `sys.dm_os_waiting_tasks`, the `blocking_session_id` column is very useful when you are troubleshooting active blocking in the system.

`cpu_time`, `logical_reads`, `reads`, `writes`, `granted_query_memory`, `dop`
> Provide you with execution metrics.

```
sql_handle, plan_handle
```
   Allow you to obtain the statement and its execution plan.

Listing 2-3 shows the code that returns information about currently running CPU-intensive requests, along with connection information. This code requires SQL Server 2016 to run; you can remove the `ep.dop` column in older versions. Also, remove the `TRY_CONVERT` function if you run it on SQL Server versions earlier than 2012.

Listing 2-3. Using the `sys.dm_exec_requests` view

```
SELECT
    er.session_id
    ,er.request_id
    ,DB_NAME(er.database_id) as [database]
    ,er.start_time
    ,CONVERT(DECIMAL(21,3),er.total_elapsed_time / 1000.) AS [duration]
    ,er.cpu_time
    ,SUBSTRING(
        qt.text,
        (er.statement_start_offset / 2) + 1,
            ((CASE er.statement_end_offset
                WHEN -1 THEN DATALENGTH(qt.text)
                ELSE er.statement_end_offset
            END - er.statement_start_offset) / 2) + 1
    ) AS [statement]
    ,er.status
    ,er.wait_type
    ,er.wait_time
    ,er.wait_resource
    ,er.blocking_session_id
    ,er.last_wait_type
    ,er.reads
    ,er.logical_reads
    ,er.writes
    ,er.granted_query_memory
    ,er.dop
    ,er.row_count
    ,er.percent_complete
    ,es.login_time
    ,es.original_login_name
    ,es.host_name
    ,es.program_name
    ,c.client_net_address
    ,ib.event_info AS [buffer]
    ,qt.text AS [sql]
    ,TRY_CONVERT(XML,p.query_plan) as [query_plan]
FROM
    sys.dm_exec_requests er WITH (NOLOCK)
        OUTER APPLY sys.dm_exec_input_buffer
            (er.session_id, er.request_id) ib
```

```
        OUTER APPLY sys.dm_exec_sql_text(er.sql_handle) qt
        OUTER APPLY
            sys.dm_exec_text_query_plan
            (
                er.plan_handle
                ,er.statement_start_offset
                ,er.statement_end_offset
            ) p
        LEFT JOIN sys.dm_exec_connections c WITH (NOLOCK) ON
                er.session_id = c.session_id
        LEFT JOIN sys.dm_exec_sessions es WITH (NOLOCK) ON
                er.session_id = es.session_id
WHERE
    er.status <> 'background' AND er.session_id > 50
ORDER BY
    er.cpu_time desc
OPTION (RECOMPILE, MAXDOP 1);
```

Getting a query execution plan with the sys.dm_exec_
text_query_plan function is expensive. Comment it out if your
server is running under heavy CPU load.

sys.dm_os_schedulers

I do not use the sys.dm_os_schedulers view (*https://oreil.ly/8CfB0*) very often, only from time to time. As you can guess by the name, this view provides information about schedulers in the system. You can use it to get information about schedulers' distribution across NUMA nodes, and to analyze metrics from individual schedulers.

I showed you the code for the first use case in Chapter 1, but it is worth providing an enhanced version of this script (see Listing 2-4). Check the count of online schedulers in each NUMA node to see if the CPU affinity has been set correctly.

Listing 2-4. NUMA node scheduler statistics

```
SELECT
    parent_node_id AS [NUMA Node]
    ,COUNT(*) AS [Schedulers]
    ,SUM(IIF(status = N'VISIBLE ONLINE',1,0)) AS [Online Schedulers]
    ,SUM(IIF(status = N'VISIBLE OFFLINE',1,0)) AS [Offline Schedulers]
    ,SUM(current_tasks_count) AS [Current Tasks]
    ,SUM(runnable_tasks_count) AS [Runnable Tasks]

FROM
    sys.dm_os_schedulers WITH (NOLOCK)
WHERE
    status IN (N'VISIBLE ONLINE',N'VISIBLE OFFLINE')
```

```
GROUP BY
    parent_node_id
OPTION (RECOMPILE, MAXDOP 1);
```

The `current_tasks_count` and `runnable_tasks_count` columns provide the number of tasks in the `RUNNING` and `RUNNABLE` queues in each node. A large `runnable_tasks_count` number may indicate a CPU bottleneck. Remember, however, that the numbers show what is happening in the system *now* and may not be representative over time. It is better to see cumulative information; for example, the percentage of signal waits (see Listing 2-2) or CPU load overtime (see Chapter 6).

Many other columns in the view provide scheduler-specific statistics, such as status, number of workers and tasks in various states, number of context switches, CPU consumption, and a few others. Check the documentation for more details.

Resource Governor Overview

Resource Governor is an Enterprise Edition feature that allows you to segregate and throttle different workloads on the server. Although it's been available for quite a long time, I consider Resource Governor a niche feature: I rarely see it in the field. (You may even consider skipping this section and coming back to it later if and when you have to deal with it.) Nevertheless, remember to check whether Resource Governor is configured in the system you are troubleshooting, as an incorrect configuration can seriously impact server throughput.

When enabled, Resource Governor separates the sessions between different *workload groups* by calling the *classifier function* at the time of the session's login. The classifier function is a simple user-defined function that enables you to use various connection properties (login name, application name, client IP address, etc.) to choose between workload groups.

Each workload group has several parameters, such as `MAXDOP`, the maximum allowed CPU time for the request, and the maximum number of simultaneous requests allowed in the group. They are also associated with a resource pool, where you can customize resource usage.

The SQL Server documentation refers to *resource pools* as "the virtual SQL Server instances inside of an SQL Server instance." I do not think this is an accurate definition, though, because resource pools do not provide enough isolation from each other. However, you can control and limit CPU bandwidth and affinity, along with query memory grants (see Chapter 7).

Starting with SQL Server 2014, you can also control disk throughput by limiting resource pool IOPS. You cannot, however, control buffer pool usage. It is shared across all pools.

There are two system workload groups and resource pools: *internal* and *default*. As you can guess, the first handles internal workload. The second is responsible for all nonclassified workload. You can change the parameters of the *default* workload group without creating other user-defined workload groups and pools.

Figure 2-6 shows a Resource Governor configuration for an example scenario in which you want to separate OLTP and reporting workloads. This will reduce the impact of reporting queries on critical OLTP transactions, preventing them from saturating CPU and I/O.

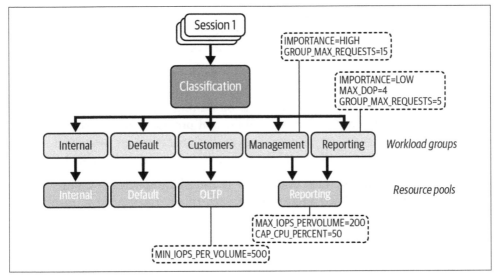

Figure 2-6. Example Resource Governor configuration

Resource Governor is useful, but it is not the easiest feature to configure and maintain. You need to do some planning and math when you want to configure resource throttling across multiple busy resource pools.

You also need to reevaluate the settings over time, because hardware and workload requirements may change. I recently had to troubleshoot a case where a major disk subsystem upgrade did not improve system performance. We found that I/O in the system had been throttled by a MAX_IOPS_PER_VOLUME setting in the resource pool.

In conclusion, Resource Governor is good in use cases where you need to segregate different workloads in a single database on a standalone server or an instance that uses Failover Clustering. It is also useful for reducing the impact of database maintenance. For example, you can limit CPU resources utilized by backup compression or I/O load from index maintenance by running them in a separate resource pool from user sessions.

I recommend looking at different technologies when you need to segregate a different workload in the Always On Availability Groups setup. The readable secondaries may provide better scalability in the long term. Also, when you need to segregate workloads from multiple databases running on a single SQL Server instance, it's usually better to split the databases across multiple instances, and potentially virtualize them.

Summary

SQLOS is the vital subsystem responsible for scheduling and resource management in SQL Server. At startup, it creates schedulers—one per logical CPU—and allocates the pool of worker threads to each scheduler to manage. User and system tasks are assigned to the worker threads, which perform the actual work.

SQL Server uses cooperative scheduling, with workers voluntarily yielding every 4 ms. The tasks constantly migrate through the RUNNING, SUSPENDED, and RUNNABLE states while they are running on the CPU or waiting for the CPU and resources. SQL Server tracks the different types of waits and provides that information in the sys.dm_os_wait_tasks view. You can analyze the most common waits and identify bottlenecks in the system with the troubleshooting process called Wait Statistics.

Be careful when analyzing waits; don't jump to immediate conclusions. Many performance issues may be related and can mask each other. You'll need to identify and confirm the root cause of the problem as part of your analysis.

In the next chapter, we will dive deeper into troubleshooting particular issues, starting with the disk, and learn how to diagnose and address them.

Troubleshooting Checklist

- ☐ Look at the waits in the system. Make sure the wait statistics are representative.
- ☐ Analyze percentages of signal and resource waits.
- ☐ Validate the Resource Governor configuration when present.
- ☐ Triage the waits, looking for bottlenecks.

CHAPTER 3

Disk Subsystem Performance

SQL Server is a very I/O-intensive application: it is constantly reading data from and writing data to disk. Good I/O throughput is essential for SQL Server performance and health. Unfortunately, many SQL Server installations are I/O bound, even with modern flash-based storage.

In this chapter, I will show you how to analyze and troubleshoot disk subsystem performance issues. You will learn how SQL Server processes I/O requests internally and how to identify and detect possible bottlenecks through the entire I/O stack, on the SQL Server, OS, virtualization, and storage levels.

Next, I will talk about checkpoint process tuning, a common source of I/O bottlenecks in busy OLTP systems.

Finally, I will cover the most common I/O-related waits you may encounter in your system.

Anatomy of the SQL Server I/O Subsystem

SQL Server never works with data pages directly in database files. Every time a data page needs to be read or modified, SQL Server reads that page to memory and caches it in the *buffer pool*. Each page in a buffer pool is referenced by a *buffer structure*, sometimes simply called a *buffer*. It includes the page's address in the data file, a pointer to the data page in the memory, status information, and the page latching queue.

SQL Server uses *latches* to protect internal objects in memory, preventing them from corruption when multiple threads are modifying them simultaneously. The two most common types of latch are *exclusive*, which blocks any access to the object, and *shared*, which allows simultaneous reads but prevents the objects from being modified.

Conceptually, latches are similar to *critical sections* or *mutexes* in application development languages. I will talk about latches in detail in Chapter 10.

The location of data pages in a buffer pool does not represent the order in which they are stored in the database files. SQL Server, however, can efficiently locate the page in the buffer pool when needed. Every time SQL Server accesses the page there, it performs a *logical read*. When the page is not present in memory and needs to be read from disk, the *physical read* also occurs.

When data needs to be modified, SQL Server generates and writes log records to the transaction log file and then changes the pages in the buffer pool, marking them as *dirty*. It saves dirty pages to the data files asynchronously in *checkpoint* and, sometimes, *lazy writer* processes. We'll discuss both of these processes later in this chapter and transaction logs in Chapter 11. For now, remember that data modifications require SQL Server to *read* data pages from disk if they have not already been cached.

Now let's look in more detail at how SQL Server works with I/O.

Scheduling and I/O

As you may remember from Chapter 2, SQL Server uses cooperative scheduling, with multiple workers running on CPUs in a rotating fashion. The workers voluntarily yield when the short 4 ms quantum expires, allowing other workers to proceed. This model requires SQL Server to use asynchronous I/O as much as possible—it is impossible for workers to wait until the I/O request is completed, preventing other workers from executing.

By default, all SQL Server schedulers handle I/O requests. You can override this behavior and bind I/O to specific CPUs by setting the affinity I/O mask. In theory, this may help improve I/O throughput in very busy OLTP systems; however, I rarely find it necessary. In most cases, you'll achieve better results by performing optimizations and reducing CPU and I/O load.

 You can read about affinity I/O masking in the Microsoft documentation (*https://oreil.ly/DXXmP*).

Every scheduler has a dedicated I/O queue. When a worker needs to perform an I/O operation, it creates an *I/O request structure*, adds it to the scheduler's queue, and issues an asynchronous OS API I/O call. It does not wait until the request is completed; it either continues to run, doing other things, or suspends itself, moving to the SUSPENDED queue.

When a new worker starts to run on the scheduler (switching to the RUNNING state), it goes through the scheduler's I/O queue. The I/O request structures contain enough information to check whether the asynchronous OS API call has been completed, and include a pointer to a callback function the worker calls to complete the I/O request.

I know this sounds complicated; please bear with me and we'll look at the details in the next section. Following are the key things I'd like you to remember:

- All active schedulers are handling I/O requests by default.
- Most I/O requests in SQL Server use asynchronous OS API calls. This is true even for write-ahead logging—the worker that issues the COMMIT statement may be suspended until the log record is written to disk; however, the OS API write command will be executed asynchronously.
- The I/O request may be completed by a different worker than the one that issued it.

You can see a list of pending I/O requests in the sys.dm_io_pending_io_requests view (*https://oreil.ly/wOFuw*). The io_pending_ms_ticks column provides the duration of that request. The io_pending column indicates if the OS API call has been completed and if the request is waiting for a worker to finish it. This may help you determine if request latency is being affected by CPU load in the system.

Now, as promised, let's look at that process again, with more concrete examples of reading data pages from disk.

Data Reads

When SQL Server needs to access a data page, it checks if the page already exists in the buffer pool. If it does not, the worker allocates the buffer for the page, protecting it with an exclusive latch. This prevents workers from accessing the page until it is read—they will be blocked, waiting for the latch to clear.

Next, the worker creates the I/O request structure, puts it in the scheduler I/O queue, and initiates an OS API read request. Then it tries to acquire another shared latch on the buffer, which is blocked by the incompatible, exclusive latch held there. The worker then suspends itself with a PAGEIOLATCH wait (Figure 3-1 illustrates this state).

When another worker switches to a RUNNING state, it checks to see if any I/O requests in the scheduler's queue have been completed. If so, the worker calls the callback function to finalize the operation: this function validates that the page is not corrupted and removes the exclusive latch from the buffer. The worker that submitted the I/O request can then resume and access the data page (Figure 3-2).

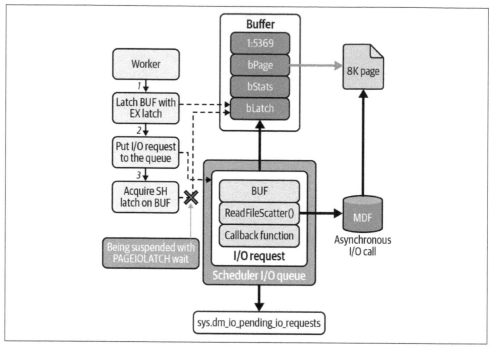

Figure 3-1. Reading a data page from disk: initiating the read

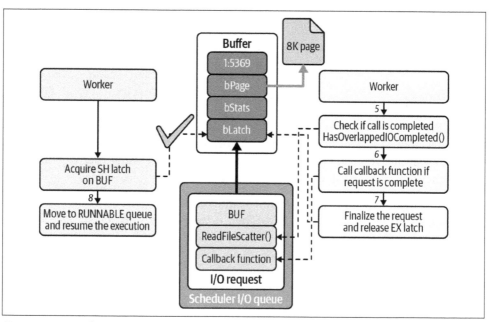

Figure 3-2. Reading a data page from disk: completing the read

Several errors may occur during I/O requests. All of them are severe, and you need to set up alerts in the system for them:

- Error 823 indicates that the OS I/O API call was not successful. This is often a sign of hardware issues.

- Errors 605 and 824 indicate logical consistency issues with the data pages. If you encounter either of these errors, immediately check whether the database is corrupted, using the DBCC CHECKDB command. You may also encounter these errors in the case of faulty I/O drivers, which can corrupt data pages during transfer.

- Error 833 tells you that an I/O request (OS API call) took longer than 15 seconds to return. This is abnormal; check the health of the disk subsystem when you see this error.

- Error 825 indicates that an I/O request failed and had to be retried in order to succeed. As with Error 833, check the health of the disk subsystem.

When troubleshooting these errors, you can look for the details in your SQL Server error log (use the code from Listing 1-4) and system event log.

It is very common for SQL Server to read multiple data pages in a single I/O request. For example, it uses *read-ahead* logic, reading multiple data pages during scans. As a result, the query may perform thousands of logical reads with just a handful of physical reads. Another example is *ramp-up reads*, which occur when SQL Server reads a large number of pages on each I/O request, trying to fill the buffer pool quickly on startup.

Data Writes

SQL Server handles data writes very similarly to data reads. In most cases, data writes are done asynchronously using a scheduler's I/O queues, as you just saw in the previous examples. Obviously, the callback function will be implemented differently in different I/O operations.

When you change some data in the database, SQL Server modifies the data pages in the buffer pool, reading pages from disk if needed. It generates log records for the modifications and saves them to the transaction log. The transaction is not considered to have been committed until the log records are hardened on disk. While *technically* you can treat write-ahead logging as synchronous writes, SQL Server uses an asynchronous I/O pattern for log writes.

SQL Server writes modified data pages in databases asynchronously during the *checkpoint process*. This process finds dirty data pages in the buffer pool and saves them to disk. It tries to minimize the number of disk requests by combining and writing adjacent modified pages together in a single I/O operation when possible.

Another SQL Server process, called *lazy writer*, periodically sweeps the buffer pool to remove data pages that have not been recently accessed, freeing up the memory. In normal circumstances, the lazy writer process skips dirty data pages; however, it may also write them to disk if there is memory pressure in the system.

There are, as always, some exceptions. For example, during a bulk import operation, SQL Server allocates a set of buffers in the buffer pool and reuses them, writing data to the database outside the checkpoint. This preserves the content of the buffer pool so that it isn't flushed by massive data imports.

Checkpoint I/O may introduce issues on busy systems. I'll talk about checkpoint tuning later in this chapter, but first, let's take a holistic look at the entire storage subsystem.

The Storage Subsystem: A Holistic View

Troubleshooting slow I/O performance in SQL Server is not an easy task. I've seen many heated discussions between database and infrastructure teams about this very issue. The database engineers generally complain about slow disk performance, while the storage engineers analyze the submillisecond latency metrics from SAN devices and insist that all issues are on the SQL Server side. Neither team is right. They usually make the same mistake: oversimplifying the storage subsystem to just a couple of components. It is not the case.

Figure 3-3 shows a very high-level diagram of the network-based storage subsystem, with many details missing. (It also references some troubleshooting tools. We'll get to those, but don't focus on them yet.) The point here is that bad I/O performance can be caused by any component, so you need to analyze *all* layers in the stack.

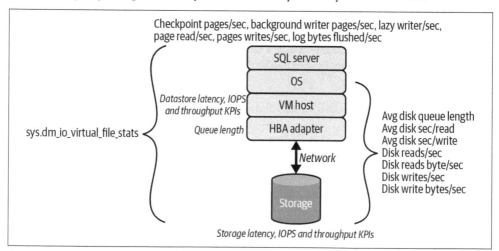

Figure 3-3. Storage subsystem (network based)

There is also the option of using direct-attached storage (DAS). In this configuration, the storage is either installed locally on the server (think about NVMe drives) or directly connected to it. This setup eliminates the network from the storage path and may provide better I/O performance. As a downside, you lose the flexibility of external storage, where you can add additional space and perform maintenance transparently to the server.

Every storage subsystem has a "tipping point" after which the latency of I/O requests will start to grow exponentially with increases in throughput and IOPS. For example, you may get a 1-millisecond response with an IOPS workload of 1,000 and a 3-millisecond response with an IOPS workload of 50,000. However, you might cross the tipping point at 100,000 IOPS and start to get double-digit or even triple-digit latency.

Every component in the stack will have its own tipping point. For example, low queue depth in the HBA adapter may lead to queueing on the controller level as the number of I/O requests increases. In this case, SQL Server will suffer from high latency and poor I/O performance; however, all SAN metrics will be perfectly healthy, with no latency at all.

You can use the `DiskSpd` utility to test storage subsystem performance. This utility emulates SQL Server's workload in the system. You can download it from GitHub (*https://aka.ms/diskspd*).

As I've noted, you'll need to look at all storage subsystem components when you troubleshoot bad I/O performance. Nevertheless, the place to start is analyzing overall storage latency and the number of data SQL Server reads and writes. You can do this by looking at the `sys.dm_io_virtual_file_stats` view.

sys.dm_io_virtual_file_stats view

The `sys.dm_io_virtual_file_stats` view (*https://oreil.ly/mJCKm*) is the most important tool in SQL Server I/O performance troubleshooting. This view provides I/O statistics by database file, including the number of I/O operations, the amount of data read and written, and information about *stalls*, or the time it takes for I/O requests to complete. (I use the terms *latency* and *stalls* interchangeably throughout this book.)

The data in this view is cumulative and is calculated from the time of the SQL Server restart. Take two snapshots of the data and calculate the delta between them (Listing 3-1 shows the code to do this). This code filters out database files with low I/O activity, since their metrics are usually skewed and not very useful.

Listing 3-1. Using the sys.dm_io_virtual_file_stats view

```
DROP TABLE IF EXISTS #Snapshot;
GO

CREATE TABLE #Snapshot
(
    database_id SMALLINT NOT NULL,
    file_id SMALLINT NOT NULL,
    num_of_reads BIGINT NOT NULL,
    num_of_bytes_read BIGINT NOT NULL,
    io_stall_read_ms BIGINT NOT NULL,
    num_of_writes BIGINT NOT NULL,
    num_of_bytes_written BIGINT NOT NULL,
    io_stall_write_ms BIGINT NOT NULL
);

INSERT INTO #Snapshot(database_id,file_id,num_of_reads,num_of_bytes_read
    ,io_stall_read_ms,num_of_writes,num_of_bytes_written,io_stall_write_ms)
    SELECT database_id,file_id,num_of_reads,num_of_bytes_read
        ,io_stall_read_ms,num_of_writes,num_of_bytes_written,io_stall_write_ms
    FROM sys.dm_io_virtual_file_stats(NULL,NULL)
OPTION (RECOMPILE);

-- Set test interval (1 minute).
WAITFOR DELAY '00:01:00.000';

;WITH Stats(db_id, file_id, Reads, ReadBytes, Writes
    ,WrittenBytes, ReadStall, WriteStall)
as
(
    SELECT
        s.database_id, s.file_id
        ,fs.num_of_reads - s.num_of_reads
        ,fs.num_of_bytes_read - s.num_of_bytes_read
        ,fs.num_of_writes - s.num_of_writes
        ,fs.num_of_bytes_written - s.num_of_bytes_written
        ,fs.io_stall_read_ms - s.io_stall_read_ms
        ,fs.io_stall_write_ms - s.io_stall_write_ms
    FROM
        #Snapshot s JOIN sys.dm_io_virtual_file_stats(NULL, NULL) fs ON
            s.database_id = fs.database_id and s.file_id = fs.file_id
)
SELECT
    s.db_id AS [DB ID], d.name AS [Database]
    ,mf.name AS [File Name], mf.physical_name AS [File Path]
    ,mf.type_desc AS [Type], s.Reads
    ,CONVERT(DECIMAL(12,3), s.ReadBytes / 1048576.) AS [Read MB]
    ,CONVERT(DECIMAL(12,3), s.WrittenBytes / 1048576.) AS [Written MB]
    ,s.Writes, s.Reads + s.Writes AS [IO Count]
    ,CONVERT(DECIMAL(5,2),100.0 * s.ReadBytes /
            (s.ReadBytes + s.WrittenBytes)) AS [Read %]
```

```
        ,CONVERT(DECIMAL(5,2),100.0 * s.WrittenBytes /
                (s.ReadBytes + s.WrittenBytes)) AS [Write %]
        ,s.ReadStall AS [Read Stall]
        ,s.WriteStall AS [Write Stall]
        ,CASE WHEN s.Reads = 0
            THEN 0.000
            ELSE CONVERT(DECIMAL(12,3),1.0 * s.ReadStall / s.Reads)
        END AS [Avg Read Stall]
        ,CASE WHEN s.Writes = 0
            THEN 0.000
            ELSE CONVERT(DECIMAL(12,3),1.0 * s.WriteStall / s.Writes)
        END AS [Avg Write Stall]
FROM
    Stats s JOIN sys.master_files mf WITH (NOLOCK) ON
        s.db_id = mf.database_id and
        s.file_id = mf.file_id
    JOIN sys.databases d WITH (NOLOCK) ON
        s.db_id = d.database_id
WHERE -- Only display files with more than 20MB throughput
    (s.ReadBytes + s.WrittenBytes) > 20 * 1048576
ORDER BY
    s.db_id, s.file_id
OPTION (RECOMPILE);
```

Figure 3-4 shows the output from the view.

The goal is to keep stalls/latency metrics as low as possible. It is impossible to define thresholds that can be applied to all systems, but my rule of thumb is not to exceed 1–2 ms write stalls for transaction logs and 3–5 ms read and write stalls for data files when network storage is used. The latency should be even lower, in submillisecond range, when you are using modern direct-attached drives.

Next, analyze throughput in the system. High stalls with low throughput usually indicate performance issues outside of SQL Server. Don't forget to look at throughput across all files that share the same drive or controller. High throughput in some files may impact the metrics in others that share the same resource.

There is usually a correlation between throughput and stalls: the more data you are reading and writing, the higher latency you'll have. This correlation is usually linear until you reach the tipping point, after which latency increases very quickly.

A large number of reads and read stalls in the data files is often accompanied by a significant percentage of PAGEIOLATCH waits and a low Page Life Expectancy performance counter value. This indicates that a large amount of data is constantly being read from disk. You need to understand why that is happening. In most cases, it's due to nonoptimized queries that perform large scans reading data from disk. We will talk about how to detect these queries in Chapter 4.

	DB ID	Database	File Name	File Path	Type	Reads	Read MB	Written MB	Writes
1	2	tempdb	tempdev	T:\SQLDa...	ROWS	279	17.375	17.563	281
2	2	tempdb	templog	T:\SQLDa...	LOG	0	0.000	76.727	1311
3	2	tempdb	temp2	T:\SQLDa...	ROWS	278	17.086	17.211	276
4	2	tempdb	temp3	T:\SQLDa...	ROWS	292	17.836	18.000	290
5	2	tempdb	temp4	T:\SQLDa...	ROWS	295	18.031	18.273	294
6	2	tempdb	temp5	T:\SQLDa...	ROWS	307	18.617	18.742	301
7	2	tempdb	temp6	T:\SQLDa...	ROWS	287	17.664	17.914	287
8	2	tempdb	temp7	T:\SQLDa...	ROWS	284	17.625	17.750	284
9	11				ROWS	76	1.578	88.719	7551
10	11				LOG	0	0.000	142.578	31166
11	11				ROWS	1111	9.453	38.422	4420
12	11				ROWS	2505	44.227	345.977	37251

	IO Count	Read %	Write %	Read Stall	Write Stall	Avg Read Stall	Avg Write Stall
1	560	49.73	50.27	205	322	0.735	1.146
2	1311	0.00	100.00	0	1191	0.000	0.908
3	554	49.82	50.18	195	308	0.701	1.116
4	582	49.77	50.23	206	322	0.705	1.110
5	589	49.67	50.33	206	323	0.698	1.099
6	608	49.83	50.17	225	343	0.733	1.140
7	574	49.65	50.35	214	308	0.746	1.073
8	568	49.82	50.18	208	299	0.732	1.053
9	7627	1.75	98.25	60	6847	0.789	0.907
10	31166	0.00	100.00	0	16944	0.000	0.544
11	5531	19.75	80.25	1994	3806	1.795	0.861
12	39756	11.33	88.67	2252	29908	0.899	0.803

Figure 3-4. Sample output from `sys.dm_io_virtual_file_stats`

Don't discount the possibility that the server is underprovisioned and doesn't have enough memory to accommodate an active data set, though, as this is also entirely possible. In either case, adding extra memory may be a completely acceptable solution that will reduce I/O load and improve system performance. It is obviously not the best solution, but in many cases it's easier and cheaper to use hardware to solve the problem.

In users' databases, a large number of writes and write stalls in data files often indicate an inefficient checkpoint configuration. You may get some improvements by tuning the checkpoint configuration, as I will show later in this chapter. In the longer term, you may need to analyze whether it is possible to reduce the number of data pages SQL Server writes to disk. Some ways to do this include removing unnecessary indexes; reducing page splits by changing the FILLFACTOR and tuning the index maintenance strategy; decreasing the number of data pages by implementing data compression; and, potentially, refactoring database schema and applications.

When you see large throughput and stalls in tempdb, identify what causes them. The three most common causes are version store activity, massive tempdb spills, and excessive usage of temporary objects. I will talk about these in Chapter 9.

Finally, you can also get an idea of I/O latency by analyzing resource wait time in PAGEIOLATCH and other I/O-related waits. This won't give you detailed information on a per-file basis, but it may be a good metric when you look at system-wide I/O performance.

Performance Counters and OS Metrics

The sys.dm_io_virtual_file_stats view provides useful and detailed information and points you in the right direction for further I/O troubleshooting, but it has one limitation: it averages data over the sampling interval.

This is completely acceptable when I/O latency is low. However, if latency numbers are high, you'll want to determine if performance is *generally* slow or if the numbers have been skewed by some bursts in activity. You can do this by looking at the performance counters correlating SQL Server and disk metrics.

The troubleshooting process will vary slightly between Windows and Linux. In Windows, the simplest way to analyze the metrics is to use the well-known PerfMon (Performance Monitor) utility. You can look at the SQL Server and I/O performance counters together and correlate data from them.

Table 3-1 lists performance counters to analyze.

Table 3-1. I/O-related performance counters

Performance object	Performance counters	Description
Physical disk	Avg Disk Queue Length Avg Disk Read Queue Length Avg Disk Write Queue Length	Provide the average number of I/O requests (total, read, and write, respectively) queued during the sampling interval. Those numbers should be as low as possible. Spikes indicate that I/O requests are being queued at the OS level.
	Current Disk Queue Length	Gives you the size of the I/O request queue when the metric was collected.
	Avg Disk sec/Transfer Avg Disk sec/Read Avg Disk sec/Write	Indicate average latency for disk operations during the sampling interval. These numbers are usually similar to latency/stall metrics from the sys.dm_io_virtual_file_stats view when sampled over the same period. However, because you typically measure sys.dm_io_virtual_file_stats over larger intervals, these counters will show you if I/O stalls were always high or if data has been affected by latency spikes.
	Disk Transfers/sec Disk Reads/sec Disk Writes/sec Disk Bytes/sec Disk Read Bytes/sec Disk Write Bytes/sec	Display the number of I/O operations and throughput at the time of the reading. Similar to latency counters, you can use them to analyze the uniformity of the disk workload.
	Avg Disk Bytes/Transfer Avg Disk Bytes/Read Avg Disk Bytes/Write	Show the average size of I/O requests, which can help you understand I/O patterns in the system.
SQL Server: Buffer Manager	Checkpoint pages/sec Background writer pages/sec	Show the number of dirty pages written by the checkpoint process.
	Lazy writer/sec	Provides the number of pages written by the lazy writer process.
	Page reads/sec Page writes/sec	Display the number of physical reads and writes.
	Readahead pages/sec	Shows the number of pages read by the read-ahead process.
SQL Server: Databases	Log Bytes Flushed/sec Log Flush Write Time (ms) Log Flushes/sec	Provide you with data about throughput, latency, and number of write requests for transaction log writes. Use these counters to understand log generation uniformity when you troubleshoot high log write latency.
SQL Server: SQL Statistics	Batch Requests/sec	While these two counters are not I/O related, they can be used to analyze spikes in system workload that may lead to bursts in I/O activity.
SQL Server: Databases	Transactions/sec	

Usually, I start by looking at the Avg Disk sec/Read and Avg Disk sec/Write latency counters, along with Avg Disk Queue Length. If I see any spikes in their values, I add SQL Server–specific counters to identify what processes may be leading to the bursts in activity.

Figure 3-5 illustrates one such example. You can see the correlation between Check point pages/sec and high Avg Disk sec/Write and Avg Disk Queue Length values. This leads to the simple conclusion that the I/O subsystem cannot keep up with bursts of writes from the checkpoint process.

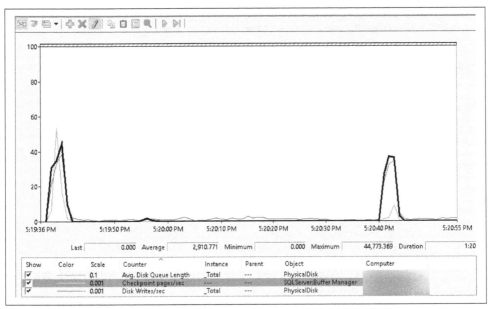

Figure 3-5. Checkpoint and disk queueing

Pay attention to other applications installed on the server. It is possible that they are responsible for I/O activity bursts or other issues.

Linux doesn't offer the standard PerfMon utility; however, plenty of free and commercially available monitoring tools are available. You can also use tools like iostat, dstat, and iotop, which are included in major Linux distributions. They provide general disk performance metrics on a per-process or system level.

On the SQL Server side, you can access performance counters through the sys.dm_os_performance_counters view (*https://oreil.ly/DJ4f5*). Listing 3-2 shows you how to do this. As a note, you will need to change the SQLServer prefix in the object_name column to MSSQL$*YOUR_INSTANCE_NAME* if you are running it on a named instance of SQL Server.

Listing 3-2. Using the sys.dm_os_performance_counters view

```sql
DROP TABLE IF EXISTS #PerfCntrs;
GO

CREATE TABLE #PerfCntrs
(
    collected_time DATETIME2(7) NOT NULL DEFAULT SYSDATETIME(),
    object_name SYSNAME NOT NULL,
    counter_name SYSNAME NOT NULL,
    instance_name SYSNAME NOT NULL,
    cntr_value BIGINT NOT NULL,
    PRIMARY KEY (object_name, counter_name, instance_name)
);

;WITH Counters(obj_name, ctr_name)
AS
(
    SELECT C.obj_name, C.ctr_name
    FROM
    (
        VALUES
            ('SQLServer:Buffer Manager','Checkpoint pages/sec')
            ,('SQLServer:Buffer Manager','Background writer pages/sec')
            ,('SQLServer:Buffer Manager','Lazy writes/sec')
            ,('SQLServer:Buffer Manager','Page reads/sec')
            ,('SQLServer:Buffer Manager','Page writes/sec')
            ,('SQLServer:Buffer Manager','Readahead pages/sec')
            ,('SQLServer:Databases','Log Flushes/sec') -- For all DBs
            ,('SQLServer:Databases','Log Bytes Flushed/sec') -- For all DBs
            ,('SQLServer:Databases','Log Flush Write Time (ms)') -- For all DBs
            ,('SQLServer:Databases','Transactions/sec') -- For all DBs
            ,('SQLServer:SQL Statistics','Batch Requests/sec')
    ) C(obj_name, ctr_name)
)
INSERT INTO #PerfCntrs(object_name,counter_name,instance_name,cntr_value)
    SELECT
        pc.object_name, pc.counter_name, pc.instance_name, pc.cntr_value
    FROM
        sys.dm_os_performance_counters pc WITH (NOLOCK) JOIN Counters c ON
            pc.counter_name = c.ctr_name AND pc.object_name = c.obj_name;

WAITFOR DELAY '00:00:01.000';

;WITH Counters(obj_name, ctr_name)
AS
(
    SELECT C.obj_name, C.ctr_name
    FROM
    (
        VALUES
            ('SQLServer:Buffer Manager','Checkpoint pages/sec')
```

```
            ,('SQLServer:Buffer Manager','Background writer pages/sec')
            ,('SQLServer:Buffer Manager','Lazy writes/sec')
            ,('SQLServer:Buffer Manager','Page reads/sec')
            ,('SQLServer:Buffer Manager','Page writes/sec')
            ,('SQLServer:Buffer Manager','Readahead pages/sec')
            ,('SQLServer:Databases','Log Flushes/sec') -- For all DBs
            ,('SQLServer:Databases','Log Bytes Flushed/sec') -- For all DBs
            ,('SQLServer:Databases','Log Flush Write Time (ms)') -- For all DBs
            ,('SQLServer:Databases','Transactions/sec') -- For all DBs
            ,('SQLServer:SQL Statistics','Batch Requests/sec')
    ) C(obj_name, ctr_name)
)
SELECT
    pc.object_name, pc.counter_name, pc.instance_name
    ,CASE pc.cntr_type
        WHEN 272696576 THEN
            (pc.cntr_value - h.cntr_value) * 1000 /
                DATEDIFF(MILLISECOND,h.collected_time,SYSDATETIME())
        WHEN 65792 THEN
            pc.cntr_value
        ELSE NULL
    END as cntr_value
FROM
    sys.dm_os_performance_counters pc WITH (NOLOCK) JOIN Counters c ON
        pc.counter_name = c.ctr_name AND pc.object_name = c.obj_name
    JOIN #PerfCntrs h ON
        pc.object_name = h.object_name AND
        pc.counter_name = h.counter_name AND
        pc.instance_name = h.instance_name
ORDER BY
    pc.object_name, pc.counter_name, pc.instance_name
OPTION (RECOMPILE);
```

You can also bring the sys.dm_io_virtual_file_stats view to the analysis, sampling its data and performance counters together every second. The approach is the same one we just discussed: you'll look at the correlation between disk latency and activity and evaluate the general performance of the I/O subsystem, identifying tipping points in the load.

Virtualization, HBA, and Storage Layers

There are several layers in the storage stack you may need to analyze in addition to the OS. They include virtualization, the HBA/SCSI controller configuration, and the storage array itself.

SQL Server mostly operates in shared environments. It shares storage and network infrastructure with other clients, and when virtualized, it runs on the same physical host with other VMs. As I said earlier in this book, when virtualization is being used, be sure to validate that the host is not overcommitted, which could lead to all sorts of performance issues.

Unless you have a very simple SQL Server setup that uses local storage, I/O requests will be serialized and sent over the network. There are two typical problems here.

The first is *insufficient queue depth* somewhere in the I/O path. Unfortunately, the default query depth may not be enough for a highly demanding I/O workload. You'll need to check and potentially increase it in the datastore, vSCSI controller, and HBA adapter settings. The typical sign of insufficient queue depth is low latency on the storage combined with much higher latency in the virtual machine (VM) and/or OS, with disk queueing present.

The second problem is *noisy neighbors*. Multiple I/O-intensive VMs running on the same host may affect each other. Similarly, multiple high-throughput servers sharing the same network and storage may overload them. Unfortunately, troubleshooting the noisy neighbor problem is never easy, and you need to analyze multiple components in the infrastructure to detect it.

 Storage arrays have a limit on the number of outstanding requests they can handle. Increasing queue depth on a busy server could increase the number of outstanding requests on the storage. You might shift the bottleneck from one layer to another, especially if the storage serves requests from many busy systems.

The virtualization host and storage both expose throughput, IOPS, and latency metrics for analysis. On the virtualization layers, the metrics may vary based on technology. For example, in Hyper-V you can use regular disk performance counters on the host. In VMware you can get the data from the ESXTOP utility, which I will cover in Chapter 15. In either case, the troubleshooting approach is very similar to what we have already discussed. Look at the available metrics, correlate data from them, and detect the bottlenecks in the I/O path.

Finally, check the storage configuration. Storage vendors usually publish best practices for SQL Server workloads: they are a good starting point. Pay attention to the alignment of the allocation unit size with the RAID stripe size and partition offset, though.

For example, a 1024 MB partition offset, 4 KB disk block, 64 KB allocation unit, and 128 KB RAID stripes are perfectly aligned, with each I/O request served by a single disk. On the other hand, 96 KB RAID stripes will spread 64 KB allocation units across two disks, which leads to extra I/O requests and can seriously impact performance.

Again, it is *always* beneficial to work together with infrastructure and storage engineers. They are the subject matter experts and may help you find the root cause of the problem faster than when you are working alone.

Finally, the best approach to get predictable performance in critical systems is to use a dedicated environment. Run SQL Server on dedicated hardware with DAS to get the best performance possible.

Checkpoint Tuning

As we all know, SQL Server uses write-ahead logging. Transactions are considered to be committed only after the log records are hardened in the transaction logs. SQL Server does not need to save dirty data pages to disk at the same time; it can reapply the changes by replaying log records if needed.

The checkpoint process saves data pages into the data files. The main goal of checkpoint is to reduce recovery time in the event of an SQL crash or failover: the fewer changes that need to be replayed, the faster the recovery will be. The maximum *desired* recovery time is controlled at either the server level or the database level. By default, both of them are 60 seconds.

You should not consider the recovery target to be a hard value. In many cases, the database will recover much more quickly than that. It is also possible for bursts of activity and long-running transactions to prolong recovery beyond the target time.

There are four different types of checkpoints:

Internal checkpoints
> These occur during some SQL Server operations, such as starting a database backup or creating a database snapshot.

Manual checkpoints
> This occurs when users trigger it with the CHECKPOINT command.

Automatic checkpoint
> Historically, SQL Server used automatic checkpoints, with the recovery interval controlled at the server level. The checkpoint process wakes up once or a few times during each recovery interval and flushes dirty data pages to disk. Unfortunately, this approach can lead to bursts of data writes, which can be problematic in busy systems.

Indirect checkpoint
> With this method, available in SQL Server 2012 and later, SQL Server tries to balance I/O load by executing checkpoints much more frequently; in some cases, even continuously. This helps mitigate bursts of data writes, making the I/O

load much more balanced. Use it instead of an automatic checkpoint whenever possible.

The *indirect checkpoint* is controlled on a per-database basis and is enabled by default in databases created in SQL Server 2016 and later. However, SQL Server does *not* enable indirect checkpoint automatically when you upgrade an SQL Server instance, or in SQL Server 2012 and 2014. You can do this manually by setting up a recovery target at the database level with the `ALTER DATABASE SET TARGET_RECOVERY_TIME` command.

Let me show you an example from one system I worked with. The sample of data from the `sys.dm_io_virtual_file_stats` view over 1 minute had very high write latency for the data files. However, the smaller samples (1 to 3 seconds) rarely showed any activity at all.

Figure 3-6 shows the data, with the 1-minute sample at the top and the 1-second sample at the bottom.

	File Path	Reads	Read MB	Written MB	Writes	IO Count	Read Stall
1	File1.NDF	3098	91.867	1404.727	138564	141622	11708
2	File2.NDF	47398	2104.140	9648.797	1113960	1161098	466594

Write Stall	Avg Read Stall	Avg Write Stall
8287158	3.779	59.807
74303099	9.773	66.750

	File Path	Reads	Read MB	Written MB	Writes	IO Count	Read Stall
1	File1.NDF	14	0.641	0.000	0	14	14
2	File2.NDF	552	27.399	0.000	0	552	471

Write Stall	Avg Read Stall	Avg Write Stall
1.000	0.000	0.000
0.000	0.853	0.000

Figure 3-6. Sample `sys.dm_io_virtual_file_stats` with automatic checkpoint

This behavior led me to believe that the issue was related to the checkpoint. I confirmed this hypothesis by looking at the Checkpoint pages/sec, Disk Writes/sec, and Avg Disk Queue Length performance counters. You can clearly see the burst of disk writes from the checkpoint process in Figure 3-5 earlier in the chapter, which shows the screenshot from PerfMon.

Although this instance ran SQL Server 2016, it used an automatic checkpoint, because all databases had been upgraded from the earlier version of SQL Server. Enabling an indirect checkpoint in the system immediately changed the I/O pattern, making it much more balanced.

You can see the performance counters in Figure 3-7. Notice that with the indirect checkpoint, you should use the Background writer pages/sec counter instead of the Checkpoint pages/sec counter.

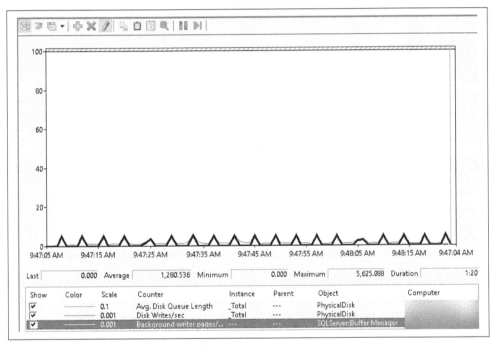

Figure 3-7. Indirect checkpoint performance counters

Figure 3-8 shows the output from a 1-minute sample in the sys.dm_io_vir tual_file_stats view. As you can see, latency went back to normal.

Indirect checkpoints do not completely eliminate I/O bursts. You can still have them, especially if the system has some spikes in data modifications. However, they are less frequent than with automatic checkpoints.

You may also need to tune the recovery target to get the most balanced I/O load. In the preceding case, I got the best results with a 90-second target. Of course, high values may increase recovery time in the system.

	File Path	Reads	Read MB	Written MB	Writes	IO Count
1	File1.NDF	2987	89.121	1367.542	135039	138026
2	File2.NDF	48212	2140.134	10944.122	1182783	1230995

Read Stall	Write Stall	Avg Read Stall	Avg Write Stall
3065	264675	1.026	1.960
66195	2280405	1.373	1.928

Figure 3-8. Sample `sys.dm_io_virtual_file_stats` with indirect checkpoint

I/O Waits

SQL Server uses several different wait types related to I/O operations. It is very common to see all of them present when the disk subsystem is not fast enough. Let's look at five of the most common ones: ASYNC_IO_COMPLETION, IO_COMPLETION, WRITELOG, WRITE_COMPLETION, and PAGEIOLATCH.

ASYNC_IO_COMPLETION Waits

This wait type occurs when SQL Server waits for asynchronous I/O operations (read or write) for pages other than buffer pool pages to complete. Examples include:

Regular checkpoint
Internal checkpoint when you start a database backup or run DBCC CHECKDB

Reading GAM pages from data files
Reading data pages from the database during a database backup (unfortunately, this tends to skew the average wait time, making it harder to analyze)

When I see a significant presence of both ASYNC_IO_COMPLETION and PAGEIOLATCH waits in the system, I perform general I/O troubleshooting. If PAGEIOLATCH waits are not present, I look at how often ASYNC_IO_COMPLETION occurs. I may ignore that wait if its percentage is not very significant and disk latency is low.

IO_COMPLETION Waits

The IO_COMPLETION wait type occurs during synchronous reads and writes in data files and during some read operations in the transaction log. Here are a few examples:

- Reading allocation map pages from the database
- Reading the transaction log during database recovery
- Writing data to `tempdb` during sort spills

When you see significant percentages of this wait type in the system, perform general disk-performance troubleshooting. Pay specific attention to `tempdb` latency and throughput; in my experience, bad `tempdb` performance is the most common reason for this wait. I will talk more about `tempdb` troubleshooting in Chapter 9.

WRITELOG Waits

As you can guess by the name, this wait occurs when SQL Server writes log records to the transaction log. It is normal to see this wait in any system; however, a large percentage may indicate a transaction log bottleneck.

Look at average wait time and transaction log write latency in the `sys.dm_io_vir tual_file_stats` view during troubleshooting. High numbers are impactful and may affect throughput in the system.

In addition to optimizing disk subsystem throughput, there are several other things you can do to reduce this wait. I will discuss them in Chapter 11.

WRITE_COMPLETION Waits

This wait occurs during synchronous write operations in database and log files. In my experience, it is most common with database snapshots.

SQL Server maintains database snapshots by persisting versions of data pages that existed when the snapshot was created. At a checkpoint, SQL Server reads old copies of data pages from data files and saves them into a snapshot before saving dirty pages to disk. This can significantly increase the amount of I/O in the system.

When you see this wait, check if there are database snapshots present. Remember that some internal processes, like `DBCC CHECKDB`, also create internal database snapshots.

When snapshots are present and their usage is legitimate, you may need to analyze how to improve disk performance to support them. In other cases, you may need to remove them from the system if storage cannot keep up.

PAGEIOLATCH Waits

As you already know, `PAGEIOLATCH` waits occur when SQL Server reads data pages from disk. These waits are very common and are present in every system. Technically, there are six such waits, but only three of them are actually noticeable:

PAGEIOLATCH_EX

Occurs when the worker wants to update the data page and is waiting for the page to be read from disk to the buffer pool

PAGEIOLATCH_SH

Occurs when the worker wants to read the data page and is waiting for the page to be read from disk to the buffer pool

PAGEIOLATCH_UP

Occurs when the worker wants to update a system page (e.g., the allocation map) and is waiting for the page to be read from disk to the buffer pool

Excessive numbers of PAGEIOLATCH waits show that SQL Server is constantly reading data from disk. This usually occurs under two conditions. The first condition is an under-provisioned SQL Server: when the active data does not fit into the memory. The second, and more prevalent, condition indicates the presence of nonoptimized queries that scan unnecessary data, flushing the contents of the buffer pool.

You can cross-check the data by looking at the Page Life Expectancy performance counter, which shows how long data pages stay in the buffer pool. As a baseline, you can generally use the value of 300 seconds per 4 GB of buffer pool memory: for example, 7,500 seconds on the server with a 100 GB buffer pool.

You can see the value of Page Life Expectancy in the PerfMon utility or with the sys.dm_os_performance_counters view, as shown in Listing 3-3. It also returns values for individual NUMA nodes in the system.

Listing 3-3. Getting Page Life Expectancy in the system

```
SELECT object_name, counter_name, instance_name, cntr_value as [PLE(sec)]
FROM sys.dm_os_performance_counters WITH (NOLOCK)
WHERE counter_name = 'Page life expectancy'
OPTION (RECOMPILE);
```

A large percentage of PAGEIOLATCH waits always require troubleshooting. While this does not always introduce customer-facing problems, especially with low-latency flash-based disk arrays, the data growth may push the disk subsystem over the limit, which can become a problem that quickly affects the entire system.

You can reduce the impact of PAGEIOLATCH waits by upgrading the disk subsystem or adding more memory to the server. However, the best approach is to reduce the amount of data to read from disk by detecting and optimizing inefficient queries. We'll look at how to detect these queries in the next chapter.

Summary

SQL Server uses cooperative scheduling and, in the majority of cases, asynchronous I/O when it reads and writes data. By default, each scheduler has its own I/O queue and handles I/O in the system.

The `sys.dm_io_virtual_file_stats` view provides I/O throughput and latency metrics per database file. In a properly tuned system, the latency of transaction log writes should not exceed 1 to 2 milliseconds, and the latency of reads and writes to data files should not exceed 3 to 5 milliseconds with network-based storage and should be even lower with DAS.

Look at the *entire* I/O stack when troubleshooting bad I/O performance. The problem may be anywhere: in the OS, virtualization, network path, or storage layer.

In many cases, high I/O latency is introduced by bursts in I/O activity. Analyze and tune the checkpoint process. It is one of the most common offenders in busy systems.

In many cases, reducing disk activity will help you improve disk latency and system performance. Query optimization is one of the best ways to achieve this. We will look at how to detect nonoptimized queries in the system in the next chapter.

Troubleshooting Checklist

- ☐ Analyze disk subsystem latency with the `sys.dm_io_virtual_file_stats` view.
- ☐ Check if high latency is caused by bursts in I/O activity by analyzing SQL Server and OS performance counters.
- ☐ Review I/O metrics at the VM and storage levels, paying attention to noisy neighbors in your setup.
- ☐ Check disk queue depth settings in the I/O stack.
- ☐ Troubleshoot SQL Server checkpoint performance and switch to indirect checkpoints.
- ☐ Troubleshoot log performance if you see significant `WRITELOG` waits (see Chapter 11).
- ☐ Troubleshoot `tempdb` performance if you see significant `IO_COMPLETION` waits and high `tempdb` usage and latency (see Chapter 9).
- ☐ Detect and optimize inefficient queries if you see high `PAGEIOLATCH` waits in the system.

CHAPTER 4

Inefficient Queries

Inefficient queries exist in every system. They impact performance in many ways, most notably by increasing I/O load, CPU usage, and blocking. It is essential to detect and optimize them.

This chapter discusses inefficient queries and their potential impact on your system, and provides guidelines for detecting them, starting with an approach that uses plan cache–based execution statistics. It also covers Extended Events, SQL Traces, and the Query Store, and ends with a few thoughts on third-party monitoring tools. We will cover strategies for optimizing inefficient queries in subsequent chapters.

The Impact of Inefficient Queries

During my career as a database engineer, I have yet to see a system that wouldn't benefit from query optimization. I'm sure they exist; after all, no one calls me in to look at perfectly healthy systems. Nevertheless, they are few and far between, and there are always opportunities to improve and optimize.

Not every company prioritizes query optimization, though. It's a time-consuming and tedious process, and in many cases it's cheaper, given the benefits of speeding up development and time to market, to throw hardware at the problem than to invest hours in performance tuning.

At some point, however, that approach leads to scalability issues. Poorly optimized queries impact systems from many angles, but perhaps the most obvious is disk performance. If the I/O subsystem cannot keep up with the load of large scans, the performance of your entire system will suffer.

You can mask this problem to a degree by adding more memory to the server. This increases the size of the buffer pool and allows SQL Server to cache more data, reducing physical I/O. As the amount of data in the system grows over time, however, this approach may become impractical or even impossible—especially in non-Enterprise editions of SQL Server that restrict the maximum buffer pool size.

Another effect to watch for is that nonoptimized queries burn CPU on the servers. The more data you process, the more CPU resources you consume. A server might spend just a few microseconds per logical read and in-memory data-page scan, but that quickly adds up as the number of reads increases.

Again, you can mask this by adding more CPUs to the server. (Note, however, that you need to pay for additional licenses and also would have limits on the maximum number of CPUs in non-Enterprise editions.) Moreover, adding CPUs may not always solve the problem, as nonoptimized queries will still contribute to blocking. While there are ways to reduce blocking without performing query tuning, this can change system behavior and has performance implications.

The bottom line is this: when you troubleshoot a system, always analyze whether queries are poorly optimized. Once you've done that, estimate the impact of those inefficient queries.

While query optimization always benefits a system, it is not always simple, nor does it always provide the best ROI for your efforts. Nevertheless, more often than not, you will at least need to tune some queries.

To put things into perspective, I perform query tuning when I see high disk through-put, blocking, or high CPU load in the system. However, I may initially focus my efforts elsewhere if data is cached in the buffer pool and the CPU load is acceptable. I have to be careful and think about data growth, though; it is possible that active data will one day outgrow the buffer pool, which could lead to a sudden and serious performance impact.

Fortunately, query optimization does not require an all-or-nothing approach! You can achieve dramatic performance improvements by optimizing just a handful of frequently executed queries. Let's look at a few methods for detecting them.

Plan Cache–Based Execution Statistics

In most cases, SQL Server caches and reuses execution plans for queries. For each plan in the cache, it also maintains execution statistics, including the number of times the query ran, the cumulative CPU time, and the I/O load. You can use this information to quickly pinpoint the most resource-intensive queries for optimization. (I will discuss plan caching in more detail in Chapter 6.)

Analyzing plan cache–based execution statistics is not the most comprehensive detection technique; it has quite a few limitations. Nevertheless, it is very easy to use, and in many cases it is *good enough*. It works in all versions of SQL Server and it is always present in the system. You don't need to set up any additional monitoring to collect the data.

You can get execution statistics using the `sys.dm_exec_query_stats` view (*https://oreil.ly/waA0W*), as shown in Listing 4-1. This query is a bit simplistic, but it demonstrates the view in action and shows you the list of metrics exposed in the view. I will use it to build a more sophisticated version of the code later in the chapter. Depending on your SQL Server version and patching level, some of the columns in the scripts in this and other chapters may not be supported. Remove them when this is the case.

The code provides you the execution plans of the queries. There are two functions that allow you to obtain them:

`sys.dm_exec_query_plan`
> This function (*https://oreil.ly/xeQEf*) returns the execution plan of the entire execution batch in XML format. Due to internal limitations of the function, the size of the resultant XML cannot exceed 2 MB, and the function may return NULL for the complex plans.

`sys.dm_exec_text_query_plan`
> This function (*https://oreil.ly/utOjM*), which I am using in Listing 4-1, returns a text representation of the execution plan. You can obtain it for the entire batch or for a specific statement from the batch by providing the statement's offset as a parameter to the function.

> In Listing 4-1, I am converting plans to XML representation using the TRY_CON VERT function, which returns NULL if the size of XML exceeds 2 MB. You can remove the TRY_CONVERT function if you need to deal with large plans or if you run the code in SQL Server 2005 through 2008R2.

Listing 4-1. Using the `sys.dm_exec_query_stats` *view*

```
;WITH Queries
AS
(
    SELECT TOP 50
        qs.creation_time AS [Cached Time]
        ,qs.last_execution_time AS [Last Exec Time]
        ,qs.execution_count AS [Exec Cnt]
        ,CONVERT(DECIMAL(10,5),
            IIF
            (
```

```
                    DATEDIFF(SECOND,qs.creation_time, qs.last_execution_time) = 0
                    ,NULL
                    ,1.0 * qs.execution_count /
                        DATEDIFF(SECOND,qs.creation_time, qs.last_execution_time)
            )
        ) AS [Exec Per Second]
        ,(qs.total_logical_reads + qs.total_logical_writes) /
            qs.execution_count AS [Avg IO]
        ,(qs.total_worker_time / qs.execution_count / 1000)
            AS [Avg CPU(ms)]
        ,qs.total_logical_reads AS [Total Reads]
        ,qs.last_logical_reads AS [Last Reads]
        ,qs.total_logical_writes AS [Total Writes]
        ,qs.last_logical_writes AS [Last Writes]
        ,qs.total_worker_time / 1000 AS [Total Worker Time]
        ,qs.last_worker_time / 1000 AS [Last Worker Time]
        ,qs.total_elapsed_time / 1000 AS [Total Elapsed Time]
        ,qs.last_elapsed_time / 1000 AS [Last Elapsed Time]
        ,qs.total_rows AS [Total Rows]
        ,qs.last_rows AS [Last Rows]
        ,qs.total_rows / qs.execution_count AS [Avg Rows]
        ,qs.total_physical_reads AS [Total Physical Reads]
        ,qs.last_physical_reads AS [Last Physical Reads]
        ,qs.total_physical_reads / qs.execution_count
            AS [Avg Physical Reads]
        ,qs.total_grant_kb AS [Total Grant KB]
        ,qs.last_grant_kb AS [Last Grant KB]
        ,(qs.total_grant_kb / qs.execution_count)
            AS [Avg Grant KB]
        ,qs.total_used_grant_kb AS [Total Used Grant KB]
        ,qs.last_used_grant_kb AS [Last Used Grant KB]
        ,(qs.total_used_grant_kb / qs.execution_count)
            AS [Avg Used Grant KB]
        ,qs.total_ideal_grant_kb AS [Total Ideal Grant KB]
        ,qs.last_ideal_grant_kb AS [Last Ideal Grant KB]
        ,(qs.total_ideal_grant_kb / qs.execution_count)
            AS [Avg Ideal Grant KB]
        ,qs.total_columnstore_segment_reads
            AS [Total CSI Segments Read]
        ,qs.last_columnstore_segment_reads
            AS [Last CSI Segments Read]
        ,(qs.total_columnstore_segment_reads / qs.execution_count)
            AS [AVG CSI Segments Read]
        ,qs.max_dop AS [Max DOP]
        ,qs.total_spills AS [Total Spills]
        ,qs.last_spills AS [Last Spills]
        ,(qs.total_spills / qs.execution_count) AS [Avg Spills]
        ,qs.statement_start_offset
        ,qs.statement_end_offset
        ,qs.plan_handle
        ,qs.sql_handle
    FROM
```

```
        sys.dm_exec_query_stats qs WITH (NOLOCK)
    ORDER BY
        [Avg IO] DESC
)
SELECT
    SUBSTRING(qt.text, (qs.statement_start_offset/2)+1,
    ((
        CASE qs.statement_end_offset
            WHEN -1 THEN DATALENGTH(qt.text)
            ELSE qs.statement_end_offset
        END - qs.statement_start_offset)/2)+1) AS SQL
    ,TRY_CONVERT(xml,qp.query_plan) AS [Query Plan]
    ,qs.*
FROM
    Queries qs
        OUTER APPLY sys.dm_exec_sql_text(qs.sql_handle) qt
        OUTER APPLY
            sys.dm_exec_text_query_plan
            (
                qs.plan_handle
                ,qs.statement_start_offset
                ,qs.statement_end_offset
            ) qp
OPTION (RECOMPILE, MAXDOP 1);
```

You can sort data differently based on your tuning goals: by I/O when you need to reduce disk load, by CPU on CPU-bound systems, and so on.

Figure 4-1 shows partial output of the query from one of the servers. As you can see, it is easy to choose queries to optimize based on the frequency of query executions and resource consumption data in the output.

The execution plans you get in the output do not include actual execution metrics. In this respect, they are similar to estimated execution plans. You'll need to take this into consideration during optimization (I'll talk more about this in Chapter 5).

This problem can be addressed in SQL Server 2019 and later, and in Azure SQL Databases where you can enable collection of the last *actual* execution plan for the statement in the databases with compatibility level 150. You also need to enable the LAST_QUERY_PLAN_STATS database option. As with any data collection, enabling this option would introduce overhead in the system; however, this overhead is relatively small.

You can access the last actual execution plan through the sys.dm_exec_query _plan_stats function (*https://oreil.ly/Rdf3U*). You can replace the sys.dm_exec _text_query_plan function with the new function in all code examples in this chapter—they will continue to work.

There are several other important limitations to remember. First and foremost, you won't see any data for the queries that do not have execution plans cached. You may miss some infrequently executed queries with plans evicted from the cache. Usually, this is not a problem; infrequently executed queries rarely need to be optimized at the beginning of tuning.

	SQL	Query Plan	Cached Time	Last Exec Time	Exec Cnt
1	Select * in	≤ShowPlanXML	2022-02-22 12:01:11.1	2022-02-22 12:01:13.0	1
2	merge bi.or	≤ShowPlanXML	2022-02-22 11:51:59.9	2022-02-22 11:52:03.3	1
3	insert into	≤ShowPlanXML	2022-02-22 11:05:15.6	2022-02-22 11:05:17.6	1
4	select * in	≤ShowPlanXML	2022-02-22 11:02:07.3	2022-02-22 11:02:07.3	1
5	select * in	≤ShowPlanXML	2022-02-22 11:03:37.4	2022-02-22 11:03:38.6	1
6	With PreQ a	NULL	2022-02-22 11:11:19.6	2022-02-22 11:16:16.7	3
7	UPDATE bi …	≤ShowPlanXML	2022-02-20 21:34:13.9	2022-02-22 11:59:48.2	9
8	insert into	≤ShowPlanXML	2022-02-19 01:12:05.5	2022-02-22 11:56:58.5	169
9	Merge bi.ac	≤ShowPlanXML	2022-02-22 12:30:42.5	2022-02-22 12:30:42.6	1
10	insert into	≤ShowPlanXML	2022-02-21 06:19:44.3	2022-02-22 12:31:25.5	64

Exec Per Second	Avg IO ⌄	Avg CPU(ms)	Total Reads	Last Reads	Total Writes
0.50000	635122575	4687180	635120267	635120267	2308
0.25000	150500130	237832	150209652	150209652	290478
0.50000	67049164	156828	66824528	66824528	224636
NULL	22608784	35622	22555427	22555427	53357
1.00000	20763067	67591	20719876	20719876	43191
0.01010	20455292	60050	61346943	20456593	18934
0.00007	16741751	56048	150667788	16642890	7972
0.00057	11209013	14492	1891521510	12295322	2801826
NULL	10895279	8734	10868145	10868145	27134
0.00059	6982600	31306	424448642	6609908	22437782
NULL	5756177	30600	5754720	5754720	1448

Figure 4-1. Partial output from the `sys.dm_exec_query_stats` *view*

There is another possibility, however. SQL Server won't cache execution plans if you are using a statement-level recompile with ad-hoc statements or executing stored procedures with a `RECOMPILE` clause. You need to capture those queries using the Query Store or Extended Events, which I will discuss later in this chapter.

If you are using a statement-level recompile in stored procedures or other T-SQL modules, SQL Server will cache the execution plan of the statement. The plan, however, is not going to be reused, and execution statistics will have the data only from the single (last) execution.

The second problem is related to how long plans stay cached. This varies by plan, which may skew the results when you sort data by *total* metrics. For example, a query with lower *average* CPU time may show a higher *total* number of executions and CPU time than a query with higher *average* CPU time, depending on the time when both plans were cached.

You can use either of these metrics, but neither approach is perfect. When you sort data by *average* values, you may see infrequently executed queries at the top of the list. Think about resource-intensive nightly jobs as an example. On the other hand, sorting by *total* values may omit the queries with the plans that had been recently cached.

You can look at the creation_time and last_execution_time columns, which show the last time when plans were cached and executed, respectively. I usually look at the data sorted based on both *total* and *average* metrics, taking the frequency of executions (the total and the average number of executions per second) into consideration. I collate the data from both outputs before deciding what to optimize.

The final problem is more complicated: it is possible to get multiple results for the same or similar queries. This can happen with ad-hoc workloads, with clients that have different SET settings in their sessions, when users run the same queries with slightly different formatting, and in many other cases. This may also occur in databases with compatibility level 160 (SQL Server 2022) due to the parameter-sensitive plan optimization feature (more on this in Chapter 6).

Fortunately, you can address that problem by using two columns, query_hash and query_plan_hash, both exposed in the sys.dm_exec_query_stats view. The same values in those columns would indicate similar queries and execution plans. You can use those columns to aggregate data.

 The DBCC FREEPROCCACHE statement clears the plan cache to reduce the size of the output in the demo. Do not run the code from Listing 4-2 on production servers!

Let me demonstrate with a simple example. Listing 4-2 runs three queries and then examines the content of the plan cache. The first two queries are the same—they just have different formatting. The third one is different.

Listing 4-2. The `query_hash` and `query_plan_hash` queries in action

```
DBCC FREEPROCCACHE -- Do not run in production!
GO
SELECT /*V1*/ TOP 1 object_id FROM sys.objects WHERE object_id = 1;
GO
SELECT /*V2*/ TOP 1 object_id
FROM sys.objects
WHERE object_id = 1;
GO
SELECT COUNT(*) FROM sys.objects
GO

SELECT
    qs.query_hash, qs.query_plan_hash, qs.sql_handle, qs.plan_handle,
    SUBSTRING(qt.text, (qs.statement_start_offset/2)+1,
    ((
        CASE qs.statement_end_offset
            WHEN -1 THEN DATALENGTH(qt.text)
            ELSE qs.statement_end_offset
        END - qs.statement_start_offset)/2)+1
    ) as SQL
FROM
    sys.dm_exec_query_stats qs
        CROSS APPLY sys.dm_exec_sql_text(qs.sql_handle) qt
ORDER BY query_hash
OPTION (MAXDOP 1, RECOMPILE);
```

You can see the results in Figure 4-2. There are three execution plans in the output. The last two rows have the same `query_hash` and `query_plan_hash` values and different `sql_handle` and `plan_handle` values.

	query_hash	query_plan_hash	sql_handle
1	0xABDF4B6F62E6CAB0	0xADFF8147759B43B8	0x0200000016AE0C0B001D08E62EFCC38CF0A7C26D920AB
2	0xC4EB59564B047EB4	0xF75077CD192BF0C4	0x020000007F0DE40F795F3792B222370C41D02238CAB50
3	0xC4EB59564B047EB4	0xF75077CD192BF0C4	0x02000000E145B236E584443C694C2299F79EE505355D5I

plan_handle	SQL
0x0600010016AE0C0B9010C2DE5602000001000000000€	SELECT COUNT(*) FROM sys.objects
0x060001007F0DE40FE00CC2DE5602000001000000000€	SELECT /*V2*/ TOP 1 object_id FROM sys.objects
0x06000100E145B2363009C2DE5602000001000000000€	SELECT /*V1*/ TOP 1 object_id FROM sys.objects

Figure 4-2. Multiple plans with the same `query_hash` and `query_plan_hash` values

Listing 4-3 provides a more sophisticated version of the script from Listing 4-1 by aggregating statistics from similar queries. The statement and execution plans are picked up randomly from the first query in each group, so factor that into your analysis.

Listing 4-3. Using the sys.dm_exec_query_stats view with query_hash aggregation

```
;WITH Data
AS
(
    SELECT TOP 50
        qs.query_hash
        ,COUNT(*) as [Plan Count]
        ,MIN(qs.creation_time) AS [Cached Time]
        ,MAX(qs.last_execution_time) AS [Last Exec Time]
        ,SUM(qs.execution_count) AS [Exec Cnt]
        ,SUM(qs.total_logical_reads) AS [Total Reads]
        ,SUM(qs.total_logical_writes) AS [Total Writes]
        ,SUM(qs.total_worker_time / 1000) AS [Total Worker Time]
        ,SUM(qs.total_elapsed_time / 1000) AS [Total Elapsed Time]
        ,SUM(qs.total_rows) AS [Total Rows]
        ,SUM(qs.total_physical_reads) AS [Total Physical Reads]
        ,SUM(qs.total_grant_kb) AS [Total Grant KB]
        ,SUM(qs.total_used_grant_kb) AS [Total Used Grant KB]
        ,SUM(qs.total_ideal_grant_kb) AS [Total Ideal Grant KB]
        ,SUM(qs.total_columnstore_segment_reads)
            AS [Total CSI Segments Read]
        ,MAX(qs.max_dop) AS [Max DOP]
        ,SUM(qs.total_spills) AS [Total Spills]
    FROM
        sys.dm_exec_query_stats qs WITH (NOLOCK)
    GROUP BY
        qs.query_hash
    ORDER BY
        SUM((qs.total_logical_reads + qs.total_logical_writes) /
            qs.execution_count) DESC
)
SELECT
    d.[Cached Time]
    ,d.[Last Exec Time]
    ,d.[Plan Count]
    ,sql_plan.SQL
    ,sql_plan.[Query Plan]
    ,d.[Exec Cnt]
    ,CONVERT(DECIMAL(10,5),
        IIF(datediff(second,d.[Cached Time], d.[Last Exec Time]) = 0,
            NULL,
            1.0 * d.[Exec Cnt] /
                datediff(second,d.[Cached Time], d.[Last Exec Time])
        )
    ) AS [Exec Per Second]
```

```
        ,(d.[Total Reads] + d.[Total Writes]) / d.[Exec Cnt] AS [Avg IO]
        ,(d.[Total Worker Time] / d.[Exec Cnt] / 1000) AS [Avg CPU(ms)]
        ,d.[Total Reads]
        ,d.[Total Writes]
        ,d.[Total Worker Time]
        ,d.[Total Elapsed Time]
        ,d.[Total Rows]
        ,d.[Total Rows] / d.[Exec Cnt] AS [Avg Rows]
        ,d.[Total Physical Reads]
        ,d.[Total Physical Reads] / d.[Exec Cnt] AS [Avg Physical Reads]
        ,d.[Total Grant KB]
        ,d.[Total Grant KB] / d.[Exec Cnt] AS [Avg Grant KB]
        ,d.[Total Used Grant KB]
        ,d.[Total Used Grant KB] / d.[Exec Cnt] AS [Avg Used Grant KB]
        ,d.[Total Ideal Grant KB]
        ,d.[Total Ideal Grant KB] / d.[Exec Cnt] AS [Avg Ideal Grant KB]
        ,d.[Total CSI Segments Read]
        ,d.[Total CSI Segments Read] / d.[Exec Cnt] AS [AVG CSI Segments Read]
        ,d.[Max DOP]
        ,d.[Total Spills]
        ,d.[Total Spills] / d.[Exec Cnt] AS [Avg Spills]
FROM
    Data d
        CROSS APPLY
        (
            SELECT TOP 1
                SUBSTRING(qt.text, (qs.statement_start_offset/2)+1,
                ((
                    CASE qs.statement_end_offset
                        WHEN -1 THEN DATALENGTH(qt.text)
                        ELSE qs.statement_end_offset
                    END - qs.statement_start_offset)/2)+1
                ) AS SQL
                ,TRY_CONVERT(XML,qp.query_plan) AS [Query Plan]
            FROM
                sys.dm_exec_query_stats qs
                    OUTER APPLY sys.dm_exec_sql_text(qs.sql_handle) qt
                    OUTER APPLY sys.dm_exec_text_query_plan
                    (
                        qs.plan_handle
                        ,qs.statement_start_offset
                        ,qs.statement_end_offset
                    ) qp
            WHERE
                qs.query_hash = d.query_hash AND ISNULL(qt.text,'') <> ''
        ) sql_plan
ORDER BY
    [Avg IO] DESC
OPTION (RECOMPILE, MAXDOP 1);
```

Starting with SQL Server 2008, you can get execution statistics for stored procedures through the sys.dm_exec_procedure_stats view (*https://oreil.ly/B2Xyg*). You can use the code from Listing 4-4 to do this. As with the sys.dm_exec_query_stats view, you can sort data by various execution metrics, depending on your optimization strategy. It is worth noting that the execution statistics include the metrics from dynamic SQL and other nested modules (stored procedures, functions, triggers) called from the stored procedures.

Listing 4-4. Using the sys.dm_exec_procedure_stats view

```
SELECT TOP 50
    IIF (ps.database_id = 32767,
        'mssqlsystemresource',
        DB_NAME(ps.database_id)
    ) AS [DB]
    ,OBJECT_NAME(
        ps.object_id,
        IIF(ps.database_id = 32767, 1, ps.database_id)
    ) AS [Proc Name]
    ,ps.type_desc AS [Type]
    ,ps.cached_time AS [Cached Time]
    ,ps.last_execution_time AS [Last Exec Time]
    ,qp.query_plan AS [Plan]
    ,ps.execution_count AS [Exec Count]
    ,CONVERT(DECIMAL(10,5),
        IIF(datediff(second,ps.cached_time, ps.last_execution_time) = 0,
            NULL,
            1.0 * ps.execution_count /
                datediff(second,ps.cached_time, ps.last_execution_time)
        )
    ) AS [Exec Per Second]
    ,(ps.total_logical_reads + ps.total_logical_writes) /
        ps.execution_count AS [Avg IO]
    ,(ps.total_worker_time / ps.execution_count / 1000)
        AS [Avg CPU(ms)]
    ,ps.total_logical_reads AS [Total Reads]
    ,ps.last_logical_reads AS [Last Reads]
    ,ps.total_logical_writes AS [Total Writes]
    ,ps.last_logical_writes AS [Last Writes]
    ,ps.total_worker_time / 1000 AS [Total Worker Time]
    ,ps.last_worker_time / 1000 AS [Last Worker Time]
    ,ps.total_elapsed_time / 1000 AS [Total Elapsed Time]
    ,ps.last_elapsed_time / 1000 AS [Last Elapsed Time]
    ,ps.total_physical_reads AS [Total Physical Reads]
    ,ps.last_physical_reads AS [Last Physical Reads]
    ,ps.total_physical_reads / ps.execution_count AS [Avg Physical Reads]
    ,ps.total_spills AS [Total Spills]
    ,ps.last_spills AS [Last Spills]
    ,(ps.total_spills / ps.execution_count) AS [Avg Spills]
FROM
```

```
    sys.dm_exec_procedure_stats ps WITH (NOLOCK)
        CROSS APPLY sys.dm_exec_query_plan(ps.plan_handle) qp
ORDER BY
    [Avg IO] DESC
OPTION (RECOMPILE, MAXDOP 1);
```

Figure 4-3 shows partial output of the code. As you can see in the output, you can get execution plans for the stored procedures. Internally, the execution plans of stored procedures and other T-SQL modules are just collections of each statement's individual plan. In some cases—for example, when the size of the execution plan exceeds 2 MB—the script would not include a plan in the output.

	DB	Proc Name	Type	Cached Time	Last Exec Time
1		IndexOptimize	SQL_STORED_PROCEDURE	2021-01-03 01:05:01.067	2021-01-10 01:05:00.640
2		archive_data	SQL_STORED_PROCEDURE	2021-01-10 05:45:00.503	2021-01-12 05:45:00.367
3		archive_misc	SQL_STORED_PROCEDURE	2021-01-03 05:47:42.547	2021-01-12 05:49:36.920
4		AGGREGATE_LI…	SQL_STORED_PROCEDURE	2021-01-10 03:01:48.407	2021-01-12 18:19:46.477
5		archive_orde…	SQL_STORED_PROCEDURE	2021-01-10 05:45:03.197	2021-01-12 05:45:06.397
6		archive_inte…	SQL_STORED_PROCEDURE	2021-01-11 05:47:20.680	2021-01-12 05:48:32.947

Plan	Exec Count	Exec Per Second	Avg IO	Avg CPU(ms)
NULL	2	0.00000	997605286	3231184
<ShowPlanXML xmlns="http:/…	3	0.00002	177832619	940548
<ShowPlanXML xmlns="http:/…	10	0.00001	80059850	677919
<ShowPlanXML xmlns="http:/…	404	0.00177	44012127	117734
NULL	3	0.00002	43522659	73929
<ShowPlanXML xmlns="http:/…	2	0.00002	23452696	40479

Figure 4-3. Partial output of the sys.dm_exec_procedure_stats *view*

Listing 4-5 helps address this. You can use it to get cached execution plans and their metrics for individual statements from T-SQL modules. You need to specify the name of the module in the WHERE clause of the statement when you run the script.

Listing 4-5. Getting the execution plan and statistics for stored procedure statements

```
SELECT
    qs.creation_time AS [Cached Time]
    ,qs.last_execution_time AS [Last Exec Time]
    ,SUBSTRING(qt.text, (qs.statement_start_offset/2)+1,
    ((
        CASE qs.statement_end_offset
            WHEN -1 THEN DATALENGTH(qt.text)
            ELSE qs.statement_end_offset
        END - qs.statement_start_offset)/2)+1) AS SQL
    ,TRY_CONVERT(XML,qp.query_plan) AS [Query Plan]
```

```
    ,CONVERT(DECIMAL(10,5),
        IIF(datediff(second,qs.creation_time, qs.last_execution_time) = 0,
            NULL,
            1.0 * qs.execution_count /
                datediff(second,qs.creation_time, qs.last_execution_time)
        )
    ) AS [Exec Per Second]
    ,(qs.total_logical_reads + qs.total_logical_writes) /
        qs.execution_count AS [Avg IO]
    ,(qs.total_worker_time / qs.execution_count / 1000)
        AS [Avg CPU(ms)]
    ,qs.total_logical_reads AS [Total Reads]
    ,qs.last_logical_reads AS [Last Reads]
    ,qs.total_logical_writes AS [Total Writes]
    ,qs.last_logical_writes AS [Last Writes]
    ,qs.total_worker_time / 1000 AS [Total Worker Time]
    ,qs.last_worker_time / 1000 AS [Last Worker Time]
    ,qs.total_elapsed_time / 1000 AS [Total Elapsed Time]
    ,qs.last_elapsed_time / 1000 AS [Last Elapsed Time]
    ,qs.total_rows AS [Total Rows]
    ,qs.last_rows AS [Last Rows]
    ,qs.total_rows / qs.execution_count AS [Avg Rows]
    ,qs.total_physical_reads AS [Total Physical Reads]
    ,qs.last_physical_reads AS [Last Physical Reads]
    ,qs.total_physical_reads / qs.execution_count
        AS [Avg Physical Reads]
    ,qs.total_grant_kb AS [Total Grant KB]
    ,qs.last_grant_kb AS [Last Grant KB]
    ,(qs.total_grant_kb / qs.execution_count)
        AS [Avg Grant KB]
    ,qs.total_used_grant_kb AS [Total Used Grant KB]
    ,qs.last_used_grant_kb AS [Last Used Grant KB]
    ,(qs.total_used_grant_kb / qs.execution_count)
        AS [Avg Used Grant KB]
    ,qs.total_ideal_grant_kb AS [Total Ideal Grant KB]
    ,qs.last_ideal_grant_kb AS [Last Ideal Grant KB]
    ,(qs.total_ideal_grant_kb / qs.execution_count)
        AS [Avg Ideal Grant KB]
    ,qs.total_columnstore_segment_reads
        AS [Total CSI Segments Read]
    ,qs.last_columnstore_segment_reads
        AS [Last CSI Segments Read]
    ,(qs.total_columnstore_segment_reads / qs.execution_count)
        AS [AVG CSI Segments Read]
    ,qs.max_dop AS [Max DOP]
    ,qs.total_spills AS [Total Spills]
    ,qs.last_spills AS [Last Spills]
    ,(qs.total_spills / qs.execution_count) AS [Avg Spills]
FROM
    sys.dm_exec_query_stats qs WITH (NOLOCK)
        OUTER APPLY sys.dm_exec_sql_text(qs.sql_handle) qt
        OUTER APPLY sys.dm_exec_text_query_plan
```

```
        (
            qs.plan_handle
            ,qs.statement_start_offset
            ,qs.statement_end_offset
        ) qp
WHERE
    OBJECT_NAME(qt.objectid, qt.dbid) = <SP Name> -- Add SP Name here
ORDER BY
    qs.statement_start_offset, qs.statement_end_offset
OPTION (RECOMPILE, MAXDOP 1);
```

Starting with SQL Server 2016, you can get execution statistics for triggers and scalar user-defined functions, using `sys.dm_exec_trigger_stats` (*https://oreil.ly/EVobu*) and `sys.dm_exec_function_stats` (*https://oreil.ly/mZEJO*) views, respectively. You can use the same code as in Listing 4-4; just replace the DMV name there. You can also download the code from this book's companion material.

Finally, it is worth mentioning that SQL Server may cache thousands of execution plans. Moreover, the functions to obtain query plans and SQL statements are resource intensive; thus, I am using the `MAXDOP 1` query hint to reduce the overhead. In some cases, it may be beneficial to save the content of the plan cache to a separate database using `SELECT INTO` statements and analyze the data on nonproduction servers.

Troubleshooting based on plan cache–based execution statistics has several limitations, and you may miss some queries. Nevertheless, it is a great starting point. Most importantly, the data is collected automatically, and you can access it immediately, without setting up additional monitoring tools.

Extended Events and SQL Traces

I am sure that every SQL Server engineer is aware of SQL Traces and Extended Events (xEvents). They allow you to capture various events in a system for analysis and troubleshooting in real time. You can also use them to capture long-running and expensive queries, including those that don't cache execution plans and are therefore missed by the `sys.dm_exec_query_stats` view.

I'd like to start this section with a warning, though: do *not* use SQL Traces and xEvents for this purpose unless it is *absolutely necessary*. Capturing executed statements is an expensive operation that may introduce significant performance overhead in busy systems. (You saw one such example in Chapter 1.)

It does not matter how much data you collect. You can exclude most statements from the output by filtering out queries with low resource consumption. But SQL Server will still have to capture *all* statements to evaluate, filter, and discard unnecessary events.

Don't collect unnecessary information in events you are collecting or in xEvent actions you are capturing. Some actions—for example, `callstack`—are expensive and lead to a serious performance hit when enabled. When possible, use xEvents instead of SQL Traces. They are lighter and introduce less overhead in the system.

Table 4-1 shows several Extended and SQL Trace events that can be used to detect inefficient queries. Each of them, except `sqlserver.attention`, has a corresponding event that fires at the beginning of the execution. Sometimes you need to capture them to correlate workloads from multiple sessions.

Table 4-1. Extended and SQL Trace events to detect inefficient queries

xEvent	SQL Trace event	Comments
`sqlserver.sql_statement_completed`	`SQL:StmtCompleted`	Fired when the statement finishes the execution.
`sqlserver.sp_statement_completed`	`SP:StmtCompleted`	Fired when the SQL statement within the T-SQL module completes the execution.
`sqlserver.rpc_completed`	`RPC:Completed`	Fired when a remote procedure call (RPC) completes. RPCs are parameterized SQL requests, such as calls of stored procedures or parameterized batches, sent from applications. Many client libraries will run queries via `sp_executesql` calls, which can be captured by that event.
`sqlserver.module_end`	`SP:Completed`	Fired when the T-SQL module completes the execution.
`sqlserver.sql_batch_completed`	`SQL:BatchCompleted`	Fired when the SQL batch completes the execution.
`sqlserver.attention`	`Error:Attention`	Occur when the client cancels a query execution, either due to a timeout or explicitly (e.g., using the red cancel button in SSMS).

Your choice of what events to capture depends on the system workload, the data access tier's design, and your troubleshooting strategy. For example, the events `sqlserver.sql_statement_completed` and `sqlserver.sp_statement_completed` allow you to detect inefficient ad-hoc and T-SQL module queries. Alternatively, you can capture inefficient batches and stored procedures by using the `sqlserver.rpc_completed` and `sqlserver.sql_batch_completed` events, reducing overhead.

The same applies to choosing xEvent actions to capture. For example, you might ignore user and client application information if you don't need it during troubleshooting. Alternatively, you could decide to collect `query_hash` and `query_plan_hash` actions and use them to identify the cumulative impact of similar queries and execution plans.

There are two scenarios in which I usually capture inefficient queries. I may run a session for a few minutes, capturing results into the `ring_buffer` target. Usually, I do this when the workload in the system is relatively static and can be represented by a small sample. Alternatively, I might run an xEvent session for a few hours, using `event_file` as the target.

Listing 4-6 shows the latter approach of saving data to the *C:\ExtEvents* folder (change it in your system). It captures statements that consume more than 5,000 ms of CPU time or produce more than 50,000 logical reads or writes. The code in Listing 4-6 and Listing 4-7 will work in SQL Server 2012 and later; it may require modifications in SQL Server 2008, which works differently with the file target and lacks `query_hash` and `query_plan_hash` actions.

As a word of caution, this session introduces overhead. How much overhead you have will depend on the workload and the amount of data you are capturing. Do not keep this session active unless you are troubleshooting performance issues. Furthermore, tune the `cpu_time`, `logical_reads`, and `writes` threshold values to your workload, and avoid capturing an excessive number of queries.

Similarly, define a list of xEvents actions based on your troubleshooting strategy. For example, there is no need to collect `plan_handle` if you are going to perform the analysis on another server and would be unable to obtain execution plans from the plan cache.

Listing 4-6. Capturing CPU- and I/O-intensive queries

```
CREATE EVENT SESSION [Expensive Queries]
ON SERVER
ADD EVENT sqlserver.sql_statement_completed
(
    ACTION
    (
        sqlserver.client_app_name
        ,sqlserver.client_hostname
        ,sqlserver.database_id
        ,sqlserver.plan_handle
        ,sqlserver.query_hash
        ,sqlserver.query_plan_hash
        ,sqlserver.sql_text
        ,sqlserver.username
    )
    WHERE
    (
        (
            cpu_time >= 5000000 or -- Time in microseconds
            logical_reads >= 50000 or
            writes >= 50000
        ) AND
```

```
            sqlserver.is_system = 0
    )
)
,ADD EVENT sqlserver.sp_statement_completed
(
    ACTION
    (
        sqlserver.client_app_name
        ,sqlserver.client_hostname
        ,sqlserver.database_id
        ,sqlserver.plan_handle
        ,sqlserver.query_hash
        ,sqlserver.query_plan_hash
        ,sqlserver.sql_text
        ,sqlserver.username
    )
    WHERE
    (
        (
            cpu_time >= 5000000 or -- Time in microseconds
            logical_reads >= 50000 or
            writes >= 50000
        ) AND
        sqlserver.is_system = 0
    )
)
ADD TARGET package0.event_file
(
    SET FILENAME = 'C:\ExtEvents\Expensive Queries.xel'
)
WITH
(
    event_retention_mode=allow_single_event_loss
    ,max_dispatch_latency=30 seconds
);
```

Listing 4-7 provides the code to parse the collected data. As a first step, it loads the collected events into a temporary table using the `sys.fn_xe_file_target_read_file` function (*https://oreil.ly/L6sG8*). The asterisk at the end of the filename tells SQL Server to load all rollover files from the xEvent session.

Second, the code parses the collected events, saving the results to another temporary table. You may need to adjust the code in the `EventInfo` CTE based on the xEvent fields and actions you need for troubleshooting. Do not parse unnecessary information—shredding XML is an expensive and time-consuming operation.

Finally, if you run this code on SQL Server 2016 or earlier versions, you need to modify it and obtain the time of the event from the `event_data` XML. In SQL Server 2017, the `sys.fn_xe_file_target_read_file` function returns this as part of the output.

Listing 4-7. Parsing collected xEvent data

```
CREATE TABLE #EventData
(
  event_data XML NOT NULL,
  file_name NVARCHAR(260) NOT NULL,
  file_offset BIGINT NOT NULL,
  timestamp_utc datetime2(7) NOT NULL -- SQL Server 2017+
);

INSERT INTO #EventData(event_data, file_name, file_offset, timestamp_utc)
  SELECT CONVERT(XML,event_data), file_name, file_offset, timestamp_utc
  FROM sys.fn_xe_file_target_read_file
    ('c:\extevents\Expensive Queries*.xel',NULL,NULL,NULL);

;WITH EventInfo([Event],[Event Time],[DB],[Statement],[SQL],[User Name]
  ,[Client],[App],[CPU Time],[Duration],[Logical Reads]
  ,[Physical Reads],[Writes],[Rows],[Query Hash],[Plan Hash]
  ,[PlanHandle],[Stmt Offset],[Stmt Offset End],File_Name,File_Offset)
AS
(
  SELECT
    event_data.value('/event[1]/@name','SYSNAME') AS [Event]
    ,timestamp_utc AS [Event Time] -- SQL Server 2017+
    /*,event_data.value('/event[1]/@timestamp','DATETIME')
        AS [Event Time] -- Prior SQL Server 2017 */
    ,event_data.value
      ('(((/event[1]/action[@name="database_id"]/value/text())[1])'
        ,'INT') AS [DB]
    ,event_data.value
      ('(((/event[1]/data[@name="statement"]/value/text())[1])'
        ,'NVARCHAR(MAX)') AS [Statement]
    ,event_data.value
      ('(((/event[1]/action[@name="sql_text"]/value/text())[1])'
        ,'NVARCHAR(MAX)') AS [SQL]
    ,event_data.value
      ('(((/event[1]/action[@name="username"]/value/text())[1])'
        ,'NVARCHAR(255)') AS [User Name]
    ,event_data.value
      ('(((/event[1]/action[@name="client_hostname"]/value/text())[1])'
        ,'NVARCHAR(255)') AS [Client]
    ,event_data.value
      ('(((/event[1]/action[@name="client_app_name"]/value/text())[1])'
        ,'NVARCHAR(255)') AS [App]
    ,event_data.value
      ('(((/event[1]/data[@name="cpu_time"]/value/text())[1])'
        ,'BIGINT') AS [CPU Time]
    ,event_data.value
      ('(((/event[1]/data[@name="duration"]/value/text())[1])'
        ,'BIGINT') AS [Duration]
    ,event_data.value
      ('(((/event[1]/data[@name="logical_reads"]/value/text())[1])'
```

```
        ,'INT') AS [Logical Reads]
    ,event_data.value
        ('((/event[1]/data[@name="physical_reads"]/value/text())[1])'
            ,'INT') AS [Physical Reads]
    ,event_data.value
        ('((/event[1]/data[@name="writes"]/value/text())[1])'
            ,'INT') AS [Writes]
    ,event_data.value
        ('((/event[1]/data[@name="row_count"]/value/text())[1])'
            ,'INT') AS [Rows]
    ,event_data.value(
        'xs:hexBinary(((/event[1]/action[@name="query_hash"]/value/text())[1]))'
            ,'BINARY(8)') AS [Query Hash]
    ,event_data.value(
        'xs:hexBinary(((/event[1]/action[@name="query_plan_hash"]/value/text())[1]))'
            ,'BINARY(8)') AS [Plan Hash]
    ,event_data.value(
        'xs:hexBinary(((/event[1]/action[@name="plan_handle"]/value/text())[1]))'
            ,'VARBINARY(64)') AS [PlanHandle]
    ,event_data.value
        ('((/event[1]/data[@name="offset"]/value/text())[1])'
            ,'INT') AS [Stmt Offset]
    ,event_data.value
        ('((/event[1]/data[@name="offset_end"]/value/text())[1])'
            ,'INT') AS [Stmt Offset End]
    ,file_name
    ,file_offset
  FROM
    #EventData
)
SELECT
  ei.*
  ,TRY_CONVERT(XML,qp.Query_Plan) AS [Plan]
INTO #Queries
FROM
  EventInfo ei
    OUTER APPLY
      sys.dm_exec_text_query_plan
      (
        ei.PlanHandle
        ,ei.[Stmt Offset]
        ,ei.[Stmt Offset End]
      ) qp
OPTION (MAXDOP 1, RECOMPILE);
```

Now you can work with raw data from the #Queries table, detecting the most inefficient queries for optimization. In many cases, it is also beneficial to aggregate the data based on a statement, query hash, or plan hash, analyzing the cumulative impact of the queries.

The companion materials to this book include a script that you can use to capture the workload into the `ring_buffer` target. There is an important limitation, however: the `sys.dm_xe_session_targets` view, which provides the collected data from the target, can only output 4 MB of XML. This may lead to a situation when you don't see some collected events.

Again: *beware of the overhead that xEvents and SQL Traces introduce in systems*. Do *not* create and run those sessions permanently. In many cases, you can get enough troubleshooting data by enabling the session or trace for just a few minutes.

Query Store

So far, we have discussed two approaches to detecting inefficient queries in this chapter. Both have limitations. Plan cache–based data may miss some queries; SQL Traces and xEvents require you to perform complex analysis of the output and may have significant performance overhead in busy systems.

The Query Store, introduced in SQL Server 2016, helps address those limitations. You can think of it as something like the flight data recorders (or "black boxes") in airplane cockpits, but for SQL Server. When the Query Store is enabled, SQL Server captures and persists the runtime statistics and execution plans of the queries in the database. It shows how the execution plans perform and how they evolve over time. Finally, it allows you to force specific execution plans to queries addressing parameter-sniffing issues, which we will discuss in Chapter 6.

 The Query Store is disabled by default in the on-premises version of SQL Server up to SQL Server 2019. It is enabled by default in Azure SQL Databases, Azure SQL Managed Instances, and new databases created in SQL Server 2022.

The Query Store is fully integrated into the query processing pipeline, as illustrated by the high-level diagram in Figure 4-4.

When a query needs to be executed, SQL Server looks up the execution plan from the plan cache. If it finds a plan, SQL Server checks if the query needs to be recompiled (due to statistics updates or other factors), if a new forced plan has been created, and if an old forced plan has been dropped from the Query Store.

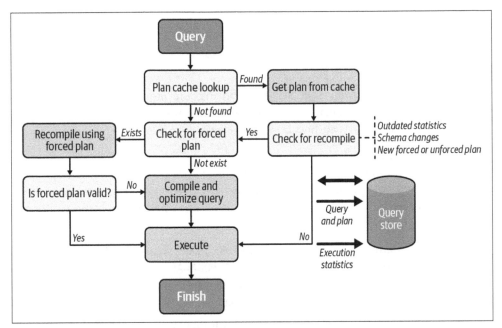

Figure 4-4. Query processing pipeline

During compilation, SQL Server checks if the query has a forced plan available. When this happens, the query essentially gets compiled with the forced plan, much like when the USE PLAN hint is used. If the resultant plan is valid, it is stored in the plan cache for reuse.

If the forced plan is no longer valid (e.g., when a user drops an index referenced in the forced plan), SQL Server does not fail the query. Instead, it compiles the query again without the forced plan and without caching it afterward. The Query Store, on the other hand, persists both plans, marking the forced plan as invalid. All of that happens transparently to the applications.

In SQL Server 2022 and SQL Azure Database, the Query Store allows you to add query-level hints using the sp_query_store_set_hints stored procedure (*https://oreil.ly/xI3nA*). With Query Store hints, SQL Server will compile and execute queries as if you were providing the hints using the OPTION query clause. This gives you additional flexibility during query tuning without the need to change the applications.

Despite its tight integration with the query processing pipeline and various internal optimizations, the Query Store still adds overhead to the system. Just how much overhead depends on the following two main factors:

Number of compilations in the system
> The more compilations SQL Server performs, the more load the Query Store must handle. In particular, the Query Store may not work very well in systems that have a very heavy, ad-hoc, nonparameterized workload.

Data collection settings
> The Query Store's configurations allow you to specify if you want to capture all queries or just expensive ones, along with aggregation intervals and data retention settings. If you collect more data and/or use smaller aggregation intervals, you'll have more overhead.
>
> Pay specific attention to the QUERY_CAPTURE_MODE setting, which controls what queries are captured. With QUERY_CAPTURE_MODE=ALL (the default in SQL Server 2016 and 2017), the Query Store captures all queries in the system. This can have an impact, especially on an ad-hoc workload.
>
> With QUERY_CAPTURE_MODE=AUTO (the default in SQL Server 2019 and later), the Query Store does not capture small or infrequently executed queries. This is the best option in most cases.
>
> Finally, starting with SQL Server 2019, you can set QUERY_CAPTURE_MODE=CUSTOM and customize criteria when queries are captured even further.

When properly configured, the overhead introduced by the Query Store is usually relatively small. However, it may be significant in some cases. For example, I've been using the Query Store to troubleshoot the performance of one process that consists of a very large number of small ad-hoc queries. I captured all the queries in the system using the QUERY_CAPTURE_MODE=ALL mode, collecting almost 10 GB of data in the Query Store. The process took 8 hours to complete with the Query Store enabled, compared to 2.5 hours without it.

Nevertheless, I suggest enabling the Query Store if your system can handle the overhead. For example, some features from the Intelligent Query Processing (IQP) family rely on the Query Store and will benefit from it. It also simplifies query tuning and may save you many hours of work when enabled.

 Monitor QDS* waits when you enable the Query Store. Excessive QDS* waits may be a sign of higher Query Store overhead in the system. Ignore QDS_PERSIST_TASK_MAIN_LOOP_SLEEP and QDS_ASYNC_QUEUE waits; they are benign.

There are two important trace flags that you should consider enabling if you are using the Query Store:

T7745

> To reduce overhead, SQL Server caches some Query Store data in memory periodically, flushing it to the database. The flush interval is controlled by the DATA_FLUSH_INTERVAL_SECONDS setting, which dictates how much Query Store data you can lose in the event of a SQL Server crash. In normal circumstances, however, SQL Server would save in-memory Query Store data during SQL Server shutdown or failover.
>
> This behavior may prolong shutdown and failover times in busy systems. You can disable this with trace flag T7745 as the loss of a small amount of telemetry is usually acceptable.

T7752 *(SQL Server 2016 and 2017)*

> SQL Server loads some Query Store data into memory on database startup, keeping the database unavailable during that time. With large Query Stores, this may prolong SQL Server restart or failover time and impact the user experience.
>
> The trace flag T7752 forces SQL Server to load Query Store data asynchronously, allowing queries to execute in parallel. The telemetry will not be collected during the load; however, it is usually an acceptable price to pay for faster startup.
>
> You can analyze the impact of a synchronous Query Store load by looking at the wait time for the QDS_LOADDB wait type. This wait occurs only at database startup, so you need to query the sys.dm_os_wait_stats view and filter the output by wait type to get the number.

As a general rule, do not create a very large Query Store. Also, consider monitoring Query Store size, especially in very busy systems. In some cases, SQL Server may not be able to clean up data quickly enough, especially if you are using the QUERY_CAP TURE_MODE=ALL collection mode.

Finally, apply the latest SQL Server updates, especially if you are using SQL Server 2016 and 2017. Multiple Query Store scalability enhancements and bug fixes were published after the initial release of the feature.

You can work with the Query Store in two ways: through the graphics UI in SSMS or by querying dynamic management views directly. Let's look at the UI first.

Query Store SSMS Reports

After you enable the Query Store in the database, you'll see a *Query Store* folder in the *Object Explorer* (Figure 4-5). The number of reports in the folder will depend on the versions of SQL Server and SSMS in your system. The rest of this section will walk you through the seven reports shown in Figure 4-5.

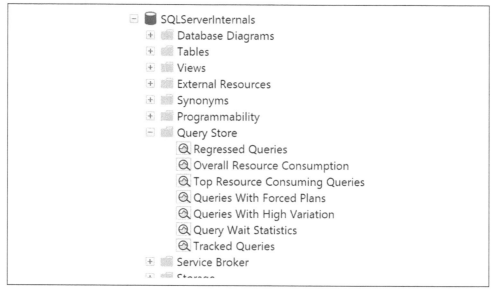

Figure 4-5. Query Store reports in SSMS

Regressed Queries

This report, shown in Figure 4-6, shows queries whose performance has regressed over time. You can configure the time frame and regression criteria (such as disk operations, CPU consumption, and number of executions) for analysis.

Choose the query in the graph in the upper-left portion of the report. The upper-right portion of the report illustrates collected execution plans for the selected query. You can click on the dots, which represent different execution plans, and see the plans at the bottom. You can also compare different execution plans.

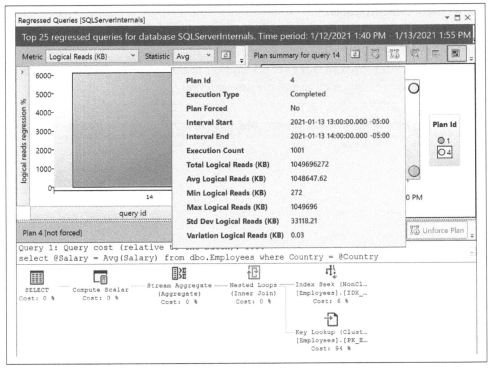

Figure 4-6. Regressed Queries report

The *Force Plan* button allows you to force a selected plan for the query. It calls the `sys.sp_query_store_force_plan` stored procedure (*https://oreil.ly/pnBff*) internally. Similarly, the *Unforce Plan* button removes a forced plan by calling the `sys.sp_query_store_unforce_plan` stored procedure (*https://oreil.ly/wa4i9*).

The Regressed Queries report is a great tool for troubleshooting issues related to parameter sniffing, which we will discuss in Chapter 6, and fixing them quickly by forcing specific execution plans.

Top Resource Consuming Queries

This report (Figure 4-7) allows you to detect the most resource-intensive queries in the system. While it works similarly to the data provided by the sys.dm _exec_query_stats view, it does not depend on the plan cache. You can customize the metrics used for data sorting and the time interval.

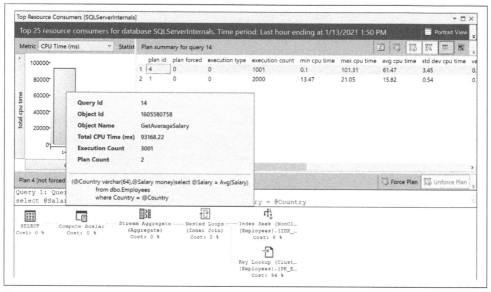

Figure 4-7. Top Resource Consuming Queries report

Overall Resource Consumption

This report shows the workload's statistics and resource usage over the specified time intervals. It allows you to detect and analyze spikes in resource usage and drill down to the queries that introduce such spikes. Figure 4-8 shows the output of the report.

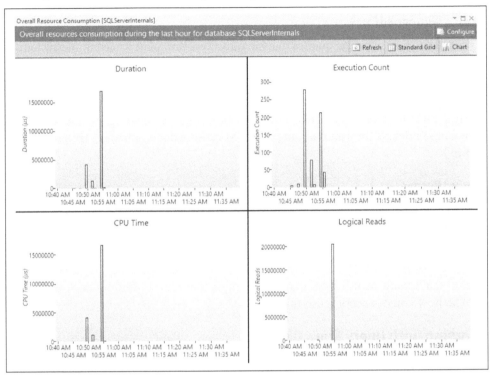

Figure 4-8. Overall Resource Consumption report

Queries With High Variation

This report allows you to pinpoint queries with high performance variation. You can use it to detect anomalies in the workload, along with possible performance regressions. To save space in the book, I am not including screenshots of every report.

Queries With Forced Plans

This report shows you the queries that have an execution plan forced in the system.

Query Wait Statistics

This report allows you to detect queries with high waits. The data is grouped by several categories (such as CPU, disk, and blocking), depending on the wait type. You can see details on wait mapping in the Microsoft documentation (*https://oreil.ly/ HmiJy*).

Tracked Queries

Finally, the Tracked Queries report allows you to monitor execution plans and statistics for individual queries. It provides similar information to the Regressed Queries and Top Resource Consuming Queries reports, at the scope of individual queries.

These reports will give you a large amount of data for analysis. However, in some cases, you'll want to use T-SQL and work with the Query Store data directly. Let's look at how you can accomplish this.

Working with Query Store DMVs

The Query Store dynamic management views are highly normalized, as shown in Figure 4-9. Execution statistics are tracked for each execution plan and grouped by collection intervals, which are defined by the INTERVAL_LENGTH_MINUTES setting. The default interval of 60 minutes is acceptable in most cases.

As you can guess, the smaller the intervals you use, the more data will be collected and persisted in the Query Store. The same applies to the system workload: an excessive number of ad-hoc queries may balloon the Query Store's size. Keep this in mind when you configure the Query Store in your system.

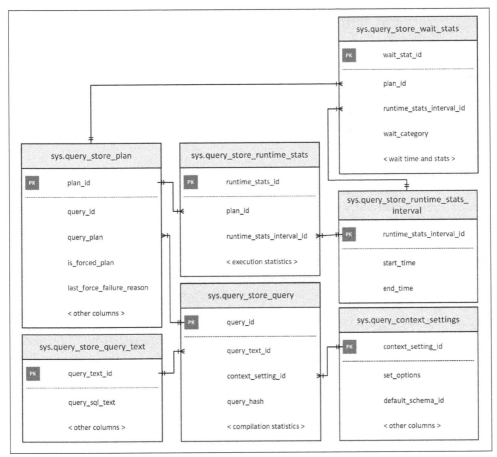

Figure 4-9. Query Store DMVs

You can logically separate DMVs into two categories: plan store and runtime statistics. Plan store DMVs include the following views:

sys.query_store_query
  The sys.query_store_query view (*https://oreil.ly/arFQS*) provides information about queries and their compilation statistics, as well as the time of the last execution.

sys.query_store_query_text
  The sys.query_store_query_text view (*https://oreil.ly/Add1d*) shows information about the query text.

sys.query_context_setting
  The sys.query_context_setting view (*https://oreil.ly/gcu4z*) contains information about context settings associated with the query. It includes SET options,

default schema for the session, language, and other attributes. SQL Server may generate and cache separate execution plans for the same query when those settings are different.

sys.query_store_plan

The sys.query_store_plan view (*https://oreil.ly/EnY5C*) provides information about query execution plans. The is_forced_plan column indicates whether the plan is forced. The last_force_failure_reason tells you why a forced plan was not applied to the query.

As you can see, each query can have multiple entries in the sys.query_store_query and sys.query_store_plan views. This will vary based on your session context options, recompilations, and other factors.

Three other views represent runtime statistics:

sys.query_store_runtime_stats_interval

The sys.query_store_runtime_stats_interval view (*https://oreil.ly/Aa8Wy*) contains information about statistics collection intervals.

sys.query_store_runtime_stats

The sys.query_store_runtime_stats view (*https://oreil.ly/Icoax*) references the sys.query_store_plan view and contains information about runtime statistics for a specific plan during a particular sys.query_store_runtime _stats_interval interval. It provides information about execution count, CPU time and call durations, logical and physical I/O statistics, transaction log usage, degree of parallelism, memory grant size, and a few other useful metrics.

sys.query_store_wait_stats

Starting with SQL Server 2017, you can get information about query waits with the sys.query_store_wait_stats view (*https://oreil.ly/HmiJy*). The data is collected for each plan and time interval and grouped by several wait categories, including CPU, memory, and blocking.

Let's look at a few scenarios for working with Query Store data.

Listing 4-8 provides code that returns information about the system's 50 most I/O-intensive queries. Because the Query Store persists execution statistics over time intervals, you'll need to aggregate data from multiple sys.query_store_runtime _stats rows. The output will include data for all intervals that ended within the last 24 hours, grouped by queries and their execution plans.

It's worth noting that the Query Store date/time information uses the data type datetimeoffset. Keep this in mind when you filter the data.

Listing 4-8. Getting information about expensive queries from the Query Store

```
SELECT TOP 50
  q.query_id, qt.query_sql_text, qp.plan_id, qp.query_plan
  ,SUM(rs.count_executions) AS [Execution Cnt]
  ,CONVERT(INT,SUM(rs.count_executions *
    (rs.avg_logical_io_reads + avg_logical_io_writes)) /
      SUM(rs.count_executions)) AS [Avg IO]
  ,CONVERT(INT,SUM(rs.count_executions *
    (rs.avg_logical_io_reads + avg_logical_io_writes))) AS [Total IO]
  ,CONVERT(INT,SUM(rs.count_executions * rs.avg_cpu_time) /
    SUM(rs.count_executions)) AS [Avg CPU]
  ,CONVERT(INT,SUM(rs.count_executions * rs.avg_cpu_time)) AS [Total CPU]
  ,CONVERT(INT,SUM(rs.count_executions * rs.avg_duration) /
    SUM(rs.count_executions)) AS [Avg Duration]
  ,CONVERT(INT,SUM(rs.count_executions * rs.avg_duration))
    AS [Total Duration]
  ,CONVERT(INT,SUM(rs.count_executions * rs.avg_physical_io_reads) /
    SUM(rs.count_executions)) AS [Avg Physical Reads]
  ,CONVERT(INT,SUM(rs.count_executions * rs.avg_physical_io_reads))
    AS [Total Physical Reads]
  ,CONVERT(INT,SUM(rs.count_executions * rs.avg_query_max_used_memory) /
    SUM(rs.count_executions)) AS [Avg Memory Grant Pages]
  ,CONVERT(INT,SUM(rs.count_executions * rs.avg_query_max_used_memory))
    AS [Total Memory Grant Pages]
  ,CONVERT(INT,SUM(rs.count_executions * rs.avg_rowcount) /
    SUM(rs.count_executions)) AS [Avg Rows]
  ,CONVERT(INT,SUM(rs.count_executions * rs.avg_rowcount)) AS [Total Rows]
  ,CONVERT(INT,SUM(rs.count_executions * rs.avg_dop) /
    SUM(rs.count_executions)) AS [Avg DOP]
  ,CONVERT(INT,SUM(rs.count_executions * rs.avg_dop)) AS [Total DOP]
FROM
  sys.query_store_query q WITH (NOLOCK)
    JOIN sys.query_store_plan qp WITH (NOLOCK) ON
      q.query_id = qp.query_id
    JOIN sys.query_store_query_text qt WITH (NOLOCK) ON
      q.query_text_id = qt.query_text_id
    JOIN sys.query_store_runtime_stats rs WITH (NOLOCK) ON
      qp.plan_id = rs.plan_id
    JOIN sys.query_store_runtime_stats_interval rsi WITH (NOLOCK) ON
      rs.runtime_stats_interval_id = rsi.runtime_stats_interval_id
WHERE
  rsi.end_time >= DATEADD(DAY,-1,SYSDATETIMEOFFSET())
GROUP BY
  q.query_id, qt.query_sql_text, qp.plan_id, qp.query_plan
ORDER BY
  [Avg IO] DESC
OPTION (MAXDOP 1, RECOMPILE);
```

Obviously, you can sort data by different criteria than average I/O. You can also add predicates to the WHERE and/or HAVING clause of the query to narrow down the results. For example, you can filter by *DOP* columns if you want to detect queries that use parallelism in an OLTP environment and fine-tune the *Cost Threshold for Parallelism* setting.

Another example is for detecting queries that balloon the plan cache. The code in Listing 4-9 provides information about queries that generate multiple execution plans due to different context settings. The two most common reasons for this are sessions that use different SET options and queries that reference objects without schema names.

Listing 4-9. Queries with different context settings

```
SELECT
    q.query_id, qt.query_sql_text
    ,COUNT(DISTINCT q.context_settings_id) AS [Context Setting Cnt]
    ,COUNT(DISTINCT qp.plan_id) AS [Plan Count]
FROM
    sys.query_store_query q WITH (NOLOCK)
        JOIN sys.query_store_query_text qt WITH (NOLOCK) ON
            q.query_text_id = qt.query_text_id
        JOIN sys.query_store_plan qp WITH (NOLOCK) ON
            q.query_id = qp.query_id
GROUP BY
    q.query_id, qt.query_sql_text
HAVING
    COUNT(DISTINCT q.context_settings_id) > 1
ORDER BY
    COUNT(DISTINCT q.context_settings_id)
OPTION (MAXDOP 1, RECOMPILE);
```

Listing 4-10 shows you how to find similar queries based on the query_hash value (SQL in the output represents one randomly selected query from the group). Usually, those queries belong to a nonparameterized ad-hoc workload in the system. You can parameterize those queries in the code. If that's not possible, consider using forced parameterization, which I will discuss in Chapter 6.

Listing 4-10. Detecting queries with duplicated query_hash values

```
;WITH Queries(query_hash, [Query Count], [Exec Count], qtid)
AS
(
    SELECT TOP 100
        q.query_hash
        ,COUNT(DISTINCT q.query_id)
        ,SUM(rs.count_executions)
        ,MIN(q.query_text_id)
```

```
    FROM
        sys.query_store_query q WITH (NOLOCK)
            JOIN sys.query_store_plan qp WITH (NOLOCK) ON
                q.query_id = qp.query_id
            JOIN sys.query_store_runtime_stats rs WITH (NOLOCK) ON
                qp.plan_id = rs.plan_id
    GROUP BY
        q.query_hash
    HAVING
        COUNT(DISTINCT q.query_id) > 1
)
SELECT
    q.query_hash
    ,qt.query_sql_text AS [Sample SQL]
    ,q.[Query Count]
    ,q.[Exec Count]
FROM
    Queries q CROSS APPLY
    (
        SELECT TOP 1 qt.query_sql_text
        FROM sys.query_store_query_text qt WITH (NOLOCK)
        WHERE qt.query_text_id = q.qtid
    ) qt
ORDER BY
    [Query Count] DESC, [Exec Count] DESC
OPTION(MAXDOP 1, RECOMPILE);
```

As you can see, the possibilities are endless. Use the Query Store if you can afford its overhead in your system.

Finally, the DBCC CLONEDATABASE command (*https://oreil.ly/2jYGV*) allows you to generate a schema-only clone of the database and use it to investigate performance problems. By default, a clone will include Query Store data. You can restore it and perform an analysis on another server to reduce overhead in production.

Third-Party Tools

As you've now seen, SQL Server provides a very rich and extensive set of tools to locate inefficient queries. Nevertheless, you may also benefit from monitoring tools developed by other vendors. Most will provide you with a list of the most resource-intensive queries for analysis and optimization. Many will also give you the baseline, which you can use to analyze trends and detect regressed queries.

I am not going to discuss specific tools; instead, I want to offer you a few tips for choosing and using tools.

The key to using any tool is to understand it. Research how it works and analyze its limitations and what data it may miss. For example, if a tool gets data by polling the sys.dm_exec_requests view on a schedule, it may miss a big portion of small but frequently executed queries that run in between polls. Alternatively, if a tool determines inefficient queries by session waits, the results will greatly depend on your system's workload, the amount of data cached in the buffer pool, and many other factors.

Depending on your specific needs, these limitations might be acceptable. Remember the Pareto Principle: you do not need to optimize all inefficient queries in the system to achieve a desired (or acceptable) return on investment. Nevertheless, you may benefit from a holistic view and from multiple perspectives. For example, it is very easy to cross-check a tool's list of inefficient queries against the plan cache–based execution statistics for a more complete list.

There is another important reason to understand your tool, though: estimating the amount of overhead it could introduce. Some DMVs are very expensive to run. For example, if a tool calls the `sys.dm_exec_query_plan` function during each `sys.dm_exec_requests` poll, it may lead to a measurable increase in overhead in busy systems. It is also not uncommon for tools to create traces and xEvent sessions without your knowledge.

Do not blindly trust whitepapers and vendors when they state that a tool is harmless. Its impact may vary in different systems. It is always better to test the overhead with your workload, baselining the system with and without the tool. Keep in mind that the overhead is not always static and may increase as the workload changes.

Finally, consider the security implications of your choice of tools. Many tools allow you to build custom monitors that execute queries on the server, opening the door to malicious activity. Do not grant unnecessary permissions to the tool's login, and control who has access to manage the tool.

In the end, choose the approach that best allows you to pinpoint inefficient queries and that works best with your system. Remember that query optimization will help in any system.

Summary

Inefficient queries impact SQL Server's performance and can overload the disk subsystem. Even in systems that have enough memory to cache data in the buffer pool, those queries burn CPU, increase blocking, and affect the customer experience.

SQL Server keeps track of execution metrics for each cached plan and exposes them through the `sys.dm_exec_query_stats` view. You can also get execution statistics for stored procedures, triggers, and user-defined scalar functions with the `sys.dm_exec_procedure_stats`, `sys.dm_exec_trigger_stats`, and `sys.dm_exec_function_stats` views, respectively.

Your plan cache–based execution statistics will not track runtime execution metrics in execution plans, nor will they include queries that do not have plans cached. Make sure to factor this into your analysis and query-tuning process.

You can capture inefficient queries in real time with Extended Events and SQL Traces. Both approaches introduce overhead, especially in busy systems. They also provide raw data, which you'll need to process and aggregate for further analysis.

In SQL Server 2016 and later, you can utilize the Query Store. This is a great tool that does not depend on the plan cache and allows you to quickly pinpoint plan regressions. The Query Store adds some overhead; this may be acceptable in many cases, but monitor it when you enable the feature.

Finally, you can use third-party monitoring tools to find inefficient queries. Remember to research how a tool works and understand its limitations and overhead.

In the next chapter, I will discuss a few common techniques that you can use to optimize inefficient queries.

Troubleshooting Checklist

- ☐ Get the list of inefficient queries from the `sys.dm_exec_query_stats` view. Sort the data according to your troubleshooting strategy (CPU, I/O, and so forth).
- ☐ Detect the most expensive stored procedures with the `sys.dm_exec _procedure_stats` view.
- ☐ Consider enabling the Query Store in your system and analyzing the data you collect. (This may or may not be feasible if you already use external monitoring tools.)
- ☐ Enable trace flags T7745 and 7752 to improve SQL Server shutdown and startup performance when you use the Query Store.
- ☐ Analyze data from third-party monitoring tools and cross-check it with SQL Server data.
- ☐ Analyze the overhead that inefficient queries introduce in the system. Correlate the queries' resource consumption with wait statistics and server load.
- ☐ Optimize queries if you determine this is needed.

CHAPTER 5

Data Storage and Query Tuning

The topic of query optimization and tuning could easily fill another book. Indeed, there are many books available already, and I encourage you to read them and master your skills. I will not try to duplicate them here; instead, this chapter will cover some of the most important concepts you need to understand to tune queries.

You cannot master the process of query optimization without understanding the internal index structure and patterns that SQL Server uses to access data. This chapter thus begins with a high-level overview of B-Tree indexes along with seek and scan operations.

Next, I discuss statistics and cardinality estimations, along with ways to read and analyze execution plans.

Finally, I cover several common issues you might encounter during the query tuning process, offering advice on how to address them and index the data.

Data Storage and Access Patterns

Modern SQL Server versions support three data storage and processing technologies. The oldest and most commonly used one is *row-based storage*. With row-based storage, all table columns are combined into the data rows that reside on 8 KB data pages. Logically, those data rows belong to *B-Tree indexes* or *heaps* (which we'll discuss in a moment).

Starting with SQL Server 2012, you can store some indexes or entire tables in columnar format using *column-based storage* and *columnstore indexes*. The data in such indexes is heavily compressed and stored on a per-column basis. This technology is optimized and provides great performance for read-only analytical queries that scan large amounts of data. Unfortunately, it does not scale well in an OLTP workload.

Finally, starting with SQL Server 2014, you can use *In-Memory OLTP* and store data in *memory-optimized tables*. The data in such tables resides completely in memory and is great for heavy OLTP workloads.

> You can use all three technologies—row-based, column-based, and memory-optimized tables—together, partitioning data among them. This approach is extremely useful when you need to support heavy OLTP and analytical workloads in the same system. I cover this architecture pattern in detail in my book *Pro SQL Server Internals* (Apress, 2016).

Row-based storage is the default and, by far, the most common storage technology in SQL Server. The CREATE TABLE and CREATE INDEX statements will store data in a row-based format unless you specify otherwise. Row-based storage can handle moderate OLTP and analytical workloads and introduces less database administration overhead than columnstore indexes and In-Memory OLTP.

In this chapter, I will focus on row-based storage and queries that work with B-Tree Indexes. We'll start with a look at how SQL Server stores data in row-based storage.

Row-Based Storage Tables

Internally, the structure of a row-based table consists of multiple elements and internal objects, as shown in Figure 5-1.

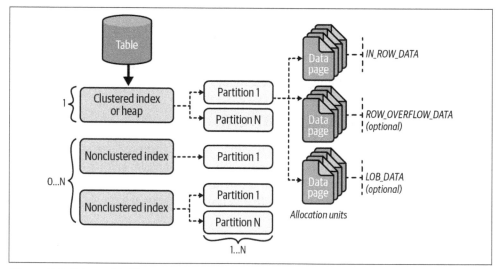

Figure 5-1. Internal table structure

The data in the tables is stored either completely unsorted (those tables are called *heap tables* or *heaps*) or sorted based on the value of a clustered index key, when such an index is defined.

I am not going to dive deep into the details, and instead will say that as a general rule, it is better to avoid heaps and define clustered indexes on your tables. There are some edge cases when heap tables may outperform tables with clustered indexes; nevertheless, heaps have several shortcomings. In most cases, you'll get better performance when tables have clustered indexes defined.

In addition to a single clustered index, every table may have a set of *nonclustered indexes*: separate data structures that store copies of the data from a table sorted according to index key columns. For example, if a column is included in two nonclustered indexes, SQL Server would store that data three times: once in a clustered index or heap, and once in each of the two nonclustered indexes.

While SQL Server allows you to create large numbers of nonclustered indexes, doing so is not a good idea, especially in OLTP systems with volatile data. In addition to storage overhead, SQL Server needs to insert, update, or delete rows in each nonclustered index during data modifications, maintaining multiple copies of the data.

 Although creating large numbers of nonclustered indexes is not a good idea, this is not to say that you should start thoughtlessly dropping indexes. There is no threshold of how many indexes a table should have, and you need to keep enough indexes to support system workload.

I will discuss how to analyze index usage in Chapter 14.

Internally, each index (and heap) consists of one or more partitions. You can think of each partition as an internal data structure (index or heap) that is independent from other partitions in the table. You can use a different partition strategy for every index in the table; however, it is usually beneficial to partition all indexes in the same way, aligning them with each other.

As I mentioned earlier, the actual data is stored in data rows on 8 KB data pages with 8,060 bytes available to users. The data from all columns is stored together, except for when column data does not fit on the data page.

The data pages combine into three different categories called *allocation units*.

IN_ROW_DATA allocation unit pages store the main data row objects, which consist of internal attributes and the data from fixed-length columns (such as int, datetime, float, etc.). The in-row part of a data row must fit on a single data page, so it cannot exceed 8,060 bytes. The data from variable-length columns, such as (n)var char(max), varbinary(max), xml, and others, may also be stored in-row in the main row object when it fits into this limit.

When variable-length data does not fit in-row, SQL Server stores it off-row on different data pages, referencing them through in-row pointers. Variable-length data that exceeds 8,000 bytes is stored on LOB_DATA allocation unit data pages (LOB stands for *large objects*). Otherwise, the data is stored in ROW_OVERFLOW_DATA allocation unit pages.

 Data from (n)text and image columns is stored in LOB_DATA allocation units by default. You can override it with the sp_tableop tion stored procedure (*https://oreil.ly/7WTZi*).

I'd like to repeat a well-known piece of advice here: do *not* retrieve unnecessary columns in SELECT statements, especially with the SELECT * pattern. This may lead to additional I/O operations to get data from off-row pages, and may also defer usage of covered indexes, as you'll see later in this chapter.

Finally, SQL Server logically groups sets of eight pages into 64 KB units called *extents*. Two types of extents are available. *Mixed extents* store data that belongs to different objects. *Uniform extents* store the data for the same object. By default, when a new object is created, SQL Server stores the first eight object pages in mixed extents. After that, all subsequent space allocation for that object is done with uniform extents.

You can disable mixed extents allocation with the server-level trace flag T1118. In SQL Server 2016 and later, you can control mixed extents allocation on the database level with the MIXED_PAGE_ALLOCATION database option. Turning mixed extents off will reduce the number of modifications in the system tables when a new table is created. Doing this rarely gives noticeable benefits in users' databases; however, it may significantly improve tempdb throughput in busy OLTP systems. You should disable mixed extents allocation with the T1118 trace flag in old versions of SQL Server (prior to 2016). From SQL Server 2016 on, tempdb stopped using mixed extents, so you don't need to enable that trace flag in the system.

Now let's look at the structure of the indexes.

B-Tree Indexes

Clustered and nonclustered indexes have a very similar internal format, called *B-Tree*. Let's create an example table called `Customers`, defined in Listing 5-1. The table has the clustered index defined on `CustomerId` and the nonclustered index on `Name` columns.

Listing 5-1. The `Customers` table

```
CREATE TABLE dbo.Customers
(
    CustomerId INT NOT NULL,
    Name NVARCHAR(64) NOT NULL,
    Phone VARCHAR(32) NULL,
    /* Other Columns */
);

CREATE UNIQUE CLUSTERED INDEX IDX_Customers_CustomerId
ON dbo.Customers(CustomerId);

CREATE NONCLUSTERED INDEX IDX_Customers_Name
ON dbo.Customers(Name);
```

Constraints Versus Indexes

As you may have noticed, I defined the clustered index on the table instead of creating the primary key constraint. I did this on purpose. I always consider constraints to be the part of a logical database design that defines entities and their key attributes. Indexes, on the other hand, belong to the physical database design and physical data structures of the database.

By default, SQL Server creates unique clustered indexes for primary key constraints. However, you can—and in many cases should—mark primary keys as nonclustered, which will make them unique nonclustered indexes.

With the exception of a few SQL Server features that require you to define primary keys, the choice between constraints and indexes is a matter of personal preference. Primary and unique constraints are implemented as indexes internally and behave the same way. During performance tuning, you'll work with indexes, so I am not going to reference primary keys and unique constraints in this book. Their absence from the discussion does not mean you should not use constraints in your databases, though.

The logical structure of the clustered index is shown in Figure 5-2.

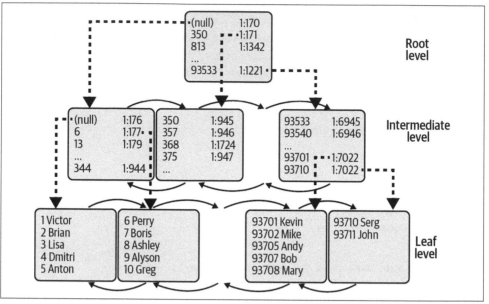

Figure 5-2. B-Tree Index

The bottom level of the index is called the *leaf level*. It stores the data sorted according to the index key value. If it is a clustered index, the leaf level stores all the data from the table, sorted based on the clustered key. To be more specific, the leaf level includes IN_ROW data only, which may reference off-row column data on the other pages.

If all the data in the index fits into a single data page, the index will consist of that single leaf page. Otherwise, SQL Server will start to build *intermediate levels* of the index. Each row on an intermediate level page references the page from the level below and contains the minimal value of the key in the referenced page, as well as its physical address (FileId:PageId) in the database. The only exception is the very first row, which stores NULL instead of the minimal value of the key.

SQL Server continues to build intermediate levels until it reaches a level with a single page. This level is called the *root level*; it is the entry point to the index.

The pages on each level of the index are linked into the double-linked list. Each page knows the previous page and the next page in the index. This allows SQL Server to scan the indexes forward and backward. (Keep in mind, however, that the backward scan may be less efficient, since SQL Server does not use parallelism during that operation.)

SQL Server can access data in the index through either *index scan* or *index seek*. With scans, there are two ways SQL Server can do this.

The first is through an *allocation order scan*. SQL Server tracks the extents that belong to each index in the database through system pages called *Index Allocation Maps* (IAMs). It reads the data pages from the index in random order according to index allocation data. SQL Server uses this method only under certain circumstances, because it could introduce data consistency problems.

The second, more common method is called an *ordered scan*. Let's assume that you want to run the SELECT Name FROM dbo.Customers query. All data rows reside on the leaf level of the index, and SQL Server can scan that level and return the rows to the client.

SQL Server starts with the root page of the index and reads the first row from there. That row references the intermediate page with the minimum key value from the table. SQL Server reads that page and repeats the process until it finds the first page on the leaf level. Then SQL Server starts to read rows one by one, moving through the linked list of the pages until all the rows have been read (Figure 5-3).

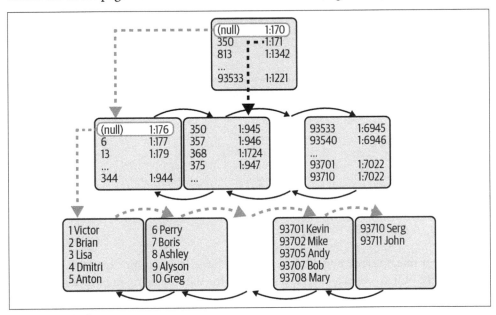

Figure 5-3. Index scan

Obviously, in real life this may become more complicated. For example, in some cases, a query may simultaneously scan multiple parts of the index with parallel execution plans. In others, SQL Server may combine multiple index scans of simultaneously running queries together into the single physical index scan. Nevertheless, when you see the *Index Scan* operator in the execution plan, you can assume that this operator will access all data from the index.

There is one exception, however: when the plan has an index scan immediately following the *Top* operator. In that case, the scan operator will stop after it returns the number of rows requested by TOP and will not access the entire table. Usually, this happens if your query does not have an ORDER BY clause, or if the ORDER BY clause matches the index key.

Figure 5-4 shows part of the execution plan of the SELECT TOP 3 Name FROM dbo.Customers ORDER BY CustomerId query. The *Number of Rows Read* and *Actual Number of Rows* properties in the *Index Scan* operator indicate that the scan stopped after it read three rows.

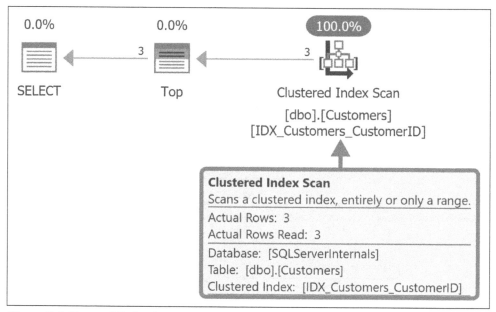

Figure 5-4. Top and Index Scan operators

As you can imagine, reading all data from the large index is an expensive operation. Fortunately, SQL Server can access a subset of the data by using the *index seek* operation. Say you want to run the following query: SELECT Name FROM dbo.Customers WHERE CustomerId BETWEEN 4 AND 7. Figure 5-5 illustrates how SQL Server might process it.

In order to read the range of rows from the table, SQL Server needs to find the row with the minimum value of the key from the range, which is 4. SQL Server starts with the root page, where the second row references a page with a minimum key value of 350. This value is greater than the key value you're looking for, so SQL Server reads the intermediate-level data page (1:170) referenced by the first row on the root page.

Similarly, the intermediate page leads SQL Server to the first leaf-level page (1:176). SQL Server reads that page, then it reads the rows with CustomerId equal to 4 and 5, and finally, it reads the two remaining rows from the second page.

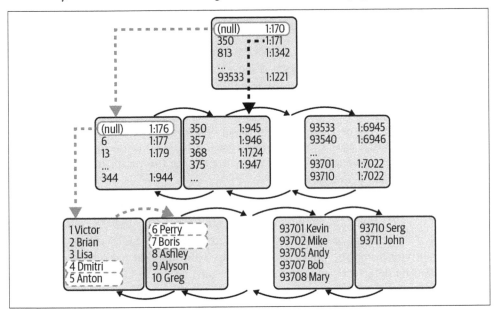

Figure 5-5. Index Seek operator

Technically speaking, there are two kinds of index seek operations:

Point-lookup
    With the point-lookup operation (also called a singleton lookup) SQL Server seeks and returns a single row: for example, the WHERE CustomerId = 2 predicate is a point-lookup operation.

Range scan
    The range scan operation requires SQL Server to find the lowest or highest value of the key and scan the set of rows (either forward or backward) until it reaches the end of the scan range. The predicate WHERE CustomerId BETWEEN 4 AND 7 leads to the range scan. Both cases are shown as Index Seek operators in the execution plans.

As you can guess, index seek is more efficient than index scan because SQL Server usually processes just a subset of rows and data pages, rather than scanning the entire index. However, the *Index Seek* operator in the execution plan may be misleading and represent an inefficient range scan that reads a large number of rows, or even the entire index. I will talk about this condition later in this chapter.

There is a concept in relational databases called *SARGable predicates*, which stands for *Search Argument-able*. SARGable predicates allow SQL Server to isolate a subset of the index key to process. In a nutshell, with a SARGable predicate, SQL Server can determine a single key value or a range of index key values to read during a predicate evaluation and utilize the Index Seek operation when the index exists.

Obviously, it is beneficial to write queries using SARGable predicates and utilize index seek whenever possible. This is done using operators, which include =, >, >=, <, <=, IN, BETWEEN, and LIKE (for prefix matching). Non-SARGable operators include NOT, <>, LIKE (when not prefix matching), and NOT IN.

Predicates are also non-SARGable when using functions—system functions or user-defined functions that are not inlined—against the table columns. SQL Server must call the function for every row it processes to evaluate the predicate. This prevents SQL Server from using an index seek.

The same applies to data type conversions where SQL Server uses the internal function CONVERT_IMPLICIT. One common example is using the unicode nvarchar parameter in the predicate with a varchar column that uses SQL collation. Another case is when you have different data types in the columns that participate in the join predicate (some data types and implicit conversions could be OK). Both cases could lead to an index scan, even when the predicate operator appears to be SARGable.

Composite Indexes

Indexes with multiple key columns are called *composite indexes*. The data in the composite indexes is sorted per column, from left to right. Figure 5-6 shows the structure of a composite index defined on the LastName and FirstName columns in the table. The data is sorted first on LastName (the leftmost column) and then on FirstName within each LastName value.

The SARGability of a composite index depends on the SARGability of the predicates on the leftmost index columns, which allow SQL Server to determine and isolate the range of the index keys to process.

Table 5-1 shows examples of SARGable and non-SARGable predicates, using the index from Figure 5-6.

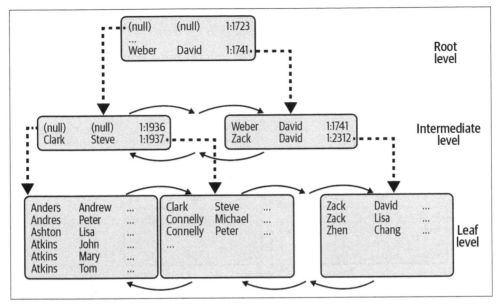

Figure 5-6. Composite indexes

Table 5-1. Composite index and SARGability

SARGable predicates	Non-SARGable predicates
`LastName = 'Clark' AND FirstName = 'Steve'`	`LastName <> 'Clark' AND FirstName = 'Steve'`
`LastName = 'Clark' AND FirstName <> 'Steve'`	`LastName LIKE '%ar%' AND FirstName = 'Steve'`
`LastName = 'Clark'`	`FirstName = 'Steve'`
`LastName LIKE 'Cl%'`	

Nonclustered Indexes

Whereas a clustered index specifies how data rows are sorted in a table, nonclustered indexes define a separate sorting order for a column or set of columns, storing them as separate data structures.

Think about a book, for example. Its page numbers represent the book's *clustered* index. The term *index*—that's the one labeled "Index" at the end of the book—lists terms from the book in alphabetical order. Each term references the numbers of each page where the term is mentioned. It is thus a *nonclustered* index of the terms.

When you need to find a term in the book, you can look it up in the term index. It is a fast and efficient operation because terms are sorted in alphabetical order. Next, you can quickly find the pages on which the terms are mentioned using the page numbers specified there. Without the term index, your only choice would be to read the entire book, page by page, until you find all references to the term.

As I have noted, clustered and nonclustered indexes use a similar B-Tree structure. Figure 5-7 shows the structure of a nonclustered index (top) on the Name column we created in Listing 5-1. It also shows the clustered index (bottom), for reference.

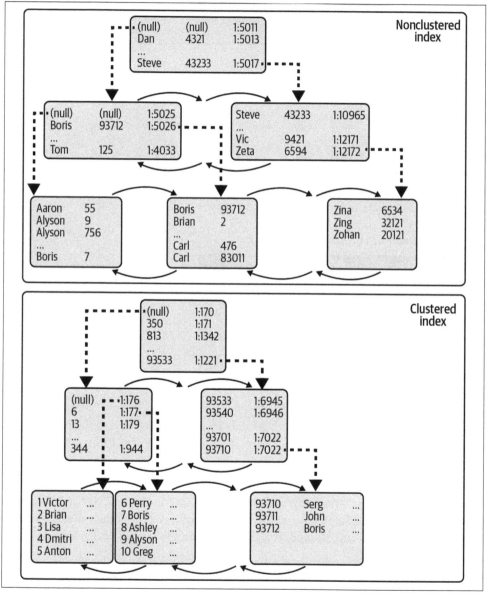

Figure 5-7. Clustered and nonclustered indexes in the Customers table

The leaf level of the nonclustered index is sorted based on the value of the index key (Name). Every row on the leaf level includes the key value and the *row-id* value. For tables with a clustered index, row-id represents the value of the clustered index key of the row.

This is a very important thing to remember: nonclustered indexes do *not* store information about physical row location when a table has a clustered index defined. They store the *value of the clustered index key* instead. This also means nonclustered indexes include the data from clustered index key columns *even if you don't explicitly add those columns* to the index definition.

Like clustered indexes, the intermediate and root levels of nonclustered indexes store one row per page from the level they reference. That row consists of the physical address and the minimum value of the key from the page. In nonunique indexes, it also stores the row-id of such a row.

Let's look at how SQL Server uses nonclustered indexes. I'll run the following query: SELECT Name, Phone FROM dbo.Customers WHERE Name = 'Boris'. Figure 5-8 shows that process.

Similar to the clustered index, SQL Server starts with the root page of the non-clustered index. The key value *Boris* is less than *Dan*, so SQL Server goes to the intermediate page referenced from the first row in the root-level page.

The second row of the intermediate page indicates that the minimum key value on the page is *Boris*, although the index had not been defined as unique and SQL Server does not know if there are other *Boris* rows stored on the first page. As a result, it goes to the first leaf page of the index and finds the row with the key value *Boris* and a row-id of 7.

In our case, the nonclustered index does not store any data besides CustomerId and Name, and SQL Server needs to traverse the clustered index tree and obtain the data for the Phone column from there. This operation is called *key lookup* (*RID lookup* in heap tables).

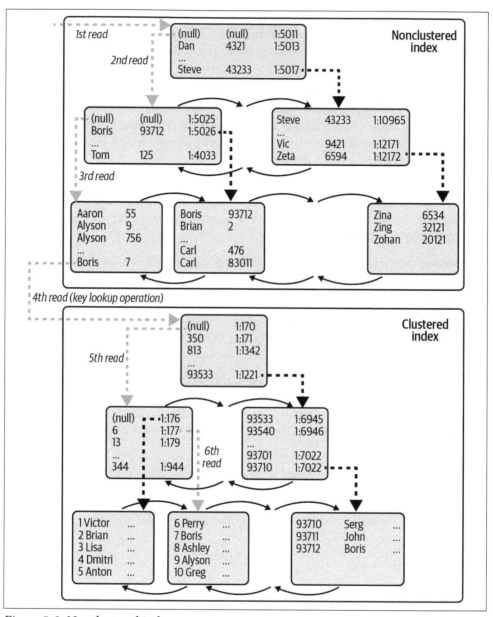

Figure 5-8. Nonclustered index usage, part 1

In the next step shown in Figure 5-9, SQL Server comes back to the nonclustered index and reads the second page from the leaf level. It finds another row with the key value *Boris* and a row-id of 93712, and it performs the key lookup again.

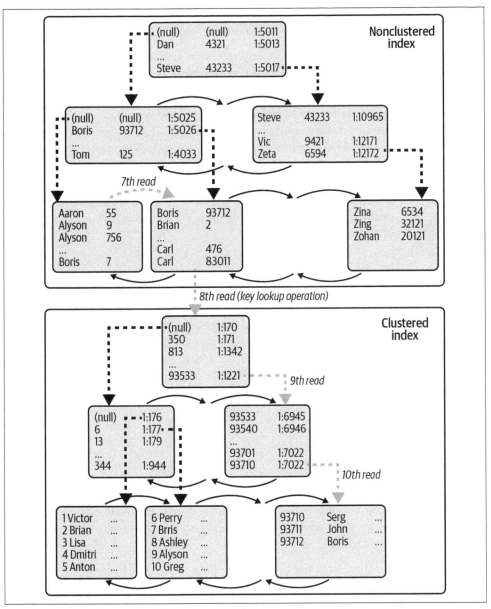

Figure 5-9. Nonclustered index usage, part 2

As you can see in Figure 5-9, SQL Server had to perform 10 reads even though the query returned just two rows. The number of I/O operations can be calculated based on the following formula:

(# of levels in nonclustered index) + (number of pages read from the leaf level of nonclustered index) + (number of rows found) * (# of levels in clustered index)

A large number of rows found (key lookup operations) leads to a large number of I/O operations, which makes using a nonclustered index inefficient.

As a result, SQL Server is very conservative in choosing nonclustered indexes when it expects that a large number of key lookup operations will be required. It may choose to scan a clustered or another nonclustered index instead. The threshold when SQL Server decides not to use a nonclustered index with key lookup varies, but it is very low—often a fraction of a percent of the total number of rows in the table.

 I have included a script in the book's companion materials demonstrating this inefficiency and SQL Server query optimization behavior.

The same applies to RID lookup operations. Nonclustered indexes in heap tables store the physical address of the row in the row-id. Technically, SQL Server can access the row in a heap through a single read operation; however, it is still expensive. Moreover, if the new version of the row does not fit into the old data page during an update, SQL Server will move it to another place, referencing it through another structure called a *forwarding pointer*, which contains the address of the new (updated) version of the row. Nonclustered indexes will continue to reference forwarding pointers in the row-id, and the RID lookup may lead to multiple read operations to access the row.

Index Fragmentation

Even though index fragmentation is not directly related to the topic of query tuning, it is worth covering while I am talking about indexes. After all, improving index maintenance strategy and reducing index fragmentation are essential parts of SQL Server performance tuning.

SQL Server always maintains the order of the data in the index, inserting new rows on the data pages to which they belong. If the data page does not have enough free space, SQL Server allocates a new page and places the row there, adjusting the pointers in the double-linked page list to maintain logical sorting order in the index. This operation is called *page split*, and it leads to index fragmentation, as you'll see in this section.

Figure 5-10 illustrates this condition. When the original page does not have enough space to accommodate the new row, SQL Server performs a page split, moving about half of the data from the original page to the new page and adjusting page pointers afterward.

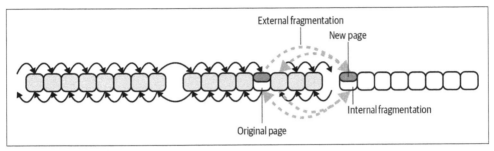

Figure 5-10. Page split

Page splits can also occur during data modifications. When an update cannot be done in place—for example, during a data row size increase—SQL Server performs a page split and moves updated and subsequent rows from that page to another page. It maintains the index sorting order through the page pointers.

There are two kinds of index fragmentation:

External
> External fragmentation means that the logical order of the pages does not match their physical order in the data files, and/or that logically subsequent pages are not located in the same or adjacent extents. External fragmentation forces SQL Server to jump around while reading the data from the disk, which makes read-ahead less efficient and increases the number of physical reads required. The impact is much higher with magnetic drives where random I/O is less efficient than sequential I/O.

Internal
> Internal fragmentation, on the other hand, means data pages in the index have free space. As a result, the index uses more data pages to store data, which in turn increases the number of logical reads during query execution. In addition, SQL Server uses more memory in the buffer pool to cache index pages.

> Sometimes a small degree of internal fragmentation is good. It reduces page splits during insert and update operations, when data is inserted into or updated in different pages in the index. A large degree of internal fragmentation, however, wastes index space and reduces system performance.

You can analyze index fragmentation in the system with the sys.dm_db_index _physical_stats function (*https://oreil.ly/YC90O*) (you have to call the function in DETAILED mode, which requires SQL Server to scan the entire table). The three most important columns from the result set are:

avg_page_space_used_in_percent
Shows the average percentage of the data storage space used on the page. This value shows you the internal index fragmentation.

avg_fragmentation_in_percent
Provides you with information about external index fragmentation. For tables with clustered indexes, it indicates the percentage of out-of-order pages when the next physical page allocated in the index is different from the page referenced by the next-page pointer of the current page. For heap tables, it indicates the percentage of out-of-order extents, when extents are not residing continuously in data files.

fragment_count
Indicates how many continuous data fragments the index has. Every fragment constitutes the group of extents adjacent to each other. Adjacent data increases the chances that SQL Server will use sequential I/O and read-ahead while accessing the data.

The impact of index fragmentation can be offset by modern hardware, when servers have enough memory to cache the data in the buffer pool and fast flash-based I/O subsystems to read the data. While it is always beneficial to reduce fragmentation in the system, you need to analyze its impact when designing your index maintenance strategy.

To put things into perspective, if your system has low-activity hours during nights or weekends, use them for index maintenance. However, if your system handles thousands of transactions per second around the clock, do the analysis and estimate the benefits and downsides of different index maintenance strategies. Remember that index maintenance is an expensive operation and will add overhead to the system while it's running.

There are two index maintenance methods that reduce fragmentation—index reorganize and index rebuild:

Index reorganize
Often called index defragmentation, this method reorders leaf-level data pages into their logical order. It also tries to compress pages, reducing their internal fragmentation. This is an online operation that can be interrupted at any time without losing the operation's progress up to the point of interruption. You can reorganize indexes with the ALTER INDEX REORGANIZE command.

Index rebuild

This method creates another copy of the index in the table. It is an offline operation that will lock the table in non-Enterprise editions of SQL Server. In the Enterprise Edition it can be done online, though it will still require a short table-level lock at the beginning and end of execution. You can rebuild indexes with the `ALTER INDEX REBUILD` command.

The Microsoft documentation (*https://oreil.ly/61dzF*) recommends rebuilding indexes if their external fragmentation (`avg_fragmentation_in_percent`) exceeds 30% and reorganizing indexes for fragmentation between 5% and 30%. You can use those values as a rule of thumb; however, as I mentioned, it may be better to analyze and tune for your own use cases.

The Enterprise Edition of SQL Server 2017 and later and Azure SQL Database allow you to pause and resume online index creation and rebuild operations (resumable online index creation requires SQL Server 2019). This gives you more flexibility in designing an index maintenance strategy and allows you to truncate the transaction log (see Chapter 11) in the middle of an operation at the cost of the additional storage space the operation requires.

Pay attention to the `FILLFACTOR` index property, which allows you to reserve some free space during index creation or rebuild, reducing page splits afterward. Unless you have an ever-increasing append-only index, you should set `FILLFACTOR` to less than 100%. I usually start with 85% or 90% and fine-tune the values to get the least internal and external fragmentation in the index.

Finally, in heap tables, the `sys.dm_db_index_physical_stats` view provides the information about forwarding pointers with the `forwarded_record_count` column. Tables with a large number of forwarding pointers are inefficient and need to be rebuilt with the `ALTER TABLE REBUILD` operation. However, the better option in most cases is to convert them into clustered index tables. I'll discuss how to detect inefficient heap tables in more detail in Chapter 14.

Ola Hallengren has provided a set of scripts (*https://oreil.ly/hz0R2*) that have become the de facto standard for database maintenance tasks. Consider using them in your systems.

Statistics and Cardinality Estimation

SQL Server stores information about data distribution in the index in internal objects called *statistics*. By default, SQL Server creates statistics for each index in the database and uses them during query optimization. Let's look at what information is stored in the statistics first.

Listing 5-2 creates a table with clustered and nonclustered indexes and populates it with some data. Finally, it provides information about the statistics using the DBCC SHOW_STATISTICS command.

Listing 5-2. Examining statistics

```
CREATE TABLE dbo.DBObjects
(
    ID INT NOT NULL IDENTITY(1,1),
    Name SYSNAME NOT NULL,
    CreateDate DATETIME NOT NULL
);

CREATE UNIQUE CLUSTERED INDEX IDX_DBObjects_ID
ON dbo.DBObjects(ID);

INSERT INTO dbo.DBObjects(Name,CreateDate)
    SELECT name, create_date FROM sys.objects ORDER BY name;

-- Creating some duplicate values
INSERT INTO dbo.DBObjects(Name, CreateDate)
    SELECT t1.Name, t1.CreateDate
    FROM dbo.DBObjects t1 CROSS JOIN dbo.DBObjects t2
    WHERE t1.ID = 5 AND t2.ID between 1 AND 20;

CREATE NONCLUSTERED INDEX IDX_DBObjects_Name_CreateDate
ON dbo.DBObjects(Name, CreateDate);

DBCC SHOW_STATISTICS('dbo.DBObjects','IDX_DBObjects_Name_CreateDate');
```

Figure 5-11 shows the output of the code example (you may get different results in your system).

As you can see, the DBCC SHOW_STATISTICS command returns three result sets. The first contains general metadata information about statistics, such as name, update date, and number of rows in the index at the time the statistics were updated.

The second result set, called the *density vector*, contains information about density for the combination of key values from the statistics (index). It is calculated based on the formula 1 / number of distinct values, and it indicates how many rows on average every combination of key values has. It is worth noting that although the IDX_DBObjects_Name_CreateDate index has two index keys, row-id (clustered index column)- ID- also presents in the index and is returned in the density vector.

The last and most important result set is called the *histogram*, which you can also obtain by querying the sys.dm_db_stats_histogram (*https://oreil.ly/Tk0tv*) view. It provides information about data distribution in the index. Each record in the histogram, called a *histogram step*, includes the sample key value from the leftmost column from the statistics (index) and information about data distribution in the interval of values from the preceding to the current RANGE_HI_KEY value. It also includes the estimated number of rows in the interval (RANGE_ROWS), number of rows with key value equal to RANGE_HI_KEY (EQ_ROWS), number of distinct key values in the interval (DISTINCT_RANGE_ROWS), and average number of rows per distinct key value (AVG_RANGE_ROWS).

	Name	Updated	Rows	Rows Sampled	Steps	Density
1	IDX_DBObjects_Name_CreateDate	Apr 23 2022 9:36AM	136	136	111	1

Average key length	String Index	Filter Expression	Unfiltered Rows	Persisted Sample Percent
37.27941	YES	NULL	136	0

	All density	Average Length	Columns
1	0.00862069	25.279411	Name
2	0.00862069	33.27941	Name, CreateDate
3	0.007352941	37.27941	Name, CreateDate, ID

	RANGE_HI_KEY	RANGE_ROWS	EQ_ROWS	DISTINCT_RANGE_ROWS	AVG_RANGE_ROWS
1	_trusted_assemblies	0	1	0	1
2	EventNotificationErrorsQueue	0	1	0	1
3	external_library_setup_failur	0	1	0	1
4	MSreplication_options	0	1	0	1
5	P1	0	21	0	1
6	P2	0	1	0	1
7	P2a	0	1	0	1
8	P3	0	1	0	1
9	persistent_version_store	0	1	0	1

Figure 5-11. Statistics

SQL Server uses statistics information during query optimization to estimate the number of rows each operator in the execution plan would process and return to the next operator there. This process is called *cardinality estimation*.

Cardinality estimation greatly affects the execution plan. SQL Server uses it to choose the sequence of operators in the plan, indexes to access the data, type of join operators, and many other things. The efficiency of its execution plans greatly depends on the correctness of its cardinality estimation, and therefore on accurate statistics in the system.

There are three things you need to remember about statistics. First, and most important, SQL Server maintains the histogram and has information about data distribution only for the leftmost column of the index. There is no information about data distribution for other index columns or for combinations of index column values.

The common advice you'll hear suggests using the most selective column as the leftmost column in the composite indexes. While following this advice may improve the quality of cardinality estimations, don't follow it blindly. You need to analyze the queries, making sure the predicates in the leftmost columns are SARGable and support efficient index seek operations.

The second important thing to remember about statistics is that the histogram stores, at most, 200 steps, regardless of the table size and whether the table is partitioned or not. This can affect cardinality estimations in large tables with uneven data distribution, since each step stores information about larger key intervals.

Finally, you need to know how SQL Server updates statistics. In databases with a compatibility level below 130 (as of SQL Server 2016), statistics are *only* updated automatically after 20% of the data in the index has changed. For example, in a table with 100 million rows, you would need to insert, delete, or update index key columns in 20 million rows before an automatic update is triggered. This means that in large tables, statistics are rarely updated automatically and tend to become inaccurate over time.

Starting with a database compatibility level of 130, the statistics update threshold becomes dynamic. The percentage of changes that trigger the statistics update becomes smaller as the amount of data in the table grows. You can force the same behavior for databases with older compatibility levels and in old versions of SQL Server with the trace flag T2371. This is one of the trace flags I enable in every system.

Statistics Maintenance

Accurate, up-to-date statistics improve system performance. Analyze the statistics maintenance strategy when you perform system troubleshooting, and validate whether it provides you with accurate information.

You can rely on automatic statistics updates, maintain statistics manually, or combine both approaches. Index maintenance also affects your statistics maintenance strategy, since index rebuild automatically updates statistics in the index. Index reorg, on the other hand, does not update it.

You can control whether SQL Server creates and updates statistics automatically at the database level with the *Auto Create Statistics* and *Auto Update Statistics* database options. When these are enabled, SQL Server automatically maintains statistics on all indexes except those that have the STATISTICS_NORECOMPUTE option enabled (it is disabled by default).

SQL Server may use different methods to update statistics. By default, it just samples the data from the index. This approach is lightweight, but it does not always provide accurate results. Alternatively, you can update statistics using the UPDATE STATISTICS WITH FULLSCAN statement, which will read the entire index.

You can also update the statistics, specifying a percentage or number of rows to sample with an UPDATE STATISTICS WITH SAMPLE statement. Obviously, the more data you read, the more I/O overhead you'll have on large indexes *and* the more accurate your results will be. It is beneficial to update statistics with FULLSCAN or large samples if you can afford the overhead—for example, if you can run it during a time of low activity.

During query compilation, SQL Server detects whether statistics are outdated and may update them synchronously or asynchronously, based on the selected *Auto Update Statistics Asynchronously* database option. With synchronous updates, the Query Optimizer defers query compilation until the update is done. With asynchronous updates, the query is optimized using old statistics while statistics are updated in the background. You can keep your default synchronous statistics update unless your system requires extremely low response time from the queries.

The default thresholds that trigger automatic statistics updates are acceptable in many cases, as long as the database has a compatibility level of 130 or above, or T2371 is set. However, in some cases, you can also update the statistics of the key indexes manually and/or run a statistics update with FULLSCAN after hours.

It is usually beneficial to update statistics on the filtered indexes manually. Modifications of filtered columns do not count toward the statistics update threshold, which may make automatic statistics maintenance inefficient. The book's companion materials include a script that demonstrates this behavior.

 Filtered indexes allow you to filter subsets of data in the table, reducing index size and index maintenance cost. Read about this in the Microsoft documentation (*https://oreil.ly/OZRtC*).

Listing 5-3 shows you how to view statistics properties, such as when statistics were last updated and how many changes in the data have occurred since the last update. You can use it as part of your custom statistics maintenance in the system, if needed.

Listing 5-3. Analyzing statistics properties

```
SELECT
    s.stats_id AS [Stat ID]
    ,sc.name + '.' + t.name AS [Table]
    ,s.name AS [Statistics]
    ,p.last_updated
    ,p.rows
    ,p.rows_sampled
    ,p.modification_counter AS [Mod Count]
FROM
    sys.stats s JOIN sys.tables t ON
        s.object_id = t.object_id
    JOIN sys.schemas sc ON
        t.schema_id = sc.schema_id
    OUTER APPLY
        sys.dm_db_stats_properties(t.object_id,s.stats_id) p
ORDER BY
    p.last_updated
```

 This section barely scratches the surface of statistics and their maintenance. I strongly recommend reading the Microsoft documentation (*https://oreil.ly/w268o*) to learn more about it.

Cardinality Estimation Models

As you already know, the quality of query optimization depends on accurate cardinality estimations. SQL Server must correctly estimate the number of rows in each step of query execution to generate an efficient execution plan. Accurate statistics go a long way toward improving the estimations; however, they are just part of the picture.

During the cardinality estimation process, the Query Optimizer relies on a set of assumptions that cover a number of things, including the following:

- Data distribution in the tables
- Impact of different operators and predicates on the size of the output
- Relationship between multiple predicates in a single table
- Correlation of the data in multiple tables during joins

These assumptions, along with cardinality estimation algorithms, define the cardinality estimation model used during optimization.

The original (legacy) cardinality estimation model was initially developed for SQL Server 7.0 and was used exclusively until the release of SQL Server 2014. Aside from some minor improvements across versions, the model remained conceptually the same.

In SQL Server 2014, Microsoft released a new cardinality estimation model enabled in databases with a compatibility level of 120. This model uses different assumptions, which lead to different cardinality estimations and execution plans.

It is impossible to tell which model is better. Some queries behave better with the new model; others may regress when you upgrade. You can continue to use the legacy cardinality estimation model with new versions of SQL Server; however, it is beneficial to upgrade at some point. Microsoft says it is not going to remove the legacy model from SQL Server in the future, but it won't be enhanced, either.

Unfortunately, upgrading to the new model is easier said than done, especially in large, complex systems. Changing the model may lead to massive changes in the execution plans, so you need to be prepared to detect and address regressions quickly. Fortunately, Query Store can simplify the process. You can collect the data before the change and force SQL Server to use old execution plans for those queries that regressed under the new model. Obviously, you'll still need to analyze and optimize them later.

You can control the cardinality estimation model with the database compatibility level. Keep in mind that the new model may behave slightly differently in each compatibility level, starting with 120 (SQL Server 2014). Legacy models, on the other hand, will behave the same in each SQL Server version. Enabling the QUERY_OPTI MIZER_HOTFIXES database setting or setting the T4199 trace flag (both were discussed in Chapter 1) may also affect the estimations.

In SQL Server 2014, you can control the model with database compatibility levels or with trace flags. T2312 and T9481 force SQL Server to use new and legacy models, respectively, ignoring the database compatibility level. In SQL Server 2016 and later, you can keep using the legacy model with new database compatibility levels by setting the LEGACY_CARDINALITY_ESTIMATION database option.

When you perform the SQL Server version upgrade, I recommend doing it in phases to reduce the risk of regression. First, upgrade the server version, keeping the old cardinality estimation model in place. Validate that everything works as expected after the upgrade. Then you can consider changing the model. As mentioned, use Query Store as part of that process.

As a general rule, I do not recommend switching to the new cardinality estimation model in SQL Server 2014. I encountered several bugs in early builds of this version, which led to more regressed queries. If you do switch, install the latest service pack, enable T4199, and carefully test the system. It is also worth noting that the lack of Query Store in SQL Server 2014 usually makes the switch much more complicated.

Finally, a new feature in the intelligent query processing family, *cardinality estimation feedback*, is available in databases with compatibility level 160 (SQL Server 2022) and above. When SQL Server detects significant cardinality estimation errors during query execution, it may recompile the query using different cardinality model assumptions. Next, SQL Server validates if the new plan performs better and either keeps or discards it based on the results.

Cardinality estimation feedback relies on Query Store hints and requires Query Store to be enabled in the database. Moreover, SQL Server does not apply it to every query —the cardinality estimation error needs to be significant, and the query should be frequently executed to trigger the action. Nevertheless, it is worth trying to switch databases to the latest compatibility level, since it may benefit from IQP features even if you keep the legacy cardinality estimator active.

Analyzing Your Execution Plan

The query optimization process in SQL Server, done by the Query Optimizer, generates a query execution plan. This plan consists of multiple operators that access and manipulate the data, achieving results for the query. The query tuning process, in a nutshell, requires us to analyze and improve execution plans for the queries.

Even though every database engineer is familiar with execution plans, I'd like to discuss several things related to query tuning. First, we need to look at how SQL Server executes operators in the plan.

Row Mode and Batch Mode Execution

SQL Server has two processing methods for queries. The default, *row mode*, is traditionally used with row-based storage and B-Tree Indexes. In this mode, each operator in the execution plan processes data rows one at a time, requesting them from child operators when needed.

Let's look at the simple query shown in Listing 5-4.

Listing 5-4. Row mode execution: sample query

```
SELECT TOP 10 c.CustomerId, c.Name, a.Street, a.City, a.State, a.ZipCode
FROM
    dbo.Customers c JOIN dbo.Addresses a ON
        c.PrimaryAddressId = a.AddressId
ORDER BY
    c.Name
```

This query produces the execution plan shown in Figure 5-12. SQL Server selects all the data from the Customers table, sorts it based on the Name column, gets the first 10 rows, joins it with the Addresses data, and returns it to the client.

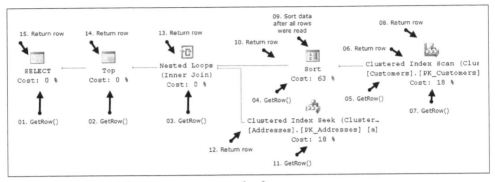

Figure 5-12. Row mode execution: getting the first row

Let's analyze how SQL Server executes a query. The *Select* operator, which is the parent operator in the execution plan, calls the GetRow() method of the *Top* operator. The *Top* operator, in turn, calls the GetRow() method of the *Nested Loop Join*.

A *Join* operator gets the data from two different inputs. First, it calls the GetRow() method of the *Sort* operator. In order to sort, SQL Server needs to read all the rows first. So, the *Sort* operation calls the GetRow() method of the *Clustered Index Scan* operator multiple times, accumulating the results. The *Scan* operator, which is the lowest operator in the execution plan tree, returns one row from the Customers table per call. Figure 5-12 shows just two GetRow() calls, for simplicity's sake.

When all the data from the Customers table has been read, the *Sort* operator performs sorting and returns the first row back to the *Join* operator, which calls the GetRow() method of the *Clustered Index Seek* operator on the Addresses table after that. If there is a match, the *Join* operator concatenates data from both inputs and passes the resultant row back to the *Top* operator, which, in turn, passes it to *Select*.

The *Select* operator returns a row to the client and requests the next row by calling the GetRow() method of the *Top* operator again. The process repeats until the first 10 rows are selected. All operators keep their state and the *Sort* operator preserves the sorted data. It does not need to access the *Clustered Index Scan* operator again, as shown in Figure 5-13.

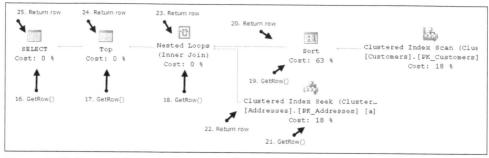

Figure 5-13. Row mode execution: getting the next row

Each operator in the execution plan has multiple properties, the names of which may vary slightly in different versions of SSMS and in other applications. Here are the most important ones:

Actual Number of Rows and Number of Rows Read
These properties illustrate how many rows were returned by the operator and how many rows were processed during execution. For example, the Index Scan operator with a predicate may process 1,000 rows, filtering out 950 of them. In this case, the properties would show 50 and 1,000 rows, respectively.

Estimated Number of Rows and Estimated Number of Rows Read
These properties provide cardinality estimation data and indicate how many rows the Query Optimizer expected the operator to return and process. The large discrepancy between estimated and actual metrics indicates a cardinality estimation error, which could lead to a suboptimal execution plan.

Number of Executions and Estimated Number of Executions
The Number of Executions metric indicates how many times the operator was executed. It does not correspond to the number of GetRow() calls, but rather indicates how many times this part of the execution plan was processed. For example, in the plan shown in Figures 5-12 and 5-13, Clustered Index Scan in the Customers table would be executed once, while Clustered Index Seek in the Addresses table would be executed 10 times.

The Estimated Number of Executions metric shows the estimate used by the Query Optimizer.

Startup Predicate
In some cases, operators may have a Startup Predicate property, which indicates the condition that needs to be met for the operator to execute. For example, a WHERE @ProvideDetails = 1 clause may generate a Filter operator with Startup Predicate @ProvideDetails = 1. The execution plan subtree after the

Filter operator may or may not be executed, depending on the `@ProvideDetails` parameter in runtime.

Unfortunately, row mode execution and per-row processing do not scale well with large analytical queries that process millions or even billions of rows. To address this, SQL Server 2012 introduced another execution model, called *batch mode execution*. This allows operators in the execution plans to process rows in batches. The process is optimized for large amounts of data and parallel execution plans.

Until SQL Server 2019, the Query Optimizer did not consider batch mode execution unless at least one of the tables in the query had a columnstore index. This restriction was removed in the Enterprise Edition of SQL Server 2019, where batch mode can be used with row-based B-Tree Indexes in databases with a compatibility level of 150. This does not mean all execution plans will use batch mode; however, the Query Optimizer will consider batch mode during optimization.

As with any feature that affects execution plans, batch mode can introduce regressions in some cases. You can enable and disable it on the database level with the `BATCH_MODE_ON_ROWSTORE` database option or on the query level with the `ALLOW_BATCH_MODE` and `DISALLOW_BATCH_MODE` query hints.

Finally, there is a trick that may enable batch mode execution on B-Tree tables in SQL Server 2016 and 2017: you can create empty and filtered nonclustered columnstore indexes on B-Tree tables that run large analytical queries. For example, if the table has an `ID` column that stores only positive values, the following index will allow the Query Optimizer to consider batch mode during optimization: `CREATE NONCLUS TERED COLUMNSTORE INDEX NCCI ON T WHERE ID < 0.`

You can see the operator's execution mode with the *Actual Execution Mode* property in the execution plan. *Actual Number of Batches* will tell you how many batches were processed. However, the query tuning strategy would be the same regardless of the execution mode.

Live Query Statistics and Execution Statistics Profiling

Several tools allow you to analyze execution plans. In addition to the well-known SSMS, you can use another freeware tool from Microsoft—Azure Data Studio (*https://oreil.ly/We7gO*). Despite the name, it works perfectly well with on-prem instances of SQL Server and can be installed on other operating systems besides Windows.

I consider Azure Data Studio to be targeted to developers rather than database administrators. Nevertheless, it provides basic database administration and tuning features and can be expanded with multiple third-party extensions. Some extensions will even bring support of other database platforms in addition to SQL Server.

I consider SolarWinds Plan Explorer (*https://oreil.ly/TOUTS*) (formerly known as SentryOne Plan Explorer) a must-have freeware tool for query tuning. This tool focuses on execution plan analysis. I find it more advanced and easier to use than SSMS. I suggest you download and test it if you have not done so already.

SSMS has another very useful feature called *Live Query Statistics*. This feature allows you to monitor query execution in runtime, detecting possible inefficiencies in the execution plan.

Figure 5-14 shows an example of the Live Query Statistics window in SSMS (the screenshot comes from the Microsoft documentation (*https://oreil.ly/qUJOV*)). The operators with solid lines have been completed. The dotted lines represent the tree of the operators that are currently executing. You can also see the estimated progress of each active operator, along with the actual and estimated numbers of rows. All metrics are updating during query execution.

Live Query Statistics is very useful when you need to debug long-running queries. It allows you to pinpoint inefficiencies in the execution plans and speed up further query tuning. You can enable Live Query Statistics for queries you run in SSMS. You can also access it from the Active Expensive Query section of the Activity Monitor window.

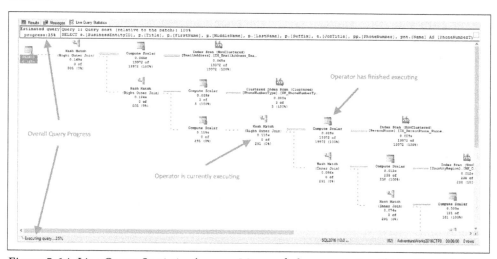

Figure 5-14. Live Query Statistics (source: Microsoft documentation (https://oreil.ly/ Rpy4O))

Live Query Statistics collects data based on *query execution statistics profiling*. There are two different methods SQL Server can use to collect the data. *Standard profiling* exists in all versions of SQL Server and has historically been used to obtain the actual execution plan for the queries. Unfortunately, this method introduces significant overhead.

Starting with SQL Server 2014 SP2, there is another option, called *lightweight profiling*. With this method, the overhead is significantly smaller; however, it does not collect runtime CPU information.

Table 5-2 illustrates how you can enable profiling in different versions of SQL Server. It also shows xEvents that enable profiling globally in the system. Live Query Statistics integrates with the latest version of profiling supported by the SQL Server instance where it runs.

Table 5-2. Query execution statistics profiling

	Type	How to enable	xEvent
Versions prior to SQL Server 2014 SP2	Standard	SET STATISTICS XML SET STATISTICS PROFILE	query_post_execution _showplan
SQL Server 2014 SP2– SQL Server 2016 RTM	Lightweight v1	Live Query Statistics	query_post_execution _showplan (less overhead compared to older versions of SQL Server)
SQL Server 2016 SP1– SQL Server 2017	Lightweight v2	T7412 QUERY_PLAN_PROFILE query hint	query_plan_profile Fires only for statements with the QUERY_PLAN_PROFILE query hint. Can be very useful when you need to capture the plan of a single query from a large batch or T-SQL module.
SQL Server 2019	Lightweight v3	Enabled by default LIGHTWEIGHT_QUERY _PROFILING database option	query_post_execution _plan_profile

The overhead of standard profiling is significant. With lightweight profiling, the overhead is lower. According to Microsoft, starting with SQL Server 2016 SP1, the overhead of continuously running lightweight profiling is about 2% to 4%, though it varies and may be significantly larger with some workloads. Be careful and measure the impact of profiling in your system, especially if you're considering running it for a prolonged amount of time.

There is another useful new function, sys.dm_exec_query_statistics_xml (*https:// oreil.ly/fwbDE*), that utilizes lightweight profiling (it returns NULL if lightweight profiling is not enabled). This function provides an in-flight execution plan for the currently running request. The result looks like the snapshot of Live Query Statistics. You can use this function together with the sys.dm_exec_requests view, as shown in Listing 5-5.

Listing 5-5. Using sys.dm_exec_query_statistics_xml

```
SELECT
    er.session_id
    ,er.request_id
    ,DB_NAME(er.database_id) as [database]
    ,er.start_time
    ,CONVERT(DECIMAL(21,3),er.total_elapsed_time / 1000.) AS [duration]
    ,er.cpu_time
    ,SUBSTRING(
        qt.text,
        (er.statement_start_offset / 2) + 1,
        ((CASE er.statement_end_offset
            WHEN -1 THEN DATALENGTH(qt.text)
            ELSE er.statement_end_offset
        END - er.statement_start_offset) / 2) + 1
    ) AS [statement]
    ,er.status
    ,er.wait_type
    ,er.wait_time
    ,er.wait_resource
    ,er.blocking_session_id
    ,er.last_wait_type
    ,er.reads
    ,er.logical_reads
    ,er.writes
    ,er.granted_query_memory
    ,er.dop
    ,er.row_count
    ,er.percent_complete
    ,es.login_time
    ,es.original_login_name
    ,es.host_name
    ,es.program_name
    ,c.client_net_address
    ,ib.event_info AS [buffer]
    ,qt.text AS [sql]
    ,p.query_plan
FROM
    sys.dm_exec_requests er WITH (NOLOCK)
        OUTER APPLY sys.dm_exec_input_buffer(er.session_id, er.request_id) ib
        OUTER APPLY sys.dm_exec_sql_text(er.sql_handle) qt
        OUTER APPLY sys.dm_exec_query_statistics_xml(er.session_id) p
        LEFT JOIN sys.dm_exec_connections c WITH (NOLOCK) ON
            er.session_id = c.session_id
        LEFT JOIN sys.dm_exec_sessions es WITH (NOLOCK) ON
            er.session_id = es.session_id
WHERE
    er.status <> 'background'
    AND er.session_id > 50
ORDER BY
```

```
     er.cpu_time desc
OPTION (RECOMPILE, MAXDOP 1);
```

Common Issues and Inefficiencies

The query optimization and tuning process may touch multiple layers in the system. For example, with third-party applications, you might not have access to the source code and must deal with a predefined set of queries. This, perhaps, is the most challenging case—where your optimization is limited to creating and modifying indexes.

The situation is much better when you are able to change queries and the database code. These changes can be time-consuming and require testing, but they yield better results and significant performance improvements.

In some cases, you need to go beyond the database code. You might need to change the database schema, the application architecture, and sometimes even the technology to scale the system. While this is an extremely complex process, it may give you the best long-term results.

I will not go that deep in this section, however. Instead, I will cover several common inefficiencies that can be addressed with indexing and code changes. Just remember that your options are not as limited in real life.

Inefficient Code

Unless you are in a situation in which you don't have access to the code, you should start the tuning by reviewing and, potentially, refactoring the queries. There are several antipatterns and issues to detect.

Non-SARGable predicates

SARGable predicates allow SQL Server to utilize the *Index Seek* operator by limiting the range of the key values to process. You need to analyze the query, detecting and removing non-SARGable predicates when possible.

One very common case that leads to non-SARGable predicates is functions. SQL Server calls the function for every row it is processing in order to evaluate the predicate. This applies to both system and scalar user-defined functions (UDFs).

SQL Server 2019 and later may inline some scalar UDFs into the query statement. However, there are many limitations that prevent inlining, so it is better to avoid scalar UDFs when possible.

Table 5-3 shows several examples of how you can refactor some predicates to make them SARGable. It is possible that some SQL Server versions may handle some non-SARGable predicates more efficiently, although it is always safer to manually adjust the queries.

Table 5-3. Examples of refactoring non-SARGable predicates into SARGable ones

Operation	Non-SARGable implementation	SARGable implementation
Mathematical calculations	`Column - 1 = @Value`	`Column = @Value + 1`
	`ABS(Column) = 1`	`Column IN (-1, 1)`
Date manipulation	`CONVERT(DATETIME, CONVERT(VARCHAR(10),Column,121)) = @Date`	`Column >= @Date AND Column < DATEADD(DAY,1,@Date)`
	`DATEPART(YEAR,Column) = @Year`	`Column >= @Year AND Column < DATEADD(YEAR,1,@Year)`
	`DATEADD(DAY,7,Column) > GETDATE()`	`Column > DATEADD(DAY,-7,GETDATE())`
Prefix search	`LEFT(Column,3) = 'ABC'`	`Column LIKE 'ABC%'`
Substring search	`Column LIKE '%ABC%'`	Use Full-Text Search or other technologies

Pay attention to the data types used in the predicates. The implicit conversion operation is, in a nutshell, a call of the system's `CONVERT_IMPLICIT` function, which in many cases would prevent index seek. Remember to analyze `JOIN` predicates in addition to `WHERE` clauses. Data type mismatches in join columns are a very common source of problems.

User-defined functions

I noted just now that system and noninlined scalar user-defined functions may prevent SQL Server from using the index seek operation. Moreover, they introduce significant performance overhead, especially in the case of user-defined functions. SQL Server calls them for every row it processes, and these calls are similar to stored procedure calls (you can confirm this by capturing an `rpc_starting` xEvent or `SP:Starting` trace event).

SQL Server optimizes the code in noninlined multistatement UDFs (scalar and table-valued) separately from the caller query. This usually leads to less efficient execution plans. More importantly, depending on the version of SQL Server, database compatibility level, and configuration settings, SQL Server estimates that multistatement table-valued functions return either 1 or 100 rows. This could completely invalidate cardinality estimations and lead to highly inefficient plans.

The latter situation is improved in SQL Server 2017. One of IQP's features, *Interleaved Execution*, defers final compilation of the query until runtime, when SQL Server can measure the actual number of rows returned by the function and finish optimization using that data. Currently, this works only with SELECT queries, although it may change in the future.

Nevertheless, it is better to avoid multistatement functions and use inline table-valued functions when possible. SQL Server embeds and optimizes them together with the caller queries. Fortunately, in many cases, scalar and multistatement table-valued functions can be converted to inline table-valued functions with very little effort.

Temporary tables and table variables

Temporary tables and table variables are very valuable during query optimization. You can use them to persist the intermediate results of queries. This allows you to simplify queries, which may improve cardinality estimations and generate more efficient execution plans.

Two common mistakes are associated with temporary tables and table variables.

The first common mistake is that some people choose table variables over temporary tables because of the common misconception that table variables are in-memory objects that don't use tempdb and are therefore more efficient than temporary tables.

This is not the case. Both objects rely on tempdb. Even though table variables are slightly more efficient than temporary tables, this efficiency comes from an important limitation: they do not maintain statistics on primary keys and indexes.

Temporary tables, on the other hand, behave like regular tables. They maintain index statistics and allow SQL Server to use them during optimization. While there are some edge cases when table variables could be the better choice, in most cases it is safer to use temporary tables. In many cases throughout my career, I've achieved great results by replacing table variables with temporary tables, without any further code or indexing changes.

The second common mistake is not indexing temporary tables, which negatively affects cardinality estimations and can lead to inefficient table scans. Treat temporary tables as regular tables and index them to support efficient querying, especially when they store significant amounts of data.

You can use a properly indexed temporary table to persist results from multistatement table-valued functions. This will improve cardinality estimations, especially in the old versions of SQL Server without interleaved execution.

Obviously, temporary tables and table variables come with a price. There is overhead involved in creating and populating them. When they are used wisely, the benefits may outweigh the downsides, but they are generally not a good choice for storing millions of rows. I'll discuss this in more depth in Chapter 9.

Stored procedures and ORM frameworks

While this topic is not directly related to query tuning, it is impossible to avoid mentioning Object Relational Mapping (ORM) frameworks. They are extremely common nowadays, and saying that all database engineers hate them would not be exaggerating. The queries generated by ORM frameworks are extremely complex and hard to optimize.

Unfortunately, we need to accept that these frameworks simplify development and reduce time and cost. In most cases, it is unrealistic and unreasonable to insist that application developers not use them. More importantly, in many cases, the performance impact from the less efficient queries that frameworks may generate is totally acceptable.

Performance-critical queries are different, though. You may not have many of them, but there are always some that will require extensive tuning and optimization. In those cases, autogenerated and/or ad-hoc queries are not the best choice. It is preferable to switch to stored procedures, which provide full flexibility and a larger set of techniques for optimization.

While this switch may require changes in the application code, in many cases it will reduce tuning time and cost. Remember this when you are choosing your tuning approach.

Inefficient Index Seek

As you already know, an index seek operation is usually more efficient than an index scan. This does not mean, however, that every index seek is efficient. SQL Server uses an index seek when query predicates allow it to isolate the range of data rows from the index during query execution. If this range is very large, this can reduce the efficiency of the operation.

Let's look at a simple example: I'll create a table and populate it with some data. Then I'll run two SELECT statements—with and without a WHERE clause—as shown in Listing 5-6.

Listing 5-6. Index seek inefficiency

```
CREATE TABLE dbo.T1
(
    IndexedCol INT NOT NULL,
    NonIndexedCol INT NOT NULL
);
CREATE UNIQUE CLUSTERED INDEX IDX_T1
ON dbo.T1(IndexedCol);

;WITH N1(C) AS (SELECT 0 UNION ALL SELECT 0) -- 2 ROWS
```

```
,N2(C) AS (SELECT 0 FROM N1 AS T1 CROSS JOIN N1 AS T2) -- 4 ROWS
,N3(C) AS (SELECT 0 FROM N2 AS T1 CROSS JOIN N2 AS T2) -- 16 ROWS
,N4(C) AS (SELECT 0 FROM N3 AS T1 CROSS JOIN N3 AS T2) -- 256 ROWS
,N5(C) AS (SELECT 0 FROM N4 AS T1 CROSS JOIN N4 AS T2) -- 65,536 ROWS
,N6(C) AS (SELECT 0 FROM N3 AS T1 CROSS JOIN N5 AS T2) -- 1,048,576 ROWS
,IDs(ID) AS (SELECT ROW_NUMBER() OVER (ORDER BY (SELECT NULL)) FROM N6)
INSERT INTO dbo.T1(IndexedCol, NonIndexedCol)
    SELECT ID, ID FROM IDs;

SET STATISTICS IO ON
SELECT COUNT(*) FROM dbo.T1;
SELECT COUNT(*) FROM dbo.T1 WHERE IndexedCol > 0;
```

Figure 5-15 shows the execution plans of both queries along with their I/O statistics. All rows in the table have positive IndexedCol values, so both queries must scan an entire index. In short, an index seek operation is identical to an index scan.

It is very common to see inefficient index seeks in multitenant systems. Take, for example, order fulfillment software, where data is generally spread across a relatively small number of warehouses. It is common to see the tenant-id (or warehouse_id, in this example) as the leftmost column in the index keys.

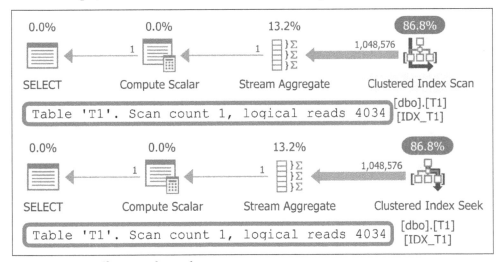

Figure 5-15. Inefficient index seek

Queries in these systems usually process data from a single tenant, using it as the predicate in the WHERE clause, which will rightfully lead to index seek operations in the execution plan. But if each tenant (or warehouse) stores very large amounts of data, you may get a perfect-looking but inefficient execution plan, even without any scans present. You'll need to use other predicates to make index seeks selective and improve performance.

You can analyze the efficiency of index seeks in the execution plan by looking at the operator's properties. Let's run the query shown in Listing 5-7 against the table we created in Listing 5-6.

Listing 5-7. Sample query

```
SELECT IndexedCol, NonIndexedCol
FROM dbo.T1
WHERE
    IndexedCol BETWEEN 100 AND 150 AND
    NonIndexedCol % 2 = 0;
```

Figure 5-16 illustrates several key properties for the analysis. The screenshot was captured in Plan Explorer; however, you'd see the same data in SSMS.

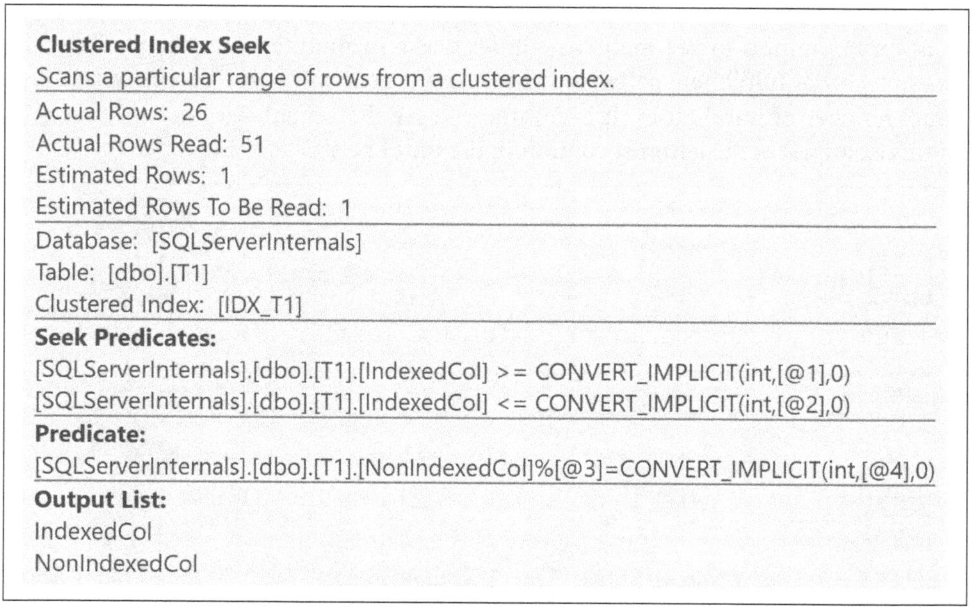

Clustered Index Seek
Scans a particular range of rows from a clustered index.

Actual Rows: 26
Actual Rows Read: 51
Estimated Rows: 1
Estimated Rows To Be Read: 1

Database: [SQLServerInternals]
Table: [dbo].[T1]
Clustered Index: [IDX_T1]

Seek Predicates:
[SQLServerInternals].[dbo].[T1].[IndexedCol] >= CONVERT_IMPLICIT(int,[@1],0)
[SQLServerInternals].[dbo].[T1].[IndexedCol] <= CONVERT_IMPLICIT(int,[@2],0)

Predicate:
[SQLServerInternals].[dbo].[T1].[NonIndexedCol]%[@3]=CONVERT_IMPLICIT(int,[@4],0)

Output List:
IndexedCol
NonIndexedCol

Figure 5-16. Index Seek operator properties

Let's look at the most important properties of the operator:

Seek predicate

This property shows the predicate(s) that SQL Server uses to limit the range of rows during the index seek. The more selective this predicate is, the more efficient index seek will be.

Predicate

The predicate illustrates additional filter criteria that SQL Server applies to every row read by an Index Seek operator. It does not reduce the size of the data the operator must process; however, it may reduce the number of rows the operator returns in the execution plan. In our case, the operator read 51 rows from the index and returned 26 rows to the next operator in the execution plan.

It is always more efficient to reduce the size of the data with an efficient seek predicate. When seek predicates are not selective enough, consider restructuring your index in a way that allows SQL Server to use regular predicates as seek predicates.

Actual rows and actual rows read
These properties are called Actual Number of Rows and Number of Rows Read in SSMS. They illustrate how many rows were returned by the operator and how many rows were processed during execution. The large value in Number of Rows Read indicates that index seek processed a large amount of data and may require further investigation. The large discrepancy between those two values shows potential index inefficiency, with a significant portion of the data being filtered out by the Predicate rather than the Seek Predicate of the operator.

Estimated rows and estimated rows to be read
These properties are called Estimated Number of Rows and Estimated Number of Rows to Be Read in SSMS. As noted, you can compare estimated and actual metrics in the execution plan to estimate the quality of the cardinality estimation data. A noticeable cardinality estimation error may indicate a wrong choice of index and/or join type (more on that later), which you will likely want to address.

When you see a large cardinality estimation error, make sure the statistics are up to date. Check the statement and remove constructs that could impact cardinality estimations (such as functions and table variables). In some cases, especially with complex queries, consider refactoring and/or splitting them, potentially using temporary tables to store intermediate data.

Obviously, it is much easier to analyze an execution plan when you have the actual execution metrics available. While estimated metrics can be useful for initial analysis, cardinality estimation errors may provide a very wrong or incomplete picture. Do additional analysis and look at the data distribution in the tables when dealing with estimated execution plans.

Incorrect Join Type

SQL Server uses many physical join operators during query execution. These belong to one of the three logical join types: *loop*, *hash*, and *merge*. Each is optimized for specific conditions, and an incorrect choice may have a serious negative impact on query performance. Unfortunately, people often don't pay attention to the join type chosen by SQL Server, overlooking opportunities for optimization.

Let's look at all three types in more detail.

Loop join

A loop join (or nested loop join) is the simplest join algorithm. As with any join type, it accepts two inputs, which are called *outer* and *inner* tables. The algorithm for the join is very simple (Listing 5-8). Briefly, SQL Server goes through the outer table, looking up rows to join in the inner table for each outer row.

Listing 5-8. Loop join algorithm (pseudocode)

```
/* Inner join */
for each row R1 in outer table
    find row(s) R2 in inner table
        if R1 joins with R2
            return join (R1, R2)

/* Outer join */
for each row R1 in outer table
    find row(s) R2 in inner table
        if R1 joins with R2
            return join (R1, R2)
        else
            return join (R1, NULL)
```

The cost of the join depends on two factors. The first is the size of the outer table. SQL Server goes through each row there, locating corresponding rows in the inner table to join. The more data it needs to process, the less efficient it will be.

The second factor is the efficiency of the inner table search. When the join column(s) in the inner table are properly indexed, SQL Server can utilize the efficient index seek operation. In that case, the cost of the inner table search on each iteration will be relatively low. Without the index, SQL Server might have to scan the inner table multiple times, once for each row from the outer table. As you can guess, this is extremely inefficient.

The loop join is optimized for conditions in which one of the tables is small and the other has an index to support an index seek operation for the join. It is impossible to define the hard threshold after which the join becomes inefficient. It may perform well with thousands and sometimes tens of thousands of rows in the outer input; however, it would not scale well with millions of rows. Nevertheless, in proper conditions, this type of join is extremely efficient. It has very little startup cost, does not use tempdb, and does not consume large amounts of memory.

Finally, loop join is the only join type that does not require an equality predicate. SQL Server may evaluate a join predicate between every row from both inputs, but it does not require a join predicate at all. For example, the CROSS JOIN operator would lead to a nested loop physical join when every row from both inputs has been joined together. Obviously, SQL Server cannot use index seek if the join predicate is not SARGable, which would lead to extremely inefficient operation with large inputs.

Merge join

A merge join works with two sorted inputs. It compares two rows, one at a time, and returns their join to the client if they are equal. If they are not, it discards the lesser value and moves on to the next row in the input. The algorithm for the join is shown in Listing 5-9.

Listing 5-9. Inner merge join algorithm (pseudocode)

```
/* Inputs I1 and I2 are sorted */
get first row R1 from input I1
get first row R2 from input I2
while not end of either input
begin
    if R1 joins with R2
    begin
        return join (R1, R2)
        get next row R2 from I2
    end
    else if R1 < R2
        get next row R1 from I1
    else /* R1 > R2 */
        get next row R2 from I2
end
```

The merge join is optimized for medium and large inputs, when both of those inputs are sorted. This means inputs need to be indexed on the join predicate columns. However, in practice, SQL Server may decide to sort inputs during query execution; the cost of the sort may thus far exceed the cost of the merge join itself. Check if that is the case and factor the cost of the Sort operator into your analysis.

There is another caveat. The merge join is less efficient in "many-to-many" join scenarios, when both inputs have duplicates in join predicate values. When this happens, SQL Server stores the duplicated values in a worktable in tempdb, which can impact join performance if a large number of duplicates are present. You can detect that a merge join is running in that mode by looking at the Many to Many property of the join operator in the execution plan.

Unfortunately, there is little you can do about it. Since merge join predicate columns are usually indexed, make sure indexes are defined as unique when the underlying data is unique.

Hash join

A hash join is designed to handle large unsorted inputs. Its algorithm consists of two different phases.

During the first, or *build*, phase, a hash join scans one of the inputs (usually the smaller one), calculates the hash values of the join key, and places them into the hash table. In the second, or *probe*, phase, it scans the second input, and checks (probes) to see if the hash value of the join key from the second input exists in the hash table. If so, SQL Server evaluates the join predicate for the row from the second input and all rows from the first input that belong to the same hash bucket. The algorithm is shown in Listing 5-10.

Listing 5-10. Inner hash join algorithm (pseudocode)

```
/* Build Phase */
for each row R1 in input I1
begin
    calculate hash value on R1 join key
    insert hash value to appropriate bucket in hash table
end

/* Probe Phase */
for each row R2 in input I2
begin
    calculate hash value on R2 join key
    for each row R1 in hash table bucket
    if R1 joins with R2
        return join (R1, R2)
end
```

A hash join requires memory to store the hash table. When there is not enough memory, the join stores some hash table buckets in tempdb. This condition is called a *spill* and can greatly affect join performance, since tempdb access is significantly slower.

Spills often happen due to incorrect memory grant estimation, which in turn may be triggered by incorrect cardinality estimation. When this is the case, make sure the statistics are up to date; consider simplifying or refactoring the query if this does not help.

Intelligent Query Processing in the Enterprise Edition of SQL Server 2017 introduced a new feature called *memory grant feedback*, which increases or decreases memory grants for a query based on memory usage in previous executions. In SQL Server 2017, this feature is limited to batch mode execution. Starting with SQL Server 2019, it is also enabled in row mode execution.

Read the Microsoft documentation (*https://oreil.ly/qyyNx*) for more information, and consider switching to a database compatibility level that supports memory grant feedback. This may reduce `tempdb` spills in the system. I'll talk more about this in Chapters 7 and 9.

Comparing join types

Table 5-4 summarizes the behavior of different join types and the use cases for which they are optimized.

Table 5-4. Join comparison

	Nested loop join	Merge join	Hash join
Best use case	At least one of the inputs is small; index on the join column(s) in another input	Medium to large inputs, sorted on index key	Medium to large inputs
Requires sorted input	No	Yes	No
Requires equality predicate	No	Yes	Yes
Blocking operator	No	No	Yes (build phase only)
Uses memory	No	No	Yes
Uses `tempdb`	No	No (sort may spill to `tempdb`)	Yes, in case of spills
Preserves order	Yes (outer input)	Yes	No

IQP, in SQL Server 2017, also introduced the concept of the *adaptive join*. With this join, SQL Server chooses to use either a loop or a hash join based on the size of the inputs at runtime. Unfortunately, in SQL Server 2017 and 2019, this works only in batch mode execution, which, in most cases, is triggered by columnstore indexes. You need to enable Live Query Statistics in SSMS to see adaptive join in the execution plan.

I mentioned just now that each type of join is optimized for specific use cases and may not perform well in other cases. Let's look at a simple example and compare the performance of different join types. Listing 5-11 creates another table (similar to the one in Listing 5-6) and populates it with the same data. Both tables have two columns each and a clustered index defined on one of the columns.

Listing 5-11. Join performance: table creation

```
CREATE TABLE dbo.T2
(
    IndexedCol INT NOT NULL,
    NonIndexedCol INT NOT NULL
);
CREATE UNIQUE CLUSTERED INDEX IDX_T2
```

```
ON dbo.T2(IndexedCol);

INSERT INTO dbo.T2(IndexedCol, NonIndexedCol)
    SELECT IndexedCol, NonIndexedCol FROM dbo.T1;
```

Next, let's compare the performance of different join types using the code in Listing 5-12. Here, I am forcing different join types with join hints (more on this later). I put the execution time of the statements in my test environment into code comments.

Listing 5-12. Join performance: test cases

```
-- Loop join with index seek in inner table
-- Elapsed time: 137ms.
SELECT COUNT(*)
FROM dbo.T1 INNER LOOP JOIN dbo.T2 ON
    T1.IndexedCol = T2.IndexedCol
WHERE
    T1.NonIndexedCol <= 100;

-- Loop join with inefficient index scan in inner table
-- Elapsed time: 16,732ms
SELECT COUNT(*)
FROM dbo.T1 INNER LOOP JOIN dbo.T2 ON
    T1.IndexedCol = T2.NonIndexedCol
WHERE
    T1.NonIndexedCol <= 100;

-- Hash join. Slower than loop join on small inputs
-- Elapsed time: 411ms.
SELECT COUNT(*)
FROM dbo.T1 INNER HASH JOIN dbo.T2 ON
    T1.IndexedCol = T2.IndexedCol
WHERE
    T1.NonIndexedCol <= 100;

-- Loop join with index seek in inner table with large input
-- Elapsed time: 1,514ms
SELECT COUNT(*)
FROM dbo.T1 INNER LOOP JOIN dbo.T2 ON
    T1.IndexedCol = T2.IndexedCol;

-- Hash join using indexed columns to join
-- Faster than loop join on large input
-- Elapsed time: 1,215ms
SELECT COUNT(*)
FROM dbo.T1 INNER HASH JOIN dbo.T2 ON
    T1.IndexedCol = T2.IndexedCol;

-- Hash join using non-indexed columns to join
-- Performance does not depend on if join columns were indexed
-- Elapsed time: 1,235ms
```

```
SELECT COUNT(*)
FROM dbo.T1 INNER HASH JOIN dbo.T2 ON
    T1.IndexedCol = T2.NonIndexedCol;

-- Merge join with pre-sorted inputs
-- Elapsed time: 440ms
SELECT COUNT(*)
FROM dbo.T1 INNER MERGE JOIN dbo.T2 ON
    T1.IndexedCol = T2.IndexedCol;

-- Merge join without pre-sorted inputs
-- Elapsed time: 774ms
SELECT COUNT(*)
FROM dbo.T1 INNER MERGE JOIN dbo.T2 ON
    T1.IndexedCol = T2.NonIndexedCol;
```

A loop join is faster than a hash join on small inputs; however, the hash join becomes more efficient as the size of the input grows. The merge join, on the other hand, is great when inputs are sorted. Otherwise, it adds a *Sort* operator to the execution plan. While this might work fine with small inputs, sorting very large inputs would not work well.

As these examples show, an incorrect choice of join type can reduce query performance dramatically. In most cases, this happens due to incorrect cardinality estimations, especially when SQL Server seriously underestimates the size of join inputs.

With hash and merge joins, this may lead to `tempdb` spills and slower join performance. However, that situation is most dangerous with the loop join, especially when the cost of inner input processing is high. (Recall that SQL Server processes the inner input for each row from the outer input, so costs add up quickly with each iteration.)

You can detect this condition by comparing actual to estimated rows in the outer input or by looking at actual versus estimated number of executions in the first operator from the inner input (see Figure 5-17). A large discrepancy would indicate a cardinality estimation error. When a cardinality estimation error leads to a high number of executions in the inner input, a loop join may be the wrong choice.

You have several options for addressing this problem. As a first step, review the query, looking for opportunities to refactor. Remove code patterns that could affect cardinality estimations, like multistatement functions and table variables. See if there is a possibility of better indexing, which could improve the execution plan.

It's worth checking whether you are being affected by parameter sniffing in parameter-sensitive plans. SQL Server sometimes caches and reuses execution plans compiled for atypical parameter values, especially when data is distributed very unevenly in the table. Think about multitenant systems where some tenants may have very little data and others a great deal. Execution plans generated for the former group of tenants would be inefficient for the latter.

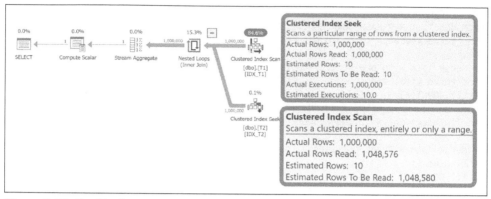

Figure 5-17. Cardinality estimation error in a loop join

When this is the case, consider using statement-level recompilation with OPTION (RECOMPILE) or disabling parameter sniffing in the database. I will discuss these and other options in more detail in the next chapter.

You can also try updating the statistics in the tables from the query. Unfortunately, this may not always help. The Query Optimizer in SQL Server does not always make the right assumptions when estimating cardinality in complex queries with multiple joins.

I have mentioned query simplification, which may help to address this problem. Consider splitting the query and persist intermediate results in the properly indexed temporary tables. SQL Server will be able to see the data distribution there and accurately estimate cardinality in the queries. Obviously, remember the overhead that temporary tables may introduce and do not use them to cache very large datasets.

As a last resort, you can force join types with query hints. This is a dangerous method, and you need to be very careful. The hints will force the Query Optimizer to perform optimization in a specific way, which may be inefficient in the future if the data distribution changes. If you do this, remember it and reevaluate periodically if hints are still required.

There are two ways to use join hints. The first is to specify a list of allowed join types in query options. The first statement in Listing 5-13 shows how to use this method to prevent the Query Optimizer from using loop joins anywhere in the query. The second option is to specify the specific type of join between the tables. The second statement in the example forces SQL Server to use a hash join between tables A and B.

Listing 5-13. Forcing join types

```
SELECT A.Col1, B.Col2
FROM
    A JOIN B ON A.ID = B.ID
    JOIN C ON B.CID = C.ID
OPTION (MERGE JOIN, HASH JOIN);

SELECT A.Col1, B.Col2
FROM
    A INNER HASH JOIN B ON A.ID = B.ID
    JOIN C ON B.CID = C.ID;
```

Unfortunately, the second approach also forces join orders for *all* joins in the query. SQL Server will always join the tables in the order they were specified in the query without trying to reorder the joins. In Listing 5-13, for instance, table A will always be joined with table B first using a hash join, and the result of their join will be joined with table C. This makes it dangerous for queries with multiple joins by preventing possible join-order optimizations. Be careful when you use them!

Excessive Key Lookups

As queries you already know, key and RID lookups[1] become extremely inefficient on a large scale. SQL Server does not use indexes for seek operations when it estimates that a large number of key or RID lookups will be required. However, you may still encounter excessive lookups in the execution plans.

This situation often occurs due to incorrect cardinality estimations. If SQL Server estimates that just a handful of key lookups will be required, it might decide to use a nonclustered index seek, and the error could lead to a large number of key lookups. That error usually happens due to cardinality estimation model limitations or parameter sniffing (in parameter-sensitive plans, about which you'll learn more in the next chapter).

You can detect this issue by analyzing estimated and actual numbers of rows in the execution plan, as shown in Figure 5-18.

SQL Server may also decide to use key lookups, choosing between bad data access strategies and worse ones. Running millions of key lookups is extremely inefficient; however, it could be better than scanning a table with billions of rows.

---

1 For the sake of brevity, from this point on I will stop referring to "key and RID lookups"; everything I say about "key lookups" applies to RID lookups as well.

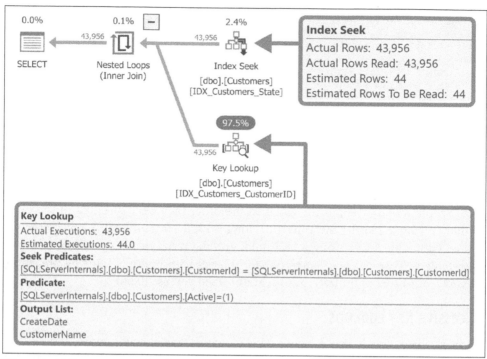

Figure 5-18. Incorrect cardinality estimation and key lookups

In many cases, you can remove key lookups with covering indexes. If all columns required for the query are present in a nonclustered index, SQL Server doesn't need to access the main data row in a clustered index or heap. By definition, it includes all columns in the nonclustered index key along with the clustered index columns in the row-id.

SQL Server allows you to include other columns in the index using the `INCLUDE` index clause. Data from these columns is stored on the leaf level only. It is not added to the index key and does not affect the sorting order of the index rows. Figure 5-19 illustrates the structure of an index with included columns, defined as `CREATE INDEX IDX_Customers_Name ON dbo.Customers(Name) INCLUDE(DateOf Birth)` on the table, which has `CustomerId` as the clustered index column.

Now, if the only columns the query references are present in the index, SQL Server can obtain all the data from the leaf level of the nonclustered index B-Tree without performing key lookups. It can use the index regardless of how many rows would be selected from there.

Turning nonclustered indexes into covering indexes is one of the most commonly used query optimization techniques. You can open the properties of the Key Lookup operator in the execution plan (see Figure 5-18) and get a list of columns from the operator's output and filter predicate. Including those columns in the nonclustered index would eliminate the need to do lookups.

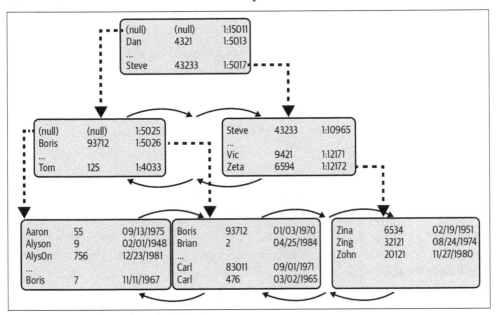

Figure 5-19. Index with included columns

Although covering indexes are a great tool for optimizing queries, they come at a cost. Every column in the index increases its row size, as well as the number of data pages it uses on disk and in memory. That introduces additional overhead during index maintenance and increases the database size. Moreover, queries need to read more pages when scanning all or part of the index. This doesn't necessarily introduce a noticeable performance impact during small-range scans, when reading a few extra pages is far more efficient than key lookups, but it can degrade the performance of queries that scan a large number of data pages or the entire index.

Covering indexes also add update overhead. By adding a column to nonclustered indexes, you store the data in multiple places. This improves the performance of queries that select the data. However, during updates, SQL Server needs to change the rows in every index where updated columns are present.

It is not a good idea to create very wide nonclustered indexes that include a majority of the columns in the table. Nor do you want to have a very large number of indexes. Both conditions will increase the size of the database and lead to excessive update overhead, especially in OLTP environments. (I will talk more about index analysis and consolidation in Chapter 14.)

Finally, I would like to state a very important and obvious thing. While excessive key lookups are bad for performance, having key lookups is *completely normal*. Doing lookups of hundreds or even thousands of rows may be a better option than creating large covering indexes.

Think about it from a different angle: the key lookup is a loop join with an efficient index seek in the inner table (clustered index). It is very fast and efficient on a small scale.

Remember, you don't have to eradicate all key lookups from the execution plan. Just analyze their efficiency and take care of the inefficient ones.

Indexing the Data

Designing proper indexes is both an art and a science. You will master this skill over time. Let me give you a few tips on how to start.

Most queries in the system have some parameters. The most selective SARGable predicates filter out most of the data; the columns in those predicates are the best candidates for the index.

Let's look at a hypothetical query that returns a list of one customer's orders (Listing 5-14).

Listing 5-14. Selecting a list of a customer's orders

```
SELECT c.CustomerName, c.CustomerNumber, o.OrderId, o.OrderDate, o.Amount
FROM
    dbo.Customers c JOIN dbo.Orders o ON
        c.CustomerId = o.CustomerId
WHERE
    c.CustomerNumber = @CustNum AND
    c.Active = 1 AND
    o.OrderDate between @StartDate AND @EndDate AND
    o.Fulfilled = 1;
```

Let's assume you run this query against tables that have no indexes except clustered indexes on the CustomerId and OrderId columns. The execution plan for the query consists of two clustered index scans and a hash join between the tables (Figure 5-20). As you can see, it is inefficient.

The natural place to start is the CustomerNumber column. The data here is likely to be unique, and the index on this column will be highly selective. The predicate Active=1 checks the status of the customer. You can expect it to be commonly used in the queries. It is a good idea to add the Active column to the index as an included column.

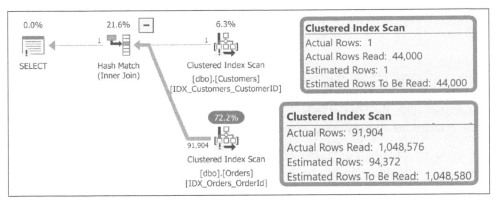

Figure 5-20. Indexing example: initial execution plan

I'd also expect `CustomerName` to often be selected alongside `CustomerNumber` data and added to the index as another included column, eliminating the need for a key lookup operation. Still, key lookups may be completely acceptable on a small scale with highly selective indexes.

Figure 5-21 shows the execution plan after you create the following index: `CREATE UNIQUE INDEX IDX_Customers_CustomerNumber ON dbo.Customers(CustomerNum ber) INCLUDE (Active, CustomerName)`.

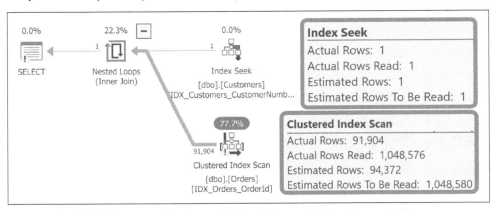

Figure 5-21. Indexing example: plan with the index on the Customers table

There are three predicates with the `Orders` table columns. Two of them—on the `CustomerId` and `OrderDate` columns—are selective, and thus are good candidates for the index. You can define the index with either the (`CustomerId`, `OrderDate`) or (`OrderDate`, `CustomerId`) column order.

To choose, consider how data will be sorted in the index. With the first option (`CustomerId`, `OrderDate`), SQL Server sorts the data by `CustomerId` first. Then the orders for each customer are sorted by OrderDate. With the second option, the data will be sorted by OrderDate across all customers.

Both indexes will allow an index seek in the Orders table. However, the first index is more efficient for our query. SQL Server will be able to do a range scan for orders that belong to this single customer for the time interval defined by @StartDate and @EndDate. With the second index, SQL Server would have to read all orders in that time interval for all customers, which would force it to scan more data.

It's good to add the Fulfilled column to the index as an included column, to evaluate the predicate as part of the seek operation. In this case, I'd also include the Amount column. It is small enough and would not increase the size of the index by much.

Figure 5-22 shows the final execution plan after the following index has been created: CREATE INDEX IDX_Orders_CustomerId_OrderDate ON dbo.Orders(CustomerId, OrderDate) INCLUDE (Fulfilled, Amount).

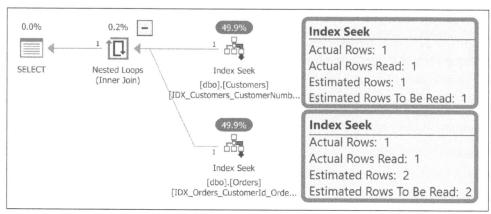

Figure 5-22. Indexing example: final execution plan

Query optimization is never boring. It constantly challenges you and helps you learn. I hope this chapter has given you some tips on where to start and has encouraged you to practice and learn more. After all, query tuning is the most efficient way to improve system performance.

A few more words of advice: don't create separate indexes for each query. Instead, analyze the workload in the system and create indexes that can be useful in multiple queries. When you start optimization, review the least efficient queries and identify common access patterns.

Also, be careful with covering indexes. Making them very wide is not a good idea. Again, there is nothing wrong with key lookups if they don't introduce a significant impact on the system.

In the next chapter, we will discuss high CPU load and options for reducing it.

Summary

SQL Server supports three data storage and processing technologies. Row-based storage, which is the most common, stores the data from all columns together in unsorted heaps or sorted B-Tree Indexes.

B-Tree Indexes sort data based on index keys. Clustered indexes store the data from all table columns. Nonclustered indexes store another copy of the data in separate physical indexes. They reference clustered indexes through the row-id, which is the clustered index key values. When data is not present in the nonclustered index, SQL Server goes through the clustered index B-Tree using the key lookup operation. This operation is expensive at scale.

SQL Server accesses data in two ways. An *index scan* usually reads all rows from the index. An *index seek* isolates and processes a subset of the index rows, which is usually more efficient than an index scan. Write your queries to allow SQL Server to utilize index seeks. You should also analyze the efficiency of your index seeks, making sure they don't process large amounts of data.

SQL Server stores information about indexes and data distribution in statistics, which it uses to estimate how many rows each operator will need to process in the execution plan. Accurate cardinality estimation helps SQL Server generate efficient execution plans. Up-to-date statistics are a key element in correct cardinality estimation.

When you analyze execution plans, pay attention to the efficiency of the Index Seek operators, the choices of join type, and the number of key and RID lookups. Check cardinality estimations too: improper cardinality estimation is one of the most common problems that lead to poor execution plans. Make sure statistics are up to date, add the required indexes, and simplify and refactor queries to address issues.

Troubleshooting Checklist

☐ Analyze your statistics maintenance strategy. Add a T2371 trace flag to reduce the automatic statistics-update threshold if the system has databases with compatibility levels below 130 (SQL Server 2016).

☐ Analyze and improve index maintenance strategies.

☐ Make sure statistics on filtered indexes are frequently updated. Optionally, consider rebuilding them frequently.

☐ Consider switching to the latest database compatibility level, especially in SQL Server 2017 and later. Pay attention to the cardinality estimation model if you do—you may need to handle it separately.

- ☐ Review temporary tables and table variable usage (more in Chapter 9).
- ☐ Refactor non-SARGable predicates when you encounter them in critical queries.
- ☐ Check the correctness of cardinality estimations. Reduce the usage of multistatement functions and constructs that could impact cardinality estimations.
- ☐ Analyze the efficiency of Index Seek operators.
- ☐ Validate that join columns have the same data types and review the choice of join types.
- ☐ Consider creating covering indexes when you see large numbers of key lookups in critical queries.

CHAPTER 6

CPU Load

My first SQL Server tuning project happened more than 20 years ago, and I've been dealing with many systems ever since. Over the years, I've noticed an interesting trend. Most of the systems I optimized in the past were I/O bound. Of course, there were other problems, but reducing I/O load through query tuning and code refactoring was usually enough to get the job done.

This started to change several years ago. While I still see nonoptimized and I/O-intensive queries, their impact is masked by high-performance, low-latency flash-based drives. Moreover, the availability of cheap hardware allows for bigger servers that can handle the load from more users. The need to reduce high CPU load is quite common nowadays.

In this chapter, I will talk about several common patterns that increase CPU load and options to address it. I will start with nonoptimized queries and inefficient database code. Next, I will cover query compilation overhead, along with plan caching, and the issues they can introduce. Finally, I will discuss the benefits and downsides of parallelism in systems and ways to tune your parallelism settings.

Nonoptimized Queries and T-SQL Code

Why does your server have a high CPU load?

There are several possibilities, but I'll start with the most obvious and common one: nonoptimized queries. It does not matter how fast the disk subsystem is. Nor does it matter whether the servers have enough memory to cache all the data in the buffer pool and eliminate all physical I/O. Nonoptimized queries *will* increase CPU load.

To put this into perspective, a query that scans 10 million data pages uses a million times more CPU resources than a query that scans just 10 pages. It does not matter that each logical read takes just a few microseconds of CPU time: it adds up quickly when multiple users are running those queries in parallel.

You can detect CPU-intensive queries using the techniques I discussed in Chapter 4, sorting data by CPU (worker) time while choosing targets for optimization. Optimizing those queries will decrease CPU load.

Don't confuse *CPU time* with *duration*, though. While queries with higher CPU time usually take longer to complete, the opposite is not true. A query may be blocked and use little CPU but still take a long time to finish.

Reducing query duration will improve the user's experience, but I rarely choose optimization targets based on this factor. Optimizing queries with high resource usage usually reduces duration as well.

Inefficient T-SQL Code

Inefficient T-SQL code also contributes to the problem. Except for natively compiled In-Memory OLTP modules, SQL Server interprets T-SQL code. This leads to additional CPU overhead.

Don't get me wrong: I don't want to discourage you from using stored procedures and T-SQL code. The benefits of properly designed and implemented T-SQL modules greatly outweigh CPU overhead. But there's one case I need to mention specifically: row-by-row processing.

Regardless of how you implement row-by-row processing—with cursors or with loops—it is inefficient. Imperative row-by-row execution will be slower and more CPU intensive than declarative set-based logic. There are some rare cases when you absolutely have to implement row-by-row processing; however, avoid it when possible.

Statements that perform row-by-row processing may not always appear to be the most resource-intensive statements. You can detect those statements with Query Store when it is enabled. Alternatively, you can look at plan cache–based execution statistics for T-SQL modules with the sys.dm_exec_procedure_stats, sys.dm_exec_function_stats, and sys.dm_exec_trigger_stats views (discussed in Chapter 4) to detect the modules with the most cumulative resource usage. Analyze what they are doing, keeping an eye on row-by-row logic.

Other T-SQL constructs contribute to CPU load too: for example, JSON and (especially) XML support are CPU intensive. It is better to parse semistructured data on the client side rather than in SQL Server. It's also easier and cheaper to scale application servers since you don't need to pay the SQL Server licensing cost.

Be aware of CLR, external languages code (*https://oreil.ly/fiZtN*), and extended stored procedures with complex logic. Avoid extensive function calls, especially with T-SQL user-defined functions. They add overhead and may lead to less efficient execution plans when they are not inlined.

Pay attention to views usage. Depending on the database schema and definition, views may introduce unnecessary joins, accessing tables the queries do not need to access. This is especially common if the tables do not have proper foreign keys defined.

Scripts for Troubleshooting High CPU Load

I'd like to provide you with a couple of scripts that are helpful when troubleshooting high CPU load. The first, in Listing 6-1, shows you CPU load on the server during the last 256 minutes. The data is measured once per minute, so it may miss short CPU load bursts that occur in between measurements.

Listing 6-1. Getting CPU load history

```
DECLARE
  @now BIGINT;

SELECT @now = cpu_ticks / (cpu_ticks / ms_ticks)
FROM sys.dm_os_sys_info WITH (NOLOCK);

;WITH RingBufferData([timestamp], rec)
AS
(
  SELECT [timestamp], CONVERT(XML, record) AS rec
  FROM sys.dm_os_ring_buffers WITH (NOLOCK)
  WHERE
    ring_buffer_type = N'RING_BUFFER_SCHEDULER_MONITOR' AND
    record LIKE N'%<SystemHealth>%'
)
,Data(id, SystemIdle, SQLCPU, [timestamp])
AS
(
  SELECT
    rec.value('(./Record/@id)[1]', 'int')
    ,rec.value
     ('(./Record/SchedulerMonitorEvent/SystemHealth/SystemIdle)[1]','int')
    ,rec.value
     ('(./Record/SchedulerMonitorEvent/SystemHealth/ProcessUtilization)[1]','int')
    ,[timestamp]
  FROM RingBufferData
)
SELECT TOP 256
  dateadd(MS, -1 * (@now - [timestamp]), getdate()) AS [Event Time]
  ,SQLCPU AS [SQL Server CPU Utilization]
```

```
  ,SystemIdle AS [System Idle]
   ,100 - SystemIdle - SQLCPU AS [Other Processes CPU Utilization]
FROM Data
ORDER BY id desc
OPTION (RECOMPILE, MAXDOP 1);
```

Figure 6-1 illustrates the output of the code. The data in the [Other Processes CPU Utilization] column shows CPU load in the system outside of SQL Server. If that load is significant, analyze what processes are running on the server and generating it.

	Event Time	SQL Server CPU Utilization	System Idle	Other Processes CPU Utilization
1	2021-03-27 09:44:52.903	61	35	4
2	2021-03-27 09:43:52.877	62	36	2
3	2021-03-27 09:42:52.863	56	42	2
4	2021-03-27 09:41:52.847	68	30	2
5	2021-03-27 09:40:52.833	77	20	3
6	2021-03-27 09:39:52.813	63	34	3
7	2021-03-27 09:38:52.800	64	33	3
8	2021-03-27 09:37:52.787	62	35	3

Figure 6-1. Script output showing CPU load history

Listing 6-2 helps you analyze CPU load per database. This may be beneficial when your server hosts multiple databases, and you are considering splitting the busy ones among different servers. (Please note: this script uses plan cache data, so the output is imprecise.)

Listing 6-2. Per-database CPU load

```
;WITH DBCPU
AS
(
    SELECT
        pa.DBID, DB_NAME(pa.DBID) AS [DB]
        ,SUM(qs.total_worker_time/1000) AS [CPUTime]
    FROM
        sys.dm_exec_query_stats qs WITH (NOLOCK)
        CROSS APPLY
        (
            SELECT CONVERT(INT, value) AS [DBID]
            FROM sys.dm_exec_plan_attributes(qs.plan_handle)
            WHERE attribute = N'dbid'
        ) AS pa
    GROUP BY pa.DBID
)
SELECT
    [DB]
    ,[CPUTime] AS [CPU Time (ms)]
```

```
      ,CONVERT(decimal(5,2), 1. * [CPUTime] /
          SUM([CPUTime]) OVER() * 100.0) AS [CPU Percent]
FROM DBCPU
WHERE DBID <> 32767 -- ResourceDB
ORDER BY [CPUTime] DESC;
```

Figure 6-2 shows the output from a production server.

	DB	CPU Time (ms)	CPU Percent
1	Appdb	55332331	73.69
2	AppDW	16190787	21.56
3	master	2264420	3.02
4	DBA	918845	1.22

Figure 6-2. Script output showing CPU load per database

Nonoptimized Query Patterns to Watch For

In the case of nonoptimized queries, there are two distinct patterns that can trigger high CPU load. I call them "the worst offenders" and "death by a thousand cuts." (This terminology is by no means standard; it's just how I like to differentiate between them.)

The worst offenders

The "worst offenders" occur when you have one or more expensive, long-running queries that generate heavy CPU load: think of nonoptimized queries with parallel execution plans that scan millions of rows and perform sorting and aggregation. They can bring a server to its knees, especially if you have several of them running simultaneously.

Fortunately, it is easy to detect the worst offenders in real time by querying the sys.dm_exec_requests view and analyzing the cpu_time column. (You can use the code from Listing 2-3 in Chapter 2 to do that.)

 A word of caution: The code in Listing 2-3 filters out system processes with a session_id below 50. In some cases, you might want to remove this filter and analyze all sessions running on the server. Keep in mind that some sessions may have been running since SQL Server startup and have high cumulative cpu_time: pay attention to the request start time.

Death by a thousand cuts

With the second pattern, "death by a thousand cuts," the load on the server is generated by a large number of simultaneously running requests. Each request may be relatively small and even optimized; however, the sheer number of requests drives CPU usage and server load up.

This case is more challenging to handle. While query optimization may help, you'll likely have to optimize a large number of queries, which will consume significant time and effort. It often requires refactoring database schemas, code, and applications on a massive scale to achieve results.

In the end, you have to reduce the load on the server to address the problem. Let's talk about several other factors that can increase that load, starting with the query compilation and plan caching processes. Reducing their overhead may help decrease the general server load.

Query Compilation and Plan Caching

Every time you submit a query to the system, SQL Server needs to compile and optimize it. This process is resource intensive, so SQL Server tries to minimize the number of compilations by caching execution plans for later reuse. In addition to regular client queries and batches, it caches plans of various objects, such as stored procedures, triggers, and user-defined functions. The memory area where these are stored is called the *plan cache.*

SQL Server uses different algorithms to determine which plans to remove from the cache in case of memory pressure. For ad-hoc queries, this selection is based on how often the plan is reused. For other types of plans, the cost of plan generation is also factored into the decision.

SQL Server recompiles queries when it suspects that currently cached plans are no longer valid. This may happen if the plan references objects whose schemas have changed, or because of stale statistics. SQL Server checks to see if the statistics are outdated when it looks up a plan from the cache, and it recompiles the query if they are. That recompilation, in turn, triggers a statistics update.

Plan caching and reuse can significantly reduce the number of compilations and the CPU load, as I will demonstrate later in this chapter. However, it can also introduce problems. Let's look at some of the most common issues that arise, starting with *parameter sensitivity* in *parameter-sensitive plans.* (This is sometimes called *parameter sniffing,* which just describes the SQL Server behavior that leads to the issue.)

Parameter-Sensitive Plans

Except for some trivial queries, SQL Server always has multiple options for generating the execution plan for the query. It can use different indexes to access data, select different join types, and choose among operators and execution strategies.

By default, SQL Server analyzes (*sniffs*) parameter values at the time of optimization and generates and caches an optimal plan for those values. Nothing is wrong with this behavior—though it can, if your data is unevenly distributed, lead to a cached plan that is optimal for atypical, rarely used parameter values but highly inefficient for queries with more common parameters.

I'm sure we've all experienced a situation where some queries or stored procedures suddenly started taking much longer to complete, even though there were no recent changes in the system. In most cases, these situations happen when queries are recompiled after a statistics update, due to parameter sniffing.

Let me show you an example. The script in Listing 6-3 creates a table and populates it with 1 million rows, evenly distributed across 10 `StoreId` values (a little more than 100,000 rows per `StoreId`), along with 10 rows with a `StoreId` of 99.

 Run this demo in a database with a compatibility level of 150 (SQL Server 2019) or below. The code may behave differently in SQL Server 2022; I will talk about this later in the chapter.

Listing 6-3. Parameter-sensitive plans: table creation

```
CREATE TABLE dbo.Orders
(
    OrderId INT NOT NULL IDENTITY(1,1),
    OrderNum VARCHAR(32) NOT NULL,
    CustomerId UNIQUEIDENTIFIER NOT NULL,
    Amount MONEY NOT NULL,
    StoreId INT NOT NULL,
    Fulfilled BIT NOT NULL
);

;WITH N1(C) AS (SELECT 0 UNION ALL SELECT 0) -- 2 rows
,N2(C) AS (SELECT 0 FROM N1 AS T1 CROSS JOIN N1 AS T2) -- 4 rows
,N3(C) AS (SELECT 0 FROM N2 AS T1 CROSS JOIN N2 AS T2) -- 16 rows
,N4(C) AS (SELECT 0 FROM N3 AS T1 CROSS JOIN N3 AS T2 CROSS JOIN N2 AS T3)
,N5(C) AS (SELECT 0 FROM N4 AS T1 CROSS JOIN N4 AS T2 ) -- 1,048,576 rows
,IDs(ID) AS (SELECT ROW_NUMBER() OVER (ORDER BY (SELECT NULL)) FROM N5)
INSERT INTO dbo.Orders(OrderNum, CustomerId, Amount, StoreId, Fulfilled)
    SELECT
        'Order: ' + CONVERT(VARCHAR(32),ID)
        ,NEWID()
```

```
         ,ID % 100
         ,ID % 10
         ,1
   FROM IDs;

INSERT INTO dbo.Orders(OrderNum, CustomerId, Amount, StoreId, Fulfilled)
   SELECT TOP 10 OrderNum, CustomerId, Amount, 99, 0
   FROM dbo.Orders
   ORDER BY OrderId;

CREATE UNIQUE CLUSTERED INDEX IDX_Orders_OrderId
ON dbo.Orders(OrderId);

CREATE NONCLUSTERED INDEX IDX_Orders_CustomerId
ON dbo.Orders(CustomerId);

CREATE NONCLUSTERED INDEX IDX_Orders_StoreId
ON dbo.Orders(StoreId);
```

Next, let's create a stored procedure that calculates the total sales amount for a specific store (Listing 6-4). I'm using a stored procedure in this example; however, parameterized queries called from client applications would behave the same way.

Listing 6-4. Parameter-sensitive plans: stored procedure

```
CREATE PROC dbo.GetTotalPerStore(@StoreId int)
AS
    SELECT SUM(Amount) as [Total Amount]
    FROM dbo.Orders
    WHERE StoreId = @StoreId;
```

With the current data distribution, when the stored procedure is called with any @StoreId other than 99, the optimal execution plan involves scanning the clustered index in the table. However, if @StoreId=99, a better execution plan would be to use an index seek on the IDX_Orders_StoreId index, with the key lookup occurring afterward.

Let's call the stored procedure twice: the first time with @StoreId=5 and the second time with @StoreId=99, as shown in Listing 6-5.

Listing 6-5. Parameter-sensitive plans: calling the procedure (test 1)

```
EXEC dbo.GetTotalPerStore @StoreId = 5;
EXEC dbo.GetTotalPerStore @StoreId = 99;
```

As you can see from the execution plan in Figure 6-3, SQL Server compiles the stored procedure, caches the plan with the first call, and reuses the plan later. Even though this plan is less efficient for the second call with @StoreId=99, it may be acceptable when those calls are rare, which is expected with such a data distribution.

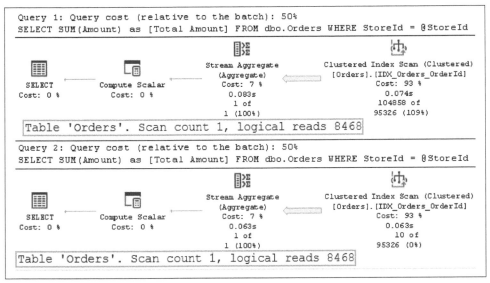

Figure 6-3. Execution plans of the queries (test 1)

Now let's take a look at what happens if we swap those calls when the plan is *not* cached (Listing 6-6). I am clearing the plan cache with the DBCC FREEPROCCACHE command—do not run this demo on a production server! Note, however, that the same thing can happen when a statistics update triggers the query to recompile.

Listing 6-6. Parameter-sensitive plans: calling the procedure (test 2)

```
DBCC FREEPROCCACHE;
EXEC dbo.GetTotalPerStore @StoreId = 99;
EXEC dbo.GetTotalPerStore @StoreId = 5;
```

As you can see in Figure 6-4, SQL Server now caches the plan compiled for the @StoreId=99 parameter value. Even though this plan is more efficient when the stored procedure is called with this parameter, it is highly inefficient for other @StoreId values.

Inefficient parameter-sensitive plans often become the "worst offender" queries that drive CPU load up. As I mentioned, you can detect those queries with the sys.dm_exec_requests view (Listing 2-3) and recompile them to remediate the issue.

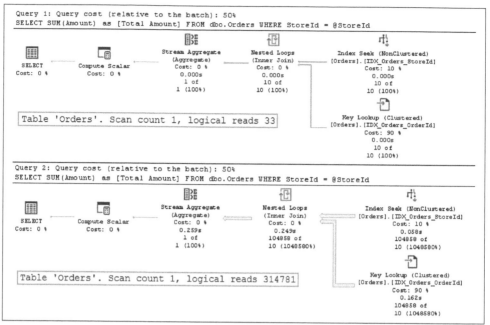

Figure 6-4. *Execution plans of the queries (test 2)*

You can force stored procedures and other T-SQL modules to recompile with the sp_recompile stored procedure. For ad-hoc queries, you can call DBCC FREEPROCCACHE, providing plan_handle or sql_handle as the parameter. Finally, if you have Query Store enabled, you can force a more efficient query execution plan there.

Obviously, it is better to address the root cause of the issue. First, see if there are any opportunities for query tuning, which would eliminate the plans' parameter sensitivity. We usually end up with parameter-sensitive plans because there are no efficient plans that do not depend on parameter values. For example, if you have the Amount column included in the IDX_Orders_StoreId index, that index would become a covering index. SQL Server can use it for all parameter values regardless of how many rows will be read, because the *Key Lookup* operation will no longer be required.

If you are using SQL Server 2017 or later, you can benefit from *automatic plan correction*, which is part of the *automatic tuning* technology. When this feature is enabled, SQL Server can detect parameter sniffing issues and automatically force the last known good plan that was used before regression occurred.

Automatic plan correction relies on the *Force Plan* feature of Query Store and, as you can guess, requires Query Store to be enabled in the database. Moreover, you need to enable it in the database with the ALTER DATABASE SET AUTOMATIC_TUNING

(FORCE_LAST_GOOD_PLAN = ON) statement. You can read more about this in the Microsoft documentation (*https://oreil.ly/GssX2*).

SQL Server 2022 introduces a new feature called *parameter-sensitive plan optimization*. In databases with compatibility level 160 and above, SQL Server may cache multiple active execution plans for parameterized SQL batches and T-SQL modules. SQL Server evaluates parameter values at runtime, choosing the optimal plan for each execution.

Parameter-sensitive plan optimization adds some slight overhead during query compilation and increases the size of the plan cache. Therefore, SQL Server will only cache multiple plans when it detects uneven data distribution, which could lead to issues in parameter-sensitive plans. There may be other cases that prevent caching of multiple plans; however, when this book went to press, this feature had not yet been released. Nevertheless, it is a valuable option to try if you are using SQL Server 2022 or Azure SQL Database.

If neither of those options works, you can force the recompilation of either stored procedure using EXECUTE WITH RECOMPILE or a statement-level recompile with OPTION (RECOMPILE) clauses. Listing 6-7 shows the latter approach.

Listing 6-7. Parameter-sensitive plans: statement-level recompile

```
ALTER PROC dbo.GetTotalPerStore(@StoreId int)
AS
    SELECT SUM(Amount) as [Total Amount]
    FROM dbo.Orders
    WHERE StoreId = @StoreId
    OPTION (RECOMPILE);
GO
EXEC dbo.GetTotalPerStore @StoreId = 99;
EXEC dbo.GetTotalPerStore @StoreId = 5;
```

Figure 6-5 shows that SQL Server recompiles the query sniffing parameters during each call.

Forcing the recompile will allow you to get the most efficient execution plans on each call—at the cost of constant recompilation overhead. This approach may be completely acceptable with infrequently executed queries; however, with frequently executed ones it may lead to a noticeable CPU increase, as I'll show later in this chapter.

You can address this by utilizing another hint: OPTIMIZE FOR. This hint allows you to specify parameter values for the Query Optimizer to use during optimization. For example, with the OPTIMIZE FOR (@StoreId=5) hint, the Query Optimizer will not sniff @StoreId, instead optimizing it for the value of 5 all the time.

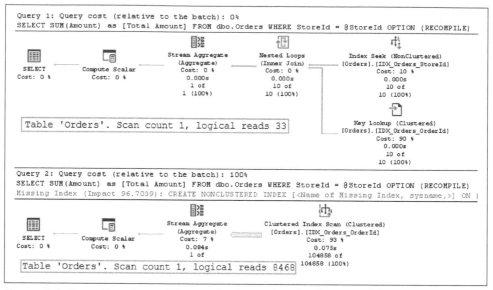

```
Query 1: Query cost (relative to the batch): 0%
SELECT SUM(Amount) as [Total Amount] FROM dbo.Orders WHERE StoreId = @StoreId OPTION (RECOMPILE)
```

		Stream Aggregate (Aggregate)	Nested Loops (Inner Join)	Index Seek (NonClustered)
SELECT	Compute Scalar	Cost: 0 %	Cost: 0 %	[Orders].[IDX_Orders_StoreId]
Cost: 0 %	Cost: 0 %	0.000s	0.000s	Cost: 10 %
		1 of	10 of	0.000s
		1 (100%)	10 (100%)	10 of
				10 (100%)

Table 'Orders'. Scan count 1, logical reads 33

Key Lookup (Clustered)
[Orders].[IDX_Orders_OrderId]
Cost: 90 %
0.000s
10 of
10 (100%)

```
Query 2: Query cost (relative to the batch): 100%
SELECT SUM(Amount) as [Total Amount] FROM dbo.Orders WHERE StoreId = @StoreId OPTION (RECOMPILE)
Missing Index (Impact 96.7039): CREATE NONCLUSTERED INDEX [<Name of Missing Index, sysname,>] ON |
```

		Stream Aggregate (Aggregate)	Clustered Index Scan (Clustered)
SELECT	Compute Scalar	Cost: 7 %	[Orders].[IDX_Orders_OrderId]
Cost: 0 %	Cost: 0 %	0.084s	Cost: 93 %
		1 of	0.075s
			104858 of
			104858 (100%)

Table 'Orders'. Scan count 1, logical reads 8468

Figure 6-5. Execution plans of the queries (statement-level recompile)

As you can guess, the danger of using the OPTIMIZE FOR hint is that data distribution may change. For example, if the store with @StoreId=5 went out of business, you'd end up with highly inefficient execution plans.

Fortunately, there is another form of this hint: OPTIMIZE FOR UNKNOWN. With this hint, SQL Server performs an optimization based on the most statistically common value in the table. In our case, this hint would lead to the plan with a clustered index scan, which is expected with data distribution in the table.

Listing 6-8 shows an example of using the OPTIMIZE FOR UNKNOWN hint. Keep in mind that you can use this hint with subsets of the parameters in the query.

Listing 6-8. Parameter-sensitive plans: OPTIMIZE FOR UNKNOWN hint

```
ALTER PROC dbo.GetTotalPerStore(@StoreId int)
AS
    SELECT SUM(Amount) as [Total Amount]
    FROM dbo.Orders
    WHERE StoreId = @StoreId
    OPTION (OPTIMIZE FOR (@StoreId UNKNOWN));
GO
```

You can use the hints OPTIMIZE FOR UNKNOWN (in all SQL Server versions after 2008) or DISABLE_PARAMETER_SNIFFING (in SQL Server 2016 and later) on the query level. Both hints are essentially the same. In SQL Server 2016, you can also control it at the database level with the PARAMETER_SNIFFING database option. Finally, you can disable parameter sniffing on the server level with the trace flag T4136. This trace flag also works in SQL Server versions prior to 2016.

 In my experience, disabling parameter sniffing leads to better and more stable execution plans in multitenant systems and in systems with very uneven data distribution. Your mileage may vary, but it's worth trying if you see a large number of parameter-sensitive plans in your system.

Caching inefficient parameter-sensitive plans increases CPU load. Unfortunately, that's not the only issue you can encounter with plan caching.

Parameter-Value Independence

Cached execution plans need to be valid for all possible combinations of parameters in future calls. As a result, even with parameter sniffing, SQL Server will not generate an execution plan that cannot be used with some parameter values in the future when SQL Server expects to cache it.

This sounds a bit confusing, so let me demonstrate it with a simple example. Listing 6-9 shows a very common and usually badly performing pattern: the stored procedure accepts optional parameters, using a single query to cover them all.

Listing 6-9. Parameter-value independence

```
CREATE PROC dbo.SearchOrders
(
    @StoreId INT = NULL
    ,@CustomerId UNIQUEIDENTIFIER = NULL
)
AS
    SELECT OrderId, CustomerId, Amount, Fulfilled
    FROM dbo.Orders
    WHERE
        ((@StoreId IS NULL) OR (StoreId = @StoreId)) AND
        ((@CustomerId IS NULL) OR (CustomerId = @CustomerId));
GO

EXEC dbo.SearchOrders
    @StoreId = 99
    ,@CustomerId = 'A65C047D-5B08-4041-B2FE-8E3DD6570B8A';
```

Regardless of what parameters you are using at the time of compilation, you will get a plan similar to the one shown in Figure 6-6. Even though there are indexes and SARGable predicates on both the CustomerId and StoreId columns, SQL Server uses the *Index Scan* operation instead of *Index Seek*. Unfortunately, SQL Server cannot use

Index Seek because the plan needs to be cached and reused in the future; this plan would not be valid if the *seek predicate* (@StoreId parameter in the following plan) was not provided.

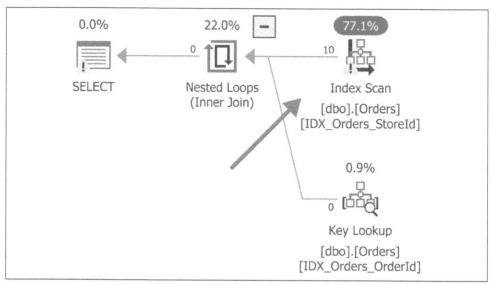

Figure 6-6. Execution plan of the stored procedure: parameter-value independence

A statement-level recompile using the OPTION (RECOMPILE) hint addresses the problem, again at the cost of additional compilation overhead. As noted, this overhead may be acceptable for infrequently executed queries.

As another option, you could rewrite the code using IF statements that cover all possible combinations of parameters. If you did, SQL Server would cache the plan for each statement. It would work in simple cases, but would quickly become unmanageable as the number of parameters grows.

Finally, writing the code using dynamic SQL is a completely valid option in many cases. Listing 6-10 shows how to do this. Be careful, of course, and utilize parameters to prevent SQL injection.

Listing 6-10. Dynamic SQL implementation

```
ALTER PROC dbo.SearchOrders
(
    @StoreId INT = NULL
    ,@CustomerId UNIQUEIDENTIFIER = NULL
)
AS
BEGIN
    DECLARE
```

```
       @SQL nvarchar(max) =
N'SELECT OrderId, CustomerId, Amount, Fulfilled
FROM dbo.Orders
WHERE
    (1=1)' +
    IIF(@StoreId IS NOT NULL, N'AND (StoreId = @StoreId)','') +
    IIF(@CustomerId IS NOT NULL, N'AND (CustomerId = @CustomerId)','');

    EXEC sp_executesql
        @SQL = @SQL
        ,@Params = N'@StoreId INT, @CustomerId UNIQUEIDENTIFIER'
        ,@StoreId = @StoreId, @CustomerId = @CustomerId;
END
```

There are other times when caching and reusing plans may lead to inefficient plans. One case, which is often overlooked, involves filtered indexes.

The query in Listing 6-11 will not use a filtered index even if you call it with the @Fulfilled = 0 value. This happens because the cached execution plan that uses the filtered index will not be valid for @Fulfilled = 1 calls.

Listing 6-11. Query that would not use filtered index

```
CREATE NONCLUSTERED INDEX IDX_Orders_ActiveOrders_Filtered
ON dbo.Orders(OrderId)
INCLUDE(Fulfilled)
WHERE Fulfilled = 0;
GO

DECLARE
    @Fulfilled bit = 0;

SELECT COUNT(*) AS [Active Order Count]
FROM dbo.Orders
WHERE Fulfilled = @Fulfilled;
```

 Always add *all* columns from the filter to either key or included columns in filtered indexes. This leads to more efficient execution plans.

Unfortunately, this problem can also occur due to auto-parameterization, especially when the database uses FORCED parameterization. I'll discuss this in more detail later in the chapter. For now, let's look at compilations and the overhead they introduce.

Compilation and Parameterization

As you know, SQL Server caches and reuses execution plans for T-SQL modules and ad-hoc client queries and batches. For ad-hoc queries, however, the plans are reused only for *identical* queries. There are a few factors that dictate that.

First, identical queries need to be *exactly* the same: a complete character-for-character match. Look at the queries in Listing 6-12. Only two are identical (the first and second), even though all the queries are logically the same.

Listing 6-12. Identical queries

```
SELECT COUNT(*) FROM dbo.Orders WHERE StoreId = 99;
SELECT COUNT(*) FROM dbo.Orders WHERE StoreId = 99;
SELECT COUNT(*) FROM dbo.Orders WHERE StoreId=99;
select count(*) from dbo.Orders where StoreId = 99;
```

In addition, some of the SET options affect plan reuse, including ANSI _NULL_DLFT_OFF, ANSI_NULL_DLFT_ON, ANSI_NULLS, ANSI_PADDING, ANSI_WARN ING, ARITHABORT, CONCAT_NULL_YELDS_NULL, DATEFIRST, DATEFORMAT, FORCEPLAN, LANGUAGE, NO_BROWSETABLE, NUMERIC_ROUNDABORT, and QUOTED_IDENTIFIER. Plans generated with one set of SET options cannot be reused by sessions that use a different set of SET options.

You've probably noticed that I keep emphasizing the point that query compilation and optimization processes are resource intensive and may introduce significant CPU load with a heavy ad-hoc workload. To demonstrate this, I have created a small application that runs simple queries from Listing 6-13 in a loop in multiple threads. You can download it from the book's companion materials.

In the first test case, the application runs ad-hoc queries using nonparameterized CustomerId values (the queries are constructed in the application). Each query in the call is unique and needs to be compiled. The second test uses a parameterized query. The plan for this query can be reused across calls.

Listing 6-13. Ad-hoc versus parameterized workload

```
-- Test Case 1
SELECT TOP 1 OrderId
FROM dbo.Orders
WHERE CustomerId = '<ID Generated in the app>';

-- Test Case 2
SELECT TOP 1 OrderId
FROM dbo.Orders
WHERE CustomerId = @CustomerId;
```

Both queries are extremely light. Moreover, I ran them in the test environment with enough memory to cache the entire table and eliminate physical I/O.

Figure 6-7 illustrates the performance metrics collected during the tests. As you can see, during the second test (on the right), the system was able to handle almost five times more requests per second than during the first test.

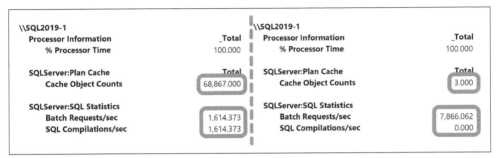

Figure 6-7. Ad-hoc versus parameterized workload throughput

Obviously, this scenario is completely fabricated; in real life, you are unlikely to see a situation where SQL Server has to spend a majority of its time compiling queries. Nevertheless, in systems with heavy ad-hoc workloads, the impact of compilations can be very significant. In addition to CPU load, there is also an impact on memory, which I will discuss in Chapter 7.

There are three `SQL Server:SQL Statistics` performance counters that can help you see the system throughput and number of compilations:

`Batch Requests/sec`
> Shows the number of batches SQL Server receives per second. Higher values indicate higher system load and throughput.

`SQL Compilations/sec`
> Shows how many compilations SQL Server performs every second. The higher this number is, the more compilations and, therefore, the more overhead you have.

`SQL Re-Compilations/sec`
> Gives you the number of recompilations for already cached execution plans. This may happen due to frequent changes in underlying data in both users and temporary tables.

In a properly tuned OLTP system, the number of compilations and recompilations should be just a fraction of the total number of batch requests. If that is not the case, analyze and reduce the compilations. (I will talk about how to analyze plan cache data in Chapter 7.)

Nonparameterized, ad-hoc client queries are the most common cause of compilations. As you can guess, the best approach is to change the queries and parameterize them. Unfortunately, this usually requires you to change the client code, which is not always possible. Fortunately, there is another option: *auto-parameterization*.

Auto-Parameterization

SQL Server tries to reduce compilation overhead by replacing constants in ad-hoc queries with parameters and cache compiled plans as if the queries were parameterized. When this happens, similar ad-hoc queries that use different constants can reuse cached plans.

Let's look at an example and run the queries in Listing 6-14. As before, I am clearing the plan cache with the DBCC FREEPROCCACHE command to reduce the size of the output.

Listing 6-14. Auto-parameterization

```
DBCC FREEPROCCACHE
GO
SELECT * FROM dbo.Orders WHERE OrderId = 1;
GO
SELECT * FROM dbo.Orders WHERE OrderId = 2;
GO

SELECT
    p.usecounts, p.cacheobjtype, p.objtype, p.size_in_bytes, t.[text]
FROM
    sys.dm_exec_cached_plans p CROSS APPLY
        sys.dm_exec_sql_text(p.plan_handle) t
WHERE
    p.cacheobjtype LIKE 'Compiled Plan%' AND
    t.[text] LIKE '%Orders%'
ORDER BY
    p.objtype DESC
OPTION (RECOMPILE);
```

Figure 6-8 shows the output of the last statement from the code. As you can see, there are three entries in the plan cache: a compiled plan used for both auto-parameterized ad-hoc queries, and two other objects called *shell queries*. Each shell query uses about 16 KB of memory, and stores information about the original ad-hoc query and links it to the compiled plan.

	usecounts	cacheobjtype	objtype	size_in_bytes	text
1	2	Compiled Plan	Prepared	40960	(@1 tinyint)SELECT * FROM [dbo].[Orders] WHERE [OrderId]=@1
2	1	Compiled Plan	Adhoc	16384	SELECT * FROM dbo.Orders WHERE OrderId = 2;
3	1	Compiled Plan	Adhoc	16384	SELECT * FROM dbo.Orders WHERE OrderId = 1;

Figure 6-8. Plan cache after auto-parameterization

Simple Parameterization

By default, SQL Server uses SIMPLE parameterization, and it is very conservative in parameterizing queries. Simple parameterization only happens when a cached plan is considered *safe to parameterize*. This means the plan would have the same shape and cardinality estimations, even when constant or parameter values change.

For example, a plan with a nonclustered index seek and key lookup on a unique index is safe because a nonclustered index seek would never return more than one row, regardless of parameter value. However, the same operation on a nonunique index is not safe. Different parameter values would lead to different cardinality estimations; this could make a clustered index scan the better option for some parameter values.

Moreover, there are many language constructs that prevent auto-parameterization, including IN, TOP, DISTINCT, JOIN, UNION, and subqueries. In practice, this means the majority of queries will not be auto-parameterized.

Forced Parameterization

Alternatively, SQL Server can use FORCED parameterization. This can be enabled at the database level with the ALTER DATABASE SET PARAMETERIZATION FORCED command, or at the query level with a PARAMETERIZATION FORCED hint. In this mode, SQL Server auto-parameterizes most ad-hoc queries (with very few exceptions).

Figure 6-9 shows results of the first test case (nonparameterized ad-hoc queries) from Listing 6-12 after I enable forced parameterization in the database. While the system throughput is still significantly lower than with a properly parameterized workload, it is much better than with the simple parameterization (Figure 6-7) that did not auto-parameterize the query. SQL Server still needs to spend CPU time to auto-parameterize queries; however, it can reuse the cached execution plan and does not need to optimize all the queries.

\\SQL2019-1	
Processor Information	**_Total**
% Processor Time	100.000
SQLServer:Plan Cache	**_Total**
Cache Object Counts	63,616.000
SQLServer:SQL Statistics	
Batch Requests/sec	4,319.563
SQL Compilations/sec	4,319.563

Figure 6-9. Throughput with forced parameterization

Enabling forced parameterization may significantly reduce compilation overhead and CPU load in systems with a heavy ad-hoc workload. You will of course get different results in different systems, but I've had a few cases where enabling forced parameterization reduced CPU load by as much as 25% to 30%.

Forced parameterization has its downsides, though. When it is enabled, SQL Server starts to auto-parameterize the majority of ad-hoc queries, which will open the door to parameter-sensitive plans and parameter sniffing–related issues. You can expect some ad-hoc queries to regress because of that.

> I recommend that you consider disabling parameter sniffing after you enable forced parameterization. While this may not be the best option for *every* system, I have found it helpful in most cases.

Fortunately, you are not always forced to take an all-or-nothing approach. As I mentioned, you can enable forced parameterization on the query level with the PARAMETERIZATION FORCED query hint. This is useful when you have just a handful of nonparameterized ad-hoc queries and do not want to enable forced parameterization globally.

If you don't have access to the source code, you can force the hint through plan guides. Listing 6-15 shows how to do that. It uses two stored procedures. The first, sp_get_query_template (*https://oreil.ly/YdXqs*), creates the query template based on the sample query provided as the parameter. You can use any constant values in an ad-hoc query for template creation. The second procedure, sp_create_plan_guide (*https://oreil.ly/cEJ4v*), creates the plan guide.

Listing 6-15. Applying forced parameterization through a plan guide

```
DECLARE
    @stmt NVARCHAR(MAX)
    ,@params NVARCHAR(MAX)
    ,@query NVARCHAR(MAX) =
N'SELECT TOP 1 OrderId FROM dbo.Orders
WHERE CustomerId = ''B970D68B-F88E-438B-9B04-6EDE47CC1D9A''';

EXEC sp_get_query_template
    @querytext = @query
    ,@templatetext = @stmt output
    ,@params = @params output;

EXEC sp_create_plan_guide
    @type = N'TEMPLATE'
    ,@name = N'forced_parameterization_plan_guide'
    ,@stmt = @stmt
    ,@module_or_batch = null
    ,@params = @params
    ,@hints = N'OPTION (PARAMETERIZATION FORCED) ';
```

You can download the test application from this book's companion materials and repeat the load tests to validate that the plan guide is working in a database that uses simple parameterization.

In some cases, you need to do the opposite and force simple parameterization for specific queries in the database that use forced parameterization. This can happen when some ad-hoc queries have parameter-sensitive plans. Listing 6-15 shows how you can force simple parameterization through the plan guide, allowing the ad-hoc query to utilize a filtered index. You need to provide the statement to the sp _create_plan_guide stored procedure as if it already had been auto-parameterized. You can obtain it from the plan cache, as shown in the example, along with the parameters of the statement.

The first query in Listing 6-16 is the one to which I am applying the plan guide.

Listing 6-16. Applying simple parameterization through a plan guide

```
SELECT OrderId
FROM dbo.Orders
WHERE Fulfilled = 0;
GO

SELECT
    SUBSTRING(qt.text, (qs.statement_start_offset/2)+1,
    ((
        CASE qs.statement_end_offset
            WHEN -1 THEN DATALENGTH(qt.text)
```

```
            ELSE qs.statement_end_offset
        END - qs.statement_start_offset)/2)+1) AS SQL
    ,qt.text AS [Full SQL]
FROM
    sys.dm_exec_query_stats qs with (nolock)
        CROSS APPLY sys.dm_exec_sql_text(qs.sql_handle) qt
WHERE
    qt.text like '%Fulfilled%'
OPTION(RECOMPILE, MAXDOP 1);

DECLARE
    @stmt NVARCHAR(MAX) =
        N'select OrderId from dbo . Orders where Fulfilled = @0'
    ,@params NVARCHAR(MAX) = N'@0 int'

-- Creating plan guide
EXEC sp_create_plan_guide
    @type = N'TEMPLATE'
    ,@name = N'simple_parameterization_plan_guide'
    ,@stmt = @stmt
    ,@module_or_batch = null
    ,@params = @params
    ,@hints = N'OPTION (PARAMETERIZATION SIMPLE)';
```

SQL Server does not auto-parameterize queries in stored procedures and other T-SQL modules. You can move some ad-hoc queries to stored procedures, avoiding parameter sensitivity issues when forced parameterization is enabled.

Finally, I'd like to reiterate: *recompilations may lead to significant CPU overhead in systems with heavy ad-hoc workloads*. Pay attention to it!

Parallelism

SQL Server uses parallelism to speed up the execution of complex queries by splitting the queries across multiple CPUs (workers). It improves the user experience by completing queries more quickly. However, there's no such thing as a free lunch: parallelism always comes with overhead. With parallel execution plans, SQL Server needs to do additional work, splitting and merging the data across multiple workers and managing their execution.

Assume that a query finishes in 1 second, with the serial execution plan using the same 1,000 ms of worker time. The same query may complete in 300 ms with a parallel four-CPU plan, consuming 1,050 ms of worker time in total. Managing parallelism requires SQL Server to perform extra work, and cumulative CPU time will always be higher than in the serial plan.

That overhead may impact throughput in busy OLTP systems. Faster execution time for a single query does not matter much, since there are many other queries waiting for CPUs in the queue. The overhead of parallelism forces them to wait longer for a CPU to become available. Although parallelism is good in complex reporting and analytical workloads, it can become a problem in OLTP systems, especially when the server operates under high CPU loads.

Unfortunately, it is extremely hard to find a system that does not mix both workloads. Even when you implement a dedicated data warehouse and operational data store (ODS), there will still be some reports and complex queries running in the source OLTP systems. Ideally, you want to separate those workloads, running them with different parallelism settings.

To make matters worse, SQL Server's default parallelism configuration is far from optimal. It allows SQL Server to utilize either all CPUs (SQL Server 2017 and earlier) or up to 16 CPUs (SQL Server 2019 and later) in parallel execution plans, and generate parallel execution plans when the cost of queries is equal to or greater than 5 (in technical terms, using the default *cost threshold for parallelisms*, or CTFP, of 5). The meaning of *cost* is synthetic: it does not represent anything meaningful and is used as a baseline metric during query optimization. Nevertheless, the value of 5 is extremely low nowadays as amounts of data grow; this value allows parallel execution plans for many queries.

Parallelism presents itself in the system with CXPACKET, CXCONSUMER, and EXCHANGE waits. It is very important to remember, however, that parallelism is not the root cause but a *symptom* of the issue. A high percentage of parallelism waits merely indicates a large number of expensive queries, which could be completely normal for a given reporting workload. In OLTP systems, on the other hand, such a figure usually means queries are not properly optimized (optimized queries would have a lower cost).

 You can see the cost of an individual statement by examining the property of the root operator in the execution plan.

When I see substantial parallelism waits in OLTP systems, I adjust the parallelism settings and continue troubleshooting and query tuning. Optimized queries have a lower cost, and therefore, reduced parallelism. In some cases, I even filter out parallelism waits from the wait statistics output, to get a more detailed picture of other waits.

There are several approaches to tuning parallelism settings. In OLTP systems I start by setting MAXDOP to one-fourth the number of available CPUs. If the server has a large number of CPUs or handles lots of OLTP requests, I may decrease the number to one-eighth that number, or even lower. In data warehouse systems, I might use half the available CPUs instead.

More importantly, I increase the CTFP. I often start with a CTFP of 50, but you can examine the cost of the queries to analyze if other thresholds would work better. The book's companion materials include a slightly modified version of Listing 4-1 that provides this information.

After the change is done, I monitor CPU load, percentage of signal waits, and parallelism waits, and I adjust the settings. One goal for these adjustments is to find the right CFTP value, which will allow SQL Server to separate different workloads and reduce or even prevent parallelism in OLTP queries.

There are other, more granular options to control parallelism. For example, you can separate OLTP and reporting workloads with Resource Governor and set different MAXDOP options for different workload groups. You could also consider setting MAXDOP to 1 in OLTP systems, enabling parallelism for reporting queries with a MAXDOP query hint. Either of those options would require you to monitor the system constantly and work closely with development teams.

In databases with compatibility levels of 160 (SQL Server 2022) and above, the IQP family adds another feature: *DOP feedback*. SQL Server monitors the execution of queries with parallel plans and may decide to decrease the degree of parallelism for individual queries. It works as if you had applied a MAXDOP query hint, although it uses a different mechanism to control parallelism internally.

This feature works similarly to the cardinality estimation feedback I covered in Chapter 5. SQL Server validates the query's performance with the new DOP value and either discards it or keeps it based on the results. It may also reevaluate the DOP, reducing it again, by up to MAXDOP = 2. It would not change the plan to become serial, though.

Whatever you do, do *not* set MAXDOP to 1 for all system workloads. This just hides the problem. Remember that parallelism is normal. You just need to make sure it is used legitimately.

Summary

Issues with high CPU load are common nowadays, as fast disk subsystems and large amounts of memory hide the impact of nonoptimized queries. Reducing CPU load often becomes the goal of the performance tuning process.

Nevertheless, nonoptimized queries are still a major factor in increasing CPU load on the server. The more data SQL Server needs to scan, the more CPU resources it uses. General query optimization helps reduce that.

In systems with heavy ad-hoc workloads, query compilation may lead to very significant CPU usage. Query parameterization in the code is the best option to address the issue. Alternatively, consider enabling forced parameterization for some queries or at the database level.

Unfortunately, parameterization may lead to issues with parameter-sensitive plans, where SQL Server compiles and caches plans for atypical parameter values. Those plans may be highly inefficient for other combinations of parameters. In many cases, disabling parameter sniffing improves the situation.

Pay attention to the amount of parallelism in your system. Parallelism is completely normal for reporting and analytical workloads; however, it is not desirable in OLTP systems, because parallelism management always adds overhead.

Remember that parallelism indicates the existence of expensive queries. You need to optimize them, instead of disabling parallelism and hiding the problem. Nevertheless, SQL Server's default parallelism settings are suboptimal and need to be tuned.

In the next chapter, you'll learn how to troubleshoot memory-related issues in SQL Server.

Troubleshooting Checklist

☐ Analyze and reduce CPU load from the processes outside of SQL Server.

☐ Detect and optimize the "worst offenders"—the queries that use the most worker time.

☐ Detect and optimize the most resource-intensive stored procedures and T-SQL modules.

☐ Review the impact of compilations. Plan cache metrics (which we'll discuss in the next chapter) may be useful in cross-checking the data.

☐ Parameterize critical queries. In the most severe cases of heavy, nonparameterized ad-hoc workloads, consider enabling forced parameterization and, potentially, disabling parameter sniffing.

☐ Tune your parallelism settings.

CHAPTER 7

Memory Issues

SQL Server can consume hundreds of gigabytes or even terabytes of memory. This is completely normal and often a good thing—using this much memory reduces the need for physical I/O and recompilations, improving server performance.

In this chapter, I will discuss how SQL Server works with memory. I will start with an overview of how SQL Server uses memory and give you a few tips on memory configuration. Next, I'll discuss the memory allocation process and show you how to analyze the memory usage of internal SQL Server components. Then I'll talk about query memory grants and the ways to troubleshoot extensive query memory usage. Finally, I'll briefly discuss memory management and potential issues with In-Memory OLTP implementation.

SQL Server Memory Usage and Configuration

SQL Server is a memory-intensive application. By default, it tries to allocate as much memory as possible and as required for the operations it performs. It does not allocate all the memory at start time; the allocation occurs as needed—for example, when it reads data pages to the buffer pool or stores compiled plans in the cache.

You can often see SQL Server consuming most of the OS memory. This is completely normal. When properly configured, SQL Server responds to OS requests and deallocates some process memory when needed. This condition is called *external memory pressure*. It usually occurs when the OS does not have enough memory for other applications. In small amounts, external memory pressure is not necessarily dangerous; however, deallocating a large amount of memory can significantly impact SQL Server's performance.

You can detect some of these events by setting up an alert on error 17890. This error indicates the most severe external memory pressure condition, when some SQL Server memory has been paged on disk. It generates the following message in the error log, providing information on how much memory had been trimmed: *A significant part of SQL Server process memory has been paged out.* I will discuss how to avoid this later in this chapter.

Another condition, *internal memory pressure*, may occur when some SQL Server components consume large amounts of memory, impacting other components on the server. In most cases, SQL Server handles those cases gracefully, dynamically adjusting internal memory usage; however, it may lead to problems. I'll show you how to troubleshoot those later in the chapter.

There are several ways to monitor memory usage on the server. The following performance counters are in the *Memory Manager* object; as a reminder, you can see them in the PerfMon utility or query the sys.dm_os_performance_counters view:

Target Server Memory (KB)
: This performance counter indicates the ideal amount of memory SQL Server should consume. It depends on configuration settings, the total amount of memory available to the OS, and a few other factors.

Total Server Memory (KB)
: This performance counter shows the amount of memory SQL Server currently uses.

In normal circumstances, the values of the two counters should stay very close. There are three cases, however, when Total Server Memory (KB) can become significantly lower than Target Server Memory (KB):

- When the server is ramping up shortly after startup. This is normal behavior.
- When hardware is over-allocated and SQL Server does not need all available memory. This is also normal, but may indicate inefficient capacity planning.
- During a memory pressure event, when SQL Server responds by trimming the memory. This condition requires further troubleshooting.

You can also get memory metrics from the sys.dm_os_sys_memory (*https://oreil.ly/xFS3u*) and sys.dm_os_process_memory (*https://oreil.ly/1IBX4*) views, which provide information about OS and SQL Server memory usage, respectively. Listing 7-1 shows the code that uses them.

Listing 7-1. Analyzing OS and SQL Server memory usage

```
SELECT
    total_physical_memory_kb / 1024 AS [Physical Memory (MB)]
    ,available_physical_memory_kb / 1024 AS [Available Memory (MB)]
    ,total_page_file_kb / 1024 AS [Page File Commit Limit (MB)]
    ,available_page_file_kb / 1024 AS [Available Page File (MB)]
    ,(total_page_file_kb - total_physical_memory_kb) / 1024
        AS [Physical Page File Size (MB)]
    ,system_cache_kb / 1024 AS [System Cache (MB)]
    /* Values: LOW/HIGH/STEADY */
    ,system_memory_state_desc AS [System Memory State]
FROM sys.dm_os_sys_memory WITH (NOLOCK);

SELECT
    physical_memory_in_use_kb / 1024
        AS [SQL Server Memory Usage (MB)]
    ,locked_page_allocations_kb / 1024
        AS [SQL Server Locked Pages Allocation (MB)]
    ,large_page_allocations_kb / 1024
        AS [SQL Server Large Pages Allocation (MB)]
    ,memory_utilization_percentage
    ,available_commit_limit_kb
    ,process_physical_memory_low /* May indicate memory pressure */
    ,process_virtual_memory_low
FROM sys.dm_os_process_memory WITH (NOLOCK);
```

You can get historical information about Target and Total Server Memory from a `system_health` xEvent session. You can also see it in the `sp_server_diagnos tics_component_result` event in the target (partial output is shown in Listing 7-2). This information may be useful when you are troubleshooting unexplained performance issues and need to check whether the server experienced memory pressure during the time the problem occurred.

This data is also captured by a hidden xEvent session and stored in XEL files in the SQL Server Log folder. The names of those files consist of the server and instance names followed by an SQLDIAG string.

Listing 7-2. The `sp_server_diagnostics_component_result` event in the sys tem_health session (partial)

```
<resource lastNotification="RESOURCE_MEM_STEADY" outOfMemoryExceptions="0"
isAnyPoolOutOfMemory="0" processOutOfMemoryPeriod="0">
  <memoryReport name="Process/System Counts" unit="Value">
    <entry description="Available Physical Memory" value="65669554176" />
    <entry description="Available Virtual Memory" value="13879244778291" />
    <entry description="Available Paging File" value="67695706112" />
    <..>
  </memoryReport>
```

```
<memoryReport name="Memory Manager" unit="KB">
  <entry description="Locked Pages Allocated" value="641593188" />
  <entry description="Large Pages Allocated" value="3248128" />
  <entry description="Target Committed" value="653261832" />
  <entry description="Current Committed" value="653263320" />
  <..>
</memoryReport>
</resource>
```

Let's look at several options you can use to configure SQL Server memory.

Configuring SQL Server Memory

There are two well-known configuration settings that control SQL Server memory usage: Maximum and Minimum Server Memory:

Maximum Server Memory

> The maximum amount of memory SQL Server can allocate. In some cases, SQL Server can allocate memory beyond this amount; if so, it will detect that condition and deallocate excess memory.

Minimum Server Memory

> The minimum amount of memory reserved for an SQL Server instance. By default, SQL Server does *not* pre-allocate memory to match the Minimum Server Memory value on startup. However, SQL Server would not deallocate the memory below it once the threshold is reached.

The default settings allow SQL Server to allocate all available memory without reserving any memory for the instance. This behavior may be sufficient in many systems with low or even mid-size loads. You may benefit, however, from tuning them (especially Maximum Server Memory) in your environment. Keep in mind that incorrect memory configuration may harm your system more than if you just keep default values.

Setting Maximum Server Memory usually requires some tuning. You can start with the base value and then adjust it by monitoring available physical memory on the server, using the `available_physical_memory_kb` column in the `sys.dm_os_sys_memory` view or the `Memory\Available MBytes` performance counter. Keep at least 512 MB of memory reserved on the small servers, and 1 GB or more reserved on servers with 128 GB of RAM or more.

You can calculate the base value to start with the following formula:

```
total_physical_memory – (4 GB + 1 GB × (total_physical_memory – 16 GB) / 8) –
memory_for_other_apps
```

If you are using a version of SQL Server older than 2012, you need to reserve additional memory, since the Maximum Server Memory setting in those versions controls memory usage of the buffer pool only.

 I am not covering memory configuration in the 32-bit version of SQL Server. If you are still using that, it's time to upgrade!

You need to properly estimate memory usage for other applications and reserve some memory for them. Those applications make memory management more complicated and can also impact system performance. I strongly recommend using dedicated SQL Servers in mission-critical systems and not running any applications (including SSIS, SSRS, and SSAS) there.

Setting Maximum Server Memory does not prevent SQL Server from responding to memory pressure. In some extreme cases, Windows can even page some of SQL Server's physical memory to a page file. You can prevent this by granting SQL Server *Lock Pages In Memory (LPIM)* permission in Group Policy.

Using LPIM may help improve SQL Server's responsiveness in the event of extreme external memory pressure. Be very careful with this setting, though, especially in nondedicated environments. It requires you to configure Maximum Server Memory properly and may lead to OS stability issues, and it even crashes if you over-allocate it. Nevertheless, I recommend enabling LPIM and properly configuring memory settings when possible.

The overhead of memory management on large servers can also increase shutdown time, which, in turn, can impact failover duration in a SQL Server Failover Cluster. You can improve this by enabling *Large Page Allocations* with trace flag T834. In this mode, SQL Server allocates memory in the larger chunks, which speeds up the process and reduces memory management overhead. This setting requires you to enable LPIM and forces SQL Server to pre-allocate all memory up to Maximum Server Memory value on startup. This may increase SQL Server startup time, especially on servers with a large amount of memory.

Test Large Page Allocations carefully before you enable it. You are unlikely to benefit from it unless the server has at least 384 GB of RAM. Do not enable it in nondedicated environments, nor in environments that use columnstore indexes. Unfortunately, those two technologies do not work well with each other.

This problem has been partially addressed in SQL Server 2019, where you can utilize some of the Large Page Allocations features in environments with columnstore indexes. You need to use trace flag T876 instead of T834 to enable this. Nevertheless, carefully test the system before switching it on.

How Much Memory Is Enough?

I discussed hardware in Chapter 1, but I'd like to repeat a few things here. Memory is the key resource in SQL Server. *Adding more memory to the servers is often the fastest and cheapest way to improve system performance.*

There are no limitations on how much memory SQL Server can utilize with Enterprise Edition. Add as much memory as your server can support, and use the fastest memory possible. Pay attention to the size of your active data—there's no need to build a server with terabytes of RAM for a 100 GB database—but keep future growth in mind and add some memory to support it.

In Standard Edition, the buffer pool size is limited to 128 GB, but you'll need additional memory for other SQL Server components and for the OS. I recommend provisioning the servers with at least 192 GB of RAM to be on the safe side.

Moreover, you will need even more memory if you are using columnstore indexes or In-Memory OLTP. The former uses an additional 32 GB per Standard Edition instance to store segment data. The latter uses up to 32 GB of RAM *per database*. Other SQL Server services, such as SSIS, SSAS, and SSRS, may also require additional memory when installed on the same box.

You can improve memory utilization by decreasing internal index fragmentation (the `avg_page_space_used_in_percent` column in the `sys.dm_db_index_physical_stats` view) and/or applying data compression. This will reduce the number of data pages and allow SQL Server to cache more data in the buffer pool.

I cannot stress it enough: memory is cheap nowadays. Benefit from it!

Memory Allocations

As I mentioned in Chapter 2, almost all memory allocations in SQL Server are done through SQLOS. Extended stored procedures and linked server providers can perform memory allocation outside of SQLOS and, therefore, would not be controlled by the Maximum Server Memory setting.

Internally, SQLOS partitions the memory into *memory nodes* based on the server's non-uniform memory access (NUMA) configuration—one memory node per NUMA node. Each memory node has a *memory allocator*, which uses various Windows and Linux API methods to allocate and deallocate the memory.

In earlier versions of SQL Server, memory allocation was carried out with single-page allocators for memory allocations less than 8 KB and with multipage allocators for any allocations greater than 8 KB. Starting with SQL Server 2012, the memory alloca-tors were consolidated into one allocator for *any size page*. You can track memory usage and allocations per memory node with the `sys.dm_os_memory_nodes` view (*https://oreil.ly/bWFG8*).

Internally, allocations become *memory objects*. Each memory object stores an alloca-ted memory along with its metadata (size, owner, etc.). You can analyze memory objects with the `sys.dm_os_memory_objects` view (*https://oreil.ly/yZYl2*), although I rarely use it during troubleshooting.

Another key element of SQL Server memory architecture is called *memory clerks*. Each major component of SQL Server has its own memory clerk, which works as the proxy between the component and the memory allocator. When a component needs memory, it sends a request to the corresponding memory clerk, which in turn gets the memory object from the memory allocator.

The last major component in SQL Server dynamic memory management is called the *memory broker*. Memory brokers supervise memory clerks by adjusting their memory usage based on available process memory, memory pressure, and other conditions. Memory brokers do not allocate or deallocate memory by themselves; however, they can send the signal to memory clerks to shrink or grow. You can look at the `sys.dm_os_memory_brokers` view (*https://oreil.ly/jDoBP*) to see the memory broker state and the amount of memory they allocate.

Figure 7-1 shows dependencies between memory management components in SQL Server.

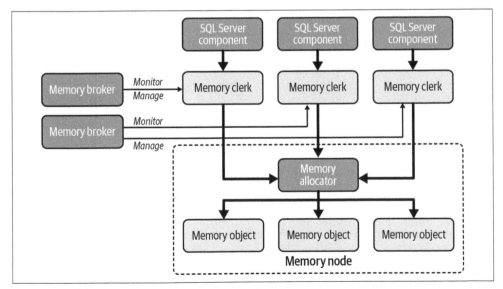

Figure 7-1. Memory management components

I usually start analyzing memory usage by looking at memory clerks using the sys.dm_os_memory_clerks view (*https://oreil.ly/i1msB*). Listing 7-3 shows how to do that. The code will work in SQL Server 2012 and later. If you are using an older version of SQL server, you should replace the single_page_kb column with the sum of the pages_kb and multi_pages_kb columns.

Listing 7-3. Analyzing memory usage

```
SELECT TOP 15
    [type] AS [Memory Clerk]
    ,CONVERT(DECIMAL(16,3),SUM(pages_kb) / 1024.0) AS [Memory Usage(MB)]
FROM sys.dm_os_memory_clerks WITH (NOLOCK)
GROUP BY [type]
ORDER BY sum(pages_kb) DESC;
```

Figure 7-2 shows the output of the script from one of the production SQL Servers that use 640 GB of RAM. The sys.dm_os_memory_clerks view provides enough information to quickly evaluate memory usage and detect potential abnormalities.

	Memory Clerk	Memory Usage (MB)
1	MEMORYCLERK_SQLBUFFERPOOL	583425.398
2	CACHESTORE_OBJCP	10116.328
3	OBJECTSTORE_LOCK_MANAGER	7620.531
4	CACHESTORE_SQLCP	4388.898
5	MEMORYCLERK_BITMAP	1542.930
6	OBJECTSTORE_XACT_CACHE	1083.602
7	MEMORYCLERK_SOSNODE	534.867
8	OBJECTSTORE_SERVICE_BROKER	423.273
9	MEMORYCLERK_SQLSTORENG	315.492
10	USERSTORE_TOKENPERM	275.320
11	MEMORYCLERK_SQLRESERVATIO	218.428

Figure 7-2. Memory usage on one of the production servers

Memory Clerks

You can see a complete list of memory clerks in the Microsoft documentation (*https://oreil.ly/9Vp3k*). Let's look at the most common memory clerks you may encounter.

MEMORYCLERK_SQLBUFFERPOOL

As you can guess by its name, MEMORYCLERK_SQLBUFFERPOOL controls memory allocation of the buffer pool. Usually, it is one of the largest memory consumers, especially when the server works with large databases.

There are no specific thresholds for *ideal* buffer pool size; it depends on your system. Large buffer pools are completely normal and mean that SQL Server just caches more data. There is nothing to worry about: when other SQL Server components need more memory, SQL Server trims the size of the buffer pool if there is no OS memory left to allocate.

Small buffer pools, on the other hand, may require some investigation. It does not necessarily present a problem—remember that SQL Server caches the *active* data the system is using. For example, even if you have a large, multiterabyte database, your buffer pool will be small if you work with a small subset of data.

You can check the *Page Life Expectancy* performance counter (Listing 3-3), the number of reads in the data files (Listing 3-1), and the percentage of PAGEIOLATCH waits, to determine if the buffer pool is constantly flushing. If this is the case, especially in OLTP systems, you should analyze the memory usage of other clerks and potential memory pressure conditions. Obviously, you should detect and optimize inefficient queries—the less data you need to scan, the less data you'd bring to the buffer pool.

Remember that non-Enterprise editions of SQL Server have limitations on the maximum buffer pool size. For example, the Standard Edition is limited to 128 GB of RAM in SQL Server 2014 and later, and to 64 GB in older versions.

Listing 7-4 shows a query that displays your buffer pool memory usage on a per-database basis. This may help you analyze when the server uses multiple databases. As a bonus, the code also returns the average time of the physical reads for data pages from disk.

Listing 7-4. Buffer pool usage on a per-database basis

```
;WITH BufPoolStats
AS
(
    SELECT
        database_id
        ,COUNT_BIG(*) AS page_count
        ,CONVERT(DECIMAL(16,3),COUNT_BIG(*) * 8 / 1024.) AS size_mb
        ,AVG(read_microsec) AS avg_read_microsec
    FROM
        sys.dm_os_buffer_descriptors WITH (NOLOCK)
    GROUP BY
        database_id
)
```

```
SELECT
    DB_NAME(database_id) AS [DB]
    ,size_mb
    ,page_count
    ,avg_read_microsec
    ,CONVERT(DECIMAL(5,2), 100. * (size_mb / SUM(size_mb) OVER()))
        AS [Percent]
FROM
    BufPoolStats
ORDER BY
    size_mb DESC
OPTION (MAXDOP 1, RECOMPILE);
```

CACHESTORE_OBJCP, CACHESTORE_SQLCP, and CACHESTORE_PHDR

The CACHESTORE and USERSTORE memory clerks are, in a nutshell, the caches for different types of data. The CACHESTORE_OBJCP, CACHESTORE_SQLCP, and CACHESTORE_PHDR memory clerks store plan cache–related objects:

CACHESTORE_PHDR
    Caches internal objects used during query compilations

CACHESTORE_OBJCP
    Stores compiled execution plans for stored procedures, functions, triggers, and other SQL objects

CACHESTORE_SQLCP
    Stores compiled execution plans for ad-hoc queries, prepared statements, and server-side cursors

CACHESTORE_PHDR clerks are most commonly used for compiling queries that reference complex views, large batches, and statements with a large number of constants in the IN clause. The objects cached by them are short-lived and are cached only during query compilation.

The CACHESTORE_PHDR clerk rarely consumes large amounts of memory. When you see high memory usage from this clerk, analyze the code and database schema to see if there are opportunities for refactoring.

In most systems, the majority of plan cache memory will be allocated by the CACHESTORE_OBJCP and CACHESTORE_SQLCP clerks. Memory consumption of CACHESTORE_OBJCP depends on the database schema and data tier architecture. Systems with a large number of actively used stored procedures and other T-SQL modules use more memory to store their execution plans. A *reasonably* high memory usage of CACHESTORE_OBJCP would not introduce any issues as long as it does not impact other components.

The situation is different with CACHESTORE_SQLCP clerks. Large memory consumption there usually indicates an excessive ad-hoc workload, which is CPU intensive and consumes plan cache memory.

You have already seen CPU overhead from ad-hoc queries in the previous chapter. Now, let me show you an example of memory overhead introduced by it. Listing 7-5 runs 1,000 simple ad-hoc queries and checks the plan cache state afterward using the sys.dm_exec_cached_plans view (*https://oreil.ly/sNg5A*). This script clears the content of the cache with the DBCC FREEPROCCACHE command—do not run it on a production server!

Listing 7-5. Running 1,000 ad-hoc queries and examining plan cache content

```
DBCC FREEPROCCACHE
GO

DECLARE
    @SQL NVARCHAR(MAX)
    ,@I INT = 0

WHILE @I < 1000
BEGIN
    SELECT @SQL =
N'DECLARE @C INT;SELECT @C=object_id FROM sys.objects WHERE object_id='
+ CONVERT(NVARCHAR(10),@I);
    EXEC(@SQL);
    SELECT @I += 1;
END;

SELECT
    p.usecounts, p.cacheobjtype, p.objtype, p.size_in_bytes, t.[text]
FROM
    sys.dm_exec_cached_plans p WITH (NOLOCK)
        CROSS APPLY sys.dm_exec_sql_text(p.plan_handle) t
WHERE
    p.objtype = 'Adhoc'
ORDER BY
    p.size_in_bytes DESC
OPTION (RECOMPILE);

SELECT
    CONVERT(DECIMAL(12,3),SUM(1. * p.size_in_bytes)/1024.) AS [Size (KB)]
FROM
    sys.dm_exec_cached_plans p WITH (NOLOCK)
WHERE
    p.objtype = 'Adhoc'
OPTION (RECOMPILE);
```

Figure 7-3 shows the content of the plan cache and its memory usage when I run a query with the Optimize for Ad-Hoc Workloads configuration setting disabled. There are 1,000 plans cached, each of which uses 48 KB of memory, or 48 MB total. Keep in mind that I ran a very simple query. Large and complex queries will use significantly more memory for the execution plans.

	usecounts	cacheobjtype	objtype	size_in_bytes	text	
1	1	Compiled Plan	Adhoc	49152	DECLARE @C INT;SELECT @C=o	.E object_id=999
2	1	Compiled Plan	Adhoc	49152	DECLARE @C INT;SELECT @C=o'	₹E object_id=998
3	1	Compiled Plan	Adhoc	49152	DECLARE @C INT;SELECT @C=o	.E object_id=997
4	1	Compiled Plan	Adhoc	49152	DECLARE @C INT;SELECT @C=c	₹E object_id=996
5	1	Compiled Plan	Adhoc	49152	DECLARE @C INT;SELECT @C=c	:E object_id=995
6	1	Compiled Plan	Adhoc	49152	DECLARE @C INT;SELECT @C=c	.E object_id=994

	Size (KB)
1	48000.000

Figure 7-3. Plan cache content when Optimize for Ad-Hoc Workloads is disabled

Figure 7-4 shows plan cache statistics after I repeat the test with the Optimize for Ad-Hoc Workloads configuration setting enabled. I still have 1,000 plans in the cache; however, memory usage is significantly lower. SQL Server caches small, 400-byte structures, called *compiled plan stubs*, instead of actual compiled plans. These structures are the placeholders that are used to keep track of which ad-hoc queries were executed. When the same query runs a second time, SQL Server replaces the compiled plan stub with the actual compiled plan and reuses it going forward.

	usecounts	cacheobjtype	objtype	size_in_bytes	text	
1	1	Compiled Plan Stub	Adhoc	456	DECLARE @C INT;SELECT @C=(	₹E object_id=999
2	1	Compiled Plan Stub	Adhoc	456	DECLARE @C INT;SELECT @C=	'E object_id=998
3	1	Compiled Plan Stub	Adhoc	456	DECLARE @C INT;SELECT @C=	₹ object_id=997
4	1	Compiled Plan Stub	Adhoc	456	DECLARE @C INT;SELECT @C=(	₹ object_id=996
5	1	Compiled Plan Stub	Adhoc	456	DECLARE @C INT;SELECT @C=(	E object_id=995
6	1	Compiled Plan Stub	Adhoc	456	DECLARE @C INT;SELECT @C=	₹ object_id=994

	Size (KB)
1	398.438

Figure 7-4. Plan cache content when Optimize for Ad-Hoc Workloads is enabled

As I already mentioned multiple times, the Optimize for Ad-Hoc Workloads setting should be enabled in most systems. It will reduce plan cache memory consumption and improve system performance.

Finally, let's repeat the same test using a parameterized query, as shown in Listing 7-6.

Listing 7-6. Running a parameterized query and examining plan cache content

```
DBCC FREEPROCCACHE
GO

DECLARE
    @SQL NVARCHAR(MAX)
    ,@I INT = 0

WHILE @I < 1000
BEGIN
    SELECT @SQL =
N'DECLARE @C INT;SELECT @C=object_id FROM sys.objects WHERE object_id=@P';
    EXEC sp_executesql @SQL=@SQL,@Params=N'@P INT',@P = @I;
    SELECT @I += 1;
END;

SELECT
    p.usecounts, p.cacheobjtype, p.objtype, p.size_in_bytes, t.[text]
FROM
    sys.dm_exec_cached_plans p WITH (NOLOCK)
        CROSS APPLY sys.dm_exec_sql_text(p.plan_handle) t
WHERE
    p.objtype = 'Prepared'
ORDER BY
    p.size_in_bytes DESC
OPTION (RECOMPILE);

SELECT
    CONVERT(DECIMAL(12,3),SUM(1. * p.size_in_bytes)/1024.) AS [Size (KB)]
FROM
    sys.dm_exec_cached_plans p WITH (NOLOCK)
WHERE
    p.objtype = 'Prepared'
OPTION (RECOMPILE);
```

As you can see in Figure 7-5, a single execution plan is cached. This reduces memory consumption and CPU load on the server.

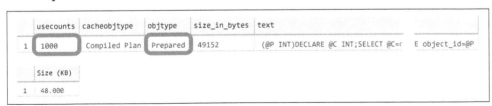

Figure 7-5. Plan cache content with parameterized query

The size and amount of memory consumed by the plan cache depends on the system workload, complexity of the execution plans, and data-tier design. It is not uncommon to see memory clerks using gigabytes or even tens of gigabytes of memory. Nevertheless, pay attention to it and analyze the content of the plan cache when you see large numbers.

This is especially important if you see high memory usage by the CACHESTORE_SQLCP clerk. More often than not, this is a sign of a heavy ad-hoc workload and a large number of single-use plans. As you saw earlier in the chapter, this impacts system performance.

There is another caveat regarding the ad-hoc workload. By default, SQL Server can cache about 160,000 objects in the plan cache. Reaching this limit may lead to additional CPU contention.

You may increase this number to about 640,000 objects by enabling trace flag T174. This may reduce CPU load in systems with very heavy ad-hoc workloads; however, it may also negatively impact performance as SQL Server would use more memory for the plan cache. Test it before deploying to production.

Listing 7-7 shows three queries you can use for plan cache analysis and troubleshooting. The first gives you the information about cached plan-cache objects grouped by their types. The data is collected from all plan cache memory clerks.

The second query gives you the number of single-used plans along with the memory they consume in plan cache. Large numbers, and especially large memory consumption, may warrant further investigation. The third query helps you detect the most memory-intensive single-used plans.

Listing 7-7. Analyzing the plan cache

```
-- Number of cached object and their memory usage grouped by type
SELECT
    cacheobjtype
    ,objtype
    ,COUNT(*) AS [Count]
    ,CONVERT(DECIMAL(15,3)
        ,SUM(CONVERT(BIGINT,size_in_bytes))/1024./1024.)
            AS [Size (MB)]
FROM
    sys.dm_exec_cached_plans WITH (NOLOCK)
GROUP BY
    cacheobjtype, objtype
ORDER BY
    [Size (MB)] DESC
OPTION (RECOMPILE);

-- Statistics on single-used execution plans
```

```
SELECT
    COUNT(*) AS [Single-used plan count]
    ,CONVERT(DECIMAL(10,3)
        ,SUM(CONVERT(BIGINT,cp.size_in_bytes))/1024./1024.)
            AS [Size (MB)]
FROM
    sys.dm_exec_cached_plans cp WITH (NOLOCK)
WHERE
    cp.objtype in (N'Adhoc', N'Prepared') AND
    cp.usecounts = 1
OPTION (RECOMPILE);

-- 25 most memory-intensive single-used plans
SELECT TOP 25
    DB_NAME(t.dbid) as [DB]
    ,cp.usecounts
    ,cp.plan_handle
    ,t.[text]
    ,cp.objtype
    ,cp.size_in_bytes
    ,CONVERT(DECIMAL(12,3),cp.size_in_bytes/1024.) as [Size (KB)]
FROM
    sys.dm_exec_cached_plans cp WITH (NOLOCK)
        CROSS APPLY sys.dm_exec_sql_text(cp.plan_handle) t
WHERE
    cp.cacheobjtype = N'Compiled Plan'
    AND cp.objtype in (N'Adhoc', N'Prepared')
    AND cp.usecounts = 1
ORDER BY
    cp.size_in_bytes DESC
OPTION (RECOMPILE);
```

You can remove individual execution plans from the cache by calling the DBCC FREEPROCCACHE statement and providing the plan handle as the parameter. This can be useful if you want to remove specific large single-used plans without affecting others. You can also do that to remove regressed parameter-sensitive plans affected by parameter sniffing.

You can also clear all plans stored by the CACHESTORE_SQLCP memory clerk with the DBCC FREESYSTEMCACHE('SQL Plans') WITH MARK_IN_USE_FOR_REMOVAL command. This removes all ad-hoc and prepared plans from the cache regardless of how often they were reused, keeping plans from stored procedures and other T-SQL modules intact.

Obviously, address the root cause of the issue when it is possible. Enable Optimize for Ad-Hoc Workloads and parameterize the queries, as I discussed in Chapter 6.

Finally, pay attention when the plan cache is small and does not use much memory. It could be completely normal when the system uses parameterized queries and stored procedures and has little ad-hoc activity. On the other hand, it may be a sign of memory pressure when the plan cache is constantly shrinking. Analyze compilation and recompilation performance counters when this is the case.

OBJECTSTORE_LOCK_MANAGER

The OBJECTSTORE_LOCK_MANAGER clerk stores lock structures that SQL Server uses to support concurrency. High memory usage of this memory clerk indicates that a large number of active locks are being held. Usually, you'd try to keep the number of active locks as small as possible; however, there are cases when you may need to acquire many row-level locks and prevent their escalation to object level.

I will talk about troubleshooting SQL Server concurrency issues in Chapter 8.

MEMORYCLERK_SQLQERESERVATIONS

The MEMORYCLERK_SQLQERESERVATIONS clerk manages *memory grants*—memory allocated to queries during their execution. It is common to see this clerk in the list of top memory consumers, especially in systems with data warehouse and reporting workloads.

I will talk about memory management during query execution and troubleshooting of extensive memory grants later in this chapter.

USERSTORE_TOKENPERM

The USERSTORE_TOKENPERM clerk provides memory for a security token store that is used to track user permissions and various other security objects. A large token store may introduce performance issues by increasing CPU load and triggering internal memory pressure by stealing the memory from other SQL Server components.

Unfortunately, this is a hard problem to address. To make it even worse, there are many known issues related to the token store in SQL Server. Some of them may be triggered by extensive usage of application roles and a heavy ad-hoc workload.

Keep an eye on the USERSTORE_TOKENPERM memory clerk. If the size is more than a few gigabytes, it may indicate that you have a problem, especially if it continues to grow. In this case, apply the latest service pack and/or cumulative update. If that does not help, consider opening a support case with Microsoft CSS.

As a temporary solution, you can clear the token store by using the DBCC FREESYS TEMCACHE ('TokenAndPermUserStore') command. In some cases, you may need to clear the token store on a regular basis by using the SQL Server Agent job, for example, until you have a permanent solution.

MEMORYCLERK_SQLCONNECTIONPOOL

The `MEMORYCLERK_SQLCONNECTIONPOOL` clerk provides memory for connection-specific objects that the client needs the server to maintain. The most common case is to use prepared statement handles that are generated by `sp_prepexecrpc` stored procedure calls during some RPC calls.

Memory consumption by this clerk is rarely a problem. It may grow, however, when client applications do not properly discard prepared handles while maintaining open connections to the database. You may have to restart the application and, in some cases, restart SQL Server to clear up the memory.

Obviously, it is better to address the root cause of the issue in the application code and close the handles after execution.

MEMORYCLERK_SQLCLR, MEMORYCLERK_SQLCLRASSEMBLY, and MEMORYCLERK_SQLEXTENSIBILITY

The `MEMORYCLERK_SQLCLR`, `MEMORYCLERK_SQLCLRASSEMBLY`, and `MEMORYCLERK_SQLEXTENSIBILITY` clerks are used for memory allocations in the Common Language Runtime (CLR) and to support language extensions (Java, R, and Python). All external languages will manage the memory and perform garbage collection automatically; however, it is possible to write code that consumes a large amount of memory during the execution. Think about processing large files or working with large documents, for example.

When you see high memory usage in those memory clerks, analyze the usage of the CLR and/or external languages. You may need to work with developers and refactor or even migrate some code to the application servers.

MEMORYCLERK_XTP

The `MEMORYCLERK_XTP` clerk controls memory allocations for In-Memory OLTP technology. When you see high memory usage in this clerk, you need to look at the memory-optimized table's memory consumption along with a few other things I will discuss later in this chapter.

High memory usage of In-Memory OLTP may be completely legitimate when memory-optimized tables store large amounts of data. More importantly, that memory is not going to be released in case of memory pressure when In-Memory OLTP is in use. You should take this into consideration when planning hardware capacity for servers (secondary Availability Groups replicas, DR servers, lower environments, etc.). The database will not start up and/or data in memory-optimized tables will become read-only if the server does not have enough memory to accommodate In-Memory OLTP data.

Wrapping up

It is impossible and unnecessary to cover all memory clerks in this section. Fortunately, Microsoft provides a comprehensive list of all memory clerks in its documentation (*https://oreil.ly/Q3gF2*). Even though the documentation does not include troubleshooting guidelines, it will help you understand what each memory clerk is responsible for and will point you in the right direction for troubleshooting.

As a word of caution, don't have tunnel vision and jump to immediate conclusions strictly based on clerks' memory usage. With very few exceptions, there are no specific guidelines on how much memory each memory clerk should use. You need to look at memory usage holistically and understand how different components impact each other.

For example, having a lot of memory reserved for query execution (MEMORY CLERK_SQLQERESERVATIONS) may be completely normal if it does not impact the buffer pool, plan cache, and other SQL Server components. On the other hand, it may be dangerous when it introduces internal memory pressure. Remember to use memory clerk information together with other metrics in your analysis.

The DBCC MEMORYSTATUS Command

If you have worked with SQL Server long enough, you are probably familiar with the DBCC MEMORYSTATUS command, which provides a snapshot of the current memory usage in SQL Server. Personally, I consider this command to be a mixed bag. Although it consolidates all memory usage information into one output of multiple result sets, it has limited ability to filter and aggregate data. More often than not, I collect the metrics using dynamic management views instead.

I am not going to cover the DBCC MEMORYSTATUS command in this book, but I'd encourage you to run it to see if you like how it presents the information and if you find it easy to interpret. It is just a different and consolidated projection of the data I've already discussed in this chapter.

Query Execution and Memory Grants

Every query in SQL Server needs to use some memory in order to run. This memory is called a *memory grant* and it is assigned to the query before it starts executing. The query will not start until the memory is available, and it may eventually time out if it cannot start.

The size of the memory grant depends on the operators in the execution plan, cardinality estimations, degree of parallelism, execution mode (row or batch mode), and a few other factors. For example, *Sort* or *Hash* operators need additional memory to support internal structures. They also benefit from extra memory to store all or a subset of the data in memory rather than spilling it to `tempdb`.

You can see memory grant information in the query execution plan. Figure 7-6 shows the information available in the query plan window in the SELECT (top plan operator) pop-up and SSMS properties window. You can also get the same data from the XML representation of the execution plan. The numbers are in kilobytes.

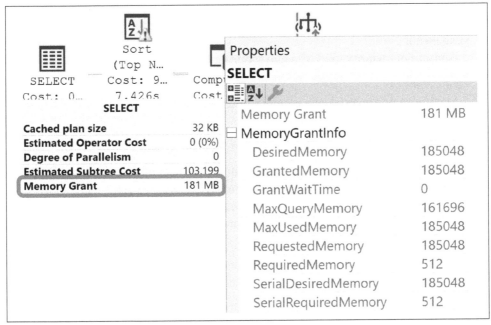

Figure 7-6. Memory grant information in SSMS

Let's look at the memory grant properties:

RequiredMemory

Absolute minimum amount of memory required for a query to execute. A query will not start until this memory is available.

SerialRequiredMemory

Absolute minimum amount of memory required for a query to execute in case of a serial execution plan. This will match `RequiredMemory` if a query runs serially.

DesiredMemory

Amount of memory the query wants in the perfect scenario. For example, if a query plan contains a *Sort* operator, `DesiredMemory` may include enough memory to sort all the data in memory based on cardinality estimations.

SerialDesiredMemory
: Desired amount of memory if the query is executed serially.

RequestedMemory
: Amount of memory the query requested from SQL Server when asking for a memory grant.

GrantedMemory
: Memory granted to a query.

MaxUsedMemory
: Amount of memory used by a query during the execution.

MaxQueryMemory
: Maximum possible size of a memory grant for a query.

GrantWait time
: Amount of time that a query waited for a memory grant.

The size of a memory grant is calculated at query optimization time and cached with the execution plan. Further executions of the queries will reuse the same grant sizes; however, SQL Server 2017 and later can recalculate the size of the memory grant based on actual memory usage from previous executions. I will cover this behavior later in this chapter.

As I mentioned earlier, memory grants are managed by a MEMORYCLERK_SQLQERESER VATIONS clerk, which uses a thread synchronization object called a *resource semaphore* to allocate the memory.

When memory cannot be allocated, the resource semaphore puts queries into the wait queue, generating RESOURCE_SEMAPHORE waits. Internally, the resource semaphore uses two wait queues and ranks queries based on their memory grant size and query cost. The first queue, called the *small-query resource semaphore*, stores queries that require less than 5 MB and costs less than three cost units. The second queue stores all other queries.

The resource semaphore processes requests on a first come, first serve basis. It favors the small-query resource queue over the other one, and reduces the waiting time for the small queries that do not require a large amount of memory.

You need to monitor situation when queries are waiting for memory grants to execute. This is unhealthy and requires investigation. The presence of RESOURCE _SEMAPHORE in noticeable amounts indicates a problem.

There are several performance counters in the Memory Management object that you can use for monitoring and troubleshooting:

Memory Grants Pending

Shows the number of memory grant requests that are currently pending. Ideally, this counter should show 0 all the time, which indicates that there are no queries waiting for memory grants.

Memory Grants Outstanding

Shows the number of currently running queries with fulfilled memory grant requests. Large values in this counter indicate a memory-intensive workload (usually queries with *Sort* and *Hash* operators). Although this can be normal in data warehouses, you need to investigate this condition in OLTP systems.

Maximum Workspace Memory

Provides the total amount of workspace memory in kilobytes.

Granted Workspace Memory

Indicates how much workspace memory in kilobytes is currently in use.

You can get more detailed information about total and granted sizes of workspace memory with the sys.dm_exec_query_resource_semaphores (*https://oreil.ly/9SuUC*) view. It provides you with statistics for both resource semaphore queues including memory information, number of queries in the waiting queue, and a few other metrics.

You can obtain information about pending and outstanding memory grants from the sys.dm_exec_query_memory_grants view (*https://oreil.ly/YRSnq*), as shown in Listing 7-8. The grant_time column shows the time when the grant was fulfilled. A NULL value in this column indicates that the grant is pending.

Listing 7-8. Memory grant information

```
SELECT
    mg.session_id
    ,t.text AS [sql]
    ,qp.query_plan AS [plan]
    ,mg.is_small  /* Resource Semaphore Queue information */
    ,mg.dop
    ,mg.query_cost
    ,mg.request_time
    ,mg.grant_time
    ,mg.wait_time_ms
    ,mg.required_memory_kb
    ,mg.requested_memory_kb
    ,mg.granted_memory_kb
    ,mg.used_memory_kb
    ,mg.max_used_memory_kb
    ,mg.ideal_memory_kb
FROM
    sys.dm_exec_query_memory_grants mg WITH (NOLOCK)
```

```
        CROSS APPLY sys.dm_exec_sql_text(mg.sql_handle) t
        CROSS APPLY sys.dm_exec_query_plan(mg.plan_handle) qp
--WHERE -- Uncomment to see only pending memory grants
--     mg.grant_time IS NULL
ORDER BY
    mg.requested_memory_kb DESC
OPTION (RECOMPILE, MAXDOP 1);
```

The `sys.dm_exec_query_memory_grants` view shows you the current status of memory grants. However, you may need to look at historical memory usage and detect the most memory-intensive queries. You can use the methods discussed in Chapter 4 to analyze memory grants data during troubleshooting.

The simplest approach, perhaps, is to use query execution statistics and the `sys.dm_exec_query_stats` view. This view includes several columns to track query memory grants and memory usage. You can use the code from Listing 4-1 to sort data by the `total_grant_kb` and/or [avg grant kb] columns and detect the most memory-intensive queries. Alternatively, you can get the data from Query Store when it is enabled.

Finally, you can track memory grant requests at runtime with xEvents. In SQL Server 2014 SP2 and later, you can use lightweight query profiling, which I discussed in Chapter 5. In older versions, you can use the `query_memory_grant_usage` event instead.

Optimizing Memory-Intensive Queries

When you detect a lot of memory-intensive queries, analyze their execution plans. In most cases, memory grants are driven by the memory usage of the *Hash* and *Sort* operators. If possible, capture actual execution plans, as they will provide you with the actual number of rows processed by operators along with their memory usage.

Unfortunately, there is no silver bullet that can magically optimize queries and reduce their memory consumption. However, there are a few things you can do instead. First, analyze if there is an opportunity for better indexing. This may eliminate unnecessary sorts and, in some cases, can change a hash join to a loop join, which does not use much memory.

Let's look at an example and create a table. The code in Listing 7-9 creates the table and populates it with some data.

Listing 7-9. Optimizing memory-intensive queries: table creation

```
CREATE TABLE dbo.Orders
(
    OrderID INT NOT NULL,
    OrderDate DATETIME2(0) NOT NULL,
```

```
    Placeholder CHAR(8000) NULL,
    CONSTRAINT PK_Orders PRIMARY KEY CLUSTERED(OrderID)
);

;WITH N1(C) AS (SELECT 0 UNION ALL SELECT 0) -- 2 ROWS
,N2(C) AS (SELECT 0 FROM N1 AS T1 CROSS JOIN N1 AS T2) -- 4 ROWS
,N3(C) AS (SELECT 0 FROM N2 AS T1 CROSS JOIN N2 AS T2) -- 16 ROWS
,N4(C) AS (SELECT 0 FROM N3 AS T1 CROSS JOIN N3 AS T2) -- 256 ROWS
,N5(C) AS (SELECT 0 FROM N4 AS T1 CROSS JOIN N4 AS T2) -- 65,536 ROWS
,IDs(ID) AS (SELECT ROW_NUMBER() OVER (ORDER BY (SELECT NULL)) FROM N5)
INSERT INTO dbo.Orders(OrderID, OrderDate)
    SELECT ID, DATEADD(day,ID % 365, '2021-01-01')
    FROM IDs;
```

Now let's run a query that returns the 200 most recent orders, as shown in Listing 7-10.

Listing 7-10. Optimizing memory-intensive queries: test query 1

```
SELECT TOP 200 OrderID, OrderDate, Placeholder
FROM dbo.Orders
ORDER BY OrderDate DESC
```

The execution plan and memory grant metrics for the query are shown in Figure 7-7. The query uses a 630 MB memory grant, which is driven by a Sort TOP N operator. This operator caches rows in memory before performing sorting.

It is worth noting that the Sort TOP N operator has internal and undocumented optimizations for cases when the TOP condition does not exceed 100 rows. In that mode, the operator uses very little memory during execution.

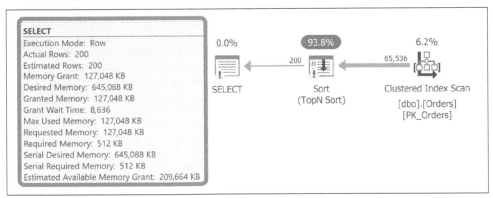

Figure 7-7. Optimizing memory-intensive queries: query execution plan

As I mentioned, you can often eliminate sorting with the proper indexing. For example, let's create the index with the `CREATE INDEX IDX_Orders_OrderDate ON dbo.Orders(OrderDate)` command and run the query from Listing 7-10 again.

Figure 7-8 shows the new execution plan. The *Sort* operator is no longer required, and the query does not require a memory grant to support it.

The size of the requested memory grant depends on the estimated number of rows and the size of the rows the operator needs to process. For example, if the Query Optimizer expects to sort 10,000 rows of 100 bytes each, it would need about 10 MB to accommodate the data in memory. Both cardinality estimation errors and row size estimation errors may lead to incorrect memory grants.

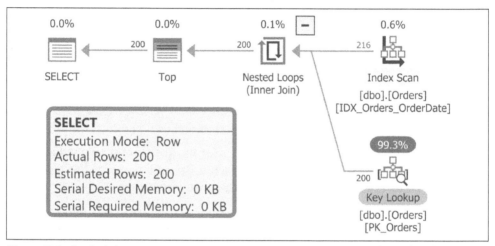

Figure 7-8. Optimizing memory-intensive queries: query execution plan after the index has been created

Let's look at the impact of cardinality estimation errors first and run another query, as shown in Listing 7-11.

Listing 7-11. Optimizing memory-intensive queries: test query 2

```
SELECT TOP 200 OrderID, OrderDate, Placeholder
FROM dbo.Orders
WHERE OrderDate BETWEEN '2021-07-01' AND '2021-08-01'
ORDER BY Placeholder;
```

Figure 7-9 shows the partial execution plan for a query along with the memory grant statistics. In this example, I just created the index and, therefore, the statistics are up to date.

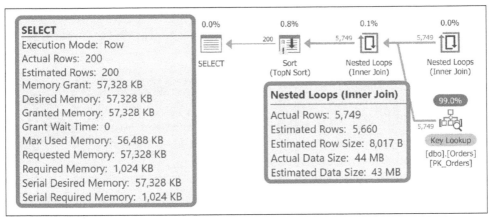

Figure 7-9. Optimizing memory-intensive queries: execution plan with up-to-date statistics

Now, let's run the code from Listing 7-12. It disables automatic statistics updates in the index and then deletes a large number of rows and clears the plan cache.

Listing 7-12. Optimizing memory-intensive queries: outdating statistics

```
ALTER INDEX IDX_Orders_OrderDate ON dbo.Orders
SET (STATISTICS_NORECOMPUTE = ON);

DELETE FROM dbo.Orders
WHERE OrderDate BETWEEN '2021-07-02' AND '2021-09-01';

DBCC FREEPROCCACHE;
```

Now let's repeat the test and run the query from Listing 7-11 again. As you can see in Figure 7-10, the cardinality estimation error led to an incorrect and excessive memory grant for the query.

Let's update the statistics with the UPDATE STATISTICS dbo.Orders IDX_Orders_OrderDate WITH FULLSCAN command and run the query again. As you can see in Figure 7-11, correct cardinality estimation led to a significantly smaller memory grant.

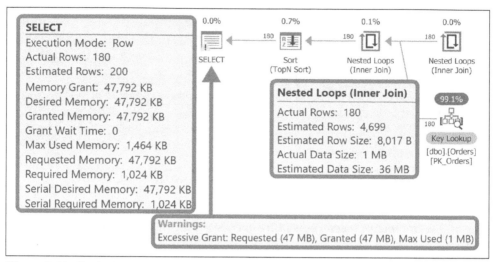

Figure 7-10. Optimizing memory-intensive queries: cardinality estimation error and memory grant

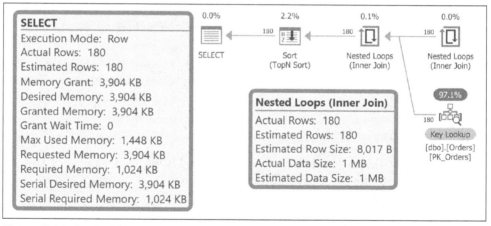

Figure 7-11. Optimizing memory-intensive queries: memory grant after UPDATE STATISTICS statement

Cardinality estimation errors are hard to deal with. Make sure the statistics are up to date and avoid any constructs that may affect cardinality estimations (table variables, multistatement table-value functions, etc.). In some cases, you can split complex queries into smaller ones and save intermediate results in temporary tables. This will lead to overhead, which I will discuss in Chapter 9; however, it may be a small price to pay for better execution plans in some cases.

Finally, let's look at another factor that contributes to the size of the memory grant, which is the data row size. SQL Server calculates it based on the data types of the columns processed by operators. For fixed-length columns the size is predefined. For example, TINYINT will use 1 byte, INT 4 bytes, and so on.

The estimations for variable-length columns, on the other hand, depend on their length in the table definition. SQL Server estimates them to be populated by 50%. For example, the column defined as VARCHAR(100) will have an estimated 50 bytes and NVARCHAR(200) an estimated 200 bytes, as Unicode characters are using 2 bytes to store the data. Finally, columns defined as (MAX) will have an estimated 4,000 bytes.

Do not select unnecessary columns, and avoid using large fixed-length (N)CHAR(N) and BINARY(N) data types, as they increase row size estimations and the size of memory grants. You can see the impact of having a large CHAR(8000) column in the previous examples. SQL Server estimated data rows being 8,017 bytes each despite the fact that the Placeholder column stored a NULL value in all the rows.

Let's change the Placeholder column data type with the ALTER TABLE dbo.Orders ALTER COLUMN Placeholder VARCHAR(32) command and run the query from Listing 7-11 again. As you can see in Figure 7-12, it changed the row size estimation from 8,017 to just 37 bytes, making the memory grant significantly smaller.

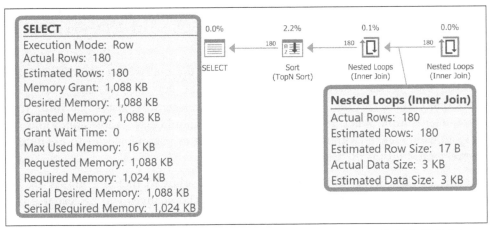

Figure 7-12. Optimizing memory-intensive queries: memory grant with VARCHAR data type

Memory Grant Feedback

The *memory grant feedback* feature, introduced in the Enterprise Edition of SQL Server 2017, allows SQL Server to dynamically adjust memory grants for cached execution plans based on memory usage from previous query executions. In SQL Server 2017, memory grant feedback works only with the queries that utilize batch-mode execution, which, in most cases, limits it to the queries that work with columnstore indexes. In SQL Server 2019, memory grant feedback was also extended to row-mode execution queries.

The memory grant feedback corrects both excessive and insufficient memory grants. For excessive memory grants, recalculation is triggered if the query uses less than 50% of granted memory. For insufficient grants, recalculation is triggered in the event of a `tempdb` spill (more on this in Chapter 9). After recalculation, SQL Server updates the memory grant parameters in the cached execution plan and uses the new values going forward.

Batch-mode memory grant feedback is enabled in databases with compatibility level 140 (SQL Server 2017) and above. For row-mode feedback, it requires compatibility level 150 (SQL Server 2019) to be set. It also works in Azure SQL Databases.

Both row- and batch-mode feedback may be disabled through the database scope configuration with the `ALTER DATABASE SCOPED CONFIGURATION` command. Row-mode feedback is controlled by the `ROW_MODE_MEMORY_GRANT_FEEDBACK` setting. For batch-mode feedback, however, the settings are different between SQL Server 2017 and 2019.

In SQL Server 2017, you can disable batch-mode feedback by setting `DISABLE_BATCH_MODE_MEMORY_GRANT_FEEDBACK` to `ON`. In SQL Server 2019, you should set `BATCH_MODE_MEMORY_GRANT_FEEDBACK` to `OFF`.

You can also disable memory grant feedback on the query level with the `DISABLE_BATCH_MODE_MEMORY_GRANT_FEEDBACK` and `DISABLE_ROW_MODE_MEMORY_GRANT_FEEDBACK` query hints. This may be useful with parameter-sensitive plans that suffer from parameter sniffing issues. Memory grant feedback should detect those conditions and stop adjusting memory grants; however, in some cases you may decide to use hints to prevent any adjustments from happening.

Finally, in SQL Server 2019 and older versions, adjusted memory grants are not persisted and are applied to cached plans only. The changes will be lost if a plan is evicted from the cache or in the event of a SQL Server restart or failover. This changed in SQL Server 2022, where memory grant information is persisted in Query Store. There are also additional improvements there, which improve the accuracy of memory grant calculations.

Controlling Memory Grant Size

SQL Server provides you with two query hints—`MIN_GRANT_PERCENT` and `MAX_GRANT_PERCENT`—that allow you to specify the minimum and maximum *percentage* of workspace memory that can be granted to a query. Unfortunately, those hints are tricky to deal with. You cannot specify memory grant size in absolute units, such as KB or MB, and you must deal with a percentage of available workspace memory, which is based on hardware and SQL Server configuration.

Workspace memory can use up to 75% of target server memory. You can track both of those metrics through the `Maximum Workspace Memory (KB)` and `Target Server Memory (KB)` performance counters. By default, the maximum size of the memory grant for individual queries is 25% of the workspace memory.

Let's assume you have the query shown in Listing 7-13.

Listing 7-13. A hypothetical query

```
SELECT Col1, Col2
FROM T1
ORDER BY Col3
OPTION(MIN_GRANT_PERCENT=0.5,MAX_GRANT_PERCENT=3);
```

In a SQL Server instance with a target server memory of 100 GB, the maximum workspace memory will be set to 75 GB by default. In that configuration, the query would get at minimum 0.5% of 75 GB, which is 0.375 GB (384 MB), and at maximum 3% of 75 GB, which is 2.25 GB, as the memory grant. It is worth noting that the size may be adjusted based on the *required memory* that is needed to start the query.

The situation becomes even more complicated when you are using Resource Governor, which allows you to separate workspace memory across multiple resource pools using the `MIN_MEMORY_PERCENT` and `MAX_MEMORY_PERCENT` resource pool settings. Moreover, you can further limit memory grants of individual requests in a resource pool's workload group by setting the `REQUEST_MAX_MEMORY_GRANT_PERCENT` property.

As an example, assume you have a resource pool with `MAX_MEMORY_PERCENT` set to 60% and a workload group with `REQUEST_MAX_MEMORY_GRANT_PERCENT` set to 10%. In this configuration, the memory grant sizes for the query from Listing 7-13 will be as follows:

- Minimum size: 75 GB workspace memory * 60% resource pool limit * 10% workload group limit * 0.5% query limit = 0.0225 GB (23.04 MB)
- Maximum size: 75 GB workspace memory * 60% resource pool limit * 10% workload group limit * 3% query limit = 0.135 GB (138.24 MB)

While Resource Governor and query hints allow you some control over memory grant size, this solution is extremely fragile. Any changes that impact memory configuration on SQL Server would lead to the different, and often unexpected, memory grant calculations. Use it with extreme care and only as a last resort when query optimization and memory grant feedback did not help. (You can read more about Resource Governor in the Microsoft documentation (*https://oreil.ly/ypXV9*).)

In-Memory OLTP Memory Usage and Troubleshooting

Our discussion about SQL Server memory management and troubleshooting would not be complete without covering In-Memory OLTP. This technology relies on memory-optimized tables. The data in those tables may be persisted on-disk for durability purposes; however, SQL Server loads entire tables into memory on database startup.

This behavior is very different when compared to regular disk-based tables. With these tables, SQL Server always loads the data to the buffer pool; however, it does not need to load and cache the entire table. Only the active portion of the data from the table needs to be in memory.

More importantly, in case of memory pressure, SQL Server can shrink the size of the buffer pool and cache less data. This may impact system performance by increasing the amount of physical I/O; nevertheless, the system will be operational if it happens.

With In-Memory OLTP, on the other hand, SQL Server loads all memory-optimized data into memory on database startup. The database will not come online if the server does not have enough memory to store the data. Moreover, if at any point SQL Server does not have enough memory to support data growth, the memory-optimized tables become read-only.

As the amount of memory consumed by In-Memory OLTP grows, it may start to impact other SQL Server components, which would then have less memory to utilize. In the Standard Edition of SQL Server, In-Memory OLTP can utilize, at most, 32 GB per database. In theory, the Enterprise Editions of SQL Server 2016 and later do not have any limits. However, in practice, In-Memory OLTP memory is limited to about 80% of the Resource Governor resource pool memory the database is bound to (or to the `DEFAULT` resource pool if it is not bound).

You can use this behavior to limit the amount of memory available to In-Memory OLTP. Listing 7-14 shows how to do this. The `sys.sp_xtp_bind_db_resource_pool` (*https://oreil.ly/27ecr*) and `sys.sp_xtp_unbind_db_resource_pool` (*https://oreil.ly/8Uo3i*) stored procedures bind and unbind the database to and from the resource pool. You may need to restart the database for the change to take effect.

Obviously, be careful and remember that In-Memory OLTP data will become read-only if you reach the limits.

Listing 7-14. Limiting the amount of memory for In-Memory OLTP

```
CREATE RESOURCE POOL InMemoryDataPool
WITH (MIN_MEMORY_PERCENT=40,MAX_MEMORY_PERCENT=40);

ALTER RESOURCE GOVERNOR RECONFIGURE;

EXEC sys.sp_xtp_bind_db_resource_pool
    @database_name = 'InMemoryOLTPDemo'
    ,@pool_name = 'InMemoryDataPool';

-- You need to take DB offline and bring it back online
-- for the changes to take effect
ALTER DATABASE MyDB SET OFFLINE;
ALTER DATABASE MyDB SET ONLINE;
```

You can monitor how much memory is consumed by In-Memory OLTP through MEMORYCLERK_XTP clerk memory consumption. In cases of high memory usage, you can analyze per-object memory consumption with the sys.dm_db_xtp_table_mem ory_stats view (*https://oreil.ly/Q77Ij*). Listing 7-15 shows you the code to do this. You can also use the *Memory Usage by Memory Optimized Objects* report in SSMS, which provides similar output.

Listing 7-15. Analyzing the memory consumption of memory-optimized tables

```
SELECT
    ms.object_id
    ,s.name + '.' + t.name AS [table]
    ,ms.memory_allocated_for_table_kb
    ,ms.memory_used_by_table_kb
    ,ms.memory_allocated_for_indexes_kb
    ,ms.memory_used_by_indexes_kb
FROM
    sys.dm_db_xtp_table_memory_stats ms WITH (NOLOCK)
        LEFT OUTER JOIN sys.tables t WITH (NOLOCK) ON
            ms.object_id = t.object_id
        LEFT OUTER JOIN sys.schemas s WITH (NOLOCK) ON
            t.schema_id = s.schema_id
ORDER BY
    ms.memory_allocated_for_table_kb DESC;
```

Analyze the amount of data stored in large memory-optimized tables. In most cases, you should not retain a lot of historical data in memory—it is better to partition it between memory-optimized and disk-based tables.

Pay attention to the schema of the tables and the (N)VARCHAR(MAX) and VARBINARY(MAX) columns. In-Memory OLTP works very differently than disk-based tables. Large object (LOB) columns introduce significant storage and performance overhead even when they are empty.

Most importantly, you need to make sure the system does not have long-running or runaway transactions. In-Memory OLTP uses row versioning. Data modifications generate the new versions of data rows that consume memory. The garbage collection process will eventually deallocate old versions and deleted data rows, but it will not process the data generated after the start time of the oldest active transaction. The memory usage will continue to grow, and it eventually may shut the system down.

Listing 7-16 shows the code that detects the 10 oldest In-Memory OLTP transactions. You can use it for troubleshooting and to build monitoring and alerting around it.

Listing 7-16. Detecting the 10 oldest In-Memory OLTP transactions

```
SELECT TOP 10
    t.session_id
    ,t.transaction_id
    ,t.begin_tsn
    ,t.end_tsn
    ,t.state_desc
    ,t.result_desc
    ,SUBSTRING(
        qt.text
        ,er.statement_start_offset / 2 + 1
        ,(CASE er.statement_end_offset
            WHEN -1 THEN datalength(qt.text)
            ELSE er.statement_end_offset
          END - er.statement_start_offset
        ) / 2 +1
    ) AS SQL
FROM
    sys.dm_db_xtp_transactions t WITH (NOLOCK)
        LEFT OUTER JOIN sys.dm_exec_requests er WITH (NOLOCK) ON
            t.session_id = er.session_id
        CROSS APPLY sys.dm_exec_sql_text(er.sql_handle) qt
WHERE
    t.state IN (0,3) /* ACTIVE/VALIDATING */
ORDER BY
    t.begin_tsn
OPTION (RECOMPILE, MAXDOP 1);
```

In-Memory OLTP is a great technology that can significantly improve the throughput of OLTP systems. It is not, however, a set-it-and-forget-it type of technology. It requires proper system and database design and adequate monitoring in production.

Consider reading my book *Expert SQL Server In-Memory OLTP, 2nd Edition* (Apress, 2017) if you want to learn more.

Summary

SQL Server is a memory-intensive application that may consume hundreds of gigabytes or terabytes of memory. This is completely normal and it can help improve SQL Server performance. Nevertheless, it is important to properly configure server memory, especially in nondedicated environments.

Set and tune the *Maximum Server Memory* setting, leaving enough memory for the OS and other applications. Consider granting the *Lock Pages In Memory* privilege to SQL Server accounts; however, remember that it may lead to system stability issues if the system is not properly configured.

You may also consider enabling *Large Page Allocations* on servers with a large amount of memory. This feature does not work well with columnstore indexes in SQL Server versions prior to 2019.

You can analyze the current memory usage by looking at the memory consumption of various memory clerks. Detect anomalies and address root causes of the issues.

Monitor the status of memory grants and the presence of RESOURCE_SEMAPHORE waits. Optimize queries with high memory grants when possible. Enable the memory grant feedback feature if it is available in your version of SQL Server.

In the next chapter, I will talk about the SQL Server concurrency model and explain how to troubleshoot blocking issues and deadlocks.

Troubleshooting Checklist

- ☐ Check and adjust the memory configuration.
- ☐ Analyze memory usage with the sys.dm_os_memory_clerks view. Address possible issues.
- ☐ Analyze plan cache memory usage.
- ☐ Analyze memory usage from single-use ad-hoc execution plans.
- ☐ Check for RESOURCE_SEMAPHORE waits. Detect and optimize the most memory-intensive queries.

CHAPTER 8

Locking, Blocking, and Concurrency

SQL Server uses locks to support transaction consistency and data isolation requirements. Locks prevent multiple active transactions from updating the same data; they reduce, or even eliminate, data consistency phenomena such as dirty, nonrepeatable, and phantom reads (more on these later).

SQL Server's concurrency model may look confusing on the surface, but it's quite logical and easy to understand after you grasp the basics. This chapter provides an overview of how the model works internally and gives guidelines on how to troubleshoot blocking and deadlocks.

I will start with an overview of SQL Server's major lock types and how they behave at different transaction isolation levels. I will explain why blocking and deadlocks occur and how to deal with them. Next, I will cover other common aspects of locking, such as lock escalation and optimistic concurrency. Finally, I will discuss locking-related wait types and typical troubleshooting strategies.

Before I begin, though, a word of caution: this chapter focuses on locking behavior in classic disk-based B-Tree tables. It does *not* touch on updatable columnstore indexes, where locking behaves slightly differently due to their more complex internal structure. Nor does it cover In-Memory OLTP, where the concurrency model behaves entirely differently. Very little of this chapter's content can be applied to memory-optimized tables.

Indeed, understanding and troubleshooting SQL Server locking behavior is a large and complex topic that can fill a book in itself—and it has. If you want to dive deeper, consider reading my book *Expert SQL Server Transaction and Locking* (Apress, 2018). For a high-level overview, read on.

Lock Types and Locking Behavior

Like many other general-purpose databases, SQL Server is designed to work in multiuser environments. It handles simultaneous workloads and keeps data consistent when multiple users query and modify it.

The field of database systems has an important concept called transactions. A *transaction* is a *single unit of work* that reads and modifies data, enforcing its consistency and durability. The four identifying characteristics of transactions are *atomicity*, *consistency*, *isolation*, and *durability*, often referenced together as *ACID*. Let's look at each of these terms:

Atomicity

Atomicity guarantees that each transaction executes as a single unit of work, using an all-or-nothing approach: all changes done within a transaction are either committed or rolled back in full.

Consider the classic example of transferring money between bank accounts. This action consists of two separate operations: decreasing the balance of one account and increasing the balance of another. Transaction atomicity guarantees that both operations either succeed or fail together so that the system will never end up in a situation where the total balance becomes inconsistent.

Consistency

Consistency ensures that every database transaction brings the database from one consistent state to another without violating any of the database's defined constraints.

Isolation

Isolation ensures that changes made in a transaction are isolated and invisible to other transactions until the transaction has been committed. In theory, transaction isolation should guarantee that concurrently executing multiple transactions should bring the system to the same state it would reach if those transactions had been executed serially. However, in most database systems, this requirement is often relaxed and controlled instead by transaction isolation levels.

Durability

Durability guarantees that after a transaction is committed, all changes done by that transaction are permanent and will survive a system crash. SQL Server achieves durability by using Write-Ahead Logging (WAL) to harden log records in the transaction log. A transaction is not considered to be committed until all the log records it has generated are hardened in the log file. I will talk more about this in Chapter 11.

SQL Server uses locking to support the isolation requirements of transactions. Locks are acquired and held on *resources*, such as data rows, pages, partitions, tables (objects), and databases. Internally, locks are in-memory structures managed by the SQL Server component called the *Lock Manager*.

Major Lock Types

The key attribute in the lock structure is a *lock type*. Internally, SQL Server uses more than 20 different lock types. Fortunately, in most cases you'll need to deal with just a subset of them. Let's look at the six most common ones you may encounter.

Exclusive (X) locks

Exclusive (X) locks are acquired by *writers*: INSERT, UPDATE, DELETE, and MERGE queries that modify data. As you can guess by the name, *exclusive* means *exclusive*: only one session can hold an (X) lock on a resource at any given time.

This behavior enforces the most important concurrency rule: *multiple sessions cannot modify the same data simultaneously*. No other sessions can acquire (X) locks on the row until the first transaction is complete and releases its (X) lock on the modified row.

You need to remember two very important things about exclusive locks. First, transaction isolation levels do not affect the behavior of (X) locks. They are acquired at all isolation levels, even in READ UNCOMMITTED.

Second, (X) locks are always held until the end of the transaction. The longer the transaction, the longer the (X) locks are held, increasing the chances of blocking. As a general rule, to reduce blocking make transactions as short as possible and update data closer to the end of the transaction, minimizing the time to hold (X) locks.

Shared (S) locks

Shared (S) locks are acquired by readers: SELECT queries. Again, as the name suggests, multiple sessions can acquire and hold an (S) lock on the same resource simultaneously.

When shared locks are acquired and how long they exist depends on transaction isolation levels. I will talk about this shortly.

Intent Shared (IS), Intent Update (IU), and Intent Exclusive (IX) locks

SQL Server uses row-level locking and usually acquires locks on the data rows. This reduces the chance that multiple sessions will have to compete for locks on the same resources, improving concurrency. However, keeping the locks only at the row level would degrade performance.

Think about a situation where the session needs exclusive access to the table: for example, when altering it. If only row-level locking existed, the session would have to scan the entire table for row-level locks from other sessions. This would be extremely inefficient, especially on large tables.

SQL Server addresses this problem by using intent locks, which are held at the data page and table levels and indicate the existence of locks on the child objects. When a session needs to obtain object- or page-level locks, it checks their compatibility with the other locks (intent or full) held on the table or page, instead of scanning the table or page and checking row-level locks there.

 You'll see the terms *full lock* and *regular lock* in documentation and online resources. These terms are used to differentiate between intent locks and other lock types, but this separation is not *technically* correct. Internally, intent locks are no different from other lock types.

Figure 8-1 shows an example of four sessions that acquired and held two exclusive and two shared locks on the data. You can see two (X) and two (S) locks on data rows, two pairs of intent exclusive (IX) and intent shared (IS) locks on the data pages, and four intent locks at the table level.

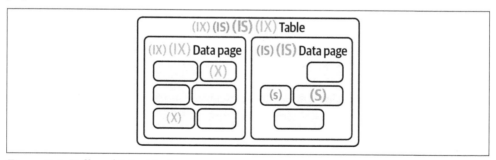

Figure 8-1. Full and intent locks

There is another important thing to remember: *row-level locking in SQL Server is neither documented nor guaranteed.* In some cases, SQL Server may choose to use a lower locking granularity.

For example, when you run the SELECT COUNT(*) FROM T statement, SQL Server needs to scan the entire table. It might use page-level or even table-level shared (S) locks instead of row-level locks. This would guarantee the required data consistency, preventing other sessions from acquiring incompatible intent locks on the pages or table and reducing the overhead of row-level locking.

Nevertheless, the lock compatibility rules always apply. This allows you to trouble-shoot locking issues.

Update (U) locks

SQL Server uses another lock type, update (U) locks, during data modifications. It acquires them during *update scans* for rows that need to be updated or deleted. Once the update (U) lock is acquired, SQL Server reads the row and checks the row data against query predicates to evaluate whether to modify (or delete) it. If so, SQL Server converts the update lock to an exclusive lock and performs the modification. Otherwise, it releases the update lock.

Figure 8-2 shows output from an xEvents session that has captured the lock_acquired and lock_released events from the UPDATE statement that modified two rows in the table. SQL Server acquired an intent exclusive (IX) lock on the table first. It next acquired intent update (IU) and update (U) locks on the data pages and rows, and finally converted them to (IX) and (X) locks.

name	mode	resource_description	resource_type
lock_acquired	IX		OBJECT
lock_acquired	IU	3:352896	PAGE
lock_acquired	U	(8194443284a0)	KEY
lock_acquired	IX	3:352896	PAGE
lock_acquired	X	(8194443284a0)	KEY
lock_acquired	IU	3:356269	PAGE
lock_acquired	U	(0855854e442a)	KEY
lock_acquired	IX	3:356269	PAGE
lock_acquired	X	(0855854e442a)	KEY
lock_released	X	(0855854e442a)	KEY
lock_released	IX	3:356269	PAGE
lock_released	X	(8194443284a0)	KEY
lock_released	IX	3:352896	PAGE
lock_released	IX		OBJECT

Figure 8-2. Update locks during data modifications

The behavior of update locks depends on the execution plan. In some cases, SQL Server acquires update locks on all rows first, then converts them to exclusive locks. In other cases (e.g., when you update only one row based on the clustered index key value), SQL Server may acquire an exclusive lock without an update lock at all.

The number of locks to acquire also greatly depends on the execution plan. SQL Server cannot evaluate whether a row needs to be modified until it acquires an update lock and reads the row. A nonoptimized DELETE statement that scans the table may delete just a single row; however, it can acquire millions of (U) locks during its update scan, searching for the rows that need to be deleted. As you will see many times in this chapter, nonoptimized queries greatly contribute to concurrency issues.

Similar to exclusive locks, update locks are acquired at all transaction isolation levels, even READ UNCOMMITTED. The only exception is SNAPSHOT isolation, where writers rely on row versioning during update scans. I will talk about this later in the chapter.

Lock Compatibility

Now it is time to look at lock compatibility in more detail. Table 8-1 shows a compatibility matrix for the major lock types. The entries in boldface signify the most important rules.

Table 8-1. Lock compatibility matrix

	(IS)	(IU)	(IX)	(S)	(U)	(X)
(IS)	Yes	Yes	Yes	Yes	Yes	No
(IU)	Yes	Yes	Yes	Yes	No	No
(IX)	Yes	Yes	Yes	No	No	No
(S)	Yes	Yes	No	**Yes**	**Yes**	**No**
(U)	Yes	No	No	**Yes**	**No**	**No**
(X)	No	No	No	**No**	**No**	**No**

There are four key compatibility rules:

Intent locks are compatible with each other
> They indicate the existence of locks on child objects. Multiple sessions can hold intent object- and page-level locks on the same resources simultaneously.

Exclusive locks are incompatible with each other and any other lock types
> Multiple sessions cannot update the same data simultaneously. Moreover, readers that acquire shared locks cannot read uncommitted rows that hold exclusive locks.

Update locks are incompatible with each other and with exclusive locks
> Writers cannot simultaneously evaluate whether a row needs to be updated, nor can they access any row that holds an exclusive lock.

Update locks are compatible with shared locks
> Writers can evaluate whether a row needs to be updated without blocking or being blocked by readers. In fact, the compatibility of (S) and (U) locks is

the main reason SQL Server uses update locks internally: they reduce blocking between readers and writers.

Lock compatibility rules are always enforced, regardless of the type of resource on which the locks are acquired. Remember this during troubleshooting. For example, it is common at the page level for a reader trying to get an (S) lock to be blocked by another session with an (IX) lock on the page.

Transaction Isolation Levels and Locking Behavior

Every statement in SQL Server executes within a transaction. There are three types of transactions in SQL Server: explicit, implicit, and auto-committed.

Explicit transactions

Explicit transactions include multiple statements within *explicitly* specified BEGIN TRAN and COMMIT blocks. Explicit transactions are managed through code, and it is a good idea to use them. They help keep data consistent and have less overhead than auto-committed transactions.

Implicit transactions

When implicit transactions are enabled, SQL Server automatically starts a transaction when you execute DML and DDL statements (INSERT, UPDATE, DELETE, MERGE, SELECT, CREATE, and a few others). The transaction stays active until you finish it with a COMMIT or ROLLBACK statement, similar to what you do with explicit transactions.

Implicit transactions are rarely used in SQL Server, and they need to be enabled with SET IMPLICIT_TRANSACTIONS ON or SET ANSI_DEFAULTS ON statements.

Auto-committed transactions

When you run a statement outside of an explicit or implicit transaction, SQL Server treats the statement as if it had been executed in its own transaction. It will behave as if you had run a BEGIN TRAN command right before and a COMMIT command right after the statement. It is worth noting that code in triggers executes in the context of the same auto-committed transaction as the main statement. The same applies to stored procedure code in an INSERT INTO .. EXEC statement.

Multistatement auto-committed transactions are less efficient during data modifications, as they introduce transaction log overhead. They will also lead to extra log-related I/O operations (see Chapter 11). It is better to use explicit transactions when possible, unless you have specific business reasons not to.

When you run SELECT statements outside of explicit or implicit transactions, SQL Server will internally use lightweight auto-committed transactions, which do not generate any transaction log activity.

Every transaction runs at a specific transaction isolation level, which controls data consistency rules within the transaction. SQL Server supports six transaction isolation levels, which can be split into two categories based on how they enforce data consistency. *Pessimistic* isolation levels—READ UNCOMMITTED, READ COMMITTED, REPEAT ABLE READ, and SERIALIZABLE—rely on blocking. *Optimistic* isolation levels—READ COMMITTED SNAPSHOT (RCSI) and SNAPSHOT—use row versioning.

At all transaction isolation levels, writers will block writers. Multiple sessions cannot update the same data. Also, with the exception of the SNAPSHOT level, update scans from multiple sessions will block each other. I will cover the behavior of SNAPSHOT and optimistic isolation levels later in this chapter.

Blocking between readers and writers depends on the isolation level that controls the *behavior and lifetime of shared* (S) *locks—and only shared locks—within the transaction*. In terms of concurrency, the isolation level does not determine the behavior of any other lock types (except in SNAPSHOT isolation, which also changes the behavior of update locks).

The SET TRANSACTION ISOLATION LEVEL statement allows you to set the isolation level for the transaction (most SQL Server client libraries use READ COMMITTED by default). You can override this at the table level in each individual statement with locking hints. Table 8-2 shows the shared lock behavior each transaction isolation level introduces.

Table 8-2. Transaction isolation levels and shared (S) lock behavior

Transaction isolation level	Table hint	Shared lock behavior
READ UNCOMMITTED	(NOLOCK) or (READUNCOMMITTED)	(S) locks are not acquired.
READ COMMITTED (default)	(READCOMMITTEDLOCK)	(S) locks are acquired and released immediately.
REPEATABLE READ	(REPEATABLEREAD)	(S) locks are acquired and held until the end of the transaction.
SERIALIZABLE	(SERIALIZABLE) or (HOLDLOCK)	Range shared locks are acquired and held until the end of the transaction.
READ COMMITTED SNAPSHOT	N/A	(S) locks are not acquired. Row versioning is used instead.
SNAPSHOT	N/A in disk-based tables. The (SNAPSHOT) hint is supported in memory-optimized tables, which are beyond the scope of this chapter.	(S) locks are not acquired. Row versioning is used instead.

At the READ UNCOMMITTED isolation level, shared locks are not acquired. Readers can read rows that have been modified by other sessions and hold exclusive locks. This isolation level reduces blocking by eliminating conflicts between readers and writers—but at the cost of data consistency. Readers will read the current (modified) version of the row regardless of what happens next—even if changes are rolled back or a row is modified multiple times. That's why this isolation level is often called a *dirty read*.

 The famous NOLOCK hint forces SQL Server to read the data from the table in READ UNCOMMITTED mode. This does not change the writers' behavior—for example, the hint in the UPDATE WITH (NOLOCK) statement would be ignored.

At the READ COMMITTED isolation level, SQL Server acquires shared locks before reading the row and releases them immediately after the row is read or, in some cases, after the SELECT statement finishes. This guarantees that transactions cannot read uncommitted data from other sessions.

At the REPEATABLE READ isolation level, SQL Server acquires shared locks and holds them until the end of the transaction. This guarantees that other sessions cannot modify the data after it has been read.

At the SERIALIZABLE isolation level, SQL Server uses another lock type, *range locks*, holding them until the end of the transaction. Range locks (both shared and exclusive) protect index key ranges rather than individual rows.

Let's say you have an Orders table that has two rows with OrderId values of 1 and 10. At the REPEATABLE READ isolation level, a SELECT statement would acquire two row-level shared locks. Other sessions would not be able to modify those rows, but they could still insert a new row in between those values, leading to *phantom reads*, which occur when the same statement running multiple times in the same transaction returns newly inserted rows in the result.

At the SERIALIZABLE isolation level, a SELECT statement acquires a range shared (RangeS-S) lock, preventing other sessions from inserting any data in between the OrderId values of 1 and 10. This eliminates phantom reads.

The optimistic isolation levels—READ COMMITTED SNAPSHOT and SNAPSHOT—do not acquire shared locks. When readers encounter a row holding an exclusive lock, they read an older (previously committed) version of that row from the version store in tempdb. Writers and uncommitted data modifications do not block readers.

In terms of blocking and concurrency, READ COMMITTED SNAPSHOT has the same behavior as READ UNCOMMITTED. Both isolation levels remove reader/writer blocking. READ COMMITTED SNAPSHOT, however, provides better data consistency by eliminating access to uncommitted data and dirty reads. In the vast majority of cases, you should not use READ UNCOMMITTED; switch to READ COMMITTED SNAPSHOT instead. Just remember that it will lead to additional `tempdb` load, which you need to monitor. I'll discuss this in the next chapter.

There are several hints that allow you to override locking behavior. You cannot force SQL Server to avoid exclusive and, in most cases, update locks during data modification. However, you can have readers and `SELECT` queries use update and exclusive locks instead of shared ones by using the `UPDLOCK` and `XLOCK` table hints. This may be beneficial when you need to prevent multiple sessions from reading the same data.

Another hint, `READPAST`, forces queries to skip rows that hold incompatible locks, instead of being blocked. The skipped rows are excluded from `SELECT` query results and will not be updated or deleted if you use this hint with `UPDATE` and `DELETE` statements.

Finally, a `SET LOCK_TIMEOUT` statement allows you to control how long sessions are blocked while waiting for locks to be granted. If locks cannot be acquired during the period you set, SQL Server will terminate the statement and raise an exception.

Now that you are familiar with locking behavior, let's discuss how to troubleshoot blocking.

Blocking Issues

Blocking occurs when multiple sessions compete for the same resource. This may be correct and expected behavior: for example, multiple sessions cannot update the same row simultaneously. However, in many cases, blocking is unexpected and occurs because queries are trying to acquire unnecessary locks.

Troubleshooting blocking issues usually consists of three steps:

- Detecting the queries involved in the blocking
- Understanding the root cause of the blocking
- Addressing the root cause

Let's look at an example. As the first step, let's create a table and populate it with some data (Listing 8-1). Note that the `OrderId` and `OrderNum` columns contain the same value, which is unique in each row.

Listing 8-1. Creating the table with test data

```sql
CREATE TABLE dbo.Orders
(
    OrderId INT NOT NULL,
    OrderNum VARCHAR(32) NOT NULL,
    OrderDate SMALLDATETIME NOT NULL,
    CustomerId INT NOT NULL,
    Amount MONEY NOT NULL,
    OrderStatus INT NOT NULL,
    Placeholder CHAR(400) NULL
);

;WITH N1(C) AS (SELECT 0 UNION ALL SELECT 0) -- 2 rows
,N2(C) AS (SELECT 0 FROM N1 AS T1 CROSS JOIN N1 AS T2) -- 4 rows
,N3(C) AS (SELECT 0 FROM N2 AS T1 CROSS JOIN N2 AS T2) -- 16 rows
,N4(C) AS (SELECT 0 FROM N3 AS T1 CROSS JOIN N3 AS T3) -- 256 rows
,N5(C) AS (SELECT 0 FROM N4 AS T1 CROSS JOIN N4) -- 65,536 rows
,IDs(ID) AS (SELECT ROW_NUMBER() OVER (ORDER BY (SELECT NULL)) FROM N5)
INSERT INTO dbo.Orders(OrderId,OrderNum,OrderDate,CustomerId,Amount,OrderStatus)
    SELECT
        ID,CONVERT(VARCHAR(32),ID),DATEADD(DAY,-ID % 365,GETDATE())
        ,ID % 512,ID % 100,0
    FROM
        IDs;

CREATE UNIQUE CLUSTERED INDEX IDX_Orders_OrderId
ON dbo.Orders(OrderId);
```

Now let's run the first two steps of the code shown in Table 8-3 from two different sessions. Do not run a ROLLBACK statement yet; we want to keep the blocking condition active.

Table 8-3. Generating blocking conditions

Session 1 (SPID = 52)	Session 2 (SPID = 53)	Comments

BEGIN TRAN
    DELETE FROM dbo.Orders
    WHERE   OrderId = 50
		Session 1 acquires an exclusive lock on the row with OrderId=50.

	SELECT OrderId, Amount FROM dbo.Orders WITH (READCOMMITTEDLOCK) WHERE OrderNum = '100'	Session 2 is blocked while trying to acquire a shared lock on the row with OrderId=50.
ROLLBACK		Session 1 releases the exclusive lock. Session 2 resumes the execution.

SQL Server provides several views that help troubleshoot blocking in real time. Let's look at them.

Troubleshooting Real-Time Blocking

The key tool in troubleshooting real-time blocking conditions is the `sys.dm_tran_locks` view (*https://oreil.ly/dXvU1*). It provides a list of active lock requests along with their type and status (`GRANT` or `WAIT`), information about the resources on which locks are being requested, and several other useful attributes.

Figure 8-3 shows partial output from the `sys.dm_tran_locks`, `sys.dm_os_waiting_tasks`, and `sys.dm_exec_requests` views at the time the blocking occurred. Session 53 is blocked, waiting for a shared (`S`) lock on the row that has an exclusive (`X`) lock held by Session 52. The `LCK_M_S` wait type indicates a shared-lock wait. I'll talk more about lock-related wait types later in this chapter.

	resource_type	request_session_id	request_mode	request_type	request_status	resource_description	resource_associated_entity_id
1	DATABASE	52	S	LOCK	GRANT		0
2	DATABASE	53	S	LOCK	GRANT		0
3	KEY	52	X	LOCK	GRANT	(f84b73ce9e8d)	72057594068729856
4	KEY	53	S	LOCK	WAIT	(f84b73ce9e8d)	72057594068729856
5	OBJECT	52	IX	LOCK	GRANT		690101499
6	OBJECT	53	IS	LOCK	GRANT		690101499
7	PAGE	52	IX	LOCK	GRANT	3:153018	72057594068729856
8	PAGE	53	IS	LOCK	GRANT	3:153018	72057594068729856

	waiting_task_address	session_id	wait_duration_ms	wait_type	blocking_session_id	resource_description
1	0x0000020A24C7D848	53	44251	LCK_M_S	52	keylock hobtid=7205759406...

	session_id	start_time	status	command	blocking_session_id	wait_type	wait_time	last_wait_type
1	53	2021-10-02 09:02:59.653	suspended	SELECT	52	LCK_M_S	292806	LCK_M_S

Figure 8-3. Output from DMVs at the time of blocking

Unfortunately, the `sys.dm_tran_locks` view alone won't give you enough information for troubleshooting. You need to combine it with the other views to get a detailed picture. You can run the code from Listing 8-2 in another session to do this.

To resolve object names correctly, you need to run the code in the context of the database involved in the blocking. Also, a statement may be blocked if you run it during DDL operations, due to the `OBJECT_NAME()` function used in the script. The locks acquired by that function are incompatible with schema modification locks from DDL statements. I'll discuss schema locks later in this chapter.

Listing 8-2. Getting additional details about a blocking condition

```
SELECT
    TL1.resource_type AS [Resource Type]
    ,DB_NAME(TL1.resource_database_id) AS [DB]
    ,CASE TL1.resource_type
        WHEN 'OBJECT' THEN
            OBJECT_NAME(TL1.resource_associated_entity_id
                ,TL1.resource_database_id)
```

```
        WHEN 'DATABASE' THEN
            'DATABASE'
        ELSE
            CASE
                WHEN TL1.resource_database_id = db_id()
                THEN
                (
                    SELECT OBJECT_NAME(object_id,TL1.resource_database_id)
                    FROM sys.partitions WITH (NOLOCK)
                    WHERE hobt_id = TL1.resource_associated_entity_id
                )
                ELSE
                    '(Run under DB context)'
            END
    END AS [Object]
    ,TL1.resource_description AS [Resource]
    ,TL1.request_session_id AS [Session]
    ,TL1.request_mode AS [Mode]
    ,TL1.request_status AS [Status]
    ,WT.wait_duration_ms AS [Wait (ms)]
    ,QueryInfo.SQL
    ,QueryInfo.query_plan
FROM
    sys.dm_tran_locks TL1 WITH (NOLOCK)
        LEFT OUTER JOIN sys.dm_os_waiting_tasks WT WITH (NOLOCK) ON
            TL1.lock_owner_address = WT.resource_address AND
            TL1.request_status = 'WAIT'
    OUTER APPLY
    (
        SELECT
            SUBSTRING(S.text, (er.statement_start_offset/2)+1,
            ((
                CASE er.statement_end_offset
                    WHEN -1 THEN DATALENGTH(S.text)
                    ELSE er.statement_end_offset
                END - er.statement_start_offset)/2)+1
            ) AS SQL
            ,TRY_CAST(qp.query_plan AS XML) AS query_plan
        FROM
            sys.dm_exec_requests er WITH (NOLOCK)
                CROSS APPLY sys.dm_exec_sql_text(er.sql_handle) S
                OUTER APPLY sys.dm_exec_text_query_plan
                (
                    er.plan_handle
                    ,er.statement_start_offset
                    ,er.statement_end_offset
                ) qp
        WHERE
            TL1.request_session_id = er.session_id
    ) QueryInfo
WHERE
    TL1.request_session_id <> @@spid
```

```
ORDER BY
    TL1.request_session_id
OPTION (RECOMPILE, MAXDOP 1);
```

Figure 8-4 shows the output of this query. It is much easier to interpret and it provides information about currently running batches and their execution plans. Keep in mind that for the sessions in which lock requests are granted, SQL and Query Plan contain the currently executing batch (NULL if the session is sleeping), rather than the batch that acquired the original lock.

	Resource Type	DB	Object	Resource	Session	Mode	Status	Wait (ms)	SQL	query_plan
1	DATABASE	SQLServerInternals	DATABASE		52	S	GRANT	NULL	NULL	NULL
2	OBJECT	SQLServerInternals	Orders		52	IX	GRANT	NULL	NULL	NULL
3	KEY	SQLServerInternals	Orders	(f84b73ce9e8d)	52	X	GRANT	NULL	NULL	NULL
4	PAGE	SQLServerInternals	Orders	3:153018	52	IX	GRANT	NULL	NULL	NULL
5	KEY	SQLServerInternals	Orders	(f84b73ce9e8d)	53	S	WAIT	15881	SELECT [OrderId],[Am	<ShowPlanXML
6	PAGE	SQLServerInternals	Orders	3:153018	53	IS	GRANT	NULL	SELECT [OrderId],[Am	<ShowPlanXML
7	DATABASE	SQLServerInternals	DATABASE		53	S	GRANT	NULL	SELECT [OrderId],[Am	<ShowPlanXML
8	OBJECT	SQLServerInternals	Orders		53	IS	GRANT	NULL	SELECT [OrderId],[Am	<ShowPlanXML

Figure 8-4. Detailed blocking information

The output of Listing 8-2 may be quite large in busy systems. This book's companion materials include an additional troubleshooting script that narrows the results to blocking and blocked sessions only.

Blocking occurs when two or more sessions are competing for the same resource. You need to answer two questions during troubleshooting:

- Why does the blocking session hold the lock on the resource?
- Why is the blocked session acquiring the lock on the resource?

Both questions are equally important; however, you may encounter a couple of challenges when analyzing blocking session data. First, as I just mentioned, the query you see in blocking session data does not always represent the statement that caused the blocking.

Consider a situation where the session runs several data modification statements in a single transaction. As you remember, SQL Server acquires and holds exclusive locks on updated rows until the end of the transaction. Each of those locks can cause blocking. Unfortunately, SQL Server does not track information about statements that acquire locks, and you cannot see it through DMVs.

The second challenge is related to *blocking chains*, which happen when the blocking session is also blocked by another session. This usually happens in busy OLTP systems and is often related to object-level locks acquired during schema alteration, index maintenance, and a few other processes.

The key thing to remember about lock compatibility is this: *in order to be granted, the lock request should be compatible with all other lock requests on the resource, regardless of whether or not those requests were granted.* When a request is incompatible, you get blocking chains.

Think about the following situation: *Session 1* is holding an intent lock on the table. This intent lock blocks *Session 2*, which is trying to obtain a full table lock; for example, during index rebuilding. The blocked lock request from *Session 2*, in turn, will block all other sessions that try to obtain incompatible intent locks on the table level. Without *Session 2*, other sessions would have been able to acquire intent locks and execute them in parallel with *Session 1*.

When this condition occurs, the output from dynamic management views will show massive blocking, with *Session 2* shown as blocking_session_id for a large number of the sessions. However, the root blocker in this chain is *Session 1*, which may appear as blocking_session_id only for one session: *Session 2*. I will come back to this condition in more detail in "Schema Locks" on page 249.

So, don't jump to immediate conclusions based on the number of blocked sessions alone! Revive the entire blocking chain and find the root blocker. (You can find a script in the book's companion materials.)

Analyzing blocking sessions is essential when you need to address blocking in real time. To find the root cause of reoccurring blocking, however, it may be easier to start troubleshooting by looking at the blocked session where you have the blocked statement and its execution plan available. In many cases, you can identify the root cause of the blocking by analyzing its execution plan.

Figure 8-5 shows the plan of the blocked statement (SPID = 53 in the code in Table 8-3).

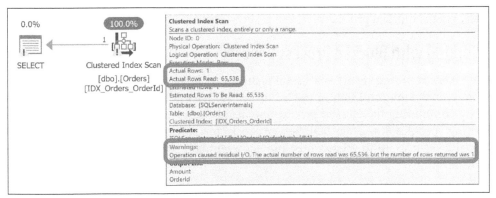

Figure 8-5. Execution plan of the blocked statement

As you can see, the blocked query is scanning the entire table looking for orders with the predicate on the OrderNum column. The query uses a READ COMMITTED transaction isolation level, and it acquires a shared lock on every row in the table as it reads them. Due to the incompatibility of the (S) and (X) locks, at some point the query is blocked by the first DELETE statement that holds an exclusive lock on one of the rows.

It is worth noting that the query was blocked even though the row with the exclusive lock held did not have OrderNum ='100'. A SELECT query cannot evaluate the predicate until it acquires a shared lock and reads the row.

 SQL Server needs to acquire a lock to evaluate whether a row needs to be read or modified. When you troubleshoot blocking, analyze what locks the query *acquires* rather than what rows it returns or modifies. It is entirely possible for queries that return a few or even zero rows to acquire millions of locks during execution.

You can resolve this problem by optimizing the query and adding the index on the OrderNum column, which will replace the clustered index scan in the execution plan with a nonclustered index seek. This will significantly reduce the number of locks the statement acquires and will eliminate lock collision and blocking between SELECT and DELETE queries, as long as they do not delete and select the same rows.

This is, perhaps, an oversimplified example; however, it demonstrates the most common cause of blocking, which is nonoptimized queries needing to scan large amounts of data and thus acquiring unnecessary locks during the scans. Optimizing queries reduces the amount of data to scan and the number of locks to acquire; therefore, it also reduces the risk of blocking conditions. In fact, query optimization will always reduce blocking and deadlocks.

Dynamic management views are very useful for troubleshooting blocking in real time. Unfortunately, they don't help much if you can't look at them at the time the blocking occurred. Fortunately, SQL Server helps capture that information automatically via the blocked process report.

Working with Blocked Process Reports

The *blocked process report* is a useful feature that allows you to capture information about a blocking condition to use in further analysis. It is disabled by default; enable it by configuring the *blocked process threshold* setting, as shown in Listing 8-3. This setting specifies how often SQL Server checks for blocking and generates a report. I usually set it to 10 to 15 seconds initially, eventually reducing it to 5 seconds after optimizations.

Listing 8-3. Setting the blocked process report threshold to 10 seconds

```
EXEC sp_configure 'show advanced options', 1;
GO
RECONFIGURE;
GO
EXEC sp_configure 'blocked process threshold', 10; -- in seconds
GO
RECONFIGURE;
GO
```

After the threshold is set, you can capture the blocked process report with a blocked_process_report xEvent or a Blocked process event SQL Trace event. Obviously, I recommend using xEvents over SQL Traces, since they introduce less overhead.

The blocked process report contains information in XML format about blocking and blocked processes. Listing 8-4 shows part of the event, with the most important elements highlighted.

Listing 8-4. A blocked process report in XML

```
<blocked-process-report monitorLoop="…">
<blocked-process>
    <process id="process3e576c928" taskpriority="0" logused="0" waitresource="KEY:
…" waittime="14102" ownerId="…" transactionname="SELECT" lasttranstarted="…"
XDES="…" lockMode="S" schedulerid="1" kpid="…" status="suspended" spid="53"
sbid="0" ecid="0" priority="0" trancount="0" lastbatchstarted="…"
lastbatchcompleted="…" lastattention="…" clientapp="…" hostname="…" hostpid="…"
loginname="…" isolationlevel="read committed (2)" xactid="…" currentdb="14"
lockTimeout="…" clientoption1="…" clientoption2="…">
        <executionStack>
            <frame line="3" stmtstart="46" sqlhandle="…"/>
            <frame line="3" stmtstart="100" sqlhandle="…"/>
        </executionStack>
        <inputbuf>
SELECT OrderId, Amount
FROM dbo.Orders WITH (READCOMMITTEDLOCK)
WHERE OrderNum = '100'
        </inputbuf>
    </process>
</blocked-process>
<blocking-process>
    <process status="sleeping" spid="54" sbid="0" ecid="0" priority="0"
trancount="1" lastbatchstarted="…" lastbatchcompleted="…" lastattention="…"
clientapp="…" hostname="…" hostpid="…" loginname="…" isolationlevel="read
uncommitted (1)" xactid="…" currentdb="14" lockTimeout="…" clientoption1="…"
clientoption2="…">
        <executionStack/>
        <inputbuf>
```

```
BEGIN TRAN
    DELETE FROM dbo.Orders
    WHERE OrderId = 50
        </inputbuf>
    </process>
</blocking-process>
</blocked-process-report>
```

As with real-time troubleshooting, you should analyze both blocking and blocked processes to find the root cause of the problem. For a *blocked* process, the most important information is as follows:

waittime
> The length of time the query is waiting, in milliseconds

lockMode
> The type of lock being waited for

isolationlevel
> The transaction isolation level

executionStack *and* inputBuf
> The query and the execution stack; you will see how to obtain the actual SQL statement involved in blocking and its execution plan in Listing 8-5

For a *blocking* process, look at the following:

status
> This indicates whether a process is *running*, *sleeping*, or *suspended*. If a process is sleeping, there is an uncommitted transaction. If a process is suspended, either the process waits for a non-lock-related resource (e.g., a page from the disk with a PAGEIOLATCH wait) or it is blocked by another session, in which case you have a blocking chain.

trancount
> Any value greater than 1 in idle (sleeping) sessions, or greater than 2 in sessions currently executing DML statements, indicates nested transactions. If this happens while the process's status is sleeping, there is a chance that the client did not commit the nested transactions correctly (e.g., the number of COMMIT statements is less than the number of BEGIN TRAN statements in the code).

executionStack *and* inputBuf
> You may need to analyze what happens in the blocking process. Some common issues include runaway transactions (e.g., missing COMMIT statements in the nested transactions); long-running transactions, perhaps with some UI involved; and excessive scans (e.g., a missing index on the referencing column in the detail table leads to scans during a referential integrity check).

Information about queries from the blocking session could be useful here. Remember that in the case of a blocking process, `executionStack` and `inputBuf` will correspond to the queries that were running when the blocked process report was generated, not when the blocking occurred.

As you already know, blocking commonly occurs because of inefficient scans in nonoptimized queries that acquire unnecessarily large numbers of locks. Check the queries' execution plans to detect and optimize them.

You can obtain the execution plan from the `sys.dm_exec_query_stats` view, based on the `sql_handle`, `stmtStart`, and `stmtEnd` elements from the execution stack section of the blocked process report. The code is shown in Listing 8-5. Keep in mind that the plan will not include actual execution metrics, such as the number of executions and the number of rows read.

Listing 8-5. Getting the execution plan and query with `sql_handle`

```
DECLARE
    @H VARBINARY(MAX) = 0x00
        /* Insert sql_handle from the top line of the execution stack */
    ,@S INT = 0
        /* Insert stmtStart from the top line of the execution stack */
    ,@E INT = 0
        /* Insert stmtEnd from the top line of the execution stack */

SELECT
    SUBSTRING(
        qt.text
        ,(qs.statement_start_offset / 2) + 1
        ,((CASE qs.statement_end_offset
            WHEN -1 THEN DATALENGTH(qt.text)
            ELSE qs.statement_end_offset
        END - qs.statement_start_offset) / 2) + 1
    ) AS SQL
    ,TRY_CAST(qp.query_plan AS XML) AS query_plan
    ,qs.creation_time
    ,qs.last_execution_time
FROM
    sys.dm_exec_query_stats qs WITH (NOLOCK)
        OUTER APPLY sys.dm_exec_sql_text(qs.sql_handle) qt
        OUTER APPLY sys.dm_exec_text_query_plan(qs.plan_handle,@S,@E) qp
WHERE
    qs.sql_handle = @H
OPTION (RECOMPILE, MAXDOP 1);
```

Unfortunately, there is a problem with this approach. As you know, the `sys.dm_exec_query_stats` view relies on the plan cache. The plan may not be available if the query uses statement-level recompile, or if the plan was evicted from the cache for any reason. The longer you wait to troubleshoot, the less chance that the plan will be available.

You can address this, to a degree, by enabling and analyzing Query Store data. Alternatively, you can automate data collection using another SQL Server technology called Event Notifications.

Event Notifications and Blocking Monitoring Framework

SQL Server allows you to obtain blocked process reports through *Event Notifications*. This technology is based on the Service Broker, and it allows you to capture information about specific SQL Server and DDL events and post the message into the Service Broker queue. You can define the activation procedure on the queue and react to events (e.g., parse a blocked process report) in near-real time. This will dramatically increase the chance of capturing the execution plans while they are still available in the cache.

I have implemented an Event Notification–based solution to capture blocking information and deadlocks, parsing and persisting the data in a utility database for further analysis. (To save space I am not showing the code here, but you can download it from my blog (*https://oreil.ly/5FQog*) and from this book's companion materials.) I call this package *Blocking Monitoring Framework*. Figure 8-6 provides a sneak peek at what collected data on blocking conditions in a utility database would look like.

	ID	EventDate		DatabaseID	Resource		WaitTime	BlockedProcessReport	BlockedSPID	BlockedXactId
1	1	2021-10-02 10:06:10.620		5	KEY: 5:7205759406872985{		1535922	<blocked-process-repo	53	241832

BlockedLockMode	BlockedIsolationLevel	BlockedSQLHandle	BlockedStmtStart	BlockedStmtEnd	BlockedQueryHash	BlockedPlanHash
S	read committed (2)	0x030005003441162	42	238	0x87D26521AC2E47,	0x73D3FD64B96F8

BlockedSql			BlockedInputBuf	BlockedQueryPlan		BlockingSPID
SELECT OrderId, Amount FROM dbo.Orders WITH (READCOMM			SELECT OrderId, Amount	<ShowPlanXML xmlns="http://schema		52

BlockingStatus	BlockingTranCount	BlockingInputBuf			BlockingSql	BlockingQueryPlan
sleeping	1	BEGIN TRAN DELETE FROM dbo.Orders		WHERE Ord	NULL	NULL

Figure 8-6. Blocking information collected by the Blocking Monitoring Framework

So far, this package has greatly simplified blocking troubleshooting for me. I have it installed on all my production servers, and I encourage you to download and try it in your environment.

Deadlocks

A *deadlock* is a special blocking case when multiple sessions or, sometimes, multiple execution threads within a single session block each other. When this happens, SQL Server terminates one of the transactions, allowing the others to continue.

Usually, the session that is chosen as the *deadlock victim* is the one that generated the fewest transaction log records before the deadlock occurred. You can control it, to a point, with the SET DEADLOCK_PRIORITY statement.

In a classic, by-the-book deadlock scenario, two or more sessions compete for the same set of resources. They may access them in the opposite order, blocking each other and creating deadlock conditions.

Classic deadlocks often occur in busy OLTP systems with volatile data. They may also be triggered by single-row UPDATE operations due to the way SQL Server handles locking with clustered and nonclustered indexes (I will talk about this shortly). However, more often than not, deadlocks are caused by excessive scans and nonoptimized queries.

Let's look at an example and run the code from Table 8-4. As before, you need to run it in two different sessions, one step at a time.

Table 8-4. Generating a deadlock

Session 1	Session 2

BEGIN TRAN
    UPDATE dbo.Orders
    SET OrderStatus = 1
    WHERE OrderId = 10;
	BEGIN TRAN
	    UPDATE dbo.Orders
	    SET OrderStatus = 1
	    WHERE OrderId = 250;

SELECT COUNT(*) AS [Cnt]
    FROM dbo.Orders WITH (READCOMMITTEDLOCK)
    WHERE CustomerId = 42;
COMMIT
	SELECT COUNT(*) AS [Cnt]
	    FROM dbo.Orders WITH (READCOMMITTEDLOCK)
	    WHERE CustomerId = 18;
	COMMIT

As you may notice, these sessions work with different data. But think about query execution plans and the way sessions access data and acquire locks.

In the first step, two UPDATE statements use a clustered index seek operation, updating two separate data rows and acquiring exclusive locks on them. Those exclusive locks will be held until the end of the transactions.

There is no index on the CustomerId column, so SELECT statements will have to perform clustered index scans, acquiring shared locks on each row in the table. Eventually, the scans in both sessions will be blocked by (S)/(X) lock incompatibility, which will lead to a deadlock. It does not matter that the updated rows holding (X) locks belong to different customers and will not be included in the COUNT(*) calculation—SQL Server cannot evaluate the predicate on a CustomerId column until it acquires an (S) lock and reads the row.

As you might guess, creating nonclustered indexes on the `CustomerId` column would solve this problem; SQL Server would not need to scan the table, and sessions would not issue incompatible locks on the same rows.

Let's look at troubleshooting deadlocks.

Troubleshooting Deadlocks

In a nutshell, troubleshooting deadlocks is very similar to troubleshooting blocking problems. You analyze the processes and queries involved in the deadlock, identify the root cause of the problem, and, finally, fix it.

The counterpart to the blocked process report here is called a *deadlock graph*, which provides information about the deadlock in XML format. There are several ways to obtain a deadlock graph:

`xml_deadlock_report` xEvent
> You can create an xEvent session to capture an `xml_deadlock_report` event. However, this event is also included in the `system_health` xEvent session, which SQL Server enables by default. This allows you to get deadlock graph information for past deadlocks without setting up any monitoring.
>
> In Azure SQL Database, an `xml_deadlock_report` is replaced with a `data base_xml_deadlock_report` event. The data provided by this event is virtually the same.

Deadlock graph SQL Trace event
> SQL Profiler displays a graphical representation of the deadlock. You can extract XML deadlock graph data by choosing the `Extract Event Data` action from the event context menu (right mouse click).

Trace flag T1222
> This trace flag saves deadlock information to the SQL Server error log. It is a perfectly safe method to use in production; however, it is redundant now due to the presence of the `system_health` session. Moreover, it pollutes the error log, making it harder to analyze.

A deadlock graph consists of two different sections, `<process-list>` and `<resource-list>`, that contain information about the processes and resources involved in the deadlock. Listing 8-6 shows the structure of a deadlock graph.

Listing 8-6. Deadlock graph structure

```
<deadlock-list>
      <deadlock victim="…">
            <process-list>
                  <process id="…">
                        …
                  </process>
                  <process id="…">
                        …
                  </process>
            </process-list>
            <resource-list>
                  <information about resource involved in the deadlock>
                        …
                  </information about resource involved in the deadlock>
                  <information about resource involved in the deadlock>
                        …
                  </information about resource involved in the deadlock>
            </resource-list>
      </deadlock>
</deadlock-list>
```

Each <process> node in the deadlock graph provides details for a specific process involved in the deadlock. Listing 8-7 shows one of the process nodes for the deadlock generated by the code from Table 8-4. I removed the values from some of the attributes to make the code easier to read and highlighted the attributes that are especially helpful during troubleshooting.

Listing 8-7. The deadlock graph <process> element

```
<process id="process3e4b29868" taskpriority="0" logused="264" waitresource="KEY: …"
waittime="…" ownerId="…" transactionname="… " lasttranstarted="…" XDES="…"
lockMode="S" schedulerid="…" kpid="…" status="suspended" spid="55" sbid="…"
ecid="…" priority="0" trancount="1" lastbatchstarted="…" lastbatchcompleted="…"
lastattention="…" clientapp="…" hostname="…" hostpid="…" loginname="…"
isolationlevel="read committed (2)" xactid="…" currentdb="…" lockTimeout="…"
clientoption1="…" clientoption2="…">
    <executionStack>
        <frame procname="adhoc" line="1" stmtstart="26" sqlhandle="…">
            SELECT COUNT(*) [Cnt] FROM [dbo].[Orders] with (REACOMMITTED) WHERE
[CustomerId]=@1
        </frame>
    </executionStack>
    <inputbuf>
            SELECT COUNT(*) AS [Cnt]
            FROM dbo.Orders WITH (REACOMMITTEDLOCK)
            WHERE CustomerId = 42;
        COMMIT
```

```
        </inputbuf>
    </process>
```

The id attribute uniquely identifies the process, while waitresource and lockMode provide information about the lock type and the resource for which the process is waiting. In this example, the process is waiting for a shared lock on one of the rows (keys). The isolationlevel attribute shows the current transaction isolation level. Finally, executionStack and inputBuf allow you to find the SQL statement that was executed when the deadlock occurred.

As opposed to the blocked process report, executionStack in the deadlock graph usually provides information about the queries and modules involved in the deadlock. However, in some cases, you may need to use the sys.dm_exec_sql_text function, which you can do with the code from Listing 8-5.

The <resource-list> section of the deadlock graph contains information about the resources involved in the deadlock. An example is shown in Listing 8-8.

Listing 8-8. The deadlock graph <resource-list> section

```
<resource-list>
    <keylock hobtid="72057594039500800" dbid="14"
objectname="SqlServerInternals.dbo.Orders" indexname="PK_Orders" id="lock3e98b5d00"
mode="X" associatedObjectId="72057594039500800">
        <owner-list>
            <owner id="process3e6a890c8" mode="X"/>
        </owner-list>
        <waiter-list>
            <waiter id="process3e4b29868" mode="S" requestType="wait"/>
        </waiter-list>
    </keylock>
    <keylock hobtid="72057594039500800" dbid="14"
objectname="SqlServerInternals.dbo.Orders" indexname="PK_Orders" id="lock3e98ba500"
mode="X" associatedObjectId="72057594039500800">
        <owner-list>
            <owner id="process3e4b29868" mode="X"/>
        </owner-list>
        <waiter-list>
            <waiter id="process3e6a890c8" mode="S" requestType="wait"/>
        </waiter-list>
    </keylock>
</resource-list>
```

The name of the XML element identifies the type of resource. Keylock, pagelock, and objectlock stand for the row-level, page, and object locks, respectively. You can also see to what objects and indexes those locks belong. Finally, the owner-list and waiter-list nodes describe the processes that own and are waiting for the locks, along with the type of locks acquired and requested. You can correlate this information with the data from the `process-list` section of the graph.

The next steps in troubleshooting are very similar to the steps in blocked process troubleshooting. You need to pinpoint the queries involved in the deadlock and find the cause.

There is one important factor to consider, however. In most cases, a deadlock involves more than one statement per session running in the same transaction. The deadlock graph provides you with the information about the *last* statement only—the one that triggered the deadlock.

You can see *signs* of the other statements in the `resource-list` node. This node shows you that processes held exclusive locks on the rows, but it does not tell you about the statements that acquired them. Identifying those statements will be useful in your root cause analysis, so you'll often need to analyze the code to do that.

You can quickly pinpoint the root cause of the deadlock from the code in Table 8-4 by looking at the execution plan of the `SELECT` statements shown at the top of Figure 8-7. It shows a clustered index scan that led to an excessive number of locks being acquired (I obtained that number by rerunning the statement after the deadlock occurred). Creating a nonclustered index on the `CustomerId` column would solve the problem, as shown at the bottom of the figure.

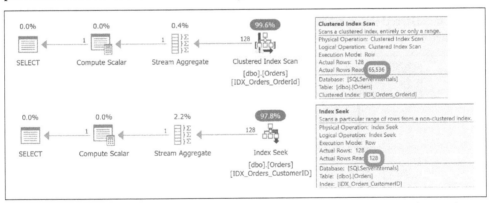

Figure 8-7. Execution plans of a SELECT statement with and without a nonclustered index

This troubleshooting approach has the same challenge as the blocked process report: you might not be able to obtain the query's execution plan in time. Fortunately, you can address this with the Blocking Monitoring Framework, which captures and parses deadlock information in real time.

Locking and Indexes

There is another thing you need to remember during deadlock troubleshooting. On a physical level, clustered and nonclustered indexes are separate objects.

Consider the table defined in Listing 8-9.

Listing 8-9. Table definition

```
CREATE TABLE T1
(
    CI_Key INT NOT NULL,
    Col1 INT NOT NULL,
    NCI_Included_Col INT NOT NULL
);
CREATE UNIQUE CLUSTERED INDEX CI ON T1(CI_Key);
CREATE NONCLUSTERED INDEX NCI ON T1(NCI_Included_Col);
```

When you update this table, SQL Server acquires an (X) lock on the row in the clustered index row first. Next, it acquires (X) locks on the nonclustered index rows, but only in the indexes that have updated columns present as either key or included columns. The process is very fast, but it is not instantaneous.

When the session reads the data through *Nonclustered Index Seek* and *Key Lookup* operations, it acquires shared locks in the opposite order: first on nonclustered and then on clustered index rows. This may lead to the classic deadlock condition shown in Figure 8-8.

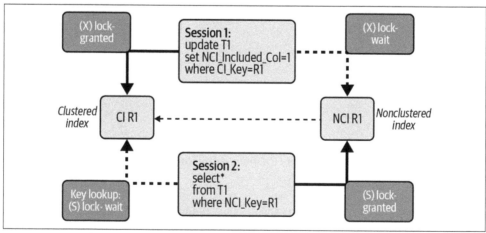

Figure 8-8. Key lookup deadlock

A similar problem may occur when you update the same row multiple times in one transaction, changing columns that belong to different nonclustered indexes. SQL Server will not obtain (X) locks in nonclustered indexes until you update the columns present there. This may trigger deadlock conditions similar to those you just saw. To address this, you can eliminate a *Key Lookup* operation with covered indexes or by switching to optimistic isolation levels. Let's discuss optimistic isolation levels next.

Optimistic Isolation Levels

Optimistic transaction isolation levels were introduced in SQL Server 2005 as a new way to deal with blocking problems, address concurrency phenomena, and simplify SQL Server migrations from Oracle. With optimistic isolation levels, queries read "old" committed versions of rows while accessing data being modified by other sessions, rather than being blocked by the incompatibility between (S) and (X) locks.

There are two optimistic transaction isolation levels: READ COMMITTED SNAPSHOT (RCSI) and SNAPSHOT. To be precise, SNAPSHOT is a separate transaction isolation level; RCSI is a database option that changes readers' behavior in the READ COMMITTED isolation level.

Both RCSI and SNAPSHOT need to be enabled. You can enable or disable RCSI with the ALTER DATABASE SET READ_COMMITTED_SNAPSHOT ON/OFF command. It is enabled by default in Azure SQL Databases and disabled in regular SQL Server instances. Switching this setting requires exclusive access to the database, so you'll have to disconnect all users to turn it on or off. You'll also need to remove the database from Always On Availability Groups when you change the setting.

Similarly, you can enable SNAPSHOT isolation with the ALTER DATABASE SET ALLOW_SNAPSHOT_ISOLATION ON command. This statement does not require an exclusive database lock and can be executed while other users are connected to the database.

When either of these optimistic transaction isolation levels is enabled, SQL Server starts to copy the "old" versions of the rows to a special part of tempdb called the *version store*. It references them by adding 14-byte *version pointers* to the modified rows. This happens with every UPDATE and DELETE query, regardless of the transaction isolation level in which it runs. In some cases, more than one version record can be stored in the version store for the row, as shown in Figure 8-9.

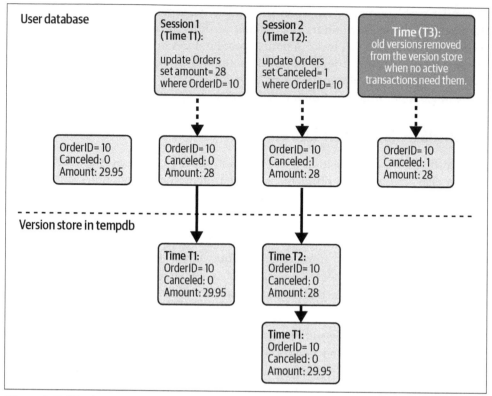

Figure 8-9. Version store

In this scenario, when readers (and sometimes writers) access a row that holds an exclusive lock, they read the old version from the version store rather than being blocked (Figure 8-10).

Optimistic isolation levels reduce blocking, although they do bring overhead. First, they increase `tempdb` load. In highly volatile systems, they can lead to heavy activity and significantly increase `tempdb`'s size. The next chapter will cover how to monitor version store size and usage.

There is also overhead during data modification and retrieval. SQL Server needs to copy the data to `tempdb` as well as maintaining a linked list of the version records. Similarly, it needs to traverse that list when reading data.

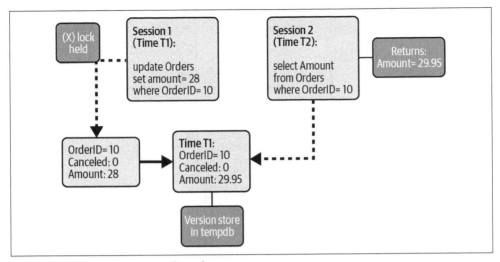

Figure 8-10. Version store and readers

Finally, optimistic isolation levels contribute to index fragmentation. When a row is modified, SQL Server increases the row size by 14 bytes due to the version pointer. If a page is tightly packed and a new version of the row does not fit, there will be a page split and further fragmentation. The book's companion materials include a curious example that demonstrates how a DELETE statement can increase a table's size on disk.

Let's discuss both transaction isolation levels.

READ COMMITTED SNAPSHOT Isolation Level

READ COMMITTED SNAPSHOT isolation (RSCI) is, as you have seen, the database option that changes the behavior of readers in READ COMMITTED mode. When it is enabled, SELECT queries do not acquire (S) locks, and they read the "old" version records rather than being blocked by (S)/(X) lock incompatibility.

Nothing changes for the writers. Data modification queries still acquire (U) and (X) locks as they do in pessimistic isolation levels, and they may block each other.

Figure 8-11 illustrates this. *Session 1* updates the row holding an (X) lock for the duration of the transaction. During this time, the SELECT statement from *Session 2* reads the old version of the row from tempdb. The UPDATE statements from *Sessions 3* and *4*, on the other hand, are blocked by the (U)/(X) and (X)/(X) locks' incompatibility with the (X) lock held by *Session 1*.

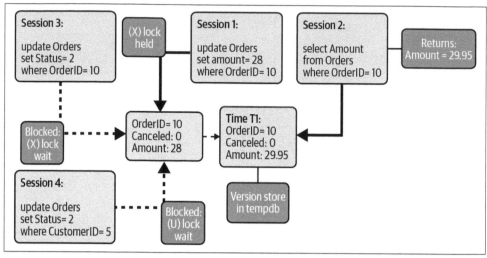

Figure 8-11. RCSI behavior

From a blocking standpoint, RCSI provides the same experience as READ UNCOMMIT TED, since both isolation levels eliminate blocking between readers and writers. There is a major difference between them, though: READ UNCOMMITTED removes blocking at the cost of data inconsistency. Many consistency anomalies are possible, including reading uncommitted data, duplicated reads, and missed rows. On the other hand, RCSI provides you with full *statement-level consistency*. Statements running at this isolation level do not access uncommitted data, nor do they see changes committed after the statement started.

As you may have already concluded, you should avoid using the (NOLOCK) hint in queries when RCSI is enabled. While using (NOLOCK) and READ UNCOMMITTED would be bad practice by itself, doing so is completely useless in RCSI mode, which causes similar nonblocking behavior without losing data consistency. It is always better to switch to RCSI when possible.

SNAPSHOT Isolation Level

SNAPSHOT is a separate transaction isolation level from RCSI. You need to set it in the code explicitly with a SET TRANSACTION ISOLATION LEVEL SNAPSHOT statement.

The SNAPSHOT isolation level gives you *transaction-level consistency*. The sessions work with a *snapshot of the data* as of the moment the SNAPSHOT transaction started. They do not see any data changes committed after that.

As with RCSI, there is no blocking between readers and writers; readers do not acquire shared locks. Moreover, blocking between writers is significantly reduced because they do not acquire update locks: they use version records from the version store during update scans instead.

Writers in SNAPSHOT isolation still acquire (X) locks when they modify data. They may be blocked by (X)/(X) incompatibility when another transaction holds an (X) lock on the row. There is another possibility, however: when a SNAPSHOT transaction tries to update a row that has been modified *after* a transaction has started, this triggers an update conflict error and terminates the transaction. You can detect this condition by capturing Error 3960 in the TRY .. CATCH block, then implement retry logic if needed.

 Switching to SNAPSHOT isolation changes the behavior of the system. Applications need to be aware about the changes and handle them properly.

Overall, optimistic isolation levels are valuable techniques for reducing blocking. Moreover, enabling RCSI can be a great emergency measure that buys you time when you see significant blocking between readers and writers at the READ COMMITTED isolation level.

Keep in mind, however, that these measures may hide the root cause of your blocking problems. Reducing blocking by performing query optimization is more time-consuming, but better in the long term.

Also, remember the overhead that optimistic isolation levels introduce. Fortunately, in most cases, this is a small price to pay to reduce concurrency issues.

Schema Locks

SQL Server needs to protect the database metadata, so it does not allow changing the table structure in the middle of query execution. This problem is more complicated than it seems. Exclusive table-level locks do not solve it, because readers at the READ UNCOMMITTED, READ COMMITTED SNAPSHOT, and SNAPSHOT isolation levels do not acquire (IS) table-level locks.

To solve this, SQL Server uses two additional lock types: *schema modification* (Sch-M) and *schema stability* (Sch-S) locks:

Schema modification locks
Think of this lock type as a super-lock. Schema modification (Sch-M) locks are acquired before any metadata changes or before execution of a TRUNCATE TABLE statement. This lock type is incompatible with all other lock types, and it completely blocks access to the object.

Like exclusive locks, schema modification locks are held until the end of the transaction. Running DDL statements within explicit transactions allows you to roll back all schema changes in case of an error, but it also prevents any access to the affected objects until the transaction is committed. Remember this, since many database schema comparison tools use explicit transactions in schema synchronization scripts.

Schema stability locks

Schema stability (Sch-S) locks are used during DML query compilation and execution if readers don't use shared locks. The only purpose they serve is to protect the table from being altered or dropped while the query accesses it. Schema stability locks are compatible with all other lock types except (Sch-M).

For all practical purposes, you can deal with schema locks as you would any other lock types and troubleshoot issues based on lock compatibility rules. However, because schema locks are acquired at the object level, blocking may have a significantly greater impact.

A key aspect of locking behavior, as noted earlier, is that a lock request, in order to be granted, must be compatible with all other lock requests on the resource, regardless of whether they have already been granted or are currently waiting in the queue. This is especially important with schema locks.

Say you want to alter a table outside of the downtime maintenance window. The ALTER TABLE statement will need to acquire a schema modification lock, which will be blocked if any other sessions hold locks on the table. This (Sch-M) lock request, in turn, will block all other sessions that are trying to access the table and acquire intent or schema stability locks there. This may lead to serious blocking issues, as illustrated in Figure 8-12.

The same may happen during index and partition maintenance. Both online index rebuilding and partition switching need to obtain schema modification locks to update table metadata. Those locks are short-lived; however, they block all other sessions while waiting to be acquired.

Fortunately, both operations support *low-priority locks*—a feature that utilizes another locking queue for schema locks. Lock requests stay there for a specified time without blocking other sessions from acquiring table-level locks. When the waiting duration expires, you can either terminate the operations or kill all sessions that hold incompatible table locks.

Low-priority locks are very useful in reducing blocking during index and partition maintenance. Utilize them when possible. You can also read about them in the Microsoft documentation (*https://oreil.ly/9p3pj*).

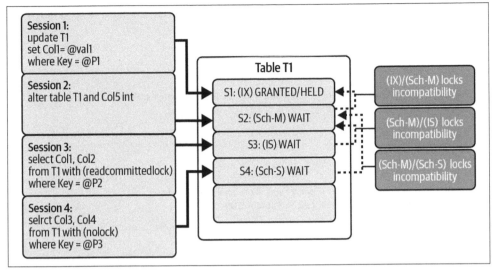

Figure 8-12. Schema locks and the locking queue

Lock Escalation

Row-level locking is great from a concurrency standpoint. Unfortunately, it is expensive. Each lock structure uses 128 bytes of memory in a 64-bit OS; keeping information about millions of row- and page-level locks would use gigabytes of RAM.

SQL Server reduces memory consumption and lock management overhead by using a technique called *lock escalation*. Once a statement acquires *at least* 5,000 row- and page-level locks on the same object (index or heap), SQL Server tries to replace those locks with a single table-level lock or, if enabled, a partition-level lock. This operation will succeed if no other sessions hold incompatible locks on the table or partition.

When the operation succeeds, SQL Server releases all row- and page-level locks held by the transaction on the object (or partition), keeping the object- (or partition-) level lock only. If the operation fails, SQL Server continues to use row-level locking and repeats its escalation attempt roughly every time 1,250 new locks are acquired.

SQL Server can also escalate locks when the total number of locks in the instance exceeds the memory or configuration thresholds. These threshold numbers (5,000 and 1,250 locks) are approximations; the numbers are usually slightly higher in real life. These thresholds are also quite small for modern workloads and may lead to unexpected blocking conditions.

Try running the code in Listing 8-10. The first ALTER TABLE statement will disable lock escalation on the Orders table, which I'll talk about later. Do not commit the transaction when you execute it so that shared locks remain held at a REPEATABLE READ isolation level.

Listing 8-10. Lock escalation demo (Session 1)

```
-- Release Lock Manager memory - do not run on production server!
-- DBCC FREESYSTEMCACHE('ALL');
GO

-- Disabling Lock Escalation
ALTER TABLE dbo.Orders SET (LOCK_ESCALATION = DISABLE);

-- Enabling Lock Escalation - uncomment for the second demo
-- ALTER TABLE dbo.Orders SET (LOCK_ESCALATION = TABLE);
GO

DECLARE
    @C int;

SET TRANSACTION ISOLATION LEVEL REPEATABLE READ
BEGIN TRAN
    SELECT @C = COUNT(*)
    FROM dbo.Orders WITH (ROWLOCK);

    SELECT
    (
        SELECT COUNT(*)
        FROM sys.dm_tran_locks WITH (NOLOCK)
        WHERE request_session_id = @@SPID
    ) AS [Lock Count]
    ,(
        SELECT SUM(pages_kb)
        FROM sys.dm_os_memory_clerks WITH (NOLOCK)
        WHERE [type] = 'OBJECTSTORE_LOCK_MANAGER'
    ) AS [Memory, KB]

-- Run Listing 8-11 Code and commit transaction afterwards
-- COMMIT
```

Figure 8-13 shows the number of locks and amount of memory the lock manager consumes.

	Lock Count	Memory, KB
1	65652	13408

Figure 8-13. Number of locks and consumed memory without lock escalation

Now, while the transaction is still active, run the code from Listing 8-11. This code inserts another row into the table without any blocking.

Listing 8-11. Lock escalation demo (Session 2)

```
INSERT INTO dbo.Orders(OrderId,OrderNum,OrderDate,CustomerId,Amount,OrderStatus)
VALUES(100000,'100000',GETDATE(),1,100,0);
```

Next, commit the transaction in the first session (Listing 8-10) and enable lock escalation on the table by changing the ALTER TABLE statement at the beginning of the script. Then repeat the test (you may also need to change the OrderId value in Listing 8-11). Now the shared locks from Session 1 will be escalated to the table level and the INSERT statement will be blocked due to (S)/(IX) lock incompatibility.

Figure 8-14 shows the number of locks and amount of memory consumed by the first session along with the status of all lock requests to the table (output from Listing 8-2).

	Lock Count	Memory, KB								
1	2	1648								
	Resource Type	DB		Object	·	Session	Mode	Status	Wait (ms)	SQL	query_plan
1	OBJECT	SQLServerInt(	Orders		51	S	GRANT	NULL	NULL	NULL
2	DATABASE	SQLServerInt(	DATABASE		51	S	GRANT	NULL	NULL	NULL
3	OBJECT	SQLServerInt(	Orders		70	IX	WAIT	72487	INSERT INTO [dbo].[Orders	<ShowPlanXML x
4	DATABASE	SQLServerInt(	DATABASE		70	S	GRANT	NULL	INSERT INTO [dbo].[Orders	<ShowPlanXML x

Figure 8-14. Locks and memory consumption with lock escalation

Lock escalation is enabled by default and can introduce blocking issues, which can be confusing for database engineers. For example, think about the purge process, which deletes large amounts of old data using a DELETE statement. If lock escalation in the purge session succeeds, the session acquires and holds a table-level (X) lock. This will block access to the table for all writers and for the readers in READ COMMITTED, REPEATABLE READ, and SERIALIZABLE levels. This happens even if those other sessions work with a completely different set of data than the set you were purging.

The same may occur with a process that inserts a large batch of rows with a single INSERT statement. Like the purge process, this can escalate an exclusive (X) lock to the table level and block the other sessions from accessing the table.

Those patterns have one thing in common: they acquire and hold large numbers of row- and page-level locks as part of a single statement. This triggers lock escalation, which succeeds if no other sessions hold incompatible locks at the table (or partition) level.

Lock escalation is triggered by the number of locks acquired by the *statement*, rather than per transaction. If the separate statements acquire fewer than 5,000 row- and page-level locks each, lock escalation is not triggered, regardless of the total number of the locks the transaction holds.

Let's look at how we can detect and address lock escalation issues.

Lock Escalation Troubleshooting

Lock escalation makes the (S) or (X) table-level lock visible in the sys.dm_tran_locks view output and the blocked process report. You can see such examples in Figure 8-14 and in Listing 8-12, which show the part of the blocked process report that includes the blocked process waiting for an intent lock on an OBJECT resource.

Listing 8-12. Blocked process report (partial)

```
<blocked-process-report>
 <blocked-process>
  <process id="…" taskpriority="0" logused="0" waitresource="OBJECT: …"
  waittime="…" ownerId="…" transactionname="user_transaction" lasttranstarted="…"
  XDES="…" lockMode="IX" schedulerid="…"  …>
```

If you have the Blocking Monitoring Framework installed, you can use parsed data to detect the tables that have the most blocking related to intent locks. (That code is included in the download package for the framework.)

Remember, however, that lock escalation is not the only reason for the sessions to acquire full object locks. Review individual blocking cases to confirm the root cause.

You can track lock escalation in real time with xEvents. Listing 8-13 shows the code that creates an xEvent session and collects the object_id of the tables where escalation has occurred. The last statement in the code parses the collected data and returns the number of lock escalations per table. As a note, you may need to change the database_id filter value in your system.

Listing 8-13. Capturing lock escalations with xEvents

```
CREATE EVENT SESSION LockEscalationTracking
ON SERVER
ADD EVENT
    sqlserver.lock_escalation
    (
        WHERE database_id = 5  -- DB_ID()
    )
ADD TARGET
    package0.histogram
    (
        SET
            SLOTS = 1024 -- Based on # of tables in the database
```

```
            ,FILTERING_EVENT_NAME = 'sqlserver.lock_escalation'
            ,SOURCE_TYPE = 0 -- event data column
            ,SOURCE = 'object_id' -- grouping column
    )
WITH
    (
        EVENT_RETENTION_MODE=ALLOW_SINGLE_EVENT_LOSS
        ,MAX_DISPATCH_LATENCY=10 SECONDS
    );

ALTER EVENT SESSION LockEscalationTracking
ON SERVER
STATE=START;
GO

-- Parsing the results
DECLARE
    @X XML;

SELECT @X = CONVERT(XML,st.target_data)
FROM
    sys.dm_xe_sessions s WITH (NOLOCK)
        JOIN sys.dm_xe_session_targets st WITH (NOLOCK) ON
            s.address = st.event_session_address
WHERE
    s.name = 'LockEscalationTracking' AND
    st.target_name = 'histogram';

;WITH EventInfo([count],object_id)
as
(
    SELECT
        t.e.value('@count','int')
        ,t.e.value('((./value)/text())[1]','int')
    FROM
        @X.nodes('/HistogramTarget/Slot') as t(e)
)
SELECT
    e.object_id
    ,s.name + '.' + t.name AS [table]
    ,e.[count]
FROM
    EventInfo e JOIN sys.tables t WITH (NOLOCK) ON
        e.object_id = t.object_id
    JOIN sys.schemas s WITH (NOLOCK) ON
        t.schema_id = s.schema_id
ORDER BY
    e.count desc
OPTION (RECOMPILE, MAXDOP 1);
```

You can also detect the tables that trigger the most lock escalation events by looking at the `index_lock_promotion_attempt_count` and `index_lock_promotion_count` columns in the `sys.dm_db_index_operational_stats` view (*https://oreil.ly/Iemz7*) (see Chapter 14).

You can control lock escalation behavior at the table level by using the `ALTER TABLE SET LOCK_ESCALATION` statement (you can see the current setting in the `lock_esca lation_desc` column in the `sys.tables` view). This option affects lock escalation behavior for all indexes defined on the table, both clustered and nonclustered. Three options are available:

DISABLE
> This option disables lock escalation for a specific table.

TABLE
> SQL Server escalates locks to the table level. This is the default option.

AUTO
> SQL Server escalates locks to the partition level when the table is partitioned or to the table level when the table is not partitioned.

There are two trace flags that allow you to disable lock escalation at the session or instance level: `T1211` and `T1224`. The `T1211` trace flag completely disables lock escalation. The `T1224` trace flag prevents lock escalation from triggering based on the number of locks acquired, allowing SQL Server to escalate locks in case of memory pressure.

These trace flags may be beneficial when you want to disable lock escalation in a particular session—for example, when the session imports or deletes a large amount of data. However, I rarely use them nowadays. In most cases, I disable lock escalations on impacted tables unless the server has very little memory or unless the code uses extremely large batch operations that cannot be properly optimized.

Finally, I would like to reiterate that lock escalation is completely normal. It helps reduce lock management overhead and memory usage, which improves system performance. Keep it enabled unless it starts to introduce noticeable blocking issues; disable it only in the tables where it becomes a problem.

You can estimate the impact of blocking in general, and lock escalation in particular, by analyzing locking-related waits in the wait statistics. Let's look at these now.

Locking-Related Waits

Every lock type has a corresponding wait type with a name starting with `LCK_M_` followed by the lock type abbreviation. For example, `LCK_M_U` and `LCK_M_IX` indicate waits for update (`U`) and intent exclusive (`IX`) locks, respectively.

These lock waits only occur during blocking, when sessions stay in a *suspended* state with lock requests waiting in the queue. SQL Server does not generate lock waits when requests are granted immediately and no blocking occurs.

As with other wait types, pay attention to both total wait time and the number of times waits occur. It is entirely possible for just a handful of long blocking events to generate waits with significant total wait time. You may decide to troubleshoot or ignore them based on your objectives.

Locking-related wait types provide a good at-a-glance picture of blocking problems and give you a direction to focus further analysis.

By now, you likely understand how different lock types are used and can guess what can be done to address concurrency problems. Nevertheless, let's summarize the approaches.

LCK_M_U Wait Type

The LCK_M_U wait type indicates a wait for update (U) locks, which SQL Server acquires during update scans. Large numbers of these waits usually indicate poorly optimized writer queries (UPDATE, DELETE, MERGE). In many cases, you'll see them alongside the PAGEIOLATCH* and CXPACKET wait types.

When I see significant LCK_M_U waits, I usually focus on query optimization (see Chapters 4 and 5). I may install the Blocking Monitoring Framework and use the collected data as another way to choose optimization targets. Again, query optimization *always* helps with reducing concurrency issues.

LCK_M_S Wait Type

The LCK_M_S wait type indicates waits for the shared (S) locks. This lock type is acquired by SELECT queries at the READ COMMITTED, REPEATABLE READ, and SERIALIZA BLE isolation levels.

In many cases, the root cause of LCK_M_S waits is similar to that of LCK_M_U waits: poorly optimized SELECT queries scan large amounts of data and are blocked by exclusive locks held by other sessions. Query optimization will help.

When queries are running at the READ COMMITTED isolation level, consider enabling the READ_COMMITTED_SNAPSHOT database option and eliminate reader/writer blocking. Remember that this approach does not address the root cause of the issue, instead masking the problems introduced by poorly optimized queries. Also remember the additional overhead that optimistic isolation levels introduce.

In some cases, LCK_M_S waits may be generated by waits for table-level locks, which SQL Server acquires during some operations. One such example is online index rebuilding, which requires a short (S) table-level lock at the beginning of its execution. This may also be caused by a (TABLOCK) hint in the queries.

Such cases may present themselves as waits with a relatively low number of occurrences and a high average wait time. Nevertheless, analyze individual blocking cases to pinpoint the root cause of the problem.

LCK_M_X Wait Type

The LCK_M_X wait type indicates waits for exclusive (X) locks. As strange as it sounds, in OLTP systems with volatile data, LCK_M_X waits may occur less frequently than LCK_M_U waits.

Unfortunately, it is hard to identify the most common pattern that leads to this type of blocking and to LCK_M_X waits. It sometimes happens when multiple sessions are working with the same data: for example, a busy *counters table* implementation can trigger it. Other common cases include excessive usage of the REPEATABLE READ and SERIALIZABLE isolation levels, inefficient transaction management and long-running transactions, and table-level locking hints such as (TABLOCKX).

When you see large numbers of LCK_M_X waits, analyze individual blocking cases to find the root cause. Again, the Blocking Monitoring Framework is extremely helpful in this situation.

LCK_M_SCH_S and LCK_M_SCH_M Wait Types

The LCK_M_SCH_S and LCK_M_SCH_M wait types indicate waits for schema stability (Sch-S) and schema modification (Sch-M) locks. Such waits should not occur on a large scale.

As noted, SQL Server acquires (Sch-M) locks during schema alterations. These locks require exclusive access to the table; the lock request will be blocked, generating a wait until all other sessions disconnect from the table.

There are several common cases when such blocking occurs. First, it can happen when database schema changes are done with other users connected to the system. In such cases, the schema modification lock is held until the end of the transaction and will generate schema stability and intent lock waits in other sessions. This can also rise during an offline index rebuild, the final phase of an online index rebuild, or a partition switch. You can reduce blocking by using low-priority locks, if they are supported.

Schema stability locks are used to avoid alterations when tables are in use. They are compatible with all other lock types except schema modification locks. LCK_M_SCH_S waits always indicate blocking introduced by schema modifications.

If you encounter many schema lock waits, identify their cause. In most cases, you can address them by changing deployment or database maintenance strategies, or by switching to low-priority locks.

Pay attention to the average wait time and number of wait occurrences. It is common to see schema lock–related wait types generated by one-off events, such as incorrectly planned deployments.

Intent LCK_M_I* Wait Types

SQL Server acquires intent locks (LCK_M_I*) at the object (table) and page levels. At the table level, blocking may occur in two conditions. The first is that the session cannot acquire an intent lock due to an incompatible schema modification lock. Usually, in such cases, you'll also see schema lock waits and will need to troubleshoot them. The second condition is when an incompatible full lock is held on the table. For example, neither intent lock can be acquired while the table has a full exclusive (X) lock held.

In some cases, this happens due to table-level locking hints in the code, such as (TAB LOCK) or (TABLOCKX). However, more often than not, it is triggered by successful lock escalation during large batch modifications. In fact, when I see a large percentage of intent waits, I immediately analyze and troubleshoot lock escalations, which are easy to detect and address, with an immediate positive impact on system performance.

Table-level locking is not the only condition where you may see intent lock waits. I've already described a situation when SQL Server decides to use full page-level locks instead of row-level locks to scan or update all rows on the page. This can trigger intent-lock blocking if another session tries to get an intent lock on the page. As usual, identify and address the cause.

Range Locks LCK_M_R* Wait Types

In addition to the SERIALIZABLE isolation level, SQL Server acquires range (LCK_M_R*) locks while maintaining nonclustered indexes that have the IGNORE_DUP_KEY=ON option set. These may lead to concurrency issues and deadlocks that are difficult to understand.

When you encounter range lock–related wait types in the system, validate individual blocking cases. Unfortunately, dealing with these waits may require you to change your transaction strategy or redesign the way data quality issues are handled.

You may encounter other lock-related wait types I have not covered in this section. Knowing the SQL Server Concurrency Model will help. Analyze the blocking conditions that may generate such lock types, and identify the cause.

Summary

SQL Server uses locks to protect the logical consistency of the data during query execution. Each lock is acquired on a resource (such as a data row, page, or object) and has a type, which defines the lock's compatibility and lifetime.

Exclusive (X) locks are acquired by writes on inserted, updated, or deleted rows. Only one session may hold an exclusive lock on a resource at any given time. Exclusive locks are acquired at all transaction isolation levels and are always held until the end of transactions. To reduce blocking, do not use long-running transactions, and modify data close to the end of the transaction.

Update (U) locks are acquired by writers during update scans at all transaction isolation levels except SNAPSHOT. Large amounts of update lock waits usually indicate the presence of nonoptimized queries.

Intent locks are acquired on the page and table levels and indicate the existence of the locks on child objects. SQL Server may escalate row-level locks to the table level during batch operations. In such cases, a full lock on the table may prevent other sessions from accessing it. Troubleshoot and disable lock escalation on affected tables when you see significant blocking related to intent locks.

Shared (S) locks are acquired by readers at the READ COMMITTED, REPEATABLE READ, and SERIALIZABLE isolation levels. The only concurrency-related aspect controlled by transaction isolation levels is the behavior of shared locks (except for the behavior of update locks in SNAPSHOT mode). Large amounts of shared lock waits are often triggered by poorly optimized queries.

When you troubleshoot concurrency issues, you need to understand why the sessions acquired locks that led to blocking and deadlocking. Nonoptimized queries that scan large amounts of data are one of the most common reasons. I'll say this once again, because it is important: optimizing queries always improves the situation.

In the next chapter, we'll look at the tempdb database, its performance, and potential issues.

Troubleshooting Checklist

☐ Collect information related to blocking and deadlocking.

☐ Review the locking wait types in the wait statistics.

☐ Analyze lock escalations if you see significant intent lock waits.

☐ Review your index and partition maintenance strategies and deployment practices if you see significant schema lock waits.

☐ Perform query optimization if you see significant update and shared lock waits.

☐ Consider enabling RCSI and utilizing optimistic isolation levels if you see shared lock waits in the READ COMMITTED isolation level.

☐ Review individual blocking and deadlock cases. Address the most common ones.

☐ In general, perform query optimization; it usually improves concurrency.

tempdb Usage and Performance

tempdb is a system database that is shared across all user and system sessions. It stores user-created and internal temporary objects and data, and is used by many processes. High tempdb performance and throughput are essential for good server performance.

I will start this chapter with an overview of tempdb consumers and usage patterns and share several best practices related to the use of temporary objects. Next, I will show how to diagnose and address common tempdb issues. Finally, I'll provide you with several tempdb configuration tips.

Temporary Objects: Usage and Best Practices

tempdb performance tuning is a complex topic. I usually like to start with an overview of usage patterns. After all, tempdb is just another database, and reducing its load usually improves its throughput. There are some internal optimizations in tempdb behavior, which I will discuss in this chapter. But for all practical purposes, you can consider tempdb to be similar to other user databases.

The tempdb database stores temporary objects created by users, internal record sets generated during query executions, the version store, and a few other objects. You can look at how much space different object types are using by running the code in Listing 9-1.

Listing 9-1. tempdb space usage

```
SELECT
    CONVERT(DECIMAL(12,3),
        SUM(user_object_reserved_page_count) / 128.
    ) AS [User Objects (MB)]
    ,CONVERT(DECIMAL(12,3),
```

```
        SUM(internal_object_reserved_page_count) / 128.
    ) AS [Internal Objects (MB)]
    ,CONVERT(DECIMAL(12,3),
        SUM(version_store_reserved_page_count) / 128.
    ) AS [Version Store (MB)]
    ,CONVERT(DECIMAL(12,3),
        SUM(unallocated_extent_page_count) / 128.
    ) AS [Free Space (MB)]
FROM
    tempdb.sys.dm_db_file_space_usage WITH (NOLOCK);
```

Let's start our discussion with the first group in that list, objects created by users.

Temporary Tables and Table Variables

Temporary tables and table variables store short-lived information and intermediate results during data processing. For the most part, temporary tables behave similarly to regular user tables. They don't support triggers and cannot be included in views; however, they support indexes and constraints and can be altered like regular tables. Altering them is not a good idea, though; I'll explain why later in this chapter.

There are two kinds of temporary tables: global and local. They differ in life span and visibility. *Global temporary tables* are created with names that start with two hash symbols (##) and are visible to all sessions. They are dropped when the session in which they were created disconnects and other sessions stop referencing them.

You can use global temporary tables to store and share temporary data between sessions. This approach, however, is fragile and prone to errors. For example, if the session that created the global temporary table loses the connection to the database, the table may be dropped at an unpredictable time. You may get better results by creating regular tables in tempdb instead.

You can create global temporary tables in startup stored procedures. Those tables will stay active and will not be dropped while SQL Server is running.

Local temporary tables are named starting with one hash symbol (#) and are visible only in the session in which they were created. When multiple sessions simultaneously create local temporary tables with the same name, every session will have its own instance of the table.

Local temporary tables are visible in the module in which they were created and in all other modules called from that module. For example, if you open a connection and create a temporary table in that session, the table will be visible everywhere in that session and will be live while the session is open. Alternatively, if you create a

---

temporary table in the stored procedure, it will be visible in that stored procedure and all other T-SQL modules or dynamic SQL called from there. It will be dropped automatically when that stored procedure completes.

You can use this behavior to pass data between T-SQL modules. Nevertheless, it has a couple of downsides. First, in SQL Server 2017 and earlier versions, it increases the number of compilations and CPU load. SQL Server will need to recompile the inner (called) module as it does not know anything about the external table until the module is called. This has been improved in SQL Server 2019, where recompilations do not happen as long as the temporary table structure stays the same.

Second, this approach is extremely fragile. Any changes in temporary table schema in the outer (calling) modules can break the inner ones. The situation will get even worse if the inner modules are executed by multiple callers—it quickly gets very hard to support. Use this approach with extreme care and only when absolutely necessary.

In contrast, table variables are visible only in the module where they were defined. You can pass them as parameters to other modules (more about this later in this chapter).[1]

Despite the old myth, regular table variables are not in-memory objects (memory-optimized table types allow you to create in-memory table variables; however, they are beyond the scope of this chapter). They use `tempdb` similarly to temporary tables. Also, they introduce less overhead than temporary tables; however, that benefit comes with a major limitation: table variables do not maintain index statistics. This can lead to significant cardinality estimation errors and highly inefficient execution plans.

Let's look at the code in Listing 9-2. Here I'm creating a temporary table and populating it with some data.

Listing 9-2. Cardinality estimations: temporary table creation

```
CREATE TABLE #TT(ID INT NOT NULL PRIMARY KEY);

;WITH N1(C) AS (SELECT 0 UNION ALL SELECT 0) -- 2 rows
,N2(C) AS (SELECT 0 FROM N1 AS T1  CROSS JOIN N1 AS T2) -- 4 rows
,N3(C) AS (SELECT 0 FROM N2 AS T1  CROSS JOIN N2 AS T2) -- 16 rows
,N4(C) AS (SELECT 0 FROM N3 AS T1  CROSS JOIN N3 AS T2) -- 256 rows
,IDs(ID) AS (SELECT ROW_NUMBER() OVER (ORDER BY (SELECT NULL)) FROM N4)
INSERT INTO #TT(ID)
    SELECT ID FROM IDs;
```

---

1 This article (*https://oreil.ly/mOOrt*) by Erland Sommarskog describes multiple methods of passing data between T-SQL modules.

As the next step, run the code in Listing 9-3. This will select the data from the temporary table and table variable and compare cardinality estimations in the queries. (Note that I am running this demo in the database with a compatibility level of 140 in SQL Server 2017. It will behave differently at compatibility level 150 or above, as in SQL Server 2019 and later; I will cover this shortly.)

Listing 9-3. Cardinality estimations: selecting data from temporary objects

```
DECLARE
    @TTV TABLE(ID INT NOT NULL PRIMARY KEY);

INSERT INTO @TTV(ID)
    SELECT ID FROM #TT;

SELECT COUNT(*) FROM #TT;
SELECT COUNT(*) FROM @TTV;
SELECT COUNT(*) FROM @TTV OPTION (RECOMPILE);
```

Figure 9-1 shows cardinality estimations for SELECT queries. As you can see, the estimation is correct for the temporary table. However, unless the statement recompiles—either with OPTION (RECOMPILE) or due to other factors that trigger recompilation—SQL Server will estimate that a table variable has only one row. Cardinality estimation errors can progress quickly through the execution plan, which means that using table variables can lead to highly inefficient plans.

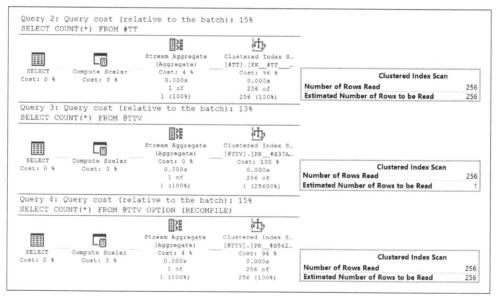

Figure 9-1. Cardinality estimations: temporary tables versus table variables

A statement recompilation with OPTION (RECOMPILE) provides Query Optimizer information about the total number of rows; however, table variables do not keep statistics or information about data distribution.

Let's repeat the test by adding a WHERE clause to the queries, as shown in Listing 9-4. All the rows in the tables have positive ID values.

Listing 9-4. Cardinality estimations: selecting data with the WHERE clause

```
DECLARE
    @TTV TABLE(ID INT NOT NULL PRIMARY KEY);

INSERT INTO @TTV(ID)
    SELECT ID FROM #TT;

SELECT COUNT(*) FROM #TT WHERE ID > 0;
SELECT COUNT(*) FROM @TTV WHERE ID > 0;
SELECT COUNT(*) FROM @TTV WHERE ID > 0 OPTION (RECOMPILE);
```

Figure 9-2 shows the cardinality estimations for the scenario in Listing 9-4. Temporary tables maintain statistics on indexes, so SQL Server was able to estimate the number of rows in the first SELECT correctly.

As before, without a statement-level recompile, SQL Server assumes the table variable has only one row. But even with a statement-level recompile, the estimations are way off. There are no statistics, and SQL Server assumes the greater-than (>) operator will filter out about 70% of the rows from the table, which is completely incorrect.

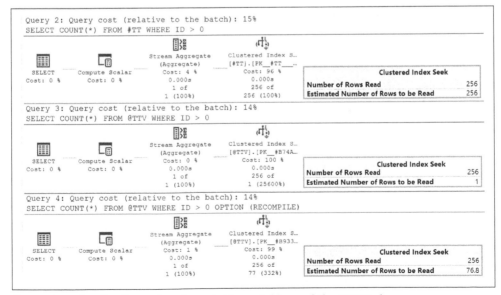

Figure 9-2. Cardinality estimations: table variables and the WHERE clause

If you run the scripts in a database with compatibility level 150 or above (SQL Server 2019), you'll get different estimations in the second query. SQL Server defers compiling statements with table variables and uses the number of rows there at the moment of compilation, caching the generated plan afterward. Nevertheless, there are still no statistics, and the estimation will not be correct when a WHERE clause is used. Remember this behavior.

> Table variables are *not* a good choice when cardinality estimation errors could impact execution plans—for example, if they store large amounts of data and participate in joins with other tables. In most cases, the Query Optimizer will choose a loop join, which is inefficient with large inputs. Use temporary tables instead—they are a *much* safer choice than table variables. In many cases, simply switching table variables to temporary tables could significantly improve query performance.

Do not forget to index temporary tables properly when you work with them. All the optimization rules you learned in Chapter 5 apply, whether you're dealing with regular or temporary tables.

Temporary tables are a great tool for improving cardinality estimations and optimizing complex queries. You can split one complex query into a few simpler ones and store the intermediate results in a temporary table. Smaller queries are easier to optimize, especially with up-to-date statistics generated in temporary tables.

As usual, this approach comes with a downside: the overhead of creating and populating temporary tables and table variables. Figure 9-3 gives a high-level overview of that process.

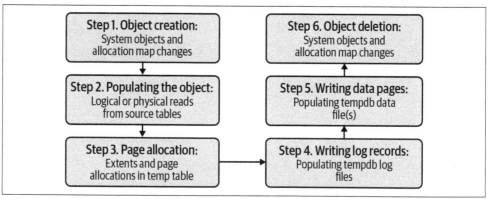

Figure 9-3. Using a temporary table to store intermediate data

Let's discuss what happens during the process pictured in Figure 9-3:

Step 1: Object creation

When SQL Server creates a temporary table or table variable, it makes several modifications in the system catalogs and allocation map pages in tempdb. This is a very fast process; however, it may become a source of contention when multiple sessions are updating system pages simultaneously.

This condition can be reduced through proper tempdb configuration, which I will cover later in this chapter. I'll also explain how to properly diagnose it in this chapter and Chapter 10.

Step 2: Populating the temporary object

Next, SQL Server is getting data to populate the temporary object by performing logical or physical reads from the source tables.

Step 3: Page allocation

SQL Server allocates data pages for the temporary object in the buffer pool and modifies them, marking them as dirty.

Step 4: Writing log records

SQL Server logs the preceding actions in the tempdb transaction log. Logging in tempdb is more efficient than in users' databases, but it still introduces overhead when you populate tempdb with temporary objects.

It is also worth mentioning that table variables use more efficient logging than temporary tables. Nevertheless, the cardinality estimation errors they introduce usually nullify that benefit.

Step 5: Writing data pages

In a separate, asynchronous process, dirty data pages will eventually be written to the data files. This might even be done after the object is dropped from the database.

Data pages that belong to temporary objects stay in the buffer pool and behave similarly to data pages from the regular tables. They consume buffer pool space and reduce the amount of memory available to cache the data from the regular tables. You can use Listing 7-4 to analyze tempdb buffer pool usage.

Step 6: Object deletion

Eventually, the temporary objects need to be deallocated. While this operation is relatively light, it also modifies the system catalogs and may lead to contention in busy systems.

As you can see, creating and populating temporary objects can be expensive, especially when you're dealing with large amounts of data. While temporary tables are a great query optimization tool for *reasonably* small intermediate results, it is usually not a good idea to store millions of rows in them.

Moreover, reading the data is significantly less expensive than writing it. It may be cheaper and faster to read large amounts of data from the regular table a few times than to write significant portions of it to the temporary table.

There are no hard thresholds for when you should or should not use temporary tables. It depends on your workload, the amount of data, your hardware configuration, and what problems you are trying to solve. Just remember the overhead that temporary tables introduce and make sure it doesn't outweigh the benefits of using them.

Temporary Object Caching

I mentioned just now that creating and deallocating temporary objects requires SQL Server to modify system catalogs and allocation map pages in tempdb. One of SQL Server's optimizations, *temporary object caching*, helps reduce that overhead.

The name of this feature is a bit confusing. It relates to caching temporary objects' *allocation* pages, not data pages. When you use temporary object caching, instead of dropping the table, SQL Server truncates it. It keeps two pages per index pre-allocated: one Index Allocation Map (IAM) and one data page. The next time the table is created, SQL Server reuses these pages, which helps reduce the number of modifications required in the allocation maps and system catalogs.

Let's look at Listing 9-5, which defines the stored procedure that creates and drops the temporary table.

Listing 9-5. Temporary object caching: the stored procedure

```
USE tempdb
GO

CREATE PROC dbo.TempTableCaching
AS
    CREATE TABLE #T(C INT NOT NULL PRIMARY KEY);
    DROP TABLE #T;
```

Next, run the stored procedure and examine the transaction log records it generates. You can see the code in Listing 9-6.

Listing 9-6. Temporary object caching: running the stored procedure

```
CHECKPOINT;
GO

EXEC dbo.TempTableCaching;

SELECT
```

```
    Operation, Context, AllocUnitName
    ,[Transaction Name], [Description]
FROM
    sys.fn_dblog(null, null);
```

You can see the output of the code in Figure 9-4. Here, the first stored procedure call produced 45 log records, most of them related to updating the allocation map pages and system tables while creating the temporary table.

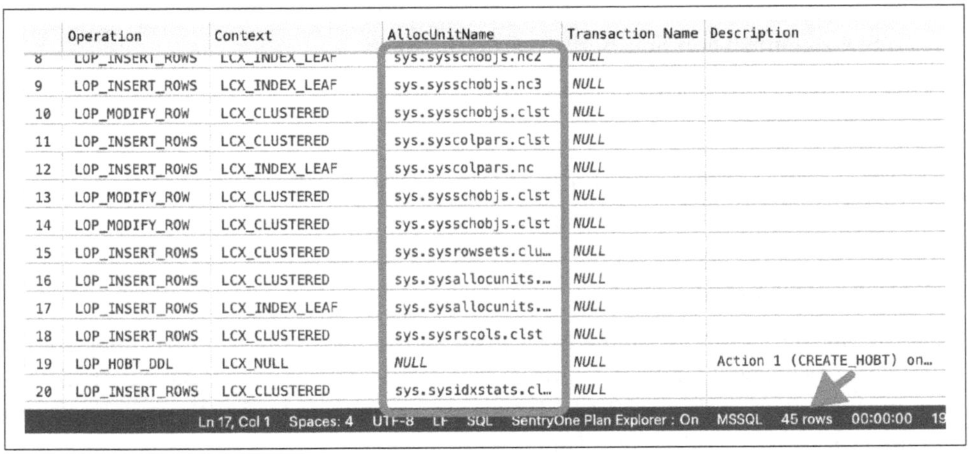

	Operation	Context	AllocUnitName	Transaction Name	Description
8	LOP_INSERT_ROWS	LCX_INDEX_LEAF	sys.sysschobjs.nc2	NULL	
9	LOP_INSERT_ROWS	LCX_INDEX_LEAF	sys.sysschobjs.nc3	NULL	
10	LOP_MODIFY_ROW	LCX_CLUSTERED	sys.sysschobjs.clst	NULL	
11	LOP_INSERT_ROWS	LCX_CLUSTERED	sys.syscolpars.clst	NULL	
12	LOP_INSERT_ROWS	LCX_INDEX_LEAF	sys.syscolpars.nc	NULL	
13	LOP_MODIFY_ROW	LCX_CLUSTERED	sys.sysschobjs.clst	NULL	
14	LOP_MODIFY_ROW	LCX_CLUSTERED	sys.sysschobjs.clst	NULL	
15	LOP_INSERT_ROWS	LCX_CLUSTERED	sys.sysrowsets.clu…	NULL	
16	LOP_INSERT_ROWS	LCX_CLUSTERED	sys.sysallocunits.…	NULL	
17	LOP_INSERT_ROWS	LCX_INDEX_LEAF	sys.sysallocunits.…	NULL	
18	LOP_INSERT_ROWS	LCX_CLUSTERED	sys.sysrscols.clst	NULL	
19	LOP_HOBT_DDL	LCX_NULL	NULL	NULL	Action 1 (CREATE_HOBT) on…
20	LOP_INSERT_ROWS	LCX_CLUSTERED	sys.sysidxstats.cl…	NULL	

Ln 17, Col 1   Spaces: 4   UTF-8   LF   SQL   SentryOne Plan Explorer : On   MSSQL   45 rows   00:00:00   19

Figure 9-4. Temporary object caching: log records after the first call

The situation changes when you run the code from Listing 9-6 a second time. Now when the temporary table is cached, table creation introduces just a few log records, all of which are against the system table, with no allocation map pages involved. You can see this in Figure 9-5.

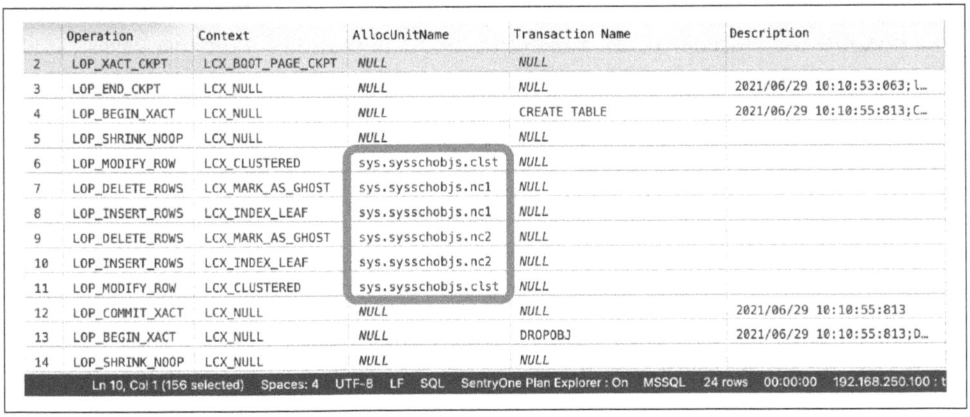

	Operation	Context	AllocUnitName	Transaction Name	Description
2	LOP_XACT_CKPT	LCX_BOOT_PAGE_CKPT	NULL	NULL	
3	LOP_END_CKPT	LCX_NULL	NULL	NULL	2021/06/29 10:10:53:063;L…
4	LOP_BEGIN_XACT	LCX_NULL	NULL	CREATE TABLE	2021/06/29 10:10:55:813;C…
5	LOP_SHRINK_NOOP	LCX_NULL	NULL	NULL	
6	LOP_MODIFY_ROW	LCX_CLUSTERED	sys.sysschobjs.clst	NULL	
7	LOP_DELETE_ROWS	LCX_MARK_AS_GHOST	sys.sysschobjs.nc1	NULL	
8	LOP_INSERT_ROWS	LCX_INDEX_LEAF	sys.sysschobjs.nc1	NULL	
9	LOP_DELETE_ROWS	LCX_MARK_AS_GHOST	sys.sysschobjs.nc2	NULL	
10	LOP_INSERT_ROWS	LCX_INDEX_LEAF	sys.sysschobjs.nc2	NULL	
11	LOP_MODIFY_ROW	LCX_CLUSTERED	sys.sysschobjs.clst	NULL	
12	LOP_COMMIT_XACT	LCX_NULL	NULL	NULL	2021/06/29 10:10:55:813
13	LOP_BEGIN_XACT	LCX_NULL	NULL	DROPOBJ	2021/06/29 10:10:55:813;D…
14	LOP_SHRINK_NOOP	LCX_NULL	NULL	NULL	

Ln 10, Col 1 (156 selected)   Spaces: 4   UTF-8   LF   SQL   SentryOne Plan Explorer : On   MSSQL   24 rows   00:00:00   192.168.250.100 : t

Figure 9-5. Temporary object caching: log records after the second call

Temporary object caching is enabled by default for all temporary objects created in stored procedures and triggers (session-level objects are not cached). However, there are a few conditions:

- The table needs to be smaller than 8 MB. Large tables are not cached.

- There can be no DDL statements that change the table structure. Any schema modification, with the exception of `DROP TABLE`, will prevent temporary object caching. However, you can create indexes and constraints inline in a `CREATE TABLE` statement and SQL Server will cache them.

- No named constraints can be defined in the table. Unnamed constraints will not prevent caching.

Consider these guidelines as you write your code. Temporary object caching is a useful performance feature, and you will benefit from it.

Table-Valued Parameters

SQL Server allows you to define table types in the database. When you declare the variable of the table type in the code, it works the same way as table variables. You can also pass the variables of the table types as parameters to T-SQL modules. Those parameters are called *table-valued parameters.*

Table-valued parameters are implemented as table variables under the hood and inherit all their benefits and limitations—most notably, missing statistics and cardinality estimation errors they may introduce. In addition, the parameters are read-only. You cannot insert, update, or delete the data from table-valued parameters in the modules they are passed to.

Listing 9-7 shows how you can use table-valued parameters. (This is just an example of a possible usage scenario, not a reference implementation for any use cases!) It also demonstrates that table variables are not transaction aware. You can use them to pass the information outside the transaction you are rolling back.

As another note, the code demonstrates that you can use table-valued parameters in dynamic SQL. Obviously, dynamic SQL is not required to pass the data between T-SQL modules.

Listing 9-7. Using table-valued parameters

```
CREATE TYPE dbo.tvpTransfers AS TABLE
(
    FromAccount BIGINT NOT NULL,
    ToAccount BIGINT NOT NULL,
    ADate DATETIME2(0) NOT NULL,
    Amount MONEY NOT NULL,
```

```
        PRIMARY KEY(FromAccount,ToAccount)
);
GO

CREATE PROC dbo.ProcessRejectedTransfers
(
    @RejectedTransfers dbo.tvpTransfers READONLY
)
AS
    SELECT FromAccount, ToAccount, ADate, Amount
    FROM @RejectedTransfers;
GO

CREATE PROC dbo.DoTransfers
(
    @Transfers dbo.tvpTransfers READONLY
)
AS
    DECLARE
        @RejectedTransfers dbo.tvpTransfers

    BEGIN TRAN
        INSERT INTO @RejectedTransfers
        (FromAccount, ToAccount, ADate, Amount)
            SELECT FromAccount, ToAccount, ADate, Amount
            FROM @Transfers
            WHERE Amount > 10000;
        /* ... */
    ROLLBACK -- Table variables are not transaction-aware.
    EXEC sp_executesql
        N'EXEC dbo.ProcessRejectedTransfers @Transfers;'
        ,N'@Transfers dbo.tvpTransfers READONLY'
        ,@Transfers = @RejectedTransfers;
GO

DECLARE
    @Transfers dbo.tvpTransfers

INSERT INTO @Transfers
    (FromAccount, ToAccount, ADate, Amount)
VALUES
    (1,2,'2021-08-01',100)
    ,(3,4,'2021-08-02',15000)
    ,(5,6,'2021-08-03',20000);

EXEC dbo.DoTransfers @Transfers;
```

Table-valued parameters are one of the fastest ways to pass a batch of rows from a client application to a T-SQL routine. They are an order of magnitude faster than separate DML statements and, in some cases, can even outperform bulk operations.

Look for opportunities to use them. They can provide significant performance improvements.

Regular Tables in tempdb and Transaction Logging

You can create and use regular tables in tempdb. The tables will be visible to all sessions and behave the same way as in the other databases. Obviously, the system needs to handle the case when those tables disappear during SQL Server restarts, when tempdb is re-created. You have two options: you can re-create them by defining them in the model database or you can use startup stored procedures.

tempdb can be a good choice as the staging area for ETL (extract, transform, load) processes in cases where you need to load and process a large amount of data *and* the process does not have High Availability (HA) requirements. Tempdb uses the SIMPLE recovery model and more efficient transaction logging. It does not need to support crash recovery, and therefore does not need to keep the REDO portion of the transaction log record, which is what allows SQL Server to reapply changes from committed transactions if it crashes before the checkpoint.

Transaction logging of local temporary tables is even more efficient. These tables are visible in the scope of a single session, which allows SQL Server to use minimally logged operations in more cases (I'll cover this in more detail in Chapter 11). You can use minimally logged operations to improve ETL performance even further. Remember, however, that temporary tables will disappear if the client loses the connection to the database.

Table 9-1 shows examples of when operations are minimally logged for regular and temporary tables in tempdb. You can use it as a reference to speed up ETL processes and the initial data load to the tables. As I stated earlier, table variables use even less logging than temporary tables; however, they open the door to cardinality estimation errors during query optimization.

Table 9-1. Minimally logged operations in tempdb

Operation	Minimally logged?
SELECT INTO dbo.RegularTable SELECT INTO #tempTable	Yes—although I don't recommend this pattern, because it does not create clustered indexes in the table
INSERT INTO dbo.RegularTable WITH (TAB LOCK) SELECT	Yes
INSERT INTO dbo.RegularTable SELECT	No
INSERT INTO #tempTable SELECT	Yes

Using `tempdb` for ETL processes may improve their performance and reduce the load on the server. In many cases, however, you can achieve even better results by using durable or non-durable memory-optimized tables and In-Memory OLTP. Consider them as options, but test implementation carefully: In-Memory OLTP behaves differently than the classic Storage Engine.

Internal tempdb Consumers

In addition to objects created by users, SQL Server uses `tempdb` to store internal objects. The two most common space consumers in this group are version store and internal row sets, which are generated by Sort, Hash, and Exchange operations that spill over to `tempdb`.

Let's look at both in detail.

Version Store

Several SQL Server features rely on row versioning. In addition to optimistic isolation levels, such as `RCSI` and `SNAPSHOT`, row versioning is used by online index rebuild, triggers, and Multiple Active Result Sets (MARS). As you learned in Chapter 8, the old versions of the rows are stored in the `tempdb` version store.

Figure 9-6 shows version store behavior with a large row-versioning transaction running in the system. You can see the growth of version store size (the `Version Store Size (KB)` performance counter), which triggers `tempdb` auto-growth events.

In this case, SQL Server cleared up the version store after the transaction completed. It took some time for cleanup to occur, however. The cleanup process is asynchronous and runs on a schedule.

Version store growth is one of the common reasons for excessive `tempdb` growth. SQL Server does not clean up the version store beyond the starting point of the oldest active row-versioning transaction. Uncommitted runaway transactions can lead to extensive version store and `tempdb` growth, even if `tempdb` does not generate row versions by itself.

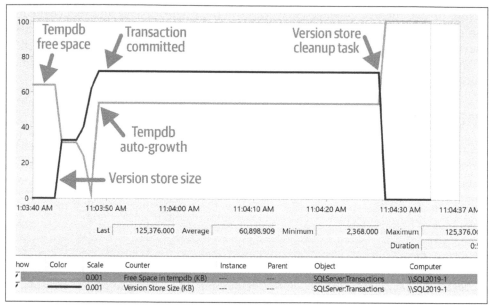

Figure 9-6. Version store growth and cleanup

Listing 9-8 shows you how to detect the five oldest row-versioning transactions using the `sys.dm_tran_active_snapshot_database_transactions` view (*https://oreil.ly/ILgAS*). You can kill the session that prevents cleanup of the version store in case of emergency.

Listing 9-8. Detecting the five oldest row-versioning transactions

```
SELECT TOP 5
    at.transaction_id
    ,at.elapsed_time_seconds
    ,at.session_id
    ,s.login_time
    ,s.login_name
    ,s.host_name
    ,s.program_name
    ,s.last_request_start_time
    ,s.last_request_end_time
    ,er.status
    ,er.wait_type
    ,er.wait_time
    ,er.blocking_session_id
    ,er.last_wait_type
    ,st.text AS [SQL]
FROM
    sys.dm_tran_active_snapshot_database_transactions at WITH (NOLOCK)
        JOIN sys.dm_exec_sessions s WITH (NOLOCK) on
```

```
        at.session_id = s.session_id
    LEFT JOIN sys.dm_exec_requests er WITH (NOLOCK) on
        at.session_id = er.session_id
    OUTER APPLY
        sys.dm_exec_sql_text(er.sql_handle) st
ORDER BY
    at.elapsed_time_seconds DESC;
```

 Long-running transactions on readable secondaries in Availability Groups can defer version store cleanup. I'll discuss this in Chapter 12.

There are several performance counters in the Transactions performance object that you can use to monitor version store behavior:

Version Store Size (KB)
: Current size of the version store.

Version Generation rate (KB/s)
: Growth rate of the version store.

Version Cleanup rate (KB/s)
: Cleanup rate of the version store.

Longest Transaction Running Time
: Duration in seconds of the oldest active transaction that is using row versioning.

Free Space in tempdb (KB)
: Amount of available space in tempdb. While this counter is not related to the version store, you can use it for general tempdb monitoring.

Listing 9-9 shows the queries you can use to analyze version store usage per database. This may be useful when you troubleshoot excessive version store growth on servers that host multiple databases.

The first query would work on SQL Server 2016 and later. The second can be used on the older versions of SQL Server. It is more resource intensive, however, and provides slightly less accurate results.

Listing 9-9. Version store usage per database

```
-- SQL Server 2016 SP2 and later
SELECT
    DB_NAME(database_id) AS [DB]
    ,database_id
    ,reserved_page_count
```

```
    ,CONVERT(DECIMAL(12,3),reserved_space_kb / 1024.)
        AS [Reserved Space (MB)]
FROM
    sys.dm_tran_version_store_space_usage WITH (NOLOCK)
OPTION (RECOMPILE);

-- SQL Server 2014 and earlier. Less accurate.
SELECT
    DB_NAME(database_id) AS [DB]
    ,database_id
    ,CONVERT(DECIMAL(12,3),
        SUM(record_length_first_part_in_bytes +
            record_length_second_part_in_bytes) / 1024. / 1024.
    ) AS [Version Store (MB)]
FROM
    sys.dm_tran_version_store WITH (NOLOCK)
GROUP BY
    database_id
OPTION (RECOMPILE, MAXDOP 1);
```

Version store is a key component for multiple SQL Server features. Monitor its size and behavior, especially looking for long-running and runaway row-versioning transactions.

Spills

As you remember from Chapter 7, Sort, Hash, and Exchange operators require memory to store the data. When the query memory grant is insufficient, they *spill* data to tempdb and perform the operation there. The spills impact query performance, since in-database data access is significantly slower than doing the operation in memory. It also adds to the tempdb load and may increase its size.

In recent versions of SQL Server, memory grant feedback can reduce the number of spills. However, it does not solve the problem completely, nor is it available in non-Enterprise editions of SQL Server. You may need to detect and optimize queries that have incorrect or excessive memory grants, using the techniques discussed in Chapter 7.

You can detect queries that spill to tempdb by using the sort_warning, hash_warning, and exchange_spill xEvents. Listing 9-10 shows the code that creates an xEvent session and the query you can use to parse the results.

Listing 9-10. Using xEvents to detect queries that spill to tempdb

```
CREATE EVENT SESSION [Spills]
ON SERVER
ADD EVENT sqlserver.hash_warning
(
```

```
    ACTION
    (
        sqlserver.database_id
        ,sqlserver.plan_handle
        ,sqlserver.session_id
        ,sqlserver.sql_text
        ,sqlserver.query_hash
        ,sqlserver.query_plan_hash
    )
    WHERE ([sqlserver].[is_system]=0)
),
ADD EVENT sqlserver.sort_warning
(
    ACTION
    (
        sqlserver.database_id
        ,sqlserver.plan_handle
        ,sqlserver.session_id
        ,sqlserver.sql_text
        ,sqlserver.query_hash
        ,sqlserver.query_plan_hash
    )
    WHERE ([sqlserver].[is_system]=0)
),
ADD EVENT sqlserver.exchange_spill
(
    ACTION
    (
        sqlserver.database_id
        ,sqlserver.plan_handle
        ,sqlserver.session_id
        ,sqlserver.sql_text
        ,sqlserver.query_hash
        ,sqlserver.query_plan_hash
    )
    WHERE ([sqlserver].[is_system]=0)
)
ADD TARGET package0.ring_buffer;
GO

-- Start xEvent Session
-- Allow it to run for some time and collect the information
ALTER EVENT SESSION [Spills]
ON SERVER
STATE = START;
GO

-- Analyze the results
DROP TABLE IF EXISTS #tmpXML;
CREATE TABLE #tmpXML
(
    EventTime DATETIME2(7) NOT NULL,
```

```
            [Event] XML
);

DECLARE
    @TargetData XML;

SELECT
    @TargetData = CONVERT(XML,st.target_data)
FROM
    sys.dm_xe_sessions s WITH (NOLOCK)
        JOIN sys.dm_xe_session_targets st WITH(NOLOCK) ON
            s.address = st.event_session_address
WHERE
    s.name = 'Spills' and st.target_name = 'ring_buffer';

INSERT INTO #tmpXML(EventTime, [Event])
    SELECT
        t.e.value('@timestamp','datetime'), t.e.query('.')
    FROM
        @TargetData.nodes('/RingBufferTarget/event') AS t(e);

;WITH EventInfo
AS
(
    SELECT
        t.EventTime
        ,t.[Event].value('/event[1]/@name','sysname') AS [Event]
        ,t.[Event].value('(/event[1]/action[@name="session_id"]/value/text())[1]'
            ,'smallint') AS [Session]
        ,t.[Event].value('(/event[1]/action[@name="database_id"]/value/text())[1]'
            ,'smallint') AS [DB]
        ,t.[Event].value('(/event[1]/action[@name="sql_text"]/value/text())[1]'
            ,'nvarchar(max)') AS [SQL]
        ,t.[Event]
            .value('(/event[1]/data[@name="granted_memory_kb"]/value/text())[1]'
                ,'bigint') AS [Granted Memory (KB)]
        ,t.[Event]
            .value('(/event[1]/data[@name="used_memory_kb"]/value/text())[1]'
                ,'bigint') AS [Used Memory (KB)]
        ,t.[Event]
    .value('xs:hexBinary((/event[1]/action[@name="plan_handle"]/value/text())[1])'
                ,'varbinary(64)') AS [PlanHandle]
        ,t.[Event].value('(/event[1]/action[@name="query_hash"]/value/text())[1]'
            ,'nvarchar(64)') AS [QueryHash]
        ,t.[Event]
            .value('(/event[1]/action[@name="query_plan_hash"]/value/text())[1]'
                ,'nvarchar(64)') AS [QueryPlanHash]
FROM
    #tmpXML t
)
SELECT
    ei.*, qp.query_plan
```

```
FROM
    EventInfo ei
        OUTER APPLY sys.dm_exec_query_plan(ei.PlanHandle) qp
OPTION (RECOMPILE, MAXDOP 1);
```

You can group the results by query hash or plan hash columns to find the queries that spill most often.

SSMS and other tools display warnings about spills in the execution plans. Figure 9-7 shows an example in SSMS. Do not ignore these warnings when you tune your queries.

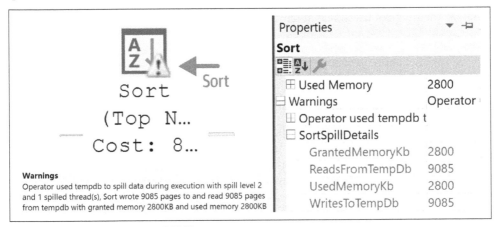

Figure 9-7. Sort warning in SSMS

Unfortunately, it is impossible to eliminate all spills. Make sure, however, that critical queries do not spill, and evaluate the impact of spills on tempdb performance.

Common tempdb Issues

Issues with tempdb performance and throughput will affect the entire system. They degrade query performance, slow down T-SQL code, and introduce other issues and side effects. Unfortunately, their impact is not easy to estimate.

I usually start my analysis by looking at the general throughput (number of reads and writes) and latency/stall metrics of tempdb database files using the sys.dm_io_vir tual_file_stats view and the code from Listing 3-1. High read and write through-put indicates heavy tempdb usage. High latency may indicate issues with tempdb configuration (more on that later) or that the disk subsystem is overloaded, poten-tially due to high throughput.

When I see high tempdb throughput, I try to pinpoint its root cause. I look at what consumes space in tempdb by running the query from Listing 9-1. The space usage of each type of object does not always correlate with the throughput it generates, but I can often get useful information by analyzing trends in how space is used over time.

I can estimate version store throughput by looking at the `Version Generation rate` and `Version Cleanup rate` performance counters. Usually, there is little you can do about the load it generates. The "solution" of switching off optimistic isolation levels is rarely appropriate. Although remember that other SQL Server features—such as triggers, online index rebuild, and MARS—use row versioning; see if you can find any opportunities to reduce the load they generate.

There are two counters in `General Statistics` performance objects that help me analyze the usage of user-created temporary objects:

`Temp Tables Creation Rate`
    Shows the count of temporary tables and table variables created per second

`Active Temp Tables`
    Provides the number of temporary tables and table variables currently in use

High numbers in those counters indicate excessive usage of temporary objects, especially when you also see high space usage of user objects in the output from Listing 9-1. You might look for opportunities to reduce usage of temporary objects: for example, by optimizing a few frequently executed stored procedures.

You can look at the following performance counters to track how often some internal objects are created in `tempdb`:

`SQLServer:Access Methods\Worktables Created/sec`
    Provides the count of internal worktables SQL Server created to support spools, cursors, and large object (LOB) and XML variables

`SQLServer:Cursor Manager By Type\Cursor worktable usage`
    Number of worktables used by cursors

Unfortunately, SQL Server does not provide performance counters to track spills. However, I can use an xEvent session to capture `sort_warning`, `hash_warning`, and `exchange_spill` events using the `event_counter` target, as shown in Listing 9-11.

Listing 9-11. Counting the number of spills

```
CREATE EVENT SESSION [Spill_Count]
ON SERVER
ADD EVENT sqlserver.exchange_spill,
ADD EVENT sqlserver.hash_warning,
ADD EVENT sqlserver.sort_warning
ADD TARGET package0.event_counter;

-- Start the session and allow it to collect the data
```

```
ALTER EVENT SESSION [Spill_Count]
ON SERVER
STATE = START;
GO

-- Analyze the data
DECLARE
    @TargetData XML

SELECT
    @TargetData = CONVERT(XML,st.target_data)
FROM
    sys.dm_xe_sessions s WITH (NOLOCK)
        JOIN sys.dm_xe_session_targets st WITH(NOLOCK) ON
            s.address = st.event_session_address
WHERE
    s.name = 'Spill_Count' and st.target_name = 'event_counter';

;WITH EventInfo
AS
(
    SELECT
        t.e.value('@name','sysname') AS [Event]
        ,t.e.value('@count','bigint') AS [Count]
    FROM
        @TargetData.nodes
            ('/CounterTarget/Packages/Package[@name="sqlserver"]/Event')
                AS t(e)
)
SELECT [Event], [Count]
FROM EventInfo
OPTION (RECOMPILE, MAXDOP 1);
```

You can achieve some benefits by optimizing queries that spill to tempdb and reducing cursor usage. Focus on the most critical and frequently executed queries and stored procedures.

That said, you can often get better ROI by scaling up your hardware. It is cheap nowadays. However, there are a couple of other common problems with tempdb that you need to be aware of.

System Page Contention

tempdb is a busy database—multiple sessions create and drop objects there all the time. During those operations, sessions make several changes in the system pages that track object allocations and metadata.

To protect the integrity of these pages, SQL Server serializes access to them: only one session may make modifications at any given time. This can lead to contention and reduce tempdb throughput in busy systems.

SQL Server enforces this serialization with internal objects called *latches*. Latches maintain the consistency of various internal data structures in SQL Server's memory, allowing only one thread to change the object at a time. (I will discuss latches in depth in Chapter 10.)

This contention presents itself with PAGELATCH waits, which are very short-lived: their duration is usually measured in microseconds. Nevertheless, they may become very noticeable in systems with large numbers of concurrent users.

Contention during system page modifications in tempdb is a common source of PAGELATCH waits. There are other cases, however, when you can see page latches and need to analyze wait resources to understand if those waits were related to tempdb. You can do this with the code in Listing 9-12, which captures current PAGELATCH waits using the sys.dm_os_waiting_tasks view.

Listing 9-12. Capturing currently waiting sessions

```
-- SQL Server 2005-2017
SELECT
    wt.session_id
    ,wt.wait_type
    ,er.wait_resource
    ,er.wait_time
FROM
    sys.dm_os_waiting_tasks wt WITH (NOLOCK)
        JOIN sys.dm_exec_requests er WITH (NOLOCK) ON
            wt.session_id = er.session_id
WHERE
    wt.wait_type LIKE 'PAGELATCH%'
OPTION (MAXDOP 1, RECOMPILE);

-- SQL Server 2019 and later
SELECT
    wt.session_id
    ,wt.wait_type
    ,er.wait_resource
    ,er.wait_time
    ,pi.database_id
    ,pi.file_id
    ,pi.page_id
    ,pi.object_id
    ,OBJECT_NAME(pi.object_id,pi.database_id) as [object]
    ,pi.index_id
    ,pi.page_type_desc
FROM
    sys.dm_os_waiting_tasks wt WITH (NOLOCK)
        JOIN sys.dm_exec_requests er WITH (NOLOCK) ON
            wt.session_id = er.session_id
        CROSS APPLY
```

```
            sys.fn_PageResCracker(er.page_resource) pc
        CROSS APPLY
            sys.dm_db_page_info(pc.db_id,pc.file_id
                ,pc.page_id,'DETAILED') pi
WHERE
    wt.wait_type LIKE 'PAGELATCH%'
OPTION (MAXDOP 1, RECOMPILE);
```

Figure 9-8 shows an example of the output. SQL Server 2019 gives you a couple of additional functions to get more detailed information. In older versions of SQL Server, you can look at the `wait_resource` column, which includes `database_id` as the first part in the resource reference. The value of 2 indicates the `tempdb`.

	session_id	wait_type	wait_resource	wait_time	database_id	file_id	page_id	object_id	object	index_id	page_type_desc
1	60	PAGELATCH_EX	2:1:118	3	2	1	118	34	sysschobjs	2	INDEX_PAGE
2	65	PAGELATCH_EX	2:1:307	0	2	1	307	34	sysschobjs	1	DATA_PAGE
3	69	PAGELATCH_EX	2:1:307	2	2	1	307	34	sysschobjs	1	DATA_PAGE
4	70	PAGELATCH_EX	2:1:118	4	2	1	118	34	sysschobjs	2	INDEX_PAGE
5	75	PAGELATCH_EX	2:1:118	2	2	1	118	34	sysschobjs	2	INDEX_PAGE
6	76	PAGELATCH_SH	2:1:118	3	2	1	118	34	sysschobjs	2	INDEX_PAGE
7	77	PAGELATCH_EX	2:3:830	0	2	3	830	34	sysschobjs	1	DATA_PAGE
8	78	PAGELATCH_EX	2:1:118	5	2	1	118	34	sysschobjs	2	INDEX_PAGE
9	80	PAGELATCH_EX	2:3:2052	3	2	3	2052	34	sysschobjs	1	DATA_PAGE
10	81	PAGELATCH_EX	2:3:830	6	2	3	830	34	sysschobjs	1	DATA_PAGE
11	82	PAGELATCH_EX	2:3:830	3	2	3	830	34	sysschobjs	1	DATA_PAGE
12	83	PAGELATCH_EX	2:3:2052	4	2	3	2052	34	sysschobjs	1	DATA_PAGE
13	84	PAGELATCH_EX	2:3:830	5	2	3	830	34	sysschobjs	1	DATA_PAGE

Figure 9-8. PAGELATCH waits

Because individual `PAGELATCH` waits are usually so short, you may miss them when you query the `sys.dm_os_waiting_tasks` view. You can run the query multiple times or use xEvents to track them.

Listing 9-13 shows the xEvents session for capturing latch waits per database. This session will introduce overhead, so don't keep it running outside of troubleshooting. Here, to reduce overhead I am limiting the number of events to collect.

Listing 9-13. Capturing latch waits

```
CREATE EVENT SESSION [Latch Waits] ON SERVER
ADD EVENT sqlserver.latch_suspend_end
ADD TARGET package0.ring_buffer
(SET max_events_limit=2000);
GO

-- The code below parses collected results
DROP TABLE IF EXISTS #tmpXML;
CREATE TABLE #tmpXML
(
    EventTime DATETIME2(7) NOT NULL,
```

```
        [Event] XML
);

DECLARE
    @TargetData XML;

SELECT
    @TargetData = CONVERT(XML,st.target_data)
FROM
    sys.dm_xe_sessions s WITH (NOLOCK)
        JOIN sys.dm_xe_session_targets st WITH(NOLOCK) ON
            s.address = st.event_session_address
WHERE
    s.name = 'Latch Waits' and st.target_name = 'ring_buffer';

INSERT INTO #tmpXML(EventTime, [Event])
    SELECT t.e.value('@timestamp','datetime'), t.e.query('.')
    FROM @TargetData.nodes('/RingBufferTarget/event') AS t(e);

;WITH EventInfo
AS
(
    SELECT
        t.[EventTime] as [Time]
        ,t.[Event].value('(/event[1]/data[@name="database_id"]/value/text())[1]'
            ,'smallint') AS [DB]
        ,t.[Event].value('(/event[1]/data[@name="duration"]/value/text())[1]'
            ,'bigint') AS [Duration]
    FROM
        #tmpXML t
)
SELECT
    MONTH([Time]) as [Month]
    ,DAY([Time]) as [Day]
    ,DATEPART(hour,[Time]) as [Hour]
    ,DATEPART(minute,[Time]) as [Minute]
    ,[DB]
    ,COUNT(*) as [Latch Count]
    ,CONVERT(DECIMAL(15,3),SUM(Duration / 1000.)) as [Duration (MS)]
FROM
    EventInfo ei
GROUP BY
    MONTH([Time]),DAY([Time]),DATEPART(hour,[Time]),DATEPART(minute,[Time]),[DB]
ORDER BY
    [Month],[Day],[Hour],[Minute],[DB]
OPTION (RECOMPILE, MAXDOP 1);
```

There are a few things you can do in cases of tempdb system page contention. In the Enterprise Edition of SQL Server 2019, you can benefit from a new feature called *memory-optimized tempdb metadata*, which converts system tables in tempdb to latch-free, nondurable, memory-optimized tables.

You can enable this feature by running the `ALTER SERVER CONFIGURATION SET MEM ORY_OPTIMIZED_TEMPDB_METADATA = ON` command. You'll need to restart the server for the change to take effect. You can check if this feature is enabled by running the `SELECT SERVERPROPERTY('IsTempdbMetadataMemoryOptimized')` command.

There are a few limitations when this feature is enabled: most notably, you cannot create columnstore indexes on `tempdb` tables. Nevertheless, it is beneficial—use it unless your server has very little memory provisioned. (You can read more about the limitations of memory-optimized `tempdb` metadata in the Microsoft documentation (*https://oreil.ly/kfkwt*).)

Unfortunately, this contention may be harder to address in previous versions of SQL Server. There are a few things you can do, however. First, check the `tempdb` configuration. Since allocations are done per file, you can reduce contention by creating multiple data files. The benefit, however, will quickly diminish as the number of files grows.

In old versions of SQL Server (prior to 2016), enable the `T1118` trace flag, which disables mixed-extent allocations. This will reduce the number of changes to the system pages during allocation and deallocation operations.

In the end, you may have to look at reducing `tempdb` usage. The less work the database performs, the less chance of contention.

Running Out of Space

Running out of space in `tempdb` is never a good thing. It usually leads to production incidents—that is, when a query that needs to write to the database fails. This can even impact sessions that don't explicitly use `tempdb`. For example, if you have optimistic isolation levels enabled, the `UPDATE` and `DELETE` statements will fail when they try to write to the version store.

You may have noticed that I keep repeating this, but it's for good reason: it is essential to implement free space monitoring. Depending on your configuration and maintenance practices, you might monitor free space on disk, available space in the database, or both. Set alerts to tell you when `tempdb` space utilization becomes critical.

Keep in mind that `tempdb` may fill up rather quickly. For example, queries that need to sort hundreds of gigabytes of data will spill to `tempdb` and may consume all available space in no time. Factor this into your capacity planning, put `tempdb` on drives with enough space, and accommodate the right thresholds in your space-monitoring alerts.

If you place the `tempdb` log file on the same drive with data files, you might also need to look at its size and the available space there. You can do this by running the `DBCC`

SQLPERF(LOGSPACE) command or using the `sys.database_files` view. I'll provide additional scripts and discuss how to troubleshoot log growth issues in Chapter 11.

You have three dynamic management views to use. The first, `sys.dm_db _file_space_usage`, provides information about space usage and available space in `tempdb` database files. Run the code from Listing 9-1 as your first step in troubleshooting.

You can follow the techniques you learned earlier in the chapter to analyze version store growth problems. Alternatively, if you see that space is consumed by user or internal temporary objects, you may need to find the sessions that consume the most space by using two other views:

`sys.dm_db_session_space_usage`

> The `sys.dm_db_session_space_usage` view (*https://oreil.ly/ojd7H*) returns the number of pages allocated and deallocated by each session in the database.

`sys.dm_db_task_space_usage`

> The `sys.dm_db_task_space_usage` view (*https://oreil.ly/mqjK8*) provides you with the allocation information for currently running tasks. This data is not reflected in the `sys.dm_db_session_space_usage` view until the task is completed.

Listing 9-14 shows you code that combines the data from both views, allowing you to detect the sessions that consume the most space in `tempdb`.

Listing 9-14. Detecting the sessions that consume the most `tempdb` *space*

```
;WITH SpaceUsagePages
AS
(
    SELECT
        ss.session_id
        ,ss.user_objects_alloc_page_count +
            ISNULL(SUM(ts.user_objects_alloc_page_count),0)
                AS [user_alloc_page_count]
        ,ss.user_objects_dealloc_page_count +
            ISNULL(SUM(ts.user_objects_dealloc_page_count),0)
                AS [user_dealloc_page_count]
        ,ss.user_objects_deferred_dealloc_page_count
                AS [user_deferred_page_count]
        ,ss.internal_objects_alloc_page_count +
            ISNULL(SUM(ts.internal_objects_alloc_page_count),0)
                AS [internal_alloc_page_count]
        ,ss.internal_objects_dealloc_page_count +
            ISNULL(SUM(ts.internal_objects_dealloc_page_count),0)
                AS [internal_dealloc_page_count]
    FROM
```

```
            sys.dm_db_session_space_usage ss WITH (NOLOCK) LEFT JOIN
                sys.dm_db_task_space_usage ts WITH (NOLOCK) ON
                    ss.session_id = ts.session_id
        GROUP BY
            ss.session_id
            ,ss.user_objects_alloc_page_count
            ,ss.user_objects_dealloc_page_count
            ,ss.internal_objects_alloc_page_count
            ,ss.internal_objects_dealloc_page_count
            ,ss.user_objects_deferred_dealloc_page_count
)
,SpaceUsage
AS
(
    SELECT
        session_id
        ,CONVERT(DECIMAL(12,3),
            ([user_alloc_page_count] - [user_dealloc_page_count]) / 128.
        ) AS [user_used_mb]
        ,CONVERT(DECIMAL(12,3),
            ([internal_alloc_page_count] - [internal_dealloc_page_count]) / 128.
        ) AS [internal_used_mb]
        ,CONVERT(DECIMAL(12,3),user_deferred_page_count / 128.)
            AS [user_deferred_used_mb]
    FROM
        SpaceUsagePages
)
SELECT
    su.session_id
    ,su.user_used_mb
    ,su.internal_used_mb
    ,su.user_deferred_used_mb
    ,su.user_used_mb + su.internal_used_mb AS [space_used_mb]
    ,es.open_transaction_count
    ,es.login_time
    ,es.original_login_name
    ,es.host_name
    ,es.program_name
    ,er.status as [request_status]
    ,er.start_time
    ,CONVERT(DECIMAL(21,3),er.total_elapsed_time / 1000.) AS [duration]
    ,er.cpu_time
    ,ib.event_info as [buffer]
    ,er.wait_type
    ,er.wait_time
    ,er.wait_resource
    ,er.blocking_session_id
FROM
    SpaceUsage su
        LEFT JOIN sys.dm_exec_requests er WITH (NOLOCK) ON
            su.session_id = er.session_id
        LEFT JOIN sys.dm_exec_sessions es WITH (NOLOCK) ON
```

```
        su.session_id = es.session_id
    OUTER APPLY
        sys.dm_exec_input_buffer(es.session_id, er.request_id) ib
WHERE
    su.user_used_mb + su.internal_used_mb >= 50
ORDER BY
    [space_used_mb] DESC
OPTION (RECOMPILE);
```

You can kill the sessions that consume the most space in `tempdb` to alleviate the problem. Obviously, it is a good idea to troubleshoot what caused the high space usage and address the root cause of the issue.

tempdb Configuration

Let's finish the chapter with a few tips on `tempdb` configuration. I've covered many aspects of it already; nevertheless, I'd like to reiterate them here.

First of all, place `tempdb` on the fastest drive possible. Use fast local storage, preferably large-capacity NVMe drives, if it's an option. This will give you lower latency and higher throughput compared to network-based storage (NAS). (See Chapter 3.)

In non-Enterprise editions, you can even consider putting `tempdb` on the RAM drive if the server has enough memory available. In the Enterprise Edition, it is usually better to leave the memory to SQL Server.

Obviously, perform capacity planning and allocate enough storage space for the `tempdb` workload. Set monitoring on available space and set alerts for when you are low on space. Running out of space in `tempdb` will lead to production incidents and potential downtime.

There is a trick you can use when you provision `tempdb` using fast storage with limited capacity: you can split `tempdb` files between fast and slow drives. Pre-allocate the files on the fast drive to the maximum possible size and disable auto-growth for them. At the same time, leave files on the slow drives very small, but keep auto-growth enabled.

In that configuration, SQL Server will favor the files on the fast drives during normal operations. However, in extreme conditions, the files on the slow drive will start to grow, which helps avoid out-of-space incidents. I do not use this configuration often; however, it may be beneficial in rare circumstances, when fast storage is big enough to handle regular `tempdb` workloads but doesn't have enough capacity for spikes.

Create multiple data files. The old, well-known advice that you should match the number of files with the number of CPUs may not be relevant anymore. My rule of thumb is:

- Match the number of files with the number of active CPU cores if the server has eight or fewer CPU cores.

- If the server has more than eight CPU cores, use either eight data files or one-fourth the number of cores, whichever is greater, rounding up in batches of four files. For example, use 8 data files in the 24-core server and 12 data files in the 40-core server.

- Add files in batches of four if you see any allocation contention or bottlenecks.

Use the same initial size and auto-growth parameters specified in megabytes for all files. If you are using SQL Server prior to 2016, set the T1118 trace flag (disable the mixed extents allocation) and, potentially, the T1117 trace flag (grow all files in the file group simultaneously). Both of these flags are server-wide and impact user databases. This is not a problem with the T1118 flag; however, do not enable T1117 if users' databases have unevenly sized data files. Rebalance the data in the users' database first.

Finally, if you are using the Enterprise Edition of SQL Server 2019 or later, consider enabling memory-optimized catalogs in tempdb, especially if you see PAGELATCH waits over tempdb allocation pages.

Summary

tempdb is a busy database that is shared among all user and system sessions. High tempdb performance and throughput are essential for good system performance.

Place tempdb on the fastest drive you have, preferably a large-capacity local NVMe drive. Make sure the database configuration is correct. Create multiple data files using the same auto-growth parameters specified in megabytes. Enable the T1118 and, potentially, T1117 flags in SQL Server versions prior to 2016.

Analyze PAGELATCH waits if you see them and detect whether they are tempdb related. In SQL Server 2019, you can mitigate them by enabling memory-optimized tempdb catalogs. In older versions of SQL Server, analyze the number of tempdb files, use temporary object caching, and reduce tempdb usage.

Troubleshoot and address excessive tempdb load. Refactor code that does not use temporary objects legitimately, and optimize queries with excessive spills.

Be aware that table variables do not store statistics; doing so leads to cardinality estimation errors and inefficient query plans. Consider using temporary tables as a safer choice.

In the next chapter, I'll talk about latches, which are synchronization objects used by SQL Server to protect internal in-memory structures.

Troubleshooting Checklist

☐ Check the `tempdb` configuration (number of files, auto-growth settings, `T1118` flag in old versions of SQL Server, etc.).

☐ Move `tempdb` to local, large-capacity NVMe drives when possible.

☐ Analyze the performance of `tempdb` storage.

☐ Review `tempdb` space consumption and usage. Address issues if feasible.

☐ Troubleshoot whether `PAGELATCH` waits are `tempdb` related.

☐ Consider enabling memory-optimized `tempdb` metadata in the Enterprise Edition of SQL Server 2019, especially if you notice `tempdb`-related `PAGELATCH` waits.

☐ Set up monitoring on `tempdb` drive space utilization.

CHAPTER 10

Latches

Latches are lightweight synchronization objects that protect the consistency of SQL Server internal data structures. As the opposite of locks, which protect transactional data consistency, latches prevent corruption of the data structures in memory.

In most cases, latches are short-lived and may be unnoticeable in systems with light loads. However, as loads grow, latch contention may become an issue and can limit system scalability and throughput. In this chapter, I will discuss how to detect and address those situations.

I will start this chapter with an overview of latches and their categories and types. Next, I will discuss page latches and several mitigation techniques to address their contention. Finally, I will cover other ways to deal with common latch types.

Introduction to Latches

There is a concept in computer science called *mutual exclusion*, which means multiple threads or processes cannot execute critical code simultaneously. Think about the multithreaded application in which threads use the shared objects. In those systems, you often need to serialize the code that accesses those objects to avoid creating race conditions when multiple threads read and update them simultaneously.[1]

Internally, SQL Server enforces mutual exclusion and protects in-memory data structures by using latches. People are often confused by latches' similarities to locks: both

---

[1] Every development language has a set of synchronization primitives: for example, mutexes and critical sections. In T-SQL, you can use application locks to serialize access to some code. I am not covering them in this book; however, you can read about them in my book *Expert SQL Server Transactions and Locking* (Apress, 2018) or in the Microsoft documentation (*https://oreil.ly/vFdLS*).

---

types of objects affect concurrency and may prevent simultaneous access to the same data. There is a subtle difference, however.

SQL Server uses locks to enforce *logical* data consistency, preventing sessions from working with transactionally inconsistent data. Latches, on the other hand, enforce the *physical* consistency of in-memory data structures, preventing corruption by multiple workers that access data structures simultaneously. Latches do not work in transaction boundaries; they are acquired when the worker needs to access an in-memory object and are released after the operation is done.

Consider a situation where multiple sessions need to update different rows on the same data page. Those sessions would not block each other with locks, as long as they don't acquire incompatible locks on the same rows. However, they might block each other with latches to prevent simultaneous updates of the in-memory data page object, which can corrupt it.

There are five different latch types in SQL Server. In terms of compatibility, they are similar to locks, but don't confuse the two, as they are different beasts:

Keep latch

> A keep latch (KP) ensures that the referenced structure cannot be destroyed. It is compatible with all other latch types except the destroy latch. This latch type has similarities to schema stability (Sch-S) locks.

Shared latch

> A shared latch (SH) is required when a thread needs to read the data structure. Shared latches are compatible with each other and with the keep and update latches.

Update latch

> An update latch (UP) allows other threads to read the structure but prevents them from updating it. SQL Server uses them in some scenarios to improve concurrency, similar to update (U) locks. Update latches are compatible with keep and shared latches and incompatible with all other types.

Exclusive latch

> An exclusive latch (EX) is required when a thread modifies the data structure. Conceptually, exclusive latches are similar to exclusive (X) locks; they are incompatible with all other latch types except keep latches.

Destroy latch

> A destroy latch (DT) is required to destroy a data structure. For example, a destroy latch would be acquired when the lazy writer process removes a data page from the buffer pool. These latches are incompatible with other latch types.

When the worker cannot obtain a latch on the data structure, it becomes suspended and generates a latch-related wait type. These wait types can belong to one of three categories:

PAGEIOLATCH

The PAGEIOLATCH waits indicate I/O-related latches. SQL Server uses these latches and wait types while waiting for data pages to be read from disk to the buffer pool. A large percentage of such waits could indicate a large number of nonoptimized queries and/or suboptimal disk subsystem performance. Chapter 3 covers how to troubleshoot these conditions, so I am not going to focus on these latches in this chapter.

PAGELATCH

PAGELATCH waits indicate latches related to the buffer pool, which occur when threads need to access or modify data and allocation map pages in the buffer pool. As you know from Chapter 9, these waits can be triggered by contention in tempdb system catalogs. I'll talk about other conditions that can trigger them later in this chapter.

LATCH

LATCH waits are all other latches not related to the buffer pool. I'll talk about them later in this chapter.

SQL Server uses different wait types for each latch type. For example, PAGELATCH_EX indicates the wait for an exclusive (EX) latch on the buffer pool page. The LATCH_SH wait type shows a shared (SH) non-buffer pool latch wait.

Let's look at the latch categories in depth.

Page Latches

SQL Server uses page latches to protect the consistency of the buffer pool pages in memory. When a worker needs to change anything on the page, it obtains an exclusive (EX) page latch. Similarly, when a worker needs to read something from the page, it acquires a shared (SH) page latch. The workers can read the data simultaneously; however, only one worker can modify the page at any given time, and only when no other workers are accessing it.

The impact of page latches greatly depends on the system load and workload patterns. SQL Server reads data from and writes data to in-memory pages very quickly; you might not notice it in a system with a light load and a small number of concurrent users. However, page latch contention increases with the number of active sessions simultaneously accessing the same data pages.

There are two common reasons for page latch contention. They are not mutually exclusive and both can contribute to a high percentage of PAGELATCH waits on the server. You need to address both when troubleshooting.

The first is related to tempdb. A heavy concurrent tempdb workload may introduce latch contention on system pages (Chapter 9 discusses how to detect and mitigate that condition).

The second most common case for page latching usually occurs in users' tables. It is called the *hotspot*. Hotspots usually occur in indexes with ever-increasing (or ever-decreasing) values, such as identities, sequences, or datetime columns that populate with the time when rows are inserted. When multiple sessions simultaneously insert data into those indexes, all rows are placed on the same page (the last one), which leads to page latch contention as workers start blocking each other.

Let's look at a hypothetical scenario in which you want to log application-request information in the database. Listing 10-1 creates a few tables to store the data.

 Do not consider this implementation a real-life example. In fact, relational databases are usually the worst place to store logs. I am using it only for the sake of demonstrating page latch contention.

Listing 10-1. Creating tables to store the logs

```
CREATE TABLE dbo.WebRequests_Disk
(
    RequestId INT NOT NULL identity(1,1),
    RequestTime DATETIME2(4) NOT NULL
        CONSTRAINT DEF_WebRequests_Disk_RequestTime
        DEFAULT SYSUTCDATETIME(),
    URL VARCHAR(255) NOT NULL,
    RequestType TINYINT NOT NULL,
    ClientIP VARCHAR(15) NOT NULL,
    BytesReceived INT NOT NULL,

    CONSTRAINT PK_WebRequests_Disk
    PRIMARY KEY NONCLUSTERED(RequestId)
);

CREATE UNIQUE CLUSTERED INDEX IDX_WebRequests_Disk_RequestTime_RequestId
ON dbo.WebRequests_Disk(RequestTime,RequestId);

CREATE TABLE dbo.WebRequestHeaders_Disk
(
    RequestId INT NOT NULL,
    HeaderName VARCHAR(64) NOT NULL,
    HeaderValue VARCHAR(256) NOT NULL,
```

```
    CONSTRAINT PK_WebRequestHeaders_Disk
    PRIMARY KEY CLUSTERED(RequestId,HeaderName)
);

CREATE TABLE dbo.WebRequestParams_Disk
(
    RequestId INT NOT NULL,
    ParamName VARCHAR(64) NOT NULL,
    ParamValue NVARCHAR(256) NOT NULL,

    CONSTRAINT PK_WebRequestParams_Disk
    PRIMARY KEY CLUSTERED(RequestId,ParamName)
);
```

Next, I will run the application, which will insert data into those tables from multiple threads simultaneously. You can get the application code from the book's companion material.

Figure 10-1 shows the metrics from my test server when the application was running. Although the duration of individual latch waits was very short—just a fraction of a millisecond—cumulatively they contributed to very large numbers and limited application throughput. CPU load had *not* been maxed out when that happened.

\\SQL2019-1	
Processor Information	**_Total**
% Processor Time	78.151
SQLServer:Latches	
Average Latch Wait Time (ms)	0.520
Latch Waits/sec	99,849.146
SQLServer:SQL Statistics	
Batch Requests/sec	6,085.086

Figure 10-1. Performance metrics during page latch contention

Figure 10-2 shows wait statistics, obtained with the code in Listing 2-1. As you can see, PAGELATCH_EX and PAGELATCH_SH waits contribute to more than 60% of the total waits.

	Wait Type	Wait Count	Wait Time	Avg Wait Time	Avg Signal Wait Time	Avg Resource Wait Time	Percent	Running Percent
1	PAGELATCH_EX	1951297	749.168	0.0	0.0	0.0	45.332	45.332
2	WRITELOG	389893	488.770	1.0	0.0	1.0	29.575	74.908
3	PAGELATCH_SH	672816	303.111	0.0	0.0	0.0	18.341	93.249

Figure 10-2. Wait statistics with page latch contention

You can detect the indexes that introduce the most page latch waits using the sys.dm_db_index_operational_stats function (*https://oreil.ly/W5Sub*). As you can guess by the name, this function tracks indexes' operational metrics, including the number of latches and their wait times.

The code in Listing 10-2 detects indexes that contribute to hotspots. This is a very simplified implementation, however; I'll provide more sophisticated code to analyze indexes' health and usage in Chapter 14.

Listing 10-2. Analyzing page latch index statistics

```
SELECT
    s.name + '.' + t.name as [table]
    ,i.index_id
    ,i.name as [index]
    ,SUM(os.page_latch_wait_count) AS [latch count]
    ,SUM(os.page_latch_wait_in_ms) as [latch wait (ms)]
FROM
    sys.indexes i WITH (NOLOCK) JOIN sys.tables t WITH (NOLOCK) on
        i.object_id = t.object_id
    JOIN sys.schemas s WITH (NOLOCK) ON
        t.schema_id = s.schema_id
    CROSS APPLY
        sys.dm_db_index_operational_stats
        (
            DB_ID()
            ,t.object_id
            ,i.index_id
            ,0
        ) os
GROUP BY
    s.name, t.name, i.name, i.index_id
ORDER BY
    SUM(os.page_latch_wait_in_ms) DESC;
```

Figure 10-3 shows the output from the code in Listing 10-2. As you can see, the data allows you to detect problematic indexes in the database quickly.

	table	index_id	index	latch count	latch wait (ms)
1	dbo.WebRequestHeaders_Disk	1	PK_WebRequestHeaders_Disk	2230279	933152
2	dbo.WebRequestParams_Disk	1	PK_WebRequestParams_Disk	356426	112319
3	dbo.WebRequests_Disk	1	IDX_WebRequests_Disk_Requ...	36621	7568
4	dbo.WebRequests_Disk	2	PK_WebRequests_Disk	984	722

Figure 10-3. Output from the sys.dm_db_index_operational_stats function

Addressing Hotspots: The OPTIMIZE_FOR_SEQUENTIAL_KEY Index Option

Unfortunately, addressing page latching due to hotspots is not an easy task, especially in old versions of SQL Server. In SQL Server 2019 and later, you can enable the OPTIMIZE_FOR_SEQUENTIAL_KEY index property. This setting will improve throughput in hotspot scenarios, but will not solve the problem completely.

Let's enable that setting, as shown in Listing 10-3, and repeat the test. I also recommend clearing wait statistics before restarting the application.

Listing 10-3. Enabling the OPTIMIZE_FOR_SEQUENTIAL_KEY option (SQL Server 2019 and later)

```
ALTER INDEX PK_WebRequestHeaders_Disk
ON dbo.WebRequestHeaders_Disk
SET (OPTIMIZE_FOR_SEQUENTIAL_KEY = ON);

ALTER INDEX PK_WebRequestParams_Disk
ON dbo.WebRequestParams_Disk
SET (OPTIMIZE_FOR_SEQUENTIAL_KEY = ON);
```

Figure 10-4 shows performance metrics when OPTIMIZE_FOR_SEQUENTIAL_KEY is enabled. As you can see, this option improves throughput; however, the latch waits are still significant.

\\SQL2019-1	
Processor Information	**_Total**
% Processor Time	93.724
SQLServer:Latches	
Average Latch Wait Time (ms)	0.306
Latch Waits/sec	13,659.224
SQLServer:SQL Statistics	
Batch Requests/sec	8,694.424

Figure 10-4. Performance metrics with OPTIMIZE_FOR_SEQUENTIAL_KEY enabled

Figure 10-5 shows the wait statistics. You can see the new wait type, BTREE_INSERT_FLOW_CONTROL, in the output. This wait type is specific to OPTIMIZE_FOR_SEQUENTIAL_KEY implementation and, for all practical purposes, masks PAGELATCH waits and latch contention in wait statistics.

	Wait Type	Wait Count	Wait Time	Avg Wait Time	Avg Signal Wait Time	Avg Resource Wait Time	Percent	Running Percent
1	WRITELOG	609044	1020.615	1.0	0.0	1.0	60.430	60.430
2	BTREE_INSERT_FLOW_CONTROL	1477495	554.722	0.0	0.0	0.0	32.845	93.275
3	PAGELATCH_EX	1128697	99.052	0.0	0.0	0.0	5.865	99.140

Figure 10-5. Wait statistics with OPTIMIZE_FOR_SEQUENTIAL_KEY enabled

While enabling OPTIMIZE_FOR_SEQUENTIAL_KEY may help improve throughput in hotspot situations, it does not completely eliminate latching. Moreover, this option is not available in older versions of SQL Server (prior to 2019). In those cases, you have very few options besides refactoring database schema and applications.

You need to detect and analyze indexes that contribute the most to latching. Review index usage (I'll share a few helpful techniques in Chapter 14) and determine if problematic indexes can be dropped or altered in ways that prevent them from constantly increasing and contributing to hotspots.

 Clustered indexes defined on identity columns in active tables are one of the most common places for hotspots. To address this, use clustered indexes that spread insert activity across the table.

Addressing Hotspots: Hash Partitioning

One technique that allows you to spread inserts across a table is called *hash partitioning*. You can partition the table and use different hash values to spread rows across multiple partitions.

Listing 10-4 shows such an example. It redefines two of the tables from Listing 10-1, partitioning them with a new HashVal column calculated as RequestId % 16. This distributes the data across 16 partitions, reducing insertion rates and latch contention on each individual partition.

Note that the HashVal column is defined as the rightmost column in the indexes, to preserve the sorting order on each individual partition.

Listing 10-4. Implementing hash partitioning

```
-- For demo purposes
TRUNCATE TABLE dbo.WebRequests_Disk;
DROP TABLE dbo.WebRequestHeaders_Disk;
DROP TABLE dbo.WebRequestParams_Disk;
GO

CREATE PARTITION FUNCTION pfHash(int)
AS RANGE LEFT FOR VALUES
(0,1,2,3,4,5,6,7,8,10,11,12,13,14,15);
```

```
CREATE PARTITION SCHEME psHash
AS PARTITION pfHash
ALL TO ([PRIMARY]);

CREATE TABLE dbo.WebRequestHeaders_Disk
(
    RequestId INT NOT NULL,
    HeaderName VARCHAR(64) NOT NULL,
    HeaderValue VARCHAR(256) NOT NULL,
    HashVal AS RequestId % 16 PERSISTED,

    CONSTRAINT PK_WebRequestHeaders_Disk
    PRIMARY KEY CLUSTERED(RequestId,HeaderName,HashVal)
    ON psHash(HashVal)
);

CREATE TABLE dbo.WebRequestParams_Disk
(
    RequestId INT NOT NULL,
    ParamName VARCHAR(64) NOT NULL,
    ParamValue nVARCHAR(256) NOT NULL,
    HashVal AS RequestId % 16 PERSISTED,

    CONSTRAINT PK_WebRequestParams_Disk
    PRIMARY KEY CLUSTERED(RequestId,ParamName,HashVal)
    ON psHash(HashVal)
);
```

Figure 10-6 shows the performance metrics on my test server with hash partitioning implemented. The insert throughput is slightly better than with the OPTIMIZE_FOR_SEQUENTIAL_KEY approach; however, the difference is relatively small. Your mileage may vary, of course, and results may differ in other use cases and workloads.

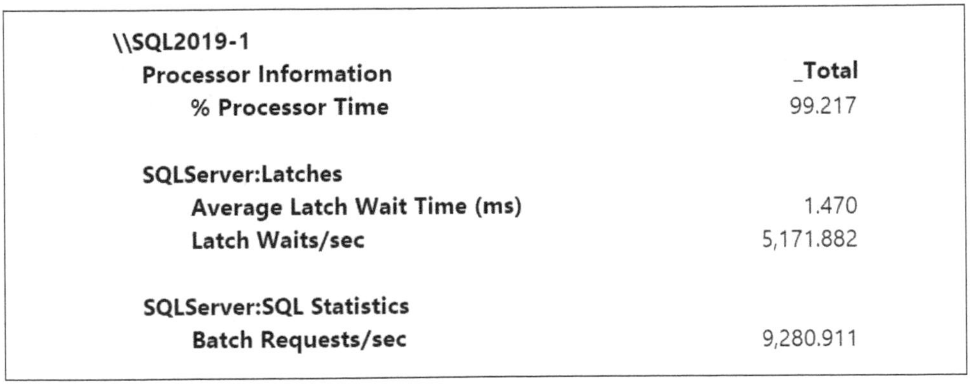

\\SQL2019-1	
Processor Information	**_Total**
% Processor Time	99.217
SQLServer:Latches	
Average Latch Wait Time (ms)	1.470
Latch Waits/sec	5,171.882
SQLServer:SQL Statistics	
Batch Requests/sec	9,280.911

Figure 10-6. Performance metrics with hash partitioning

Figure 10-7 shows the wait statistics. As you see, the page latch wait percentage is lower than it would be without partitioning (shown in Figure 10-2).

	Wait Type	Wait Count	Wait Time	Avg Wait Time	Avg Signal Wait Time	Avg Resource Wait Time	Percent	Running Percent
1	WRITELOG	331696	722.286	2.0	0.0	1.0	66.211	66.211
2	PAGELATCH_EX	1248937	291.905	0.0	0.0	0.0	26.759	92.970
3	PAGELATCH_SH	246413	68.703	0.0	0.0	0.0	6.298	99.268

Figure 10-7. Wait statistics with hash partitioning

While hash partitioning may help reduce latch contention, it is dangerous. As with any partitioning, the data will be spread across multiple internal tables (partitions). This will change execution plans and may lead to regressions in query performance.

From a contention reduction standpoint, hash partitioning will achieve the best results when the number of partitions would be equal to the number of logical CPU cores on the server. However, the larger number of partitions may increase the risk of performance regressions. Keep this in mind when you design the approach, and carefully test the system when you implement it. I consider hash partitioning a last resort when dealing with page latch contention.

In some cases, you can reduce the side effects of hash partitioning by using staging tables. In this scenario, the application may insert data into hash-partitioned staging tables and have another process running on schedule, copying data from the staging to the main tables. While this approach adds some overhead in terms of staging table management, it protects against the unanticipated performance regressions that hash partitioning can introduce.

Addressing Hotspots: In-Memory OLTP

It is impossible to discuss performance issues introduced by latching without mentioning In-Memory OLTP. After all, one of the main goals of that technology is to address latching and locking challenges with disk-based tables under heavy concurrent loads. Memory-optimized tables are free of latches and locks and would scale perfectly under a concurrent OLTP workload.

These benefits don't come for free, though. In-Memory OLTP and memory-optimized tables behave differently than classic Storage Engine and disk-based tables. You need to design the system properly and utilize technology to avoid possible side effects and issues. As with hash partitioning, you may get performance regressions if you simply switch disk-based tables to become memory-optimized tables without taking different technology behavior into consideration.

Fortunately, memory-optimized tables are perfect candidates for staging tables. You can completely eliminate hotspots and latch contention and reduce any possible side effects In-Memory OLTP may introduce. Consider it a valid implementation option to solve hotspot problems.

I will repeat my word of caution, though: you need to know how to deploy and maintain In-Memory OLTP properly before using it. You can read my book *Expert SQL Server In-Memory OLTP* (Apress, 2017) to learn more.

Other Latch Types

The third latch category, non-buffer-pool latches, presents itself with generic LATCH wait types. Similar to wait statistics, you can get information about individual latch types using the sys.dm_os_latch_stats view (*https://oreil.ly/UqHne*) shown in Listing 10-5. You can also clear latch statistics with the command DBCC SQLPERF('sys.dm_os_latch_stats', CLEAR).

Listing 10-5. Analyzing latch statistics

```
;WITH Latches
AS
(
    SELECT
        latch_class, wait_time_ms, waiting_requests_count
        ,100. * wait_time_ms / SUM(wait_time_ms) OVER() AS Pct
        ,100. * SUM(wait_time_ms) OVER(ORDER BY wait_time_ms DESC) /
            NULLIF(SUM(wait_time_ms) OVER(), 0) AS RunningPct
        ,ROW_NUMBER() OVER(ORDER BY wait_time_ms DESC) AS RowNum
    FROM
        sys.dm_os_latch_stats WITH (NOLOCK)
    WHERE
        wait_time_ms > 0 AND
        latch_class NOT IN (N'BUFFER',N'SLEEP_TASK')
)
SELECT
    l1.latch_class AS [Latch Type]
    ,l1.waiting_requests_count AS [Latch Count]
    ,CONVERT(DECIMAL(12,3), l1.wait_time_ms / 1000.0)
        AS [Wait Time]
    ,CONVERT(DECIMAL(12,1), l1.wait_time_ms / l1.waiting_requests_count)
        AS [Avg Wait Time]
    ,CONVERT(DECIMAL(6,3), l1.Pct)
        AS [Percent]
    ,CONVERT(DECIMAL(6,3), l1.RunningPct)
        AS [Running Percent]
FROM
    Latches l1
WHERE
    l1.RunningPct <= 99 OR l1.RowNum = 1
ORDER BY
```

```
    l1.RunningPct
OPTION (RECOMPILE, MAXDOP 1);
```

Figure 10-8 shows the output from one of the servers.

	Latch Type	Latch Count	Wait Time	Avg Wait Time	Percent	Running Percent
1	ACCESS_METHODS_DATASET_PARENT	3858110729	1249807.056	0.0	47.031	47.031
2	NESTING_TRANSACTION_FULL	766539824	972751.713	1.0	36.605	83.635
3	TRACE_CONTROLLER	38694619	270191.197	6.0	10.167	93.803

Figure 10-8. Latch statistics

Unfortunately, latch types are poorly documented. You often need to search multiple sources to understand the meaning of each latch. Nevertheless, let's look at a few common types you will encounter:

Parallelism-related latches

There are multiple parallelism-related latch types. The most common are ACCESS_METHOD_DATASET_PARENT, ACCESS_METHODS_SCAN_RANGE_GENERATOR, ACCESS_METHODS_SCAN_KEY_GENERATOR, and NESTING_TRANSATION_FULL. In my experience, these latches usually appear at the top of the list in the sys.dm_os_latch_stats view output.

Treat these latches as you would parallelism waits (CXPACKET, CXCONSUMER, and EXCHANGE), which often appear alongside parallelism-related latches. Analyze and tune parallelism usage to address this, as discussed in Chapter 6.

LOG_MANAGER

The LOG_MANAGER latch type indicates growth in the transaction log. You may see this latch in situations where something is regularly preventing the transaction log from being truncated. Monitor the log_reuse_wait_desc column in the sys.databases view to troubleshoot it (more on this in Chapter 11).

I have also encountered this latch type in systems that regularly shrink the transaction log after each log backup. This is a bad practice, since the log file is zero initializing at the time of growth.

ACCESS_METHODS_HOBT_VIRTUAL_ROOT

The ACCESS_METHODS_HOBT_VIRTUAL_ROOT latch is used during access to the index metadata. Significant presence of this latch indicates a large number of page splits of the root pages in B-Tree Indexes. Usually this happens in small indexes with very volatile data; for example, tables that operate as in-database queues.

You can detect potentially problematic indexes with the `tree_page_latch_wait_count` and `tree_page_latch_wait_time_ms` columns in the `sys.db_db_index_operational_stats` view (more in Chapter 14).

ACCESS_METHODS_HOBT_COUNT

The `ACCESS_METHODS_HOBT_COUNT` latch is used to update page and row count information in table metadata. Contention with this latch indicates lots of small concurrent data modifications in some tables.

Chapter 14 will discuss how to track the number of modifications in the indexes using the `sys.db_db_index_usage_stats` view. This may help you detect tables with a large number of modifications. However, it may be easier to work with the development team instead of using SQL Server views, since addressing this latch contention usually requires application changes.

FGCB_ADD_REMOVE

The `FGCB_ADD_REMOVE` latch occurs when adding, removing, growing, and shrinking files in the filegroup. Check whether *Instant File Initialization* is enabled and the *Auto Shrink* database option is disabled. Also check that auto-growth parameters are not growing files in very small chunks.

You may also see this latch in databases with a very large number of data files, especially in `tempdb`. Reevaluate database configuration to address it.

TRACE_CONTROLLER

As you can guess by the name, the `TRACE_CONTROLLER` latch indicates a large number of traces. Evaluate your monitoring strategy and remove unnecessary monitoring when you see this latch.

Similar to waits, latches are unavoidable. They are completely acceptable in small numbers; however, excessive latching is usually a sign of issues in the system. Don't jump to immediate action, though—identify and address the root causes!

Summary

Latches are lightweight synchronization objects that protect the consistency of SQL Server internal data structures. They are usually short-lived and may be unnoticeable in systems with light loads. However, as loads grow, latch contention may become an issue, limiting system scalability and throughput.

There are three categories of latches. Each latch type (shared, exclusive, etc.) has a corresponding wait type in the wait statistics.

PAGEIOLATCH waits occur when SQL Server waits for the data page to be read to the buffer pool. A significant percentage of these waits require you to troubleshoot disk subsystem load (see Chapter 3).

Page latches and corresponding `PAGELATCH` waits occur when multiple workers are simultaneously accessing and updating data pages in memory. They are usually triggered by `tempdb` system object contention or by hotspots in ever-increasing indexes in users' databases.

In SQL Server 2019 and later, you can reduce the impact of hotspots by enabling the `OPTIMIZE_FOR_SEQUENTIAL_KEY` index option. However, in many cases, you need to drop or change the index, or implement workarounds with hash partitioning and/or staging tables.

Latches not related to the buffer pool present themselves with `LATCH` wait types. You can obtain latch statistics with the `sys.dm_os_latch_stats` view. Identify and address the root cause of these issues when you troubleshoot them.

In the next chapter, we will look at transaction log problems you may encounter.

Troubleshooting Checklist

☐ Analyze the impact of page latches with `PAGELATCH` waits.

☐ Detect whether `PAGELATCH` waits are coming from `tempdb` or hotspots in users' databases.

☐ Address `tempdb` system object contention (Chapter 9).

☐ Identify indexes that contribute to hotspots with the `sys.dm_db_index_opera tional_stats` view. Analyze whether indexes can be refactored or dropped (more in Chapter 14).

☐ Enable the `OPTIMIZE_FOR_SEQUENTIAL_KEY` option in SQL Server 2019 and later.

☐ Consider refactoring the application using In-Memory OLTP, staging tables, and/or hash partitioning if neither of the other options helps with hotspots.

☐ Review latch statistics with the `sys.dm_os_latch_stats` view; troubleshoot and address issues if necessary.

CHAPTER 11

Transaction Log

Every database in SQL Server has one transaction log implemented as one or more transaction log files in addition to data files. The transaction log stores information about the changes made in the database and allows SQL Server to recover databases to a transactionally consistent state in case of an unexpected shutdown or crash. Every data modification in the database is stored there, and low transaction log latency is essential for good system performance.

In this chapter, I'll explain how SQL Server logs transactions and how the transaction log works internally. Next, I'll cover several best practices for transaction log configuration and talk about how to address "Transaction log full" situations. Finally, I'll discuss how to troubleshoot insufficient transaction log performance.

Transaction Log Internals

SQL Server uses a transaction log to keep each database in a *transactionally consistent* state, meaning that data modifications done from within transactions must be either committed or rolled back in full. SQL Server never allows data to be transactionally inconsistent by applying just a subset of the changes from uncommitted transactions.

The transaction log guarantees consistency. It stores the stream of *log records* generated by data modifications and some internal operations. Every log record has a unique, auto-incrementing *Log Sequence Number* (*LSN*) and describes the data change. It includes information about the affected row, the old and new versions of the data, the transaction that performed the modification, and so forth.

Every data page keeps the LSN of the last log record that modified it. During recovery, SQL Server can compare the LSNs of the log records and data pages and find out if the most recent changes were saved to the data files. There is enough information stored in a log record to undo or redo the operation if needed.

SQL Server uses *Write-Ahead Logging* (*WAL*), which guarantees that log records are always written to the log file *before* dirty data pages are saved to the database. Sharp-eyed readers may notice that in Chapter 3, I mentioned that log records are saved synchronously with data modifications and data pages are saved asynchronously during the checkpoint process. While that is conceptually correct, I will be more precise here: SQL Server caches the log records in small memory caches called *log buffers*, writing them in batches to reduce the number of log-write I/O operations.

Each database has its own log buffer, consisting of 60 KB structures called *log blocks*. Each log buffer (and database) can have up to 128 log blocks. SQL Server writes log blocks to the log file in a single I/O operation. However, it does not always wait until the log block is full. The typical size of a log-writing I/O operation varies, from 512 bytes to 60 KB.

Unfortunately, the SQL Server documentation is inconsistent in its terminology and often references *log blocks* as *log buffers*. Just remember that SQL Server caches the log records in memory before writing them to disk.

Data Modifications and Transaction Logging

Let's look at how SQL Server modifies data in more detail. Figure 11-1 shows a database with an empty log buffer and transaction log. The last transaction in the log has an LSN of 7314.

Let's assume there are two active transactions: T1 and T2. The BEGIN TRAN log records for both of those transactions have already been saved in the log and are not shown in the diagram.

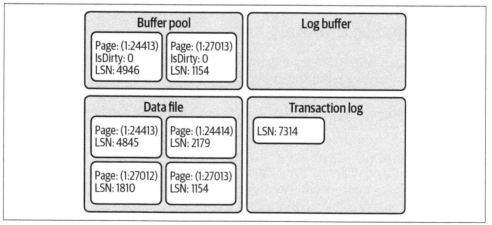

Figure 11-1. Data modifications and transaction logging: initial state

Let's assume that transaction T1 updates one of the rows on the page (1:24413). This operation generates a new log record, which will be placed into the log buffer. It will also update the data page, marking it as dirty and changing the LSN in the page header. Figure 11-2 illustrates this.

At this point, the log record has not been saved to the log file (this is often called *hardened*). It does not introduce any issues as long as the data page has not been saved in the data file. In the event of an SQL Server crash, both the log record and the modifications on the data page will be gone—which is fine, because the transaction has not been committed.

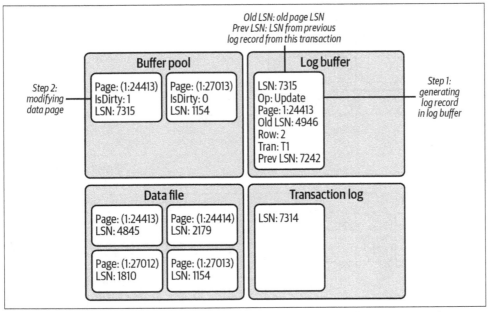

Figure 11-2. Data modifications and transaction logging: state after the first update

Next, let's assume transaction T2 inserts a new row on the page (1:27013), while transaction T1 deletes another row on the same page. These operations generate two log records that are placed into the log buffer, as shown in Figure 11-3. Right now, all log records are still in the log buffer.

Now let's assume an application commits transaction T2. This action generates a COMMIT log record and forces SQL Server to write (harden) the contents of the log block to disk. It writes *all* log records from the buffer to disk, regardless of what transaction generated them (Figure 11-4).

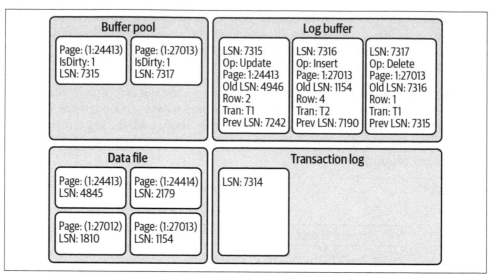

Figure 11-3. Data modifications and transaction logging: state after two data modifications

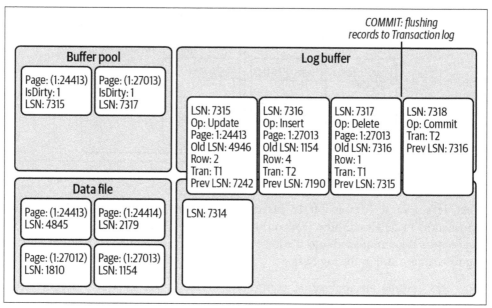

Figure 11-4. Data modifications and transaction logging: commit operation

The applications receive confirmation that the transaction has been committed *only* after all log records are hardened. Even though the data page (1:27013) is still dirty and has not been saved into the data file, the hardened log records on the disk have enough information to reapply the changes made by the committed T2 transaction if needed.

The dirty pages from the buffer pool will be saved to data files on the checkpoint. This operation also generates a CHECKPOINT log record and immediately hardens it into the log. Figure 11-5 shows this state.

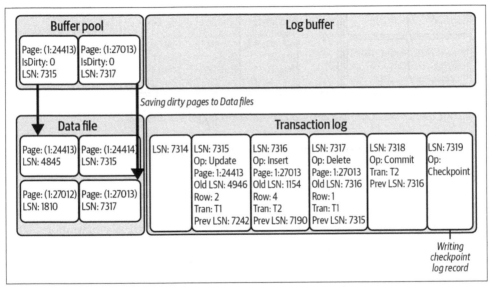

Figure 11-5. Data modifications and transaction logging: checkpoint

After the checkpoint occurs, the pages in the data file may store data from uncommitted transactions (T1 in our example). However, log records in the transaction log include enough information to undo the changes if needed. When this is the case, SQL Server performs *compensation operations*, executing actions opposite those that made the original data modifications and generating compensation log records.

Figure 11-6 shows such an example; in this case, rolling transaction T1 back. Here, SQL Server has performed a compensation update, generating a compensation log record (LSN: 7320) to reverse the changes of the original update operation (LSN: 7315). It has also generated a compensation insert (LSN: 7321) to compensate for the delete operation (LSN: 7317).

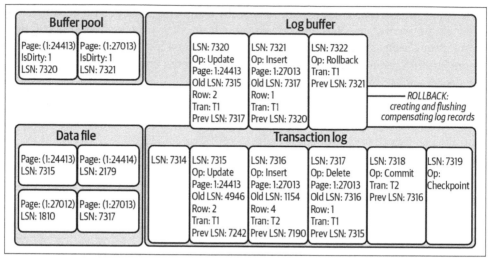

Figure 11-6. Data modifications and transaction logging: rollback

There are two transaction logging–related waits to monitor:

WRITELOG

>   WRITELOG waits occur when SQL Server is waiting for the completion of an I/O operation that writes a log block to disk. With the exception of delayed durability (covered later in this chapter), this type of wait is synchronous, since it prevents transactions from committing while the write I/O is in progress. Your goal should be to minimize this wait and improve transaction log throughput as much as possible.

LOGBUFFER

>   LOGBUFFER waits occur when SQL Server is waiting for an available log block to save the log records. In most cases, this happens due to insufficient I/O through-put, when SQL Server cannot write log blocks to disk fast enough. Usually, when LOGBUFFER waits are present, you'll also see WRITELOG waits. Improving transaction log throughput would help address that.

I will talk about how to troubleshoot and improve log file throughput later in this chapter.

You can also improve transaction log performance by reducing the amount of logging. You can do this by removing unnecessary and unused indexes (more on this in Chapter 14), tuning your index maintenance strategy to reduce page splits, and reducing the row size in frequently modified indexes.

You can also improve your transaction management strategy by avoiding auto-committed transactions. This greatly reduces the amount of logging and the number of write-log I/O requests in the system. Let's look at this in more detail.

Explicit and Auto-Committed Transactions and Log Overhead

As you learned in Chapter 8, SQL Server always executes statements in the context of a transaction. If you don't have any explicit or implicit transactions started, SQL Server runs the statement in an auto-committed transaction, as if that statement were wrapped into a `BEGIN TRAN ... COMMIT` block.

From a logging standpoint, the transaction management operators—`BEGIN TRAN`, `COMMIT`, and `ROLLBACK`—generate `BEGIN XACT`, `COMMIT XACT`, and `ROLLBACK XACT` transaction log records, respectively. In auto-committed transactions, the log records from each data modification statement also include `BEGIN XACT` and `COMMIT XACT` records. This can significantly increase the amount of logging in the system, and more importantly, it also decreases log performance, since SQL Server has to flush the log blocks after each statement on every `COMMIT` operation.

Figure 11-7 illustrates this. `INSERT_1`, `UPDATE_1`, and `DELETE_1` operations run in auto-committed transactions, generating additional log records and forcing the log buffer to flush on each `COMMIT`. Alternatively, running those operations in explicit transactions leads to more efficient logging.

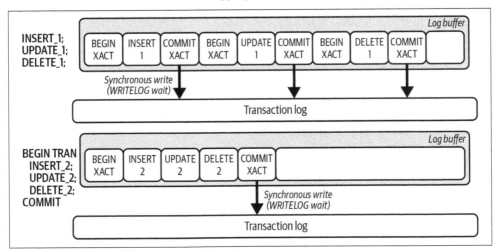

Figure 11-7. Explicit and auto-committed transactions

The code in Listing 11-1 shows the overhead involved in auto-committed transactions as compared to explicit transactions. It performs an `INSERT/UPDATE/DELETE` sequence 10,000 times in the loop, in auto-committed and explicit transactions, respectively. It then compares their execution time and transaction log throughput using the sys.dm_io_virtual_file_stats view.

Listing 11-1. Explicit and auto-committed transactions

```
CREATE TABLE dbo.TranOverhead
(
    Id INT NOT NULL,
    Col CHAR(50) NULL,
    CONSTRAINT PK_TranOverhead
    PRIMARY KEY CLUSTERED(Id)
);

-- Auto-committed transactions
DECLARE
    @Id INT = 1
    ,@StartTime DATETIME = GETDATE()
    ,@num_of_writes BIGINT
    ,@num_of_bytes_written BIGINT

SELECT @num_of_writes = num_of_writes, @num_of_bytes_written = num_of_bytes_written
FROM sys.dm_io_virtual_file_stats(db_id(),2);

WHILE @Id <= 10000
BEGIN
    INSERT INTO dbo.TranOverhead(Id, Col) VALUES(@Id, 'A');
    UPDATE dbo.TranOverhead SET Col = 'B' WHERE Id = @Id;
    DELETE FROM dbo.TranOverhead WHERE Id = @Id;

    SET @Id += 1;
END;

SELECT
    DATEDIFF(MILLISECOND,@StartTime,GETDATE())
        AS [Time(ms): Autocommitted Tran]
    ,s.num_of_writes - @num_of_writes
        AS [Number of writes]
    ,(s.num_of_bytes_written - @num_of_bytes_written) / 1024
        AS [Bytes written (KB)]
FROM
    sys.dm_io_virtual_file_stats(db_id(),2) s;
GO

-- Explicit Tran
DECLARE
    @Id INT = 1
    ,@StartTime DATETIME = GETDATE()
    ,@num_of_writes BIGINT
    ,@num_of_bytes_written BIGINT

SELECT @num_of_writes = num_of_writes, @num_of_bytes_written = num_of_bytes_written
```

```
FROM sys.dm_io_virtual_file_stats(db_id(),2);

WHILE @Id <= 10000
BEGIN
    BEGIN TRAN
        INSERT INTO dbo.TranOverhead(Id, Col) VALUES(@Id, 'A');
        UPDATE dbo.TranOverhead SET Col = 'B' WHERE Id = @Id;
        DELETE FROM dbo.TranOverhead WHERE Id = @Id;
    COMMIT
    SET @Id += 1;
END;

SELECT
    DATEDIFF(MILLISECOND,@StartTime,GETDATE())
        AS [Time(ms): Explicit Tran]
    ,s.num_of_writes - @num_of_writes
        AS [Number of writes]
    ,(s.num_of_bytes_written - @num_of_bytes_written) / 1024
        AS [Bytes written (KB)]
FROM
    sys.dm_io_virtual_file_stats(db_id(),2) s;
```

You can see the output from the code in my environment in Figure 11-8. Explicit transactions were about three times faster and generated three times less log activity than auto-committed transactions.

	Time(ms): Autocommitted Tran	Number of writes	Bytes written (KB)
1	13117	30000	15670

	Time(ms): Explicit Tran	Number of writes	Bytes written (KB)
1	4500	10000	10658

Figure 11-8. Performance of explicit and auto-committed transactions

As I have stated, proper transaction management with explicit transactions can significantly improve your transaction log throughput. Remember the impact of long-running transactions on blocking, however. Exclusive (X) locks are held until the end of the transaction. Keep this locking behavior in mind as you design your transaction strategy and write your code, as well as considering the factors discussed in Chapter 8.

Unfortunately, changing your transaction strategy in existing systems is not always possible. If your system suffers from a large number of auto-committed transactions and can tolerate a small amount of data loss, consider using another feature: *Delayed Durability*. This feature is available in SQL Server 2014 and later.

Delayed Durability

As you already know, SQL Server flushes the contents of the log block into a log file at the time of a commit. It sends a confirmation to the client only after a commit record has been hardened to disk. This may lead to a large number of small log-write I/O requests with auto-committed transactions.

Delayed durability changes this behavior, making commit operations asynchronous. The client immediately receives confirmation that the transaction has been committed, without having to wait for the commit record to be hardened to disk. The commit record stays in the log buffer until one or more of the following conditions occur:

- The log block is full.
- A fully durable transaction in the same database is committed, and its commit record flushes the contents of the log buffer to disk.
- A CHECKPOINT operation occurs.
- The sp_flush_log stored procedure is called.
- A log buffer flush operation is triggered based on the log generation rate and/or timeout thresholds.

There is obviously some risk here. If SQL Server crashes before the commit record is hardened, the data modifications from that transaction will be rolled back at recovery, as if the transaction had never been committed at all. However, other transactions would be able to see the data modifications made by the delayed durability transaction between the commit and the crash.

You can control delayed durability on both the database and transaction levels. The database option DELAYED_DURABILITY supports three different values:

DISABLED

> This is the default option. It disables delayed durability in the database regardless of the transaction durability mode. All transactions in the database are always fully durable.

FORCED

> This option forces delayed durability for all database transactions regardless of the transaction durability mode.

ALLOWED

> With this option, delayed durability is controlled at the transaction level. Transactions are fully durable unless delayed durability is specified. Listing 11-2 shows how to specify this at the transaction level.

Listing 11-2. Controlling delayed durability at the transaction level

```
BEGIN TRAN
/* Do the work */
COMMIT WITH (DELAYED_DURABILITY=ON);
```

Delayed durability may be used in chatty systems with large numbers of auto-committed transactions and insufficient log throughput. In most cases, however, I prefer to avoid it. I use it as a last resort, only when all other log throughput improvement techniques have been unsuccessful and *only* when data loss is acceptable. Use it with extreme care!

In-Memory OLTP Transaction Logging

Although covering In-Memory OLTP in detail would be beyond the scope of this book, I need to mention In-Memory OLTP transaction logging. As opposed to row-based and column-based technologies, In-Memory OLTP generates transaction log records at the time of the InCOMMIT operation and only when the transaction is successfully committed. Logging is also optimized. Transactions usually generate just one or a few transaction log records, even when they modify large amounts of data. These records are stored in the regular log file and backed up with all the other log records.

This behavior may change I/O patterns for log operations. In-Memory OLTP log writes may lead to larger write requests, especially with large In-Memory OLTP transactions. Moreover, the log files are continuously read by In-Memory OLTP's continuous checkpoint process, which parses log records and updates In-Memory OLTP data persisted on disk.

You don't need to worry about these details in most cases; just remember about I/O patterns when you design an I/O subsystem for databases that use In-Memory OLTP.

Virtual Log Files

Internally, SQL Server divides physical log files into smaller parts called *Virtual Log Files* (VLFs). SQL Server uses them as a unit of management, and they can be active or inactive.

Active VLFs store the active portion of the transaction log, which contains log records required to keep the database transactionally consistent, provide point-in-time recovery, and support active SQL Server processes that rely on log records (transactional replication and AlwaysOn Availability Groups are examples of such processes). An inactive VLF contains the truncated (inactive) and unused parts of the transaction log.

Figure 11-9 shows an example transaction log file and VLFs. The active portion of the log starts with VLF3, the oldest active transaction in the system. In case of a rollback, SQL Server would need to access log records generated by that transaction.

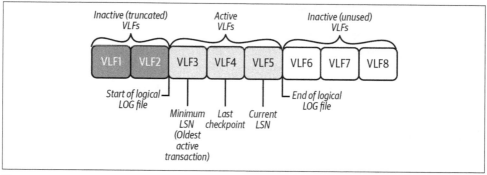

Figure 11-9. Transaction log and VLFs

In Figure 11-9, the only process that keeps VLF3 active is the active transaction. When this transaction commits, SQL Server truncates the log, marking VLF3 as inactive (Figure 11-10). Truncating the transaction log does not reduce the size of the log file on disk; it just means that parts of the transaction log (one or more VLFs) are marked as inactive and are ready for reuse. (This example is intentionally oversimplified; I will cover the conditions when log truncation occurs shortly.)

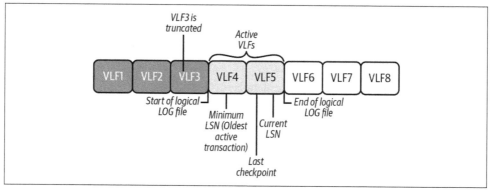

Figure 11-10. Transaction log and VLFs after the commit

SQL Server uses VLFs as the unit of truncation. A VLF cannot be marked as inactive if it contains a single log record from the active portion of the log. This is one reason why having very large VLFs is not a good idea.

Transaction log truncation behavior is controlled by the *Database Recovery Model* setting. There are three recovery models. Each guarantees that the active portion of the log has enough data to keep the database consistent; however, they may provide different levels of recoverability in case of disaster, and the SIMPLE and BULK-LOGGED models may prevent you from using some SQL Server technologies.

Let's take a look at the three recovery models in more detail:

SIMPLE

In the SIMPLE recovery model, the log is truncated at checkpoint. All data pages with LSNs prior to checkpoint LSN are saved on disk. SQL Server does not need to access log records prior to the checkpoint to reapply them to data pages in the event of an unexpected shutdown or crash. Old active transactions and transaction replication may defer truncation, keeping VLFs active.

In this recovery model, SQL Server does not use transaction log backups. The model prevents you from performing a point-in-time recovery and may lead to data loss if either of the database files (data or log) becomes corrupted. The *recovery point* (RPO) for the database, in this model, becomes the time of the last full backup.

In some cases, such as when data is static or can be re-created from other sources, the SIMPLE recovery model may be completely acceptable. However, when you encounter this model during a system health check, you need to confirm its acceptability with the system stakeholders and discuss the possibility of data loss.

FULL

In the FULL recovery model, SQL Server fully logs all operations in the database and requires you to perform transaction log backups to truncate the transaction log. Because the transaction log backups store all log records in the database, this mode supports point-in-time recovery, as long as the sequence of backup files (*backup chain*) is available. With a few exceptions, you will want to use the FULL recovery model in production databases.

To support various SQL Server features and technologies that rely on transaction log records, the FULL recovery model is required. These technologies may also defer truncation of the log, even when log backups are taken. For example, if an AlwaysOn Availability Group node goes offline, SQL Server will be unable to truncate the log until the node is back and catches up with the replication.

BULK-LOGGED

The BULK-LOGGED recovery model works similarly to the FULL model, except that some operations are minimally logged: for example, index creation or BULK INSERT statements. With minimally logged operations, SQL Server logs only the extent allocation information in the log file. While this reduces log file usage, you cannot perform a point-in-time recovery when minimally logged operations are present. As with the SIMPLE recovery model, analyze the frequency of bulk-logged operations and the risks of potential data loss when you see databases with this recovery model in production.

You can analyze VLFs by using the sys.dm_db_log_info (*https://oreil.ly/oZ7DS*) dynamic management view in SQL Server 2016 and later, or with the DBCC LOGINFO command in older versions of SQL Server. Listing 11-3 shows the code that uses this view against one of the databases.

Listing 11-3. Analyzing VLFs in the database

```
SELECT *
FROM sys.dm_db_log_info(DB_ID());

SELECT
    COUNT(*) as [VLF Count]
    ,MIN(vlf_size_mb) as [Min VLF Size (MB)]
    ,MAX(vlf_size_mb) as [Max VLF Size (MB)]
    ,AVG(vlf_size_mb) as [Avg VLF Size (MB)]
FROM sys.dm_db_log_info(DB_ID());
```

Figure 11-11 shows the output from the view for a database with an incorrect log file configuration that uses a 10% auto-growth setting. As you can see, the database has a large number of unevenly sized VLFs.

	database_id	file_id	vlf_begin_offset	vlf_size_mb	vlf_sequence_number	vlf_active	vlf_s1
35	16	2	27459584	2.62	281	1	2
36	16	2	30212096	2.87	282	1	2
37	16	2	33226752	3.18	283	1	2
38	16	2	36569088	3.5	284	1	2
39	16	2	40239104	3.87	285	1	2
40	16	2	44302336	4.25	286	1	2
41	16	2	48758784	4.68	287	1	2
42	16	2	53673984	5.12	288	1	2
43	16	2	59047936	5.62	289	1	2

	VLF Count	Min VLF Size (MB)	Max VLF Size (MB)	Avg VLF Size (MB)
1	105	0.24	1889.87	197.98695238095235

Figure 11-11. Inefficient VLF configuration

Transaction Log Configuration

SQL Server works with transaction logs sequentially while writing and reading a stream of log records. Even though the log may have multiple physical files, SQL Server does not usually benefit from them; in most cases, a single log file is easier to maintain and manage.

There are a couple of edge cases when multiple log files can be beneficial:

- SQL Server may zero-initialize a log file in parallel. This could speed up database creation or restoration if it uses large (multiterabyte) log files.

- If you want to place the transaction log on a fast but small drive, you can create a file pre-allocating the size to fill the fast drive and add another small log file on a larger and slower drive. SQL Server will use the file on the fast drive most of the time; the small file will protect you if the transaction log is full and not truncating.

It is better to manage transaction log size manually, avoiding the overhead of zero-initializing at the time of auto-growth. You can analyze a transaction log's size and re-create the log, pre-allocating the size as needed. Be sure to take log-intensive operations such as index maintenance into account when you do the analysis.

As you learned in Chapter 1, you can rebuild the log by shrinking it to the minimal size and then pre-allocating the space using chunks of 1,024 to 4,096 MB. I usually use 1,024 MB chunks, which will create 128 MB VLFs. If I need *very* large log files— hundreds of gigabytes, or even terabytes—I might use larger chunks.

Do not restrict the log's maximum size and auto-growth: you need to be able to grow the log in case of emergencies!

Log Truncation Issues

Excessive transaction log growth is a common problem that junior or accidental DBAs should be able to handle. It happens when SQL can't truncate the transaction log and reuse the space in the log file. In such cases, the log file continues to grow until it fills the entire disk, switching the database to read-only mode and raising a "Transaction log full" error (error code 9002).

The best way to handle this condition is to avoid it in the first place. As I discussed in Chapter 9, it is essential to monitor for low disk space conditions and set up alerts. Alternatively, you can pre-allocate the log file to fit the entire drive, monitor the amount of free space in the log file, and set an alert when it is low.

If you end up in a "Transaction log full" situation, my most important piece of advice is this: don't panic. First, you need to analyze the root cause of the issue and see if you can mitigate it quickly. You can do this by looking at the log_reuse_wait_desc column in the sys.databases view, either querying it directly or using the more sophisticated version shown in Listing 11-4. This column shows you why the log is not truncated.

Listing 11-4. Analyzing the log_reuse_wait_desc column in the sys.databases view

```
CREATE TABLE #SpaceUsed
(
    database_id SMALLINT NOT NULL,
    file_id SMALLINT NOT NULL,
    space_used DECIMAL(15,3) NOT NULL,
    PRIMARY KEY(database_id, file_id)
);

EXEC master..sp_MSforeachdb
N'USE[?];
INSERT INTO #SpaceUsed(database_id, file_id, space_used)
    SELECT DB_ID(''?''), file_id,
        (size - CONVERT(INT,FILEPROPERTY(name, ''SpaceUsed''))) / 128.
FROM sys.database_files
WHERE type = 1;';

SELECT
    d.database_id, d.name, d.recovery_model_desc
    ,d.state_desc, d.log_reuse_wait_desc, m.physical_name
    ,m.is_percent_growth
    ,IIF(m.is_percent_growth = 1
        ,m.growth
        ,CONVERT(DECIMAL(15,3),m.growth / 128.0)
    ) AS [Growth (MB or %)]
    ,CONVERT(DECIMAL(15,3),m.size / 128.0) AS [Size (MB)]
    ,IIF(m.max_size = -1
        ,-1
        ,CONVERT(DECIMAL(15,3),m.max_size / 128.0)
    ) AS [Max Size(MB)]
    ,s.space_used as [Space Used(MB)]
FROM
    sys.databases d WITH (NOLOCK)
        JOIN sys.master_files m WITH (NOLOCK) ON
        d.database_id = m.database_id
    LEFT OUTER JOIN #SpaceUsed s ON
        s.database_id = m.database_id AND
        s.file_id = m.file_id
ORDER BY
    d.database_id;
```

Figure 11-12 shows some sample from Listing 11-4.

database...	name	recovery...	state_desc	log_reuse_wait_desc	physical_...	is_percent_growth	Growth (MB or %)	Size (MB)	Max Size(MB)	Space Used(MB)
1	master	SIMPLE	ONLINE	NOTHING	M:\SQLDa...	1	10.000	2.250	-1.000	1.328
2	tempdb	SIMPLE	ONLINE	NOTHING	T:\SQLDa...	0	1024.000	1024.000	-1.000	966.094
2	tempdb	SIMPLE	ONLINE	NOTHING	L:\SQLDa...	0	1024.000	1024.000	2097152.000	966.094
3	model	FULL	ONLINE	LOG_BACKUP	M:\SQLDa...	0	1024.000	1024.000	-1.000	1015.336
4	msdb	SIMPLE	ONLINE	NOTHING	M:\SQLDa...	1	10.000	19.625	2097152.000	18.133
5	DBA	SIMPLE	ONLINE	NOTHING	L:\SQLDa...	0	1024.000	1024.000	2097152.000	937.281
16	LogDemo2	FULL	ONLINE	LOG_BACKUP	L:\SQLDa...	0	0.000	20769.0...	21000.000	-16.281

Figure 11-12. Analyzing `log_reuse_wait_desc` *data*

Let's look at the most common reasons for deferred log truncation and `log_reuse_wait_desc` values.

LOG_BACKUP Log Reuse Wait

The `LOG_BACKUP` log reuse wait is one of the most common waits for databases in the `FULL` and `BULK-LOGGED` recovery models. It indicates that the log cannot be truncated due to a lack of recent transaction log backups.

When you see this log reuse wait, check the status of the transaction log backup job. Make sure it is not failing due to a lack of space in the backup destination, or for any other reasons. It is also possible that log backup frequency is not fast enough during log-intensive operations. For example, index maintenance can generate an enormous number of transaction log records in a very short time.

You can mitigate the issue by performing a transaction log backup. Remember to keep the backup file if you run this operation manually using a nonstandard backup destination. The file becomes part of your backup chain and will be required for database recovery.

If you don't use any technologies that rely on the `FULL` recovery model, you can temporarily switch the database to `SIMPLE` mode, which will truncate the transaction log. Remember that this will leave you exposed to data loss. Switch back to the `FULL` recovery model as soon as possible, and immediately reinitialize the backup chain by performing `FULL` and `LOG` backups.

Finally, in many cases, this situation may be avoided by properly monitoring the health of the backup jobs. Set up alerts for continuous log backup failures.

ACTIVE_TRANSACTION Log Reuse Wait

The `ACTIVE_TRANSACTION` log reuse wait indicates that the log cannot be truncated due to the presence of the old active transaction. The most common case for this is incorrect transaction management in the application, which leads to runaway uncommitted transactions. For example, the application may issue multiple `BEGIN TRAN` statements without a corresponding `COMMIT` for each of them.

Be careful when you run explicit or implicit transactions in SQL Server Management Studio (SSMS). Unless you are using the SET XACT_ABORT ON setting, SSMS does not roll back a transaction when you terminate the batch execution.

You can see the list of active transactions using the code from Listing 11-5. The code may provide you with multiple rows for each transaction, because it gets log usage information on a per-database basis.

Listing 11-5. Getting active transactions

```
SELECT
    dt.database_id
    ,DB_NAME(dt.database_id) as [DB]
    ,st.session_id
    ,CASE at.transaction_state
        WHEN 0 THEN 'Not Initialized'
        WHEN 1 THEN 'Not Started'
        WHEN 2 THEN 'Active'
        WHEN 3 THEN 'Ended (R/O)'
        WHEN 4 THEN 'Commit Initialize'
        WHEN 5 THEN 'Prepared'
        WHEN 6 THEN 'Committed'
        WHEN 7 THEN 'Rolling Back'
        WHEN 8 THEN 'Rolled Back'
     END AS [State]
    ,at.transaction_begin_time
    ,es.login_name
    ,ec.client_net_address
    ,ec.connect_time
    ,dt.database_transaction_log_bytes_used
    ,dt.database_transaction_log_bytes_reserved
    ,er.status
    ,er.wait_type
    ,er.last_wait_type
    ,sql.text AS [SQL]
FROM
    sys.dm_tran_database_transactions dt WITH (NOLOCK)
        JOIN sys.dm_tran_session_transactions st WITH (NOLOCK) ON
            dt.transaction_id = st.transaction_id
        JOIN sys.dm_tran_active_transactions at WITH (NOLOCK) ON
            dt.transaction_id = at.transaction_id
        JOIN sys.dm_exec_sessions es WITH (NOLOCK) ON
            st.session_id = es.session_id
        JOIN sys.dm_exec_connections ec WITH (NOLOCK) ON
            st.session_id = ec.session_id
        LEFT OUTER JOIN sys.dm_exec_requests er WITH (NOLOCK) ON
            st.session_id = er.session_id
        CROSS APPLY
            sys.dm_exec_sql_text(ec.most_recent_sql_handle) sql
```

```
ORDER BY
    dt.database_transaction_begin_time;
```

You can kill the session that holds the active transaction using the KILL command. Later, you can analyze why the transaction was not properly managed.

AVAILABILITY_REPLICA Log Reuse Wait

As you can guess by the name, the AVAILABILITY_REPLICA log reuse wait may occur in systems that use AlwaysOn Availability Groups. In this technology, the primary node communicates with the secondary nodes by sending them the stream of transaction log records. The log cannot be truncated until those records have been sent and replayed on the secondaries.

AVAILABILITY_REPLICA log reuse waits usually occur during certain issues in Availability Groups: most commonly the secondary node being unavailable, replication between the nodes falling behind, or secondaries being unable to replay changes fast enough to keep up with the load.

When you see this wait, check the health of the Availability Group. In most cases, the only quick option to address the issue, besides adding more space to the log, is to remove a problematic secondary node from the Availability Group. I'll discuss Availability Groups in more detail in Chapter 12.

DATABASE_MIRRORING Log Reuse Wait

The DATABASE_MIRRORING log reuse wait occurs in systems that use database mirroring technology. This technology was a predecessor of AlwaysOn Availability Groups and behaves similarly to it, communicating through the stream of log records.

I'm not going to discuss how to troubleshoot database mirroring in this book, since this technology has long been obsolete. Conceptually, it is similar to troubleshooting Availability Group issues.

As with AVAILABILITY_REPLICA reuse waits, analyze the health of database mirroring when you see a DATABASE_MIRRORING reuse wait.

REPLICATION Log Reuse Wait

The REPLICATION log reuse wait occurs when the Log Reader agent falls behind while harvesting log records for transactional replication or Change Data Capture (CDC) processes. When you see this log reuse wait, check the status of the Log Reader agent and address the issues you discover.

One particular issue you may experience is the Log Agent query timing out. By default, it is 30 minutes, which is sufficient in most cases. However, it may not be enough when the system processes very large data modifications (millions of rows) in the replicated tables. You can increase the QueryTimeout in the Log Agent profile if this is the case. Check the Microsoft documentation (*https://oreil.ly/enaGx*) for more details.

There are two "nuclear" options: you can remove the replication or mark log records as harvested by using the sp_repldone command. Both approaches may require you to reinitialize the replication later.

ACTIVE_BACKUP_OR_RESTORE Log Reuse Wait

The ACTIVE_BACKUP_OR_RESTORE log reuse wait indicates that the log cannot be truncated due to active database backup or restore processes, regardless of what type of backup or restore is running.

One of the common cases for this wait is degraded performance of network or backup storage during the large FULL backup. Check the status of the active backup and restore jobs when you see this reuse wait.

Other Mitigation Strategies

It isn't always possible to mitigate the root cause of an issue quickly. Sometimes it isn't even feasible. For example, removing an unavailable replica from an Availability Group or disabling replication may lead to significant work rebuilding them later.

You can add another log file or expand the size of the log drive as a temporary solution. This allows the database to operate and gives you some time to mitigate the root cause of the issue.

Remember that you could have multiple issues preventing transaction log truncation simultaneously. For example, a network outage could prevent the server from communicating with Availability Group replicas and from accessing the backup destination. Check the log_reuse_wait_desc value and the amount of free space in the log file after you address each issue.

Finally, learn from the experience. "Transaction log full" issues are serious, and you should avoid them at all costs. Do the root cause analysis, evaluate your monitoring strategy, and perform capacity planning to reduce the possibility of this happening again.

Accelerated Database Recovery

Accelerated database recovery (ADR) is a new feature introduced in SQL Server 2019. It can significantly speed up database recovery time if SQL Server crashes or fails over in the middle of a long-running transaction. As another benefit, it allows SQL Server

---

to truncate a transaction log with long active transactions present, reducing or even eliminating `ACTIVE_TRANSACTION` log reuse waits.

Unfortunately, this feature adds overhead. Internally, it uses the in-database version store, which is conceptually similar to the traditional version store in `tempdb`. You may or may not notice this overhead, depending on your system workload and hardware; nevertheless, it is there.

I'd like to repeat that ADR addresses a very specific problem, which is slow database recovery related to the presence of long active transactions. It does not help in other cases; for example, if you failover an Availability Group to the secondary node that has a large redo queue present (more on this in Chapter 12). Due to the overhead that ADR introduces, do not enable it unless you need it in your system.

In my opinion, ADR is a double-edged sword. It helps mask the problem introduced by a long active transaction rather than addressing the root cause of the issue. There are some cases when long transactions may be required; however, it is always better to redesign the system and avoid them when possible.

ADR is enabled by default in Azure SQL Databases and SQL Managed Instances. You can enable it in regular SQL Server by setting the `ALTER DATABASE SET ACCELERATED_DATABASE_RECOVERY` database option. You can monitor the size of the persisted version store (PVS) in a database with the `sys.dm_tran_persistent_ver sion_store_stats` view. Read the Microsoft documentation (*https://oreil.ly/79pCX*) for more information about this feature.

Transaction Log Throughput

The impact of bad transaction log throughput is not always visible. While any operation that changes something in the database writes to the transaction log, these writes are considered part of the operation. Engineers tend to look at the "big picture" and the performance of an entire operation as a whole, overlooking the impact of individual components.

Think about index maintenance, for example. This is an extremely log-intensive operation, and bad log throughput greatly affects its performance. Nevertheless, database administrators usually try to reduce the impact and duration of index maintenance by adjusting its schedule or excluding indexes from the maintenance process, overlooking slow log writes. (There are some exceptions; however, they are few and far between.)

Slow log writes are also often overlooked with the regular workload in OLTP systems. High log-write latency increases query execution time, though people rarely look at it during query tuning. In either case, improving transaction log performance always improves system performance.

A word of caution, though: while improving transaction log performance is always beneficial, it is not a magical solution to every problem. Nor will its impact always be visible to users. You may get better ROI from addressing other bottlenecks first.

From a wait statistics standpoint, you can look at `WRITELOG` and `LOGBUFFER` waits: as I've mentioned, `WRITELOG` occurs when SQL Server waits for the log write to complete. `LOGBUFFER` happens when SQL Server does not have the available log buffer to cache the log records or can't flush log blocks to disk fast enough.

I wish I could tell you an exact percentage threshold when those waits start to represent a problem, but that would be impossible. You'll always see them in the system, but you need to look at general I/O health and throughput to estimate their impact. You'll also often see `WRITELOG` waits together with other I/O waits (`PAGEIOLATCH`, etc.), especially when log and data files are sharing the same *physical* storage and network I/O path. In most cases, this is a sign that the I/O subsystem is either overloaded or configured incorrectly.

As Chapter 3 discussed, the `sys.dm_io_virtual_file_stats` view provides information about database file latency and throughput. I generally like to see an average write latency in the log files of within 1 to 2 milliseconds when network-based storage is used.

In high-end OLTP systems, you can place log files on direct-attached storage (DAS) NMVe drives, which should bring latency into the submillisecond range. In some edge cases, you can also utilize persistent memory technologies to reduce latency even further.

Pay attention to the average size of log writes. Small writes are less efficient and may impact log throughput. In most cases, these writes are a sign of auto-committed transactions. You can reduce the number of these writes with proper transaction management or by enabling delayed durability (in cases when you can tolerate a small amount of data loss).

There are several performance counters in the `Databases` object that you can use to monitor transaction log activity in real time. These include:

Log Bytes Flushed/sec
: The `Log Bytes Flushed/sec` counter shows how much data has been written to the log file.

Log Flushes/sec
: The `Log Flushes/sec` counter indicates how many log write operations have been performed every second. You can use it with the `Log Bytes Flushed/sec` counter to estimate the average log write size.

Log Flush Write Time(ms)

The `Log Flush Write Time(ms)` counter shows the average time of a log write operation. You can use it to see log write I/O latency in real time.

Unfortunately, this counter measures time in milliseconds and will display 0 if storage system provides submillisecond latency.

Log Flush Waits/sec

The `Log Flush Waits/sec` counter provides the number of commit operations per second while waiting for the log records to be flushed. Ideally, this number should be very low. High values indicate a log throughput bottleneck.

Keep in mind that log-intensive operations may dramatically change the numbers. For example, an unthrottled index rebuild can generate an enormous number of log records very quickly, saturating your I/O subsystem and log throughput.

I like to run an SQL Agent job and collect data from the `sys.dm_io_virtual _file_stats` view every 5 to 15 minutes, then persist it in the utility database. This provides detailed information about I/O workload overtime. This information is extremely useful when you're analyzing transaction log throughput and general I/O performance.

In either case, you may need to look at a few different areas to improve transaction log performance and throughput. First, analyze the hardware. It is essential to use a fast, low-latency disk subsystem with the log files. Next, look at the log configuration, and try to reduce the overhead of a large number of VLFs and growth management. Finally, look for opportunities to reduce log generation through proper transaction management and efficient database maintenance jobs.

Summary

SQL Server uses Write-Ahead Logging to support database consistency requirements. Log records are hardened to the log file before transactions are committed. Insufficient transaction log throughput and high I/O latency impact system performance. Save transaction logs to fast, low-latency storage when possible.

Transaction log throughput issues present themselves with `WRITELOG` and `LOGBUFFER` waits. Troubleshoot log performance when these waits become noticeable. You can use the `sys.dm_io_virtual_file_stats` view and performance counters for troubleshooting.

You can improve transaction log performance by reducing the databases' log generation rate. This can be done by tuning your index maintenance strategy, removing unnecessary indexes, refactoring database schema, and improving transaction management. You can enable delayed durability for databases that handle large numbers of auto-committed transactions and can sustain small data losses.

Make sure the log file is properly configured and the number of VLFs in the file is manageable. Consider rebuilding the log if you detect a suboptimal configuration.

In the next chapter, I'll talk about AlwaysOn Availability Groups and the issues you may encounter when using them.

Troubleshooting Checklist

- ☐ Review and adjust transaction log configurations for all databases.
- ☐ Analyze the number of VLFs and rebuild logs if needed.
- ☐ Check the databases' recovery models and discuss a disaster recovery strategy with stakeholders.
- ☐ Reduce the transaction log generation rate when possible.
- ☐ Consider enabling accelerated database recovery if your system uses long active transactions and ADR overhead is acceptable.
- ☐ Analyze and improve transaction log throughput.

CHAPTER 12

AlwaysOn Availability Groups

AlwaysOn Availability Groups is the most common High Availability (HA) technology used in SQL Server. It persists multiple copies of databases, eliminating storage from being the single point of failure. It also allows you to scale the read workload through multiple readable secondary nodes.

In this chapter, I'll provide an overview of how Availability Groups work internally and explain how to troubleshoot common issues. You will learn about the overhead introduced by synchronous replicas and readable secondaries. Finally, I will discuss Availability Groups monitoring and cover how to troubleshoot failover events.

AlwaysOn Availability Groups Overview

Perhaps the easiest way to explain how AlwaysOn Availability Groups work is to look at the history of this technology. It was introduced in SQL Server 2012 as the replacement and successor to Database Mirroring, which used to have the internal Microsoft code name *Real Time Log Shipping*. That name is a good description: both Database Mirroring and Availability Groups rely on the stream of transaction log records to communicate. The primary node sends log records to secondaries, which harden them in their transaction logs and replay (redo) the changes in the databases.

Both technologies support the single primary node that handles the write workload. In SQL Server Enterprise Edition, Availability Groups can have multiple secondary nodes, of which some or all can handle read-only workloads. In the Standard Edition, the technology is limited to Basic Availability Groups, which support just a single secondary replica. This replica is used strictly for HA and/or Disaster Recovery (DR) purposes. Clients cannot connect and read data from there.

Availability Groups support automatic failover for HA. They rely on Windows Server Failover Cluster (WSFC) in Windows and on Pacemaker in Linux. Prior to SQL Server 2017, you had to have WSFC to set up Availability Groups. Starting with SQL Server 2017, you can use Availability Groups without WSFC. Automatic failover is not supported in that configuration.

Figure 12-1 shows an example of a three-node Availability Group setup in a Windows environment. Availability Group Listener is the name of the virtual network (similar to WSFC Cluster Endpoint) that provides a level of abstraction for clients' connectivity. In this configuration, clients can connect to the Availability Group without knowing which node is working as the primary at that moment.

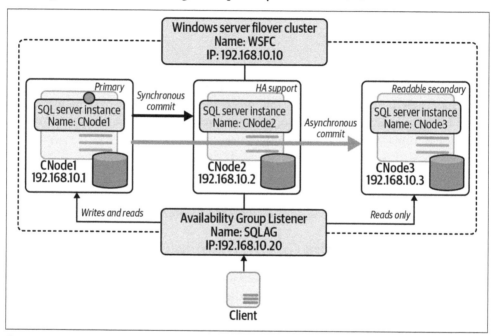

Figure 12-1. Example of an Availability Group setup

Availability Groups work on the database-group level. They replicate the group of databases, failing them over together to another node in the event of a failover. Each node in the topology stores its own copy of the data. This avoids a situation where storage can be the single point of failure.

Unfortunately, Availability Groups do not replicate instance-level objects. You need matching sets of logins, jobs, and all other instance objects on all nodes to support HA properly and ensure that it can operate after a failover. Make sure you validate the configuration as part of any system health check, and regularly test HA implementation in production systems.

The dbatools open source library (*https://dbatools.io*) provides many PowerShell cmdlets to replicate instance-level objects and validate the setup.

Now let's look at the key components of Availability Group infrastructure: send and redo queues.

Availability Group Queues

Availability Group nodes communicate through the stream of transaction log records. Secondary nodes write these records to transaction logs and asynchronously apply the changes to the databases they host.

Figure 12-2 shows a high-level view of this process.

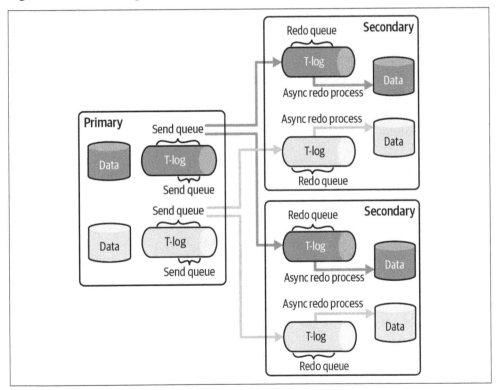

Figure 12-2. Availability Group queues

The key components here are *send queues* and *redo queues*:

Send queue

   Send queues exist on the primary node. They consist of log records that need to be sent to the secondary nodes. There are separate queues per database for each secondary node in the Availability Group.

Redo queue

   Redo queues exist on secondary nodes. They consist of the log records for changes that need to be applied to the databases by an asynchronous *redo process*. Each database on each secondary node has its own redo queue.

In a healthy Availability Group, send and redo queues stay as small as possible. A large send queue increases the amount of possible data loss in asynchronous replicas and may significantly increase blocking with synchronous ones (more on that later in this chapter). A large redo queue will impact database recovery time and increase replication latency, which in turn can affect queries on readable secondary nodes.

Finally, large send and redo queues also impact transaction log truncation. SQL Server will not truncate a log beyond the largest send queue starting point. Nor (though this is not documented) will it truncate the log beyond the oldest redo starting point across all secondary nodes.

Listing 12-1 shows you the code you can use to monitor the health of Availability Groups. You need to run this code on the primary node to get the right results. This script requires SQL Server 2014 or later. I provide a version of the script that runs on SQL Server 2012 in the book's companion materials.

Listing 12-1. Availability Group monitoring code

```
SELECT
    ar.replica_server_name as [Replica]
    ,DB_NAME(drs.database_id) AS DB
    ,drs.synchronization_state_desc as [Sync State]
    ,ars.synchronization_health_desc as [Health]
    ,ar.availability_mode as [Synchronous]
    ,drs.log_send_queue_size
    ,drs.redo_queue_size
    ,ISNULL(
        GhostReplicaState.max_low_water_mark_for_ghosts -
            drs.low_water_mark_for_ghosts,0
    ) AS [water_mark_diff]
    ,drs.log_send_rate
    ,drs.redo_rate
    ,pri.last_commit_time AS primary_last_commit_time
    ,IIF(drs.is_primary_replica = 1
        ,pri.last_commit_time
        ,drs.last_commit_time
    ) AS node_last_commit_time
    ,IIF(drs.is_primary_replica = 1
```

```
        ,0
        ,DATEDIFF(ms,drs.last_commit_time,pri.last_commit_time)
    ) AS commit_latency
FROM
    sys.availability_groups ag WITH (NOLOCK)
        JOIN sys.availability_replicas ar WITH (NOLOCK) ON
            ag.group_id = ar.group_id
        JOIN sys.dm_hadr_availability_replica_states ars WITH (NOLOCK) ON
            ar.replica_id = ars.replica_id
        JOIN sys.dm_hadr_database_replica_states drs WITH (NOLOCK) ON
            ag.group_id = drs.group_id AND
            drs.replica_id = ars.replica_id
        LEFT JOIN sys.dm_hadr_database_replica_states pri WITH (NOLOCK) ON
            pri.is_primary_replica = 1 AND
            drs.database_id = pri.database_id
        OUTER APPLY
        (
            SELECT MAX(drs2.low_water_mark_for_ghosts) AS
                    max_low_water_mark_for_ghosts
            FROM sys.dm_hadr_database_replica_states drs2 WITH (NOLOCK)
            WHERE drs.database_id = drs2.database_id
        ) GhostReplicaState
WHERE
    ars.is_local = 0
ORDER BY
    replica_server_name, DB;
```

Figure 12-3 shows the output from Listing 12-1 on one of my production servers.

	Replica	DB	Sync State	Health	Syncronous	log_send_queue_size	redo_queue_size
1			SYNCHRONIZED	HEALTHY	1	0	3605
2			SYNCHRONIZED	HEALTHY	1	0	81
3			SYNCHRONIZED	HEALTHY	1	0	0
4			SYNCHRONIZED	HEALTHY	1	0	0
5			SYNCHRONIZED	HEALTHY	1	0	0
6			SYNCHRONIZED	HEALTHY	1	0	0
7			SYNCHRONIZED	HEALTHY	1	0	0
8			SYNCHRONIZING	HEALTHY	0	60	2898
9			SYNCHRONIZING	HEALTHY	0	0	128

water_mark_diff	log_send_rate	redo_rate	primary_last_commit_time	node_last_commit_time	commit_latency
985	236939	34739	2021-05-13 07:15:08.397	2021-05-13 07:15:05.960	2436
53	0	85281	2021-05-13 07:15:08.340	2021-05-13 07:15:07.680	660
1	0	22799	2021-05-13 07:00:33.760	2021-05-13 07:00:33.760	0
1	0	0	2021-05-13 07:00:34.220	2021-05-13 07:00:34.220	0
1	0	0	2021-05-13 07:00:34.493	2021-05-13 07:00:34.493	0
1	0	0	2021-05-13 07:00:34.777	2021-05-13 07:00:34.777	0
1	0	1	2021-05-13 07:00:35.050	2021-05-13 07:00:35.050	0
38251	0	10584	2021-05-13 07:15:08.397	2021-05-13 07:15:06.483	1913
117	0	50990	2021-05-13 07:15:08.340	2021-05-13 07:15:07.510	830

Figure 12-3. Output from Availability Group monitoring script

You need to monitor several things:

Synchronization health and state
> Synchronization health and state, provided by the `synchronization_health_desc` and `synchronization_state_desc` columns, indicate whether the Availability Group is healthy and the data is synchronized. Those are the key metrics to monitor.

Send and redo queue sizes
> You can see send and redo queue sizes in the output of the `log_send_queue_size` and `redo_queue_size` columns. Both queues should be as small as possible.

Replication lag
> You can monitor replication lag by comparing the last commit times on the primary and secondary nodes. The data is available in the `last_commit_time` columns (these appear as `primary_last_commit_time` and `node_last_commit_time` columns in the script output). Both the send and redo queues affect the lag: the more data you have in the queues, the higher the lag will be. Obviously, the lag should be as small as possible, especially if you are using readable secondaries.
>
> The `sys.dm_hadr_database_replica_states` view has a `secondary_lag_seconds` column; however, I have found it to be less accurate than calculating lag based on `last_commit_time` data.

Ghost cleanup lag
> Large send and redo queues and long active transactions on the readable secondaries will defer the ghost cleanup and version store cleanup processes on the primary node, impacting system performance. From a monitoring standpoint, you can detect this condition by analyzing the difference in the `low_water_mark_for_ghosts` values between the primary and secondary nodes. This data is exposed by the `water_mark_diff` column in the script.
>
> The impact of readable secondaries on system performance is an important topic that I'll cover later in this chapter.

I'd like to repeat: it is *extremely important* to monitor the health and performance of the Availability Groups in your setup. Many things can go wrong. I'll talk about a few of them in this chapter.

You can build the monitoring code using the script from Listing 12-1. You can compare the metrics returned by the script against predefined thresholds, triggering alerts as needed. Tune the thresholds for your specific workload and infrastructure. For example, asynchronous off-site replicas may need higher send queue alert thresholds than synchronous on-site HA replicas.

You can also obtain queue sizes and several other Availability Group performance metrics through performance counters in the *Database Replica* performance object (*https://oreil.ly/mKgtk*). You can build alerting around them; however, this method is more susceptible to load spikes. For example, large batch operations may trigger short spikes in log generation, leading to unnecessary alerts.

Let's look at a few common issues you may encounter with Availability Groups.

Synchronous Replication and the Danger of the HADR_SYNC_COMMIT Wait

Availability Groups allow you to configure replication using either synchronous or asynchronous commit modes. The synchronous mode allows you to avoid data loss, but at the cost of additional commit latency.

To be exact, synchronous commit allows you to avoid data loss only when the Availability Group is healthy. By default, the primary node continues to operate even if all synchronous replicas crash. Thus, a subsequent primary node failure may lead to data loss.

In SQL Server 2017 and later, you can specify the minimum required number of healthy synchronous replicas before the primary commits a transaction with the REQUIRED_SYNCHRON IZED_SECONDARIES_TO_COMMIT Availability Group setting. If the minimum number of replicas is not available, the commit on the primary node will fail.

There is a common misconception that, in synchronous mode, data on the secondaries is updated synchronously with the primary node. This is not the case. Only the log records are hardened synchronously. The redo process will still be asynchronous and can fall behind.

Figure 12-4 shows the replication data flow in synchronous commit mode. As you can see, the client does not receive confirmation that the transaction is committed until the primary node gets acknowledgment that COMMIT log records have been hardened on the secondaries. The primary node waits for the confirmation, generating a HADR_SYNC_COMMIT wait.

This behavior introduces subtle, hard-to-understand concurrency issues. SQL Server keeps transactions active and does not release locks until it receives commit acknowledgments. This increases the chances of competing lock requests and blocking.

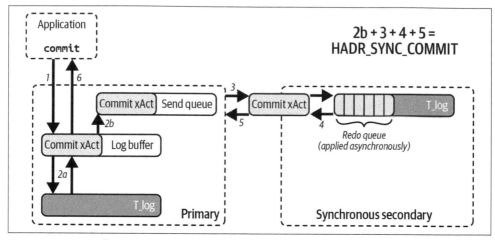

Figure 12-4. Synchronous commit data flow

This increase in transaction duration may not always be visible under normal circumstances. However, it may become an issue during log-intensive operations, when the primary node does not have enough throughput to send log records to secondaries and send queues start to grow.

You can reproduce this problem[1] by running an unthrottled clustered index rebuild on a large table with large object (LOB) columns (tables with LOB columns will produce more log records). If your server is powerful enough, you'll notice that the send queues for synchronous replicas start to grow. This will lead to extensive blocking in busy OLTP systems, consume available workers, and likely bring the system down in a short amount of time. To make matters worse, canceling the index rebuild will not solve the issue immediately, because the primary will still need to transmit all log records from the send queue.

It is common to see HADR_SYNC_COMMIT become one of the top waits in busy OLTP systems. This situation may be legitimate and does not always represent the problem. Nevertheless, you need to estimate the impact of this wait on your system and the overhead of a synchronous commit.

Look at the average resource wait time of an HADR_SYNC_COMMIT wait in the output from the sys.dm_os_wait_stats view (Listing 2-1). That value represents the average time SQL Server waits for acknowledgment that log records have been hardened on the secondary nodes. It should be as low as possible, ideally no more than a couple of milliseconds. Its duration depends on three key factors:

---

1 I created a short YouTube video (*https://oreil.ly/nH1MS*) to demonstrate.

Network performance

Both log records and acknowledgment messages go through the network, so good network throughput and low network latency are *essential* to support Availability Group replication. You can look at network performance counters, such as `Bytes Received/sec`, `Bytes Sent/sec`, and `Current Bandwidth`, to analyze and troubleshoot possible network issues.

In some cases, you might build a separate network for Availability Groups, segregating replication from client traffic. If so, make sure these networks are physically separated from each other; if they share the same physical LAN adapters, this topology would not provide you many benefits as the traffic from both networks will go to the same physical infrastructure.

I/O performance on secondary nodes

Synchronous replicas harden the log records in the log files before sending an acknowledgment back to the primary node. Insufficient I/O performance there will increase commit latency. Look at the log-write stalls in the `sys.dm_io_vir tual_file_stats` view. You can troubleshoot I/O performance using the methods discussed in Chapter 3.

CPU bandwidth

Both the primary and secondary nodes need enough CPU bandwidth to handle replication. Make sure the servers are not overloaded and the schedulers are evenly balanced across NUMA nodes (Listing 2-4).

As a general rule, I do not recommend running read workloads on *synchronous* replicas. Client queries add additional load and can impact replication throughput. Think about nonoptimized queries that overload the I/O subsystem and thus increase log-write latency. It is usually better to build separate asynchronous replicas to scale the read workload instead.

You can improve Availability Group performance by reducing the number of log records to process. I mentioned a few ways to do this in Chapter 11. All of them are applicable here.

Finally, if you are still using SQL Server 2012 or 2014, consider upgrading to a newer version. SQL Server 2016 introduced performance enhancements in many areas, including Availability Groups. Newer versions of SQL Server will provide even better results.

Figure 12-5 shows the waits on one production server before and after a SQL Server 2016 upgrade. Both snapshots were taken in the SolarWinds DPA application, with the server handling the same workload. As you can see, SQL Server 2016 reduced HADR_SYNC_COMMIT waits to less than a third of their previous levels. The upgrade also reduced CPU load by 35% without any further changes to the applications.

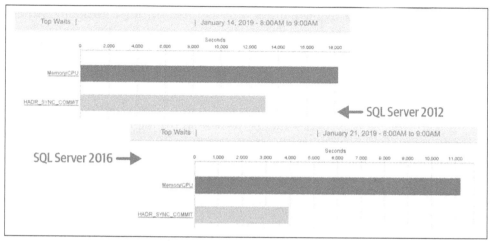

Figure 12-5. Waits before and after SQL Server 2016 upgrade

Usually, analyzing your network and I/O performance and your CPU load provides you with enough information to troubleshoot bad Availability Group throughput. In some cases, however, you need to go further and look at the performance of individual operations. You can do this by utilizing Availability Group Extended Events.

Availability Group Extended Events

SQL Server exposes a large number of xEvents that you can use while troubleshooting Availability Group performance. Table 12-1 shows the most important ones.

Table 12-1. Extended Events for Availability Group performance troubleshooting

xEvent	Location	Description
`log_flush_start`	Primary Secondary	The node starts hardening log records in the transaction log files.
`log_flush_complete`	Primary Secondary	The node finishes hardening log records in the transaction log files.
`hadr_log_block_compression`	Primary	The primary node compresses a log block.
`hadr_log_block_decompression`	Secondary	The secondary node decompresses a log block.
`hadr_capture_log_block`	Primary	The primary node captures a log block for the replication. The Mode field indicates the action: 1: Log block is captured 2: Log block is enqueued into a send queue 3: Log block is dequeued and ready to be sent 4: Log block is routed to proper replica
`ucs_connection_send_msg`	Primary Secondary	A log block is sent to transport.
`hadr_transport_receive_log_block_message`	Secondary	The secondary node receives the log block. The Mode field indicates the action: 1: Log block is received 2: Log block is enqueued in a working queue
`hadr_send_harden_lsn_message`	Secondary	The secondary node is sending acknowledgment that a log block is hardened. The Mode column indicates the action: 1: Message is created 2: Message is ready to be sent 3: Message is routed to primary node
`hadr_lsn_send_complete`	Secondary	Acknowledgment has been sent.
`hadr_receive_harden_lsn_message`	Primary	The primary node receives an acknowledge message. The Mode field indicates the action: 1: Message is received 2: Message is dequeued for processing
`hadr_db_commit_msg_harden`	Primary	Acknowledgment has been processed.
`hadr_db_commit_mgr_harden_still_waiting`	Primary	This indicates that a commit acknowledgment has not been received after 2 seconds. This should not happen under normal circumstances and usually indicates an issue with Availability Groups.

Figure 12-6 shows the sequence of events that occur during synchronous Availability Group communication. On the primary node, SQL Server starts the log flush and simultaneously sends the log block to the secondary node. The secondary node decodes the block, hardens it in the log file, and then constructs and sends an acknowledgment message back to the primary node.

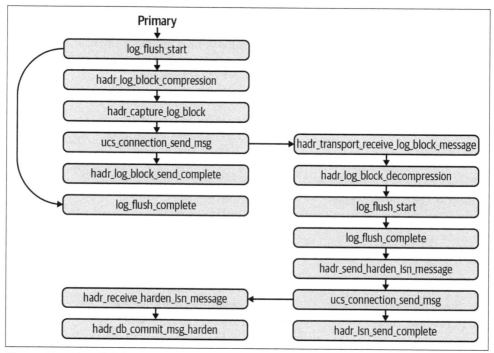

Figure 12-6. Availability Group communication flow in synchronous mode

Listing 12-2 shows two xEvent sessions you can run to capture xEvents from Table 12-1. A word of caution: those sessions can collect a large number of events. Do not keep them running outside of troubleshooting.

I am not including a `ucs_connection_send_msg` event here, because it introduces a lot of noise. Consider including it if you troubleshoot possible network performance issues.

Listing 12-2. Creating xEvent sessions for Availability Group performance troubleshooting

```
-- Create on primary node
CREATE EVENT SESSION [AlwaysOn_Tracing_Primary] ON SERVER
ADD EVENT sqlserver.hadr_capture_log_block,
ADD EVENT sqlserver.hadr_db_commit_mgr_harden,
ADD EVENT sqlserver.hadr_db_commit_mgr_harden_still_waiting,
```

```
ADD EVENT sqlserver.hadr_log_block_compression,
ADD EVENT sqlserver.hadr_log_block_send_complete,
ADD EVENT sqlserver.hadr_receive_harden_lsn_message,
ADD EVENT sqlserver.log_flush_complete,
ADD EVENT sqlserver.log_flush_start
ADD TARGET package0.ring_buffer(SET max_events_limit=(0),max_memory=(16384));
GO

-- Create on secondary node
CREATE EVENT SESSION [AlwaysOn_Tracing_Secondary] ON SERVER
ADD EVENT sqlserver.hadr_apply_log_block,
ADD EVENT sqlserver.hadr_log_block_decompression,
ADD EVENT sqlserver.hadr_lsn_send_complete,
ADD EVENT sqlserver.hadr_send_harden_lsn_message,
ADD EVENT sqlserver.hadr_transport_receive_log_block_message,
ADD EVENT sqlserver.log_flush_complete,
ADD EVENT sqlserver.log_flush_start
ADD TARGET package0.ring_buffer(SET max_events_limit=(0),max_memory=(16384));
```

You can use the `log_block_id` and `database_id` fields in both sessions to correlate session data. There is a catch, though: in `hadr_send_harden_lsn_message`, `hadr_receive_harden_lsn_message`, and `hadr_lsn_send_complete` events, the `log_block_id` will be higher than in previous events. This is due to how xEvents collects the data. The difference in values depends on the load in the database; however, it won't exceed 120.

Figure 12-7 shows the events collected in my test environment on the primary node. You may notice that a few events were collected out of order on the target. They were all fired very rapidly and have the same timestamp.

name	timestamp	mode	log_block_id
hadr_capture_log_block	2021-05-10 19:09:31.4952867	1	158913901495
hadr_capture_log_block	2021-05-10 19:09:31.4952867	2	158913901495
log_flush_start	2021-05-10 19:09:31.4952867	NULL	158913901495
hadr_log_block_compression	2021-05-10 19:09:31.4952867	NULL	158913901495
hadr_log_block_send_complete	2021-05-10 19:09:31.4952867	NULL	158913901495
log_flush_complete	2021-05-10 19:09:31.4952867	NULL	158913901495
hadr_receive_harden_lsn_message	2021-05-10 19:09:31.4962860	1	158913901496
hadr_receive_harden_lsn_message	2021-05-10 19:09:31.4962860	2	158913901496
hadr_db_commit_msg_harden	2021-05-10 19:09:31.4962860	NULL	NULL

Figure 12-7. xEvents from the primary node

Figure 12-8 shows the events collected on the secondary node. There is a small gap in timestamps with the primary node, because I was unable to synchronize time perfectly between the servers.

name	timestamp	mode	log_block_id
hadr_transport_receive_log_block_message	2021-05-10 19:09:31.5116162	1	158913901495
hadr_transport_receive_log_block_message	2021-05-10 19:09:31.5116664	2	158913901495
hadr_log_block_decompression	2021-05-10 19:09:31.5116888	NULL	158913901495
hadr_log_block_decompression	2021-05-10 19:09:31.5116967	NULL	158913901495
log_flush_start	2021-05-10 19:09:31.5117582	NULL	158913901495
log_flush_complete	2021-05-10 19:09:31.5123777	NULL	158913901495
hadr_send_harden_lsn_message	2021-05-10 19:09:31.5124051	1	158913901496
hadr_send_harden_lsn_message	2021-05-10 19:09:31.5124295	2	158913901496
hadr_send_harden_lsn_message	2021-05-10 19:09:31.5124316	3	158913901496
hadr_lsn_send_complete	2021-05-10 19:09:31.5125995	NULL	158913901496

Figure 12-8. xEvents from the secondary node

The timing of individual operations can help you identify possible bottlenecks. For example, a slow disk subsystem on the secondary node would introduce a delay between the log_flush_start and log_flush_complete events. Insufficient CPU throughput may prolong hadr_log_block_compression and hadr_log_block_decompression events when compression is used. Analyze the data and cross-check it with other metrics.

Compression behavior varies among different versions of SQL Server. SQL Server 2012 and 2014 compressed all Availability Group traffic by default. In SQL Server 2016 and later, however, compression is used only in asynchronous communication. Synchronous commit, on the other hand, does not compress the traffic. Nevertheless, you can still see compression and decompression xEvents generated even when the action is not performed.

There are three trace flags that you can use to change compression behavior in SQL Server 2016 and later:

T9592

This trace flag enables compression of the traffic between synchronous replicas. Consider enabling it if you have to support synchronous replicas over a slow network. Keep in mind that compression adds CPU overhead on both nodes and may increase HADR_SYNC_COMMIT latency in fast networks.

T1462

This trace flag disables compression of the traffic between asynchronous replicas. This may reduce CPU load on the nodes in very busy OLTP systems, at the cost of additional network traffic.

T9567

SQL Server does not use compression when it performs automatic seeding of the new nodes in Availability Groups. The T9567 flag allows you to enable it. This can speed up the automatic seeding process, but at the cost of additional CPU load on the primary node.

Note that these three trace flags may shift the workload and bottlenecks between the CPU and the network, so use them with care!

Finally, modern versions of SSMS provide tools to get similar latency data. You can do this by clicking Collect Latency Data in the Availability Group dashboard. This action creates and runs xEvent sessions on the nodes that collect Availability Group events.

The sessions will run for two minutes, using a file target to store the data. After that, SQL Server processes the data and allows you to access it through the standard reports in the Availability Group pop-up menu in SSMS Object Explorer.

There are some limitations to SSMS data collection. First, it works only when you connect to the servers using Windows Authentication and have sysadmin permissions on all replicas. Also, it relies on the SQL Server Agent running on all servers. Finally, it uses file targets, which may add overhead on busy servers with heavy Availability Group traffic. Nevertheless, SSMS data collection is often easier than manual xEvent analysis.

Asynchronous Replication and Readable Secondaries

In contrast to synchronous commit mode, in asynchronous mode the primary node does not wait for confirmation that the log records have been hardened on the secondaries. A transaction becomes committed when the COMMIT log record is saved in the primary's transaction log.

Figure 12-9 shows replication data flow in asynchronous mode. The size of the send queue on the primary node dictates possible data loss in the event of an SQL Server crash.

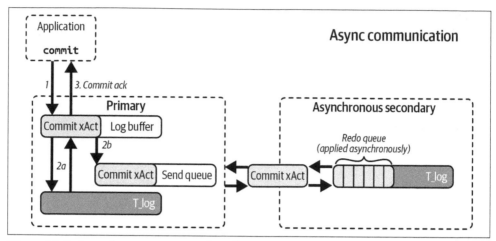

Figure 12-9. Asynchronous commit data flow

The Enterprise Edition of SQL Server allows you to scale the read workload by running queries on the secondary nodes. This is a great feature that helps improve system throughput and reduces the load on the primary node. There are a few factors you need to consider, however.

As I have mentioned, be extremely careful when querying nodes that use synchronous replication. The overhead of the queries may increase replication latency and HADR_SYNC_COMMIT waits, impacting the primary node. It is always better to leave synchronous nodes alone and build asynchronous nodes to scale the read workload.

Regardless of the replication mode, the data on secondaries will always be behind the primary node, because the redo process that applies changes to the database is asynchronous. Under normal circumstances, the lag may be very small—measured in milliseconds or even microseconds; however, it may grow during log-intensive operations such as index maintenance or large batch processing.

Do not use secondary nodes for critical queries that need up-to-date data. Remember that you cannot guarantee that the lag is always going to be small. Neither should you split the read and write queries across the nodes within a single business transaction. This will lead to inconsistent results.

Next, let's look at another, lesser-known issue related to readable secondaries that can affect the primary node in quite unexpected ways.

The Impact of Readable Secondaries

SQL Server always uses the SNAPSHOT isolation level for queries on the secondary nodes, ignoring SET TRANSACTION ISOLATION LEVEL statements and isolation-level table hints. The SNAPSHOT isolation level allows you to eliminate the possibility of readers being blocked by writers. This happens even if you do not enable the `ALLOW_SNAPSHOT_ISOLATION` database option.

Using the `SNAPSHOT` isolation level also means SQL Server will use row versioning on the secondary nodes. As you may remember from Chapter 8, SQL Server will start using the version store in `tempdb` and also maintain 14-byte version store pointers in modified data rows.

In the Availability Group infrastructure, the databases on the primary and secondary nodes are exactly the same, so it is impossible to maintain row versioning on secondary nodes only. SQL Server needs to allocate space for 14-byte version store pointers on the primary node for the databases to match, even if optimistic isolation levels are not enabled in the database.

SQL Server does not use the `tempdb` version store on primary nodes if you don't enable the `READ_COMMITTED_SNAPSHOT` or `ALLOW_SNAPSHOT_ISOLATION` option. Nevertheless, it adds an extra 14 bytes to the data rows during data modifications, which may lead to additional page splits and index fragmentation.

Unfortunately, readable secondaries also introduce another phenomenon that is less known: long-running `SNAPSHOT` transactions on secondary nodes may defer the ghost and version store cleanup tasks on the primary node. Such transactions work with a snapshot of the data at the time the transaction started. SQL Server cannot remove deleted rows and reuse the space because of the possibility that the `SNAPSHOT` transaction will need to access the old versions of the rows.

The same applies to large send and redo queues. SQL Server cannot clean up deleted rows, because the secondaries could start a `SNAPSHOT` transaction before replaying the ghost cleanup log records. This can become an issue if the replica goes offline or constantly falls behind in applying the changes.

Take a look at the code in Listing 12-3. This code will create two tables in the database. Table `T1` will have 65,536 rows and use 65,536 pages: one row per data page.

Listing 12-3. Readable secondaries: table creation

```
CREATE TABLE dbo.T1
(
    ID INT NOT NULL,
    Placeholder CHAR(8000) NULL,
    CONSTRAINT PK_T1 PRIMARY KEY CLUSTERED(ID)
);

CREATE TABLE dbo.T2
(
    Col INT
);
```

```
;WITH N1(C) AS (SELECT 0 UNION ALL SELECT 0) -- 2 rows
,N2(C) AS (SELECT 0 FROM N1 AS T1 CROSS JOIN N1 AS T2) -- 4 rows
,N3(C) AS (SELECT 0 FROM N2 AS T1 CROSS JOIN N2 AS T2) -- 16 rows
,N4(C) AS (SELECT 0 FROM N3 AS T1 CROSS JOIN N3 AS T2) -- 256 rows
,N5(C) AS (SELECT 0 FROM N4 AS T1 CROSS JOIN N4 AS T2 ) -- 65,536 rows
,IDS(ID) AS (SELECT ROW_NUMBER() OVER (ORDER BY (SELECT NULL)) FROM N5)
INSERT INTO dbo.T1(ID)
    SELECT ID FROM IDS;
```

Let's start a transaction on the secondary node and run the query against table T2, as shown in Listing 12-4. Even though I am using explicit transactions, the same behavior will occur if there is a long-running statement in an auto-committed transaction.

Listing 12-4. Readable secondaries: starting a transaction on the secondary node

```
BEGIN TRAN
    SELECT * FROM dbo.T2;
```

Next, using the code in Listing 12-5, delete all the data from the T1 table and then run the query that will do the clustered index scan on the primary node.

Listing 12-5. Readable secondaries: deleting data and performing a clustered index scan

```
DELETE FROM dbo.T1;

-- Wait 1 minute
WAITFOR DELAY '00:01:00.000';

SET STATISTICS IO ON
SELECT COUNT(*) FROM dbo.T1;
SET STATISTICS IO OFF
--Output: Table 'T1'. Scan count 1, logical reads 65781
```

Even though the table is empty, the data pages have not been deallocated. This leads to I/O overhead and a large number of logical reads on the primary node.

Finally, let's look at the index statistics, using the code from Listing 12-6.

Listing 12-6. Readable secondaries: checking the index stats

```
SELECT
    index_id, index_level, page_count
    ,record_count, version_ghost_record_count
FROM
    sys.dm_db_index_physical_stats
    (
        DB_ID()
        ,OBJECT_ID(N'dbo.T1')
```

```
    ,1
    ,NULL
    ,'DETAILED'
);
```

Figure 12-10 shows the output of the query. The leaf index level shows 65,536 rows in the `version_ghost_record_count` column. This column contains the number of ghosted rows that cannot be removed due to active transactions that rely on row versioning. In our case, this transaction runs on a different (secondary) node.

	index_id	index_level	page_count	record_count	version_ghost_record_count
1	1	0	65536	0	65536
2	1	1	243	65536	0
3	1	2	1	243	0

Figure 12-10. Index statistics

This behavior may increase I/O and CPU load, because SQL Server needs to scan ghosted data rows during query execution. It also increases the size of `tempdb` since the version store there is not being cleaned up.

The impact on I/O and CPU load may be especially high if the system is implementing message processing based on in-database queueing. The tables that store the messages are usually small, but the data there is extremely volatile. Ghost records accumulate quickly, driving up CPU and I/O load.

I encountered this issue for the first time in such a scenario. One of the tables was used for message processing, handling about 100 inserts and deletes every second. The runaway reporting transaction on the secondary node increased CPU load on the primary node by 30% overnight without any changes in the system workload. By the time I detected the issue, the table had more than a million data pages storing just a handful of rows. The queries that read the messages scanned all those data pages, driving the CPU load up.

Unfortunately, it is very common for people to offload nonoptimized reporting queries to secondary nodes without understanding the potential consequences. Remember this, and monitor ghost cleanup lag with the `water_mark_diff` column from Listing 12-1. The alert threshold will depend on your system workload. Analyze the overhead of deferred ghost cleanup and set it accordingly.

Last but not least, do not enable readable secondaries unless you are querying them. They introduce a performance impact and increase the licensing cost. There is no need to incur that unless you are using the feature.

Parallel Redo

In SQL Server 2012 and 2014, the redo process in Availability Groups used one thread per database. In high-end OLTP systems with an extremely high rate of modifications, this led to insufficient redo throughput, making it hard to use Availability Groups at all.

Starting with SQL Server 2016, the redo process may become parallel with SQL Server using multiple threads to replay the log records. The number of threads that perform the redo process depends on the number of CPUs on the server and the number of databases in the Availability Group.

In an Availability Group with multiple databases, only the first six use parallel redo. Their order usually depends on when the databases joined the Availability Group. Unfortunately, this behavior is poorly documented and may change in future versions of SQL Server.

 SQL Server 2016 and 2017 do not use parallel redo with databases that use In-Memory OLTP. This restriction has been removed in SQL Server 2019.

Parallel redo is a great feature—*when it works*. Unfortunately, it doesn't always work. I've experienced quite a few cases where it suddenly *stopped* working, leading to significant performance degradation of the redo process. Usually, it occurs in busy OLTP systems that use readable secondaries.

The issue usually presents as elevated CPU usage, with constantly growing redo queues. You are also likely to see multiple waiting tasks, usually including one or more of the following wait types in output from the `sys.dm_os_waiting_tasks` and `sys.dm_exec_requests` views:

- `DIRTY_PAGE_TABLE_LOCK`
- `DPT_ENTRY_LOCK`
- `PARALLEL_REDO_TRAN_TURN`
- `PARALLEL_REDO_FLOW_CONTROL`

You can disable parallel redo with the server-level trace flag `T3459`, using the command `DBCC TRACEON(3459,-1)`. You can make this change online without restarting the server. However, disabling the trace flag and switching back to parallel redo does require restarting in the builds prior to SQL Server 2017 CU9, SQL Server 2016 SP2 CU2, and SQL Server 2016 SP1 CU10.

As usual, apply the latest cumulative update to SQL Server. There are many fixes related to parallel redo, especially in SQL Server 2016 and 2017.

Troubleshooting Failover Events

Automatic failover is a great feature that improves High Availability. It also introduces a few tasks. When an unintended failover occurs, you'll need to find the root cause. In other cases, you may need to troubleshoot why failover did *not* occur as expected.

The troubleshooting strategy is the same in both cases: collect information, then analyze it after the failover. I will discuss the sources of that information later in this section. First, though, let's get a high-level overview of how SQL Server interacts with Windows Server Failover Cluster.

Availability Groups and Windows Server Failover Cluster

Availability Groups rely on WSFC services to support automatic failovers. They become the cluster resource in the cluster, which manages them similarly to other services. This means that if WSFC has a problem—for example, if it loses the quorum—underlying Availability Groups will also be affected.

There are two key checks in cluster resource management: `IsAlive` and `IsHealthy`. The cluster executes `IsAlive` and `IsHealthy` checks frequently, validating that the resource is online and is healthy, operating as expected.

To put things into perspective, if an `IsAlive` check fails, the cluster may initiate the failover or shut down the SQL Server instance. It could also trigger those actions if it decides that SQL Server is unhealthy, based on the results of the `IsHealthy` check; if it finds a large number of access violation errors; or if the server shows extremely high and prolonged resource consumption.

Both checks are done by the SQL Server resource DLL, which constantly communicates with the SQL Server instance. The `IsAlive` check is done through the Shared Memory protocol, which allows two processes to share memory for communication. The frequency of the communication is controlled by the `LeaseTimeout` property in the Availability Group cluster resource. By default, `LeaseTimeout` is set to 20,000 milliseconds; the `IsAlive` check runs every 5 seconds, just 25% of that value.

The lease mechanism exists only on the primary node, and you can think of it as the Availability Group's heartbeat. When the cluster does not receive confirmation that the lease is active, it considers the lease to be expired and considers the Availability Group to be unhealthy. It stops accepting write requests in order to avoid *split brain*, a condition when multiple nodes behave as the primary replica, accepting write requests. Next, the Availability Group tries to failover, assuming WSFC itself is healthy.

The IsHealthy check, on the other hand, relies on the sp_server_diagnostics stored procedure, which provides health information about the general system and Availability Group, as well as the SQL Server component status and resource utilization. The frequency of the check is controlled by the HealthCheckTimeout property in the Availability Group cluster resource. By default, it is 30,000 milliseconds; the frequency of the IsHealthy check is one-third of that value, or 10 seconds.

Another property, FailureConditionLevel, specifies the failure condition for the health check. It has the following values:

1: OnServerDown

The health check validates that the Availability Group is online. The validation succeeds if the IsAlive check passes.

2: OnServerUnresponsive

The health check fails if no data is received from the sp_server_diagnostics procedure within the time specified in HealthCheckTimeout.

3: OnCriticalServerError

The health check fails if any of the major SQL Server components returns an error. This is the default setting.

4: OnModerateServerError

The health check fails if the resource component returns an error.

5: OnAnyQualifiedFailureConditions

The health check fails if the query processing component returns an error.

As you can guess, the higher the value, the more often failover will be triggered. In most cases, you don't need to change the FailureConditionLevel parameters; however, you may decide to temporarily decrease them when you are troubleshooting failovers due to extremely high resource utilization. I do not recommend increasing the parameters unless you want to failover at the first sign of a possible issue, even when the issue could resolve itself.

You can increase LeaseTimeout if you are experiencing connectivity issues between cluster nodes. Use the following formula to determine the maximum possible value for the property:

LeaseTimeout <= (SameSubnetDelay * SameSubnetThreshold) * 2

SameSubnetDelay and SameSubnetThreshold are cluster-level properties that indicate the cluster's heartbeat frequency and the number of times it can be missed before the cluster considers it unhealthy. You can tune these parameters, as well as LeaseTimeout.

The CrossSubnetDelay and CrossSubnetThreshold parameters control the heartbeat parameters in the cross-subnet cluster. Make sure the SameSubnetDelay and SameSubnetThreshold values do not exceed them.

Increase HealthTimeout if you do not want to failover when short spikes in resource utilization cause SQL Server to become unresponsive. For example, virtualization and virtual machine (VM) backup software may pause VMs while the backup is in progress, and increasing HealthTimeout may help to avoid failovers. Be careful, though: this may delay the failover in the cluster in other legitimate situations.

As I have noted, SQL Server on Linux relies on an external service, Pacemaker, for failover support (this may change in future versions of SQL Server). Conceptually, Pacemaker behaves similarly to WSFC; however, SQL Server cannot communicate with Pacemaker directly. The implementation relies on a polling mechanism, with Pacemaker regularly querying SQL Server and database states.

Troubleshooting Failovers

So, why do failovers occur? You may have already guessed some of the reasons. The most common are:

- Hardware issues
- WSFC issues, such as cluster quorum loss due to network or connectivity problems
- Lease expiration, which can be triggered by WSFC issues like extremely high load on the server or an unresponsive OS
- Health check timeouts, often triggered by high SQL Server load (CPU and/or disk), high numbers of access violation errors and thread dumps, an unresponsive OS, a frozen VM, or other factors
- Human error during WSFC configuration or maintenance

Fortunately, SQL Server and your OS provide a lot of information to help you research the cause. Let's look at several of them now:

AlwaysOn_health *xEvent session*

The AlwaysOn_health xEvent session is started when you provision Availability Groups. This session contains the set of events that track the health of Availability Groups, the state and role changes of the nodes, and Availability Group–related DDL operations. It also includes several events that track high-severity errors: for example, the availability_group_lease_expired event is generated when the lease expires.

The AlwaysOn_health session is a great place to start troubleshooting. It may not show you the root cause of the incident, but it gives you information about what happened with the Availability Group and when, as well as what actions were taken. Finally, it allows you to pinpoint conditions when manual failover was triggered either advertently or by human error.

SQLDIAG *files*

The WSFC, as noted, uses an sp_server_diagnostics stored procedure as part of IsHealthy cluster checks. This stored procedure provides information about SQL Server component health and resource utilization, such as memory and CPU usage, the state of the deadlock monitor, and access violations and thread dumps. It also provides general health information on all Availability Groups on the server.

The data from sp_server_diagnostics is captured by a hidden xEvent session and stored in XEL files in the SQL Server Log folder. These files are extremely useful during failover troubleshooting, because they can tell you if some of the server components were overloaded or not healthy. The naming convention for the files consists of the server and instance names followed by an SQLDIAG string.

system_health *xEvent session*

The system_health xEvent session is another session that is created and runs by default in SQL Server. It provides information about general SQL Server health and high-severity errors along with component health and diagnostics data. The latter is similar to the information in the SQLDIAG files; however, the metrics are aggregated in larger intervals of five minutes.

Cluster log

The cluster log is a key source of data for troubleshooting. It contains detailed information about the errors that led to failover conditions and can help you pinpoint quorum and other cluster-related issues.

SQL Server log

The SQL Server log provides information about critical errors, the status of failovers, and the state of Availability Group replicas. Looking at the events around the time of an incident can be useful when troubleshooting.

System logs

System logs and the Windows Event Log can provide details about critical system conditions and errors, such as hardware failures.

Keep in mind that SQL Server and WSFC roll the logs and xEvent files over. You need to collect the data shortly after a failover occurs, or it may disappear. When you have collected the data, analyze it holistically to identify the problem.

When a Failover Does Not Occur

In some cases, you need to troubleshoot the opposite problem: why an Availability Group did not failover automatically when it should have. Here are a few common reasons this happens:

Incorrect configuration

The Availability Group has not been configured correctly: for example, it does not have Automatic Failover set or it has databases that joined the Availability Group on a single node only.

Communication issues

Failover may not occur if the primary node loses connectivity to the secondary node to which it is supposed to failover. Failover also requires the databases to be fully synchronized, so it might not happen if the secondary node has not caught up with replication after being offline.

Cluster issues

Some WSFC issues may prevent automatic failover, such as the SQL Server resource DLL losing its connection to SQL Server.

Availability Group exceeded maximum failover threshold

Each cluster resource has a set of properties that specify the maximum number of failovers that can occur within a specific period. In Availability Groups, the default maximum number of failovers is $N - 1$, where N is the number of nodes in the cluster. The default period is six hours.

You can change these values in the properties of the Availability Group cluster resource.

The troubleshooting approach in this case is very similar to what you did to identify an unwanted failover: look at the data from the Cluster and SQL Server logs, SQLDIAG files, and AlwaysOn_health and system_health sessions and reconstruct what happened during the incident. This usually provides enough data to help you understand the cause of the problem.

Summary

AlwaysOn Availability Groups is the most popular High Availability technology used in SQL Server. It avoids a situation where storage can be the single point of failure and, in the Enterprise Edition, allows you to scale the read workload across multiple replicas.

Availability Groups do not replicate instance-level objects, such as logins and jobs. Synchronize them across the nodes to allow systems to operate after failovers.

Replication in Availability Groups is based on the stream of transaction log records. Monitor send and redo queues and set alerts to notify you when they grow. Large queues may lead to data loss and prolong recovery time. They can also prevent log truncation and introduce other performance issues.

Synchronous commit mode helps avoid data loss, but the trade-off is additional commit latency during replication. Analyze the `HADR_SYNC_COMMIT` wait time and reduce it as much as possible.

Readable secondaries allow you to scale the read workload. However, they may defer ghost and version store cleanup tasks on the primary node, increasing CPU and I/O load there. Avoid long-running transactions on secondaries and monitor the workload there.

When you troubleshoot failover events, look at the data from `AlwaysOn_health` and `system_health` xEvent sessions; `SQLDIAG` files; and OS, SQL Server, and Cluster logs. They usually contain enough information to diagnose the problem.

In the next chapter, I'll discuss several other common wait types.

Troubleshooting Checklist

- ☐ Make sure instance-level objects are synchronized across Availability Group nodes.
- ☐ Perform failover/HA testing if possible.
- ☐ Set up Availability Group monitoring and alerting to cover queue sizes, replication latency, ghost cleanup lag, and failover events.
- ☐ Analyze the impact of commit latency if synchronous commit is used; review the `HADR_SYNC_COMMIT` resource wait time and troubleshoot replication performance if needed.
- ☐ Check whether readable secondaries are enabled. Evaluate the impact of read-only queries on synchronous readable replicas.
- ☐ Disable readable secondaries if they are not being used.

CHAPTER 13

Other Notable Wait Types

This rather short chapter covers several wait types I have not discussed yet. I will start with the ASYNC_NETWORK_IO wait type, which occurs when the client does not consume data from SQL Server fast enough. Next, I will talk about the THREADPOOL wait and the dangerous condition of worker thread starvation. After that, I will address backup-related wait types and ways to improve backup performance.

I will conclude the chapter with an overview of OLEDB and a few other preemptive wait types that occur when SQL Server calls OS API switching to preemptive execution mode.

ASYNC_NETWORK_IO Waits

ASYNC_NETWORK_IO is a common wait type I see in nearly every system. Inexperienced engineers usually guess by the wait type name, associating ASYNC_NETWORK_IO with bad network performance. This wait, however, indicates a much broader condition that occurs when SQL Server has to wait for the client application to consume data.

Slow networks can definitely trigger that condition, but more often than not, the cause is inefficient client application design. If the application reads and processes data row by row, this forces SQL Server to wait during processing.

Listing 13-1 shows the code pattern that will trigger the issue. The client application consumes and processes rows one by one, keeping SqlDataReader open. The SQL Server worker waits for the client to consume all the rows and generates the ASYNC_NETWORK_IO wait in the meantime.

Listing 13-1. Code pattern that triggers an ASYNC_NETWORK_IO wait

```
using (SqlConnection connection = new SqlConnection(connectionString))
{
    SqlCommand command = new SqlCommand(cmdText, connection);
    connection.Open();
    using (SqlDataReader reader = command.ExecuteReader())
    {
        while (reader.Read())
            ProcessRow((IDataRecord)reader);
    }
}
```

The right approach here is to read all the rows first as quickly as possible, then process them afterward, as shown in Listing 13-2. The client may need to batch the operation, if the size of the data is very large and the client does not have enough memory to cache it.

Listing 13-2. Code pattern that reduces an ASYNC_NETWORK_IO wait

```
List<Orders> orderRows = new List<Orders>();
using (SqlConnection connection = new SqlConnection(connectionString))
{
    SqlCommand command = new SqlCommand(cmdText, connection);
    connection.Open();
    using (SqlDataReader reader = command.ExecuteReader())
    {
        while (reader.Read())
            orderRows.Add(ReadOrderRow((IDataRecord)reader));
    }
}
ProcessAllOrderRows(orderRows);
```

My favorite way to prove that row-by-row processing triggers an ASYNC_NETWORK_IO wait is to run a small demo in SSMS. Connect to the local SQL Server instance— SSMS will use the *Shared Memory* protocol, which does not involve any network traffic. Next, clear the wait statistics and run the SELECT * statement from the table, selecting several thousand rows. When you check the waits after the execution, you'll see ASYNC_NETWORK_IO at the top of the list despite the total absence of network traffic.

Next, enable the "Discard results after execution" setting in the Tools > Options > Query Results > SQL Server > Results to Grid options form and repeat the test. You'll see that the ASYNC_NETWORK_IO wait is no longer present. The reason you saw the wait in the first test is due to SSMS inefficiency, which populates the results grid on a row-by-row basis. This implementation is slow, and SQL Server waits for each row to be displayed in the grid, generating the wait.

When this wait is present in significant amounts, analyze network performance first. Review network topology (remember, network throughput depends on the slowest component) and check network performance counters and metrics.

When you are confident that network performance is not an issue, analyze the situation with client applications. You might detect inefficient code with the `sys.dm_os_waiting_tasks`, `sys.dm_exec_requests`, `sys.dm_exec_sessions`, and `sys.dm_exec_connections` views. However, in some cases, it may not be feasible or even possible to change the client code.

Also, pay attention to client application performance. It is possible to see a `ASYNC_NET WORK_IO` wait generated by applications running on overloaded servers or in incorrectly configured virtual machines that don't have enough bandwidth to handle the load.

In my list, the `ASYNC_NETWORK_IO` waits belong to the "it depends" category. I sometimes ignore them if they are not very significant and the system is not operating under an extremely heavy load.

Don't take this the wrong way, though: this wait is not benign. It consumes workers on the server and introduces memory and CPU overhead. It may also prolong the time SQL Server holds locks on the rows and may lead to blocking issues. Nevertheless, usually it is not the biggest fish to fry. I typically get better ROI by focusing on other areas.

THREADPOOL Waits

In contrast to `ASYNC_NETWORK_IO waits`, `THREADPOOL` waits need to be investigated even when you see only a few. They indicate that SQL Server does not have enough worker threads to assign to tasks. When this happens, clients are unable to connect to SQL Server and will get *connection timeout* errors, as if SQL Server was down.

One situation where this may happen is when you have long blocking chains, usually with schema modification (`Sch-M`) locks involved. Follow along with me as we go through an example that emulates this condition.

First, let's reduce the number of workers on the server by running the code from Listing 13-3. This code also enables a remote Dedicated Admin Connection (DAC); more about that later.

 Do *not* execute this scenario on production servers. It will bring the server down! Also, reset the *max worker threads* value back to 0 after the test is complete.

Listing 13-3. Enabling a remote dedicated admin connection and reducing the number of workers

```
EXEC sp_configure N'max worker threads', 128;
GO
EXEC sp_configure 'remote admin connections', 1;
GO
RECONFIGURE
GO
```

Next, let's create a small table and insert into it a row that acquires an intent-exclusive (IX) lock. Run the code in Listing 13-4; do not commit the transaction and do not close the session afterward.

Listing 13-4. THREADPOOL wait: creating a test table and acquiring an intent-exclusive lock

```
CREATE TABLE dbo.ThreadPoolDemo
(
    Col1 INT
);
GO

BEGIN TRAN
    INSERT INTO dbo.ThreadPoolDemo VALUES(0);
```

Now let's open another session and run the ALTER TABLE statement shown in Listing 13-5. This statement will be blocked because the (Sch-M) and (IX) locks are incompatible.

Listing 13-5. THREADPOOL wait: altering the table

```
-- Run in a different session from Listing 13-4
ALTER TABLE dbo.ThreadPoolDemo ADD Col2 INT;
```

Now, any other sessions trying to access the table will be blocked due to the presence of the (Sch-M) lock request in the queue. They will be suspended and will wait, consuming workers on the server.

Let's emulate this condition by running the Windows Batch script shown in Listing 13-6. This script will open multiple sessions that try to select data from the table. You may need to change the server and database names in your environment.

Listing 13-6. THREADPOOL wait: generating multiple sessions and blocking

```
@ECHO OFF
SET query="SELECT * FROM SQLServerInternals.dbo.ThreadPoolDemo"
SET p1=-S
SET server=.
SET p3=-E
SET p4=-Q

FOR /L %%I IN (1,1,150) DO (
    START "" "sqlcmd.exe" %p1% %server% %p3% %p4% %query%
)
```

This will consume all available workers. Now, if you try to connect to the server from SSMS, you'll get the connection error shown in Figure 13-1 because there are no available workers in the system to pick up the connection.

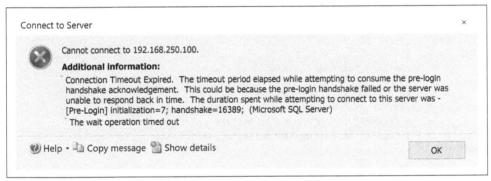

Figure 13-1. Connection error when worker pool is exhausted

When this condition occurs (and in other cases when the server stops responding), you can connect to it through a dedicated admin connection. SQL Server reserves a private scheduler and a small amount of memory for the DAC to support those troubleshooting scenarios.

You can connect to SQL Server with the DAC by using the ADMIN: prefix in the server name in the SSMS connection box or with the -A option in the sqlcmd utility. Only members of the sysadmin server role are allowed to connect, and only one session at a time can use a DAC connection. Do not connect to the DAC in the SSMS Object Explorer, which requires its own connection. Similarly, disable the IntelliSense feature in the Query window before connecting. In old versions of SSMS, you may get a benign connection error message from IntelliSense even when it is disabled.

By default, the DAC is only available locally. In some cases, when a server is completely overloaded, the OS may not respond, preventing you from utilizing it. You always need to enable remote access to the DAC during the initial server setup, as I did in Listing 13-3.

Now, connect to the server through the DAC and query the `sys.dm_os_wait` `ing_tasks` view with the code shown in Listing 13-7. Note that I filtered out system sessions from the output to focus on the blocking chain and THREADPOOL waits. I would not do that if I were troubleshooting an ongoing issue.

Listing 13-7. THREADPOOL wait: querying the `sys.dm_os_waiting_tasks` view

```
SELECT
    session_id
    ,wait_type
    ,wait_duration_ms
    ,blocking_session_id
    ,resource_description
FROM
    sys.dm_os_waiting_tasks WITH (NOLOCK)
WHERE
    (session_id > 50 OR session_id IS NULL) AND
    wait_type NOT IN (N'CLR_AUTO_EVENT',N'QDS_ASYNC_QUEUE'
        ,N'XTP_PREEMPTIVE_TASK',N'BROKER_RECEIVE_WAITFOR'
        ,N'QDS_PERSIST_TASK_MAIN_LOOP_SLEEP')
ORDER BY
    session_id,
    wait_duration_ms DESC;
```

Figure 13-2 shows the output of the code. You can see the large number of sessions waiting for a schema stability lock on the table, generating a LCK_M_SCH_S wait type. They are blocked by the session with an ALTER TABLE statement, due to incompatibility between the (Sch-S) and (Sch-M) locks. The ALTER TABLE, in turn, is blocked by the session with SPID=55 that executed an INSERT statement in the uncommitted transaction. You can terminate either the root blocker or the ALTER TABLE session with the KILL command to solve the problem.

As you may have noticed, the root blocker session with SPID=55 is not present in the output. This session has the runaway uncommitted transaction and had not been blocked in our example. You can see it in *sleeping* status with open_trans action_count=1 in the sys.dm_exec_sessions view output. You can use Listing 2-3 to obtain information about the session and client application for further troubleshooting.

	session_id	wait_type	wait_duration_ms	blocking_session_id	resource_description
9	NULL	THREADPOOL	95069	NULL	threadpool id=scheduler1d7...
10	NULL	THREADPOOL	92985	NULL	threadpool id=scheduler1d7...
11	NULL	THREADPOOL	91421	NULL	threadpool id=scheduler1d7...
12	NULL	THREADPOOL	82514	NULL	threadpool id=scheduler1d7...
13	52	LCK_M_SCH_S	106991	64	objectlock lockPartition=0...
14	60	LCK_M_SCH_S	106991	64	objectlock lockPartition=0...
15	61	LCK_M_SCH_S	106928	64	objectlock lockPartition=0...
16	63	LCK_M_SCH_S	106843	64	objectlock lockPartition=0...
17	64	LCK_M_SCH_M	303772	55	objectlock lockPartition=0...
18	76	LCK_M_SCH_S	106586	64	objectlock lockPartition=0...
19	80	LCK_M_SCH_S	106410	64	objectlock lockPartition=0...
20	81	LCK_M_SCH_S	106388	64	objectlock lockPartition=0...

Figure 13-2. Output of the sys.dm_os_waiting_tasks view

You can also see the tasks with THREADPOOL waits in the sys.dm_os_waiting_tasks view output. These tasks belong to connection requests from the clients. SQL Server does not have available workers to handle them, which will eventually trigger connection errors on the client side.

It is also worth noting that these tasks have empty session_id values, as the sessions have not been established yet. Thus, they would not appear in the sys.dm_exec_requests view output.

There are other cases that may lead to THREADPOOL waits. For example, they may occur in low memory conditions, due to inadequately provisioned servers or memory pressure. The number of workers in the system depends on the amount of memory and other factors; you may have insufficient workers to handle the load. Look at the error log for signs of memory pressure and SQL Server dumps.

It is also possible that the server cannot handle the workload because there are too many active sessions or too many concurrent queries with the parallel plans. You need to troubleshoot these conditions and potentially tune the system to reduce the overall load.

Check the max worker thread setting. It is sometimes misconfigured and set to a low number. Reset it to the default value (0) and see how that impacts the system.

You can consider increasing the max worker thread setting; however, this rarely addresses the problem. For example, massive blocking may quickly reappear, with the new workers also blocked. Don't panic! Just troubleshoot the root cause of the issue. That's always the better option.

Backup-Related Waits

As you can guess by their names, BACKUPIO and BACKUPBUFFER waits occur during backup and restore. They indicate insufficient operation throughput when SQL Server cannot write to or read from backup files fast enough. I rarely focus on these waits in the beginning of the performance tuning process; however, there are a couple of things worth analyzing if you see these waits in noticeable numbers.

It is common to see backup-, I/O-, and network-related waits together when they share the same resources. For example, a slow or overloaded disk subsystem may lead to BACKUPIO, PAGEIOLATCH, WRITELOG, and other I/O-related waits. Backup-related waits, in such cases, may become another element confirming the problem.

However, when resources are shared, check whether the backup operation impacts other components when it is running. For example, is there an increase in the number of occurrences and average wait times of PAGEIOLATCH, WRITELOG, or HADR_SYNC_COMMIT waits during that time?

Many monitoring tools collect information about waits that occur in specific time intervals, and you can use this in your analysis. Alternatively, you can build a solution by persisting sys.dm_os_wait_stats data in the utility database at regular intervals, perhaps using SQL Server Agent Job. The companion materials for this book include a script that provides a snapshot of the wait statistics for the time interval, which you can use to build your implementation.

In the end, redesign the backup process if you see an impact. Utilize differential backups, use different targets to store files, and adjust the schedule. Your strategy and options will depend on the infrastructure, your Recovery Time Objective (RTO) and Recovery Point Objective (RPO) requirements, version and edition of SQL Server, and other factors.

Improving Backup Performance

The native SQL Server backup does not provide a lot of configuration options. Nevertheless, there are some knobs you can turn to tune and improve backup performance. Let's look at them.

Backup compression

SQL Server allows you to compress backup files. In most cases, it reduces the size of the backup files, at the cost of extra CPU load introduced by the compression.

Usually, this is a good trade-off. Smaller backup files will take less time to transmit over the network, which improves recovery time in the event of a disaster. They also reduce the load and storage size on the disk subsystem.

As a general rule, unless the server is CPU bound, enable backup compression. There are a few considerations related to Transparent Data Encryption (TDE), which I will cover shortly.

Striped backups

You can split the database backup into multiple files and create a *striped backup*. This will parallelize backup and restore operations, allowing SQL Server to use multiple threads to perform them.

This feature is very beneficial for large databases and may significantly reduce backup and restore times. Keep in mind that it is resource intensive and will add load to the infrastructure. Do not configure the number of stripes above the number of logical CPU cores on the server; monitor any overhead the backup process may introduce.

You also need to analyze bottlenecks during the backup process. For example, if you are backing up the database to a network location and have high network latency or insufficient network throughput, striping the backups and parallelizing the process won't help you much. In that case, you might consider striping backups to local direct-attached storage (DAS) and copying the files to the network location later, when the backup is complete.

BUFFERCOUNT and MAXTRANSFERSIZE Options

SQL Server allows you to control the number of I/O buffers (BUFFERCOUNT option) and the maximum size of the transfer block (MAXTRANSFERSIZE option) for your backup operation. Usually, increasing both speeds up the process. You need to carefully tune them in your system, though. After a speed increase, the backup operation will consume more memory, which may impact other SQL Server components. It may even lead to an *out of memory* condition if you the set parameters incorrectly.

If you want to compress a TDE-enabled database in SQL Server 2016 or 2017, set MAXTRANSFERSIZE so that it is larger than 65,536 bytes (64 KB). This will switch SQL Server to the new and improved compression algorithm, which works with encryption. Without that, compressing an encrypted database would not save much space. This is not required in SQL Server 2019 and later, which will adjust MAXTRANSFERSIZE automatically while it compresses the TDE-enabled database.

Partial Database Backups

When you deal with large databases, it is very common for a large portion of the data to become static over time: think of scenarios with append-only tables or when the data becomes read-only after some time.

When this is the case, you can partition the data, utilizing partitioned tables and/or views. You can place the static portion of the data into separate filegroups, marking them as read-only. Those filegroups can be backed up just once and then excluded from the regular FULL backups, saving time and significantly reducing the backup's size on disk. (You can read about this implementation in more detail on my blog (*https://oreil.ly/VWS9y*) or in my book *Pro SQL Server Internals* [Apress, 2016].)

In the end, the way you tune backup and restore processes should be aligned with your organization's disaster recovery strategy. Review the requirements and the RTO and RPO policies and design an implementation that can support them.

HTBUILD and Other HT* Waits

The HTBUILD, HTDELETE, HTMEMO, HTREINIT, and HTREPARTITION waits occur during management of internal hash tables in batch-mode execution. Prior to SQL Server 2019, batch-mode execution was almost exclusively used with columnstore indexes. In SQL Server 2019 and later, it can also be used with row-based tables.

Having these waits present in small amounts does not necessarily indicate a problem. They may, however, be a sign of poorly maintained columnstore indexes. In particular, they sometimes indicate the presence of large uncompressed delta stores or of many small and unevenly sized rowgroups. Review the columnstore indexes and rebuild any partitions that have inefficiencies. You can use the sys.col umn_store_row_group view (*https://oreil.ly/BK5CL*) for the analysis.

I have yet to see these waits become an issue with batch-mode execution on row-based tables in SQL Server 2019. I'd guess, however, that inaccurate statistics may introduce them.

Finally, I'd like to note that the Microsoft documentation suggests reducing MAXDOP or increasing the cost threshold for parallelism as ways to mitigate these waits. This is not the right approach, in my opinion: it will mask the problem and disable batch-mode execution for some queries, degrading performance.

Preemptive Waits

As you remember from Chapter 2, the SQL Server OS uses cooperative scheduling. The workers voluntarily yield when their CPU time quantum expires, allowing other workers to execute.

There are some exceptions, however, when SQL Server needs to call external functions it does not control. Think about OS API calls to authenticate the user against a domain controller or extended stored procedure calls. When this happens, SQL Server switches the worker to preemptive execution mode. SQL Server does not control its scheduling anymore. The worker continues to show the RUNNING state; however, it also generates a wait of one of the preemptive types, of which there are more than 200 in SQL Server 2019. Most of them do not represent any contention and can be ignored. There are a few, however, that you need to be aware of. Let's look at them.

PREEMPTIVE_OS_WRITEFILEGATHER Wait Type

PREEMPTIVE_OS_WRITEFILEGATHER waits occur during the zero-initializing process. As you'll recall, SQL Server always zero-initializes log files and may also zero-initialize data files if instant file initialization is not enabled.

When you see this wait in the system, check and enable instant file initialization by granting "Perform volume management tasks" (SE_MANAGE_VOLUME_NAME) permission to the SQL Server startup account. Remember that there is a small security risk (discussed in Chapter 1), although it is usually not an issue in most systems.

Also, review the transaction log's auto-growth parameters. Growing the log files in large chunks can prolong zero-initializing time and lead to inefficient Virtual Log File (VLF) structure. As you learned in Chapter 11, it is better to manage transaction log size manually.

Obviously, make sure you do not have any scheduled processes that routinely shrink transaction logs. As you already know, this is a bad practice.

PREEMPTIVE_OS_WRITEFILE Wait Type

PREEMPTIVE_OS_WRITEFILE waits may indicate a bottleneck during synchronous writes to files. This wait type rarely becomes an issue; however, it may be a sign of a slow or overloaded disk subsystem on the server.

When I see this wait type present in significant amounts, I check whether the server runs multiple SQL Traces or SQL Audits using files as the targets to save data. Another occurrence of this wait may be related to database snapshot writes—either snapshots created by users or internal snapshots created by the DBCC CHECKDB operation.

Authentication-Related Wait Types

There are several wait types that occur during user authentication calls when SQL Server needs to wait for responses from the Domain Controller. Their names start with PREEMPTIVE_OS_AUTH*; and they also include PREEMPTIVE_OS_LOOKUPACCOUNT SID and PREEMPTIVE_OS_ACCEPTSECURITYCONTEXT waits.

These waits may be infrastructure related. One typical example involves cloud-based SQL Servers authenticating against remote on-premises Active Directory controllers. The latency of the calls can prolong the authentication process, leading to a high percentage of authentication-related waits.

Another possible reason is code that runs under a different execution context than the calling session. The EXECUTE AS OWNER or EXECUTE AS USER module may require constant authentication calls, which can be expensive under a heavy load.

When you see authentication-related waits in the system, check the health of the Active Directory infrastructure and the latency of authentication calls, then review how often those calls have been performed.

OLEDB Waits

OLEDB is another preemptive wait type that occurs when SQL Server is waiting for data from an OLE DB provider. Most often it happens in the following cases:

- Calls to linked servers
- Execution of some SQL Server Integration Services (SSIS) packages
- Operations during DBCC CHECKDB execution
- Queries against dynamic management views

Waits from the first two categories usually have relatively high wait times. Such cases indicate long-running remote queries and prolonged SSIS package execution. Consider troubleshooting the performance of those calls on remote servers and/or reviewing the SSIS package logic.

Waits from the DBCC CHECKDB operation and from DMV access are usually short, no more than a few milliseconds on average. The cumulative numbers will give you an idea of the overhead of the operations. You can address the DBCC CHECKDB overhead by offloading it to a backup validation server.

DMV access waits can give you an idea of the overhead of the monitoring tools that are constantly querying those views. If they produce excessive waits, you might decide to redesign your monitoring strategy and/or switch to different tools.

Finally, another known issue for OLEDB waits sometimes occurs when a remote non-SQL Server linked server does not terminate the connection properly. SQL Server will keep the connection open, generating a never-ending OLEDB wait for the session. Unfortunately, there is no easy way to fix this other than to restart SQL Server.

Wait Types: Wrapping Up

There are hundreds of wait types in SQL Server and it is impossible to cover all of them. Nor is it practical; in all likelihood, you'll never deal with most of them during system troubleshooting.

This book has so far covered the most common wait types, enough to troubleshoot most issues; however, you may encounter other wait types. Don't be confused when this happens!

Start by researching the wait type. The Microsoft documentation (*https://oreil.ly/xEUg4*) is a good place to start. Another useful resource is the SQLSkills Wait Types Library (*https://oreil.ly/ZHKse*). Obviously, use Google or Bing as well; sometimes you'll find useful information there.

The conditions when the wait type is generated will point you to the problematic areas. By now, you know enough about SQL Server's execution model and components to define your troubleshooting strategy and address issues. Just remember to look at the problem holistically and avoid tunnel vision. All of SQL Server's components work together, and issues that arise can impact many of them.

Summary

ASYNC_NETWORK_IO waits occur when SQL Server has to wait for a client application to consume the data. This wait type may indicate inefficient network throughput or issues with client applications that read and process data row by row.

The presence of THREADPOOL waits indicates the dangerous condition of worker thread starvation. When this happens, SQL Server does not have enough workers to execute client requests and becomes unresponsive. Typical issues that trigger this condition include long blocking chains, insufficient memory (due to incorrect configuration or extreme memory pressure), and heavy concurrent (and often non-optimized) load.

You can use a dedicated admin connection to troubleshoot ongoing issues when SQL Server is unresponsive and does not accept regular connections. Make sure to enable remote access to the DAC during server provisioning.

BACKUPIO and BACKUPBUFFER waits occur if SQL Server does not have enough throughput to write to or read from backup files. Analyze the infrastructure and tune the backup process when you see these wait types.

Preemptive waits occur when SQL Server needs to call external functions by switching to a preemptive execution model. You can ignore most of those waits; however, pay attention to authentication-related waits, OLEDB waits, and I/O-related preemptive wait types.

In the next chapter we'll switch gears, discussing how to detect inefficiencies in the database schema and indexing.

Troubleshooting Checklist

- ☐ Review the network topology and client implementation when you see a large number of ASYNC_NETWORK_IO waits.

- ☐ Investigate THREADPOOL waits if you see them.

- ☐ Review disaster recovery and backup strategies and tune the backup process if needed.

- ☐ Analyze the size of delta stores and the state of rowgroups in columnstore indexes if you see HTBUILD or other batch-mode execution-related waits.

- ☐ Troubleshoot preemptive and OLEDB waits if you see a noticeable number of them.

CHAPTER 14

Database Schema and Index Analysis

Until this point, most of the troubleshooting efforts described in this book have treated users' databases and applications as *black boxes*. I've focused on performance improvements that do not require any changes in the databases and applications beyond indexing and simple T-SQL code changes. This approach provides easier and faster ROI; however, it also limits the results you can accomplish.

Don't take this the wrong way: in many cases, you can achieve *good enough* results without needing to make significant database and application changes. Nevertheless, it may be beneficial to perform a high-level review of your database schema and index usage and address some of the problems you find.

I'll start this chapter with an overview of several SQL Server catalog views and show you how to detect a few database design issues. Then I'll demonstrate how to identify inefficient indexing through analysis of index usage and its operational statistics and provide a handful of scripts for this analysis, including one that lets you view at a glance several consolidated index metrics.

Database Schema Analysis

SQL Server provides quite a few catalog views (*https://oreil.ly/BIl1D*) that expose information about server- and database-level objects. They are extremely useful when you need to analyze and detect inefficiencies in the database schema.

Figure 14-1 shows several database object–related catalog views with their dependencies and key attributes. This is just a small subset of the available views, to give you an idea of how much information you can obtain.

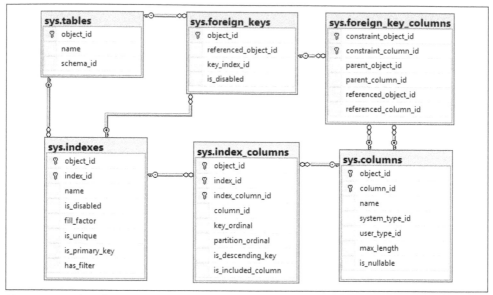

Figure 14-1. Catalog views

You can identify multiple common database design issues with these views. Let's look at some of them:

- Heap tables
- Indexes on `uniqueidentifier` columns
- Wide and nonunique clustered indexes
- Untrusted foreign keys
- Nonindexed foreign keys
- Redundant indexes
- High identity values

Let's look at each one in turn.

Heap Tables

Heap tables are a somewhat controversial subject. They certainly have their uses—for example, they may be a good choice in some ETL (extract, transform, load) processes where fast insert throughput is critical and you cannot use memory-optimized tables. However, as I briefly mentioned in Chapter 5, it is better to avoid heap tables, since tables with clustered indexes outperform them in most workloads.

When I see heap tables during my analyses, I usually review them and consider creating clustered indexes on them. If that's impossible, I look for inefficient heap tables and rebuild them.

The code in Listing 14-1 provides a list of heap tables in the database. You may want to review index usage statistics in those tables to see if there is a natural candidate for a clustered index. (I'll talk more about this later in the chapter.)

 Remove the predicates on the sys.tables.is_memory_optimized column if you run this and other scripts from this chapter in SQL Server versions prior to 2014.

Listing 14-1. Obtaining heap tables in the database

```
SELECT
    t.object_id
    ,s.name + '.' + t.name AS [table]
    ,p.rows
FROM
    sys.tables t WITH (NOLOCK)
        JOIN sys.schemas s WITH (NOLOCK) ON
            t.schema_id = s.schema_id
        CROSS APPLY
        (
            SELECT SUM(p.rows) AS [rows]
            FROM sys.partitions p WITH (NOLOCK)
            WHERE t.object_id = p.object_id AND p.index_id = 0
        ) p
WHERE
    t.is_memory_optimized = 0 AND
    t.is_ms_shipped = 0 AND
    EXISTS
    (
        SELECT *
        FROM sys.indexes i WITH (NOLOCK)
        WHERE t.object_id = i.object_id AND i.index_id = 0
    )
ORDER BY
    p.rows DESC
OPTION (RECOMPILE, MAXDOP 1);
```

There are two main metrics to monitor with heap tables. The first is the number of *forwarded records*. In contrast to B-Tree Indexes, when a heap table page does not have enough space to accommodate the new version of a row, SQL Server does not perform a page split. Instead, it puts the new row on another page and replaces the original row with a small structure called a *forwarding pointer*. Large numbers of forwarding pointers and forwarded records will reduce the performance of I/O operations on the table, because SQL Server has to perform additional reads to access the data.

The second metric is *internal fragmentation*, which is the amount of free space available on the data pages. A large degree of internal fragmentation will increase the size of the table on disk and in memory, which decreases performance.

Listing 14-2 shows how to detect inefficient heap tables. The code uses the `sys.dm_db_index_physical_stats` function (*https://oreil.ly/NlpJO*), running it in `DETAILED` mode. In this mode, the function scans the entire table, so it's better to run it in a nonproduction environment—for example, against a recent database backup restored on a nonproduction server.

The performance impact of forwarding pointers and internal fragmentation increases along with their growth, although it is hard to provide exact thresholds at which they become a problem. As a rule of thumb, the number of forwarding pointers should not exceed 2% to 3% of the total number of rows in the table. I like to see internal fragmentation be within 20% to 25%. In large tables, I like to see even lower values, especially when large amounts of data become static.

You can rebuild inefficient heap tables with the `ALTER TABLE REBUILD` statement after you detect them.

Listing 14-2. Detecting inefficient heap tables

```
SELECT TOP 25
    t.object_id
    ,s.name + '.' + t.name AS [table]
    ,SUM(ips.record_count) AS [rows]
    ,SUM(ips.forwarded_record_count)
        AS [forwarding pointers]
    ,SUM(ips.avg_page_space_used_in_percent * ips.page_count) /
        NULLIF(SUM(ips.page_count),0)
            AS [internal fragmentation %]
FROM
    sys.tables t WITH (NOLOCK)
        JOIN sys.schemas s WITH (NOLOCK) ON
            t.schema_id = s.schema_id
        CROSS APPLY
            sys.dm_db_index_physical_stats
                (DB_ID(),t.object_id,0,NULL,'DETAILED') ips
WHERE
    t.is_memory_optimized = 0 AND
    t.is_ms_shipped = 0 AND
    EXISTS
    (
        SELECT *
        FROM sys.indexes i WITH (NOLOCK)
        WHERE t.object_id = i.object_id AND i.index_id = 0
```

```
        )
GROUP BY
    t.object_id, s.name, t.name
ORDER BY
    [forwarding pointers] DESC
OPTION (RECOMPILE, MAXDOP 1);
```

Indexes with the uniqueidentifier Data Type

B-Tree Indexes that use randomly generated values for keys often cause performance problems. Random values may introduce very significant index fragmentation, and they are slow during large batch operations.

One of the most common approaches to generating random values is to use the uniqueidentifier data type. The code in Listing 14-3 detects indexes that have uniqueidentifier as the leftmost key column in the index. When you detect this, you can also look at index fragmentation with the sys.dm_db_index_physical_stats view.

Listing 14-3. Getting indexes with uniqueidentifiers in the leftmost key column

```
SELECT
    t.object_id
    ,s.name + '.' + t.name AS [table]
    ,i.name AS [index]
    ,i.is_disabled
    ,p.rows
FROM
    sys.tables t WITH (NOLOCK)
        JOIN sys.schemas s WITH (NOLOCK) ON
            t.schema_id = s.schema_id
        JOIN sys.indexes i WITH (NOLOCK) ON
            t.object_id = i.object_id
        CROSS APPLY
        (
            SELECT SUM(p.rows) AS [rows]
            FROM sys.partitions p WITH (NOLOCK)
            WHERE i.object_id = p.object_id AND i.index_id = p.index_id
        ) p
WHERE
    t.is_memory_optimized = 0 AND
    i.type in (1,2) AND /* CI and NCI */
    i.is_hypothetical = 0 AND
    EXISTS
    (
        SELECT *
        FROM
            sys.index_columns ic WITH (NOLOCK)
                JOIN sys.columns c WITH (NOLOCK) ON
                    ic.object_id = c.object_id AND
```

```
                    ic.column_id = c.column_id
        WHERE
            ic.object_id = i.object_id AND
            ic.index_id = i.index_id AND
            ic.key_ordinal = 1 AND
            c.system_type_id = 36 /* uniqueidentifier */
    )
ORDER BY
    p.[rows] DESC
OPTION (RECOMPILE, MAXDOP 1);
```

You'll need to analyze how new `uniqueidentifier` values are generated. Random values generated in the application or with the `NEWID()` function will lead to problems; however, the `NEWSEQUENTIALID()` function introduces ever-increasing GUID values that behave similarly to `identity` columns (except that they are less efficient due to their larger data type size). Keep in mind that the `NEWSEQUENTIALID()` function may generate values lower than it previously generated after an OS restart or failover.

Unfortunately, there is no simple way to address the problems introduced by indexed random keys. I recommend that you analyze the amount of fragmentation, tune the index maintenance strategy and the `FILLFACTOR` index property to minimize page splits, and consider code refactoring when it is an option.

Wide and Nonunique Clustered Indexes

For good system performance, you need efficient clustered indexes. In addition to supporting critical queries, the ideal clustered index has the following three characteristics:

Static

First, an ideal clustered index should be *static*. The goal is generally to avoid updating clustered keys, as this is a very expensive operation that requires moving data rows to another place in the B-Tree (of the clustered index) and then updating `row-ids` in all nonclustered index rows that reference modified data.

Narrow

Second, an ideal clustered index should be *narrow*. Because clustered index key columns present as `row-id` in all nonclustered indexes, wide clustered index keys lead to wide and, therefore, less efficient nonclustered indexes.

It is impossible to provide hard guidelines as to how *narrow* the index should be—this completely belongs in the "it depends" category. Just remember that narrow indexes are more efficient than wide ones. For example, 4-byte `int`- or 8-byte `bigint`-based primary keys are always more efficient than 16-byte `uniqueidentifier` keys.

Unique

Finally, an ideal clustered index should be defined as *unique*. When you don't define this, SQL Server adds another 4-byte internal column called *uniquifier* (not to be confused with *uniqueidentifier*!) that enforces the uniqueness of the clustered index keys. This column increases the size of clustered and nonclustered index keys and should be avoided when possible.

Listing 14-4 shows two queries. The first provides the 25 tables with the widest clustered index keys, based on key column data types. The second produces a list of tables with nonunique clustered indexes.

Listing 14-4. Detecting inefficient clustered indexes

```
SELECT TOP 25
    t.object_id
    ,s.name + '.' + t.name AS [table]
    ,p.rows
    ,ic.[max length]
FROM
    sys.tables t WITH (NOLOCK)
        JOIN sys.schemas s WITH (NOLOCK) ON
            t.schema_id = s.schema_id
        CROSS APPLY
        (
            SELECT SUM(p.rows) AS [rows]
            FROM sys.partitions p WITH (NOLOCK)
            WHERE t.object_id = p.object_id AND p.index_id = 1
        ) p
        CROSS APPLY
        (
            SELECT SUM(c.max_length) as [max length]
            FROM
                sys.indexes i
                    JOIN sys.index_columns ic WITH (NOLOCK) ON
                        i.object_id = ic.object_id AND
                        i.index_id = ic.index_id AND
                        ic.is_included_column = 0
                    JOIN sys.columns c WITH (NOLOCK) ON
                        ic.object_id = c.object_id AND
                        ic.column_id = c.column_id
            WHERE
                i.object_id = t.object_id AND
                i.index_id = 1 AND
                i.type = 1
        ) ic
WHERE
    t.is_memory_optimized = 0
ORDER BY
    ic.[max length] DESC
OPTION (RECOMPILE, MAXDOP 1);
```

```
-- Non-unique CI
SELECT
    t.object_id
    ,s.name + '.' + t.name AS [table]
    ,p.rows
FROM
    sys.tables t WITH (NOLOCK)
        JOIN sys.schemas s WITH (NOLOCK) ON
            t.schema_id = s.schema_id
        CROSS APPLY
        (
            SELECT SUM(p.rows) AS [rows]
            FROM sys.partitions p WITH (NOLOCK)
            WHERE t.object_id = p.object_id AND p.index_id = 1
        ) p
WHERE
    t.is_memory_optimized = 0 AND
    EXISTS
    (
        SELECT *
        FROM sys.indexes i WITH (NOLOCK)
        WHERE
            t.object_id = i.object_id AND
            i.index_id = 1 AND
            i.is_unique = 0 AND
            i.type = 1 /* CI */
    )
ORDER BY
    p.[rows] DESC
OPTION (RECOMPILE, MAXDOP 1);
```

Do not jump to conclusions based strictly on query outputs. The benefits of having the right clustered indexes to support critical queries may easily offset the overhead introduced by wide and nonunique indexes. Look at the queries and indexing holistically before making the decision to refactor database schema.

Nevertheless, it is always better to create indexes—clustered and nonclustered—as unique if data in the index key is unique. This makes the clustered index more efficient, eliminating the unnecessary overhead of a `uniquifier` column. This also helps the Query Optimizer generate more efficient execution plans.

Untrusted Foreign Keys

Aside from a very few edge cases, it's always good to define foreign key constraints in the database. They improve data quality and reduce errors and bugs. Moreover, they often improve performance—for example, the Query Optimizer can remove unnecessary joins between tables with foreign keys present.

There are two ways to create foreign key constraints. By default, they are created as *trusted* with SQL Server validating that existing data in the tables does not violate the constraint. You can also create the constraint as *untrusted* using the WITH NOCHECK clause in the ALTER TABLE statement. In this case, SQL Server enforces the constraint going forward; however, it does not validate existing data.

Unfortunately, untrusted foreign key constraints limit possible optimizations for the Query Optimizer, and it is better to validate untrusted foreign keys. Listing 14-5 allows you to detect untrusted constraints in the database.

Listing 14-5. Selecting untrusted foreign key constraints

```
SELECT
    fk.is_disabled
    ,fk.is_not_trusted
    ,fk.name AS [FK]
    ,ps.name + '.' + pt.name AS [Referencing Table / Detail]
    ,rs.name + '.' + rt.name AS [Referenced Table / Master]
    ,fk.update_referential_action_desc
    ,fk.delete_referential_action_desc
FROM
    sys.foreign_keys fk WITH (NOLOCK)
        JOIN sys.tables pt WITH (NOLOCK) ON
            fk.parent_object_id = pt.object_id
        JOIN sys.schemas ps WITH (NOLOCK) ON
            pt.schema_id = ps.schema_id
        JOIN sys.tables rt WITH (NOLOCK) ON
            fk.referenced_object_id = rt.object_id
        JOIN sys.schemas rs WITH (NOLOCK) ON
            rt.schema_id = rs.schema_id
WHERE
    fk.is_not_trusted = 1 OR fk.is_disabled = 1
OPTION (RECOMPILE, MAXDOP 1);
```

You can validate constraints with the ALTER TABLE WITH CHECK CHECK CONSTRAINT command (the CHECK keyword should appear twice in the statement). A word of caution, though: this operation scans the table, acquiring the schema modification (Sch-M) lock for the duration of the scan. Schedule it during downtime, especially with large tables.

Nonindexed Foreign Keys

Foreign key constraints require you to have an index on the constraint columns in a referenced (master) table. You are not, however, required to have an index in a referencing (detail) table. This may lead to very serious issues during referential integrity checks.

Consider the situation when you delete a row in a referenced table. SQL Server needs to check whether this operation violated the constraint and potentially perform a cascading action in the referencing table. Without the index, this would lead to a referencing table scan, which introduces performance and potential blocking issues.

Listing 14-6 returns the list of foreign key constraints that don't have corresponding indexes in referencing tables defined. With few exceptions, you want to create the indexes to support referential integrity operations.

Obviously, take potential index usage into consideration. For example, if you have foreign keys referencing static lookup tables that have never been updated or deleted, the indexes may not be needed. On the other hand, if the referenced tables are not static and you anticipate referential integrity checks or cascading operations, create indexes to support them.

Another factor is queries that join the tables, filtering data by lookup table attributes. Having indexes in the referencing tables may lead to better execution plans.

Listing 14-6. Getting nonindexed foreign key constraints

```
SELECT
    fk.is_disabled
    ,fk.is_not_trusted
    ,fk.name as [FK]
    ,ps.name + '.' + pt.name AS [Referencing Table / Detail]
    ,rs.name + '.' + rt.name AS [Referenced Table / Master]
    ,fk.update_referential_action_desc
    ,fk.delete_referential_action_desc
    ,fk_cols.cols as [fk columns]
FROM
    sys.foreign_keys fk WITH (NOLOCK)
        JOIN sys.tables pt WITH (NOLOCK) ON
            fk.parent_object_id = pt.object_id
        JOIN sys.schemas ps WITH (NOLOCK) ON
            pt.schema_id = ps.schema_id
        JOIN sys.tables rt WITH (NOLOCK) ON
            fk.referenced_object_id = rt.object_id
        JOIN sys.schemas rs WITH (NOLOCK) ON
            rt.schema_id = rs.schema_id
        CROSS APPLY
        (
            SELECT
                (
                    SELECT
                        UPPER(col.name) AS [text()]
                        ,',' AS [text()]
                    FROM
                        sys.foreign_key_columns fkc WITH (NOLOCK)
                            JOIN sys.columns col WITH (NOLOCK) ON
                                fkc.parent_object_id = col.object_id AND
```

```
                                    fkc.parent_column_id = col.column_id
                        WHERE
                            fkc.constraint_object_id = fk.object_id
                        ORDER BY
                            fkc.constraint_column_id
                        FOR XML PATH('')
                ) as cols
        ) fk_cols
WHERE
    NOT EXISTS
    (
        SELECT *
        FROM
            sys.indexes i WITH (NOLOCK)
                CROSS APPLY
                (
                    SELECT
                        (
                            SELECT
                                UPPER(col.name) AS [text()]
                                ,',' AS [text()]
                            FROM
                                sys.index_columns ic WITH (NOLOCK)
                                    JOIN sys.columns col WITH (NOLOCK) ON
                                        ic.object_id = col.object_id AND
                                        ic.column_id = col.column_id
                            WHERE
                                i.object_id = ic.object_id AND
                                i.index_id = ic.index_id AND
                                ic.is_included_column = 0
                            ORDER BY
                                ic.partition_ordinal
                            FOR XML PATH('')
                        ) AS cols
                ) idx_col
        WHERE
            i.object_id = fk.parent_object_id AND
            CHARINDEX(fk_cols.cols,idx_col.cols) = 1 AND
            i.is_disabled = 0 AND
            i.is_hypothetical = 0 AND
            i.has_filter = 0 AND
            i.type IN (1,2)
    )
ORDER BY
    [Referenced Table / Master]
OPTION (RECOMPILE, MAXDOP 1);
```

The preceding script excludes filtered indexes from the evaluation, which may incorrectly include some foreign keys in the output. Think about a scenario when a detail table has a nullable referencing column, Col, and an index defined with a Col IS NOT

NULL filter. This index will be ignored by the script even though it is perfectly valid for referential integrity support. Pay attention to this possibility during analysis.

Redundant Indexes

As you remember from Chapter 5, the data in the composite B-Tree Indexes is sorted starting from leftmost to rightmost key columns. SQL Server may use indexes for the index seek operation as long as it has SARGable predicates on the leftmost columns of the index.

Consider two indexes, IDX1(LastName) and IDX2(LastName, FirstName), as an example. The data in both indexes is sorted based on LastName. Next, IDX2 has the data sorted by FirstName within each LastName, while IDX1 would not have FirstName data sorted. Nevertheless, both indexes would support index seek on LastName data, which makes IDX1 redundant and unnecessary.

In some edge cases, you may need to keep redundant indexes with narrow index keys to support fast index scan operations. Such conditions are quite rare, though.

Listing 14-7 shows you the code you can use to detect potentially redundant indexes with matching leftmost columns. Use this script with care. It is common to have composite indexes that share the same leftmost column.

The multitenant database that stores the data from multiple customers or accounts is a perfect example of this scenario. The CustomerId or AccountId column in those systems is usually present in the WHERE clause of the queries, and it is common to see that column defined as the leftmost column in most of the indexes.

Listing 14-7. Locating potentially redundant indexes

```
SELECT
    s.name + '.' + t.name AS [Table]
    ,i1.index_id AS [I1 ID]
    ,i1.name AS [I1 Name]
    ,dupIdx.index_id AS [I2 ID]
    ,dupIdx.name AS [I2 Name]
    ,LEFT(i1_col.key_col,LEN(i1_col.key_col) - 1) AS [I1 Keys]
    ,LEFT(i1_col.included_col,LEN(i1_col.included_col) - 1) AS [I1 Included Col]
    ,i1.filter_definition AS [I1 Filter]
    ,LEFT(i2_col.key_col,LEN(i2_col.key_col) - 1) AS [I2 Keys]
    ,LEFT(i2_col.included_col,LEN(i2_col.included_col) - 1) AS [I2 Included Col]
    ,dupIdx.filter_definition AS [I2 Filter]
    ,IIF(
        CHARINDEX(i1_col.key_col, i2_col.key_col) = 1 OR
```

```
                CHARINDEX(i2_col.key_col, i1_col.key_col) = 1,'Yes','No'
        ) AS [Fully Redundant]
FROM
    sys.tables t WITH (NOLOCK)
        JOIN sys.indexes i1 wITH (NOLOCK) ON
            t.object_id = i1.object_id
        JOIN sys.index_columns ic1 WITH (NOLOCK) ON
            ic1.object_id = i1.object_id AND
            ic1.index_id = i1.index_id AND
            ic1.key_ordinal = 1
        JOIN sys.columns c WITH (NOLOCK) ON
            c.object_id = ic1.object_id AND
            c.column_id = ic1.column_id
        JOIN sys.schemas s WITH (NOLOCK) ON
            t.schema_id = s.schema_id
        CROSS APPLY
        (
            SELECT i2.index_id, i2.name, i2.filter_definition
            FROM
                sys.indexes i2 WITH (NOLOCK)
                    JOIN sys.index_columns ic2 WITH (NOLOCK) ON
                        ic2.object_id = i2.object_id AND
                        ic2.index_id = i2.index_id AND
                        ic2.key_ordinal = 1
            WHERE
                i2.object_id = i1.object_id AND
                i2.index_id > i1.index_id AND
                ic2.column_id = ic1.column_id AND
                i2.type in (1,2) AND
                i2.is_disabled = 0 AND
                i2.is_hypothetical = 0 AND
                (
                    i1.has_filter = i2.has_filter AND
                    ISNULL(i1.filter_definition,'') =
                        ISNULL(i2.filter_definition,'')
                )
        ) dupIdx
        CROSS APPLY
        (
            SELECT
                (
                    SELECT
                        col.name AS [text()]
                        ,IIF(icol_meta.is_descending_key = 1, ' DESC','')
                            AS [text()]
                        ,',' AS [text()]
                    FROM
                        sys.index_columns icol_meta WITH (NOLOCK)
                            JOIN sys.columns col WITH (NOLOCK) ON
                                icol_meta.object_id = col.object_id AND
                                icol_meta.column_id = col.column_id
                    WHERE
```

```
                            icol_meta.object_id = i1.object_id AND
                            icol_meta.index_id = i1.index_id AND
                            icol_meta.is_included_column = 0
                    ORDER BY
                        icol_meta.key_ordinal
                    FOR XML PATH('')
            ) AS key_col
            ,(
                SELECT
                    col.name AS [text()]
                    ,',' AS [text()]
                FROM
                    sys.index_columns icol_meta WITH (NOLOCK)
                        JOIN sys.columns col WITH (NOLOCK) ON
                            icol_meta.object_id = col.object_id AND
                            icol_meta.column_id = col.column_id
                WHERE
                    icol_meta.object_id = i1.object_id AND
                    icol_meta.index_id = i1.index_id AND
                    icol_meta.is_included_column = 1
                ORDER BY
                    col.name
                FOR XML PATH('')
            ) AS included_col
    ) i1_col
    CROSS APPLY
    (
        SELECT
            (
                SELECT
                    col.name AS [text()]
                    ,IIF(icol_meta.is_descending_key = 1, ' DESC','')
                        AS [text()]
                    ,',' AS [text()]
                FROM
                    sys.index_columns icol_meta WITH (NOLOCK)
                        JOIN sys.columns col WITH (NOLOCK) ON
                            icol_meta.object_id = col.object_id AND
                            icol_meta.column_id = col.column_id
                WHERE
                    icol_meta.object_id = t.object_id AND
                    icol_meta.index_id = dupIdx.index_id AND
                    icol_meta.is_included_column = 0
                ORDER BY
                    icol_meta.key_ordinal
                FOR XML PATH('')
            ) AS key_col
            ,(
                SELECT
                    col.name AS [text()]
                    ,',' AS [text()]
                FROM
```

```
                    sys.index_columns icol_meta WITH (NOLOCK)
                        JOIN sys.columns col WITH (NOLOCK) ON
                            icol_meta.object_id = col.object_id AND
                            icol_meta.column_id = col.column_id
                WHERE
                    icol_meta.object_id = t.object_id AND
                    icol_meta.index_id = dupIdx.index_id AND
                    icol_meta.is_included_column = 1
                ORDER BY
                    col.name
                FOR XML PATH('')
            ) AS included_col
        ) i2_col
WHERE
    i1.is_disabled = 0 AND
    i1.is_hypothetical = 0 AND
    i1.type in (1,2)
ORDER BY
    s.name, t.name, i1.index_id
OPTION (RECOMPILE, MAXDOP 1);
```

You can usually drop fully redundant indexes (pay attention to index filters and included columns) and perform additional analysis looking for the candidates for index consolidation. For example, you can consolidate the IDX3 and IDX4 indexes defined in Listing 14-8 into IDX5. Pay attention to index usage statistics (I will cover this later in this chapter), as they may provide you the information on which indexes are rarely used.

Listing 14-8. Examples of index consolidation

```
CREATE INDEX IDX3 ON T(LastName, FirstName) INCLUDE(Phone);
CREATE INDEX IDX4 ON T(LastName) INCLUDE (SSN);
--IDX3 and IDX4 can be consolidated to IDX5
CREATE INDEX IDX3 ON T(LastName, FirstName) INCLUDE(Phone,SSN);
```

 Analyze database schema and queries, making sure that indexes are not referenced in index hints, before dropping or disabling them!

High Identity Values

One silly but, at the same time, very dangerous condition you may encounter is running out of capacity for integer-based columns. Think about a table with an INT IDENTITY PRIMARY KEY that reaches the value of 2,147,483,647, which is the maximum that the INT data type allows you to store. All further INSERT operations to the table would fail, which could lead to a production outage.

To make matters worse, this condition is hard to recover from. While you can change the data type from INT to BIGINT, the ALTER TABLE ALTER COLUMN statement can take hours or even days to complete on large tables. Moreover, it will lock the table with a schema modification (Sch-M) lock during execution. It is sad but not uncommon to see people lose their jobs when this happens.

Listing 14-9 shows the code you can use to detect identity columns and sequences that are running out of capacity. Run it on your systems regularly and address the risks proactively when you detect issues.

Listing 14-9. Identifying identity columns with high utilization

```
DECLARE
    @Types TABLE
    (
        type_id INT NOT NULL PRIMARY KEY,
        name SYSNAME NOT NULL,
        max_val DECIMAL(38) NOT NULL
    )

INSERT INTO @Types(type_id, name, max_val)
VALUES
     (48,'TINYINT',255)
    ,(52,'SMALLINT',32767)
    ,(56,'INT',2147483647)
    ,(127,'BIGINT',9223372036854775807)
    ,(108,'NUMERIC',99999999999999999999999999999999999999)  -- 10^38-1
    ,(106,'DECIMAL',99999999999999999999999999999999999999); -- 10^38-1

DECLARE
    @percentThreshold INT = 50;

;WITH CTE
AS
(
    SELECT
        s.name + '.' + t.name AS [table]
        ,c.name AS [column]
        ,tp.name + IIF(tp.type_id IN (106,108), '(' +
            CONVERT(VARCHAR(2),c.precision) + ')','') AS [type]
        ,CONVERT(DECIMAL(38),IDENT_CURRENT(t.name)) AS [identity]
        ,CASE
            WHEN tp.type_id IN (106,108)
            THEN
                CASE
                    WHEN c.precision < 38
                    THEN POWER(CONVERT(DECIMAL(38),10),c.precision) - 1
                    ELSE tp.max_val
                END
            ELSE
```

```
                tp.max_val
            END AS [max value]
    FROM
        sys.tables t WITH (NOLOCK)
            JOIN sys.schemas s WITH (NOLOCK) ON
                t.schema_id = s.schema_id
            JOIN sys.columns c WITH (NOLOCK) ON
                c.object_id = t.object_id
            JOIN @Types tp ON
                tp.type_id = c.system_type_id
    WHERE
        c.is_identity = 1
)
SELECT
    *
    ,CONVERT(DECIMAL(6,3),[identity] / [max value] * 100.)
        AS [percent full]
FROM
    CTE
WHERE
    CONVERT(DECIMAL(6,3),[identity] / [max value] * 100.) >
        @percentThreshold
ORDER BY
    [percent full] DESC;

-- Sequences
;WITH CTE
AS
(
    SELECT
        s.name + '.' + seq.name AS [sequence]
        ,tp.name AS [type]
        ,CASE tp.type_id
            WHEN 48 THEN
                CONVERT(DECIMAL(38),CONVERT(TINYINT,seq.current_value))
            WHEN 52 THEN
                CONVERT(DECIMAL(38),CONVERT(SMALLINT,seq.current_value))
            WHEN 56 THEN
                CONVERT(DECIMAL(38),CONVERT(INT,seq.current_value))
            WHEN 127 THEN
                CONVERT(DECIMAL(38),CONVERT(BIGINT,seq.current_value))
            WHEN 106 THEN
                CONVERT(DECIMAL(38),seq.current_value)
            WHEN 108 THEN
                CONVERT(DECIMAL(38),seq.current_value)
        END as [current]
        ,CASE tp.type_id
            WHEN 48 THEN
                CONVERT(DECIMAL(38),CONVERT(TINYINT,seq.maximum_value))
            WHEN 52 THEN
                CONVERT(DECIMAL(38),CONVERT(SMALLINT,seq.maximum_value))
            WHEN 56 THEN
```

```
                CONVERT(DECIMAL(38),CONVERT(INT,seq.maximum_value))
            WHEN 127 THEN
                CONVERT(DECIMAL(38),CONVERT(BIGINT,seq.maximum_value))
            WHEN 106 THEN
                CONVERT(DECIMAL(38),seq.maximum_value)
            WHEN 108 THEN
                CONVERT(DECIMAL(38),seq.maximum_value)
        END as [max value]
    FROM
        sys.sequences seq WITH (NOLOCK)
            JOIN sys.schemas s WITH (NOLOCK) ON
                seq.schema_id = s.schema_id
            JOIN @Types tp ON
                tp.type_id = seq.system_type_id
)
SELECT
    *
    ,CONVERT(DECIMAL(6,3), [current] / [max value] * 100.) as [percent full]
FROM
    CTE
WHERE
    CONVERT(DECIMAL(6,3), [current] / [max value] * 100.) >
        @percentThreshold
ORDER BY
    [percent full] DESC;
```

Obviously, the preceding script will not catch a situation in which the values are generated in the code. Nor does it check possible out-of-capacity risks not related to identity and sequences. I included in the book's companion materials a script (created by Erland Sommarskog, who did a great job reviewing this book!) that shows the maximum values of index keys in all database indexes.

These are just a few examples of what you can do with catalog views to detect inefficiencies and issues with the database schema. Explore other views and be creative!

Now let's look at another gold mine of information: index usage and operational statistics.

Index Analysis

As we all know, indexes help improve query performance. Unfortunately, they come at a cost: they increase the amount of data in the database, consume additional memory, and add overhead during data modifications. A large number of inefficient and/or unused indexes may significantly degrade system performance.

The query optimization process is an essential part of performance tuning and often leads to the creation of new indexes in the database. However, unless you are operating in an emergency situation, I always advocate spending time analyzing and removing inefficient indexes *before* starting to create new ones. This will remove the overhead they introduce and simplify the optimization process.

SQL Server comes with two dynamic management views for index usage analysis. The first, the `sys.dm_db_index_usage_stats` view (*https://oreil.ly/IcA15*), shows you how many queries used the index for seek, scan, update, and lookup operations. The second, the `sys.dm_db_index_operational_stats` view (*https://oreil.ly/AWvEX*), gives you information on row-level access and operational metrics, including I/O, locking, latching, and a few others.

There is a key difference in how these metrics are collected. The `sys.dm_db_index_usage_stats` view provides information on the query level, while the `sys.dm_db_index_operational_stats` view works on the row level. For example, if you run a query that inserts 1,000 rows into a table, the first view will have a `user_updates` value increased by 1. In contrast, the `leaf_insert_count` column in the second view will be incremented by 1,000.

SQL Server does not persist index usage statistics. The metrics in the views will be cleared when SQL Server restarts or the database goes offline. Moreover, in some old SQL Server builds (SQL Server 2012 prior to SP2 CU12 and SP3 CU3; SQL Server 2014 prior to SP2), the metrics will be cleared when you perform an index rebuild operation. You need to factor this into your analysis, making sure the statistics are representative and do not miss important but infrequently executed queries, such as, for example, a critical process in the accounting system that runs on a schedule once per month.

You also need to look at index usage on readable secondaries in the Availability Groups setup. It is common to have some indexes to support queries on secondary nodes, and those indexes may appear as unused on the primary node.

Let's look at both views in more detail and see how we can interpret information from them.

The sys.dm_db_index_usage_stats View

The `sys.dm_db_index_usage_stats` view is one of the main index usage analysis tools. It provides data on how often the index is used or, to be precise, how many times queries utilized the index and the index appeared in the execution plans.

The data is grouped by access methods, and you'll see separate metrics for seek, scan, and lookup operations. Finally, the view also shows how often the index has been updated, which helps you estimate the update overhead it introduces.

Listing 14-10 shows you the code that utilizes this view. I am renaming some of the view columns in the output to make them more compact. I will use both the view column names and my aliases interchangeably in this chapter.

Listing 14-10. Using the sys.dm_db_index_usage_stats view

```
SELECT
    t.object_id
    ,i.index_id
    ,s.name + '.' + t.name AS [Table]
    ,i.name AS [Index]
    ,i.type_desc
    ,i.has_filter AS [Filtered]
    ,i.is_unique AS [Unique]
    ,p.rows AS [Rows]
    ,ius.user_seeks AS [Seeks]
    ,ius.user_scans AS [Scans]
    ,ius.user_lookups AS [Lookups]
    ,ius.user_seeks + ius.user_scans + ius.user_lookups AS [Reads]
    ,ius.user_updates AS [Updates]
    ,ius.last_user_seek AS [Last Seek]
    ,ius.last_user_scan AS [Last Scan]
    ,ius.last_user_lookup AS [Last Lookup]
    ,ius.last_user_update AS [Last Update]
FROM
    sys.tables t WITH (NOLOCK)
        JOIN sys.indexes i WITH (NOLOCK) ON
            t.object_id = i.object_id
        JOIN sys.schemas s WITH (NOLOCK) ON
            t.schema_id = s.schema_id
        CROSS APPLY
        (
            SELECT SUM(p.rows) AS [rows]
            FROM sys.partitions p WITH (NOLOCK)
            WHERE
                i.object_id = p.object_id AND
                i.index_id = p.index_id
        ) p
        LEFT OUTER JOIN sys.dm_db_index_usage_stats ius ON
            ius.database_id = DB_ID() AND
            ius.object_id = i.object_id AND
            ius.index_id = i.index_id
WHERE
    i.is_disabled = 0 AND
    i.is_hypothetical = 0 AND
    t.is_memory_optimized = 0 AND
    t.is_ms_shipped = 0
ORDER BY
    s.name, t.name, i.index_id
OPTION (RECOMPILE, MAXDOP 1);
```

Figure 14-2 shows the output of the code.

	object_id	index_id	Table	Index	type_desc	Filtered	Unique	Rows	Seeks	Scans	Lookups
1	5801971...	1	Table_5801	Index_1	CLUSTERED	0	1	920095	3003390844	442375	35632327
2	5801971...	3	Table_5801	Index_3	NONCLUSTERED	0	1	920095	420014	0	0
3	5801971...	7	Table_5801	Index_7	NONCLUSTERED	0	0	920095	2040257472	7	0
4	5801971...	20	Table_5801	Index_20	NONCLUSTERED	0	0	920095	1805673313	43	0
5	5801971...	22	Table_5801	Index_22	NONCLUSTERED	0	0	920095	1288379097	0	0
6	2107310...	1	Table_2107	Index_1	CLUSTERED	0	1	2701711053	136545557	44714994	104653148
7	2107310...	2	Table_2107	Index_2	NONCLUSTERED	0	0	2701711053	2090315	0	0
8	2107310...	3	Table_2107	Index_3	NONCLUSTERED	0	0	2701711053	10	0	0

Reads	Updates	Last Seek	Last Scan	Last Lookup	Last Update
3039465546	1429545988	2021-08-22 09:55:24.943	2021-08-22 09:55:14.567	2021-08-22 09:55:23.983	2021-08-22 09:55:24.923
420014	673402076	2021-08-22 09:54:39.727	NULL	NULL	2021-08-22 09:55:24.923
2040257479	1344552091	2021-08-22 09:55:24.963	2021-02-10 17:43:00.593	NULL	2021-08-22 09:55:24.923
1805673356	1344552091	2021-08-22 09:55:24.990	2021-08-20 10:56:54.933	NULL	2021-08-22 09:55:24.923
1288379097	1344552091	2021-08-22 09:55:25.027	NULL	NULL	2021-08-22 09:55:24.923
285913699	44717469	2021-08-22 09:55:21.800	2021-08-22 09:55:20.300	2021-08-22 09:55:23.583	2021-08-22 09:55:20.297
2090315	44717461	2021-08-22 09:55:04.730	NULL	NULL	2021-08-22 09:55:20.297
10	44717461	2021-07-22 13:15:04.757	NULL	NULL	2021-08-22 09:55:20.297

Figure 14-2. Output from the sys.dm_db_index_usage_stats view

Let's look at the columns in the output:

database_id, object_id, *and* index_id

> The database_id, object_id, and index_id columns reference database, table, and index, respectively. You can use them to filter the output and join them with sys.databases, sys.tables, and sys.indexes catalog views.

user_seek, user_scan, *and* user_lookup

> The user_seek, user_scan, and user_lookup columns tell you how often queries used the index in the Index Seek, Index Scan, Key Lookup, and RID Lookup operators. An efficient B-Tree Index in an OLTP system should primarily use an index seek.

> Remember, however, as I discussed in Chapter 5, that the Index Seek operators are not always efficient and may scan a very large range of rows depending on the seek predicate and the data.

user_update

> The user_update column shows how many times the index had been modified by insert, update, delete, or merge operations. In a nutshell, this allows you to estimate the overhead required for index maintenance during data modifications.

> It is very important to remember that user_update represents how many times an operation occurred rather than how many rows it changed. For example, a single DELETE call would always increment a user_update value by 1 regardless of how many rows were deleted.

last_user_seek, last_user_scan, last_user_lookup, *and* last_user_update

> The last_user_* columns tell you the time of the last corresponding operation in the index. This data is useful when SQL Server had not been restarted and usage metrics have been collected for a long time.

system_seek, system_scan, system_lookup, system_update, last_system_seek, last_system_scan, last_system_lookup, *and* last_system_update

> The system_* columns (not shown in the script or in Figure 14-2) provide statistics on index usage by system processes. They include statistics updates, index maintenance, and a few others. In most cases, you don't need to worry about these metrics.

Let's look at a few common patterns in the view output and the conclusions you can draw from them.

Unused indexes

I've performed many SQL Server health checks in the past and I've rarely seen systems that don't have unused and unnecessary indexes present. These indexes are easy to detect as the sys.dm_db_index_usage_stats view does not show any read (user_seek, user_scan, and user_lookup) activity in them.

Figure 14-3 shows an example of such output (I am removing some columns from the results of Listing 14-10 to make the output more concise). As you can see, the indexes with an index_id of 43 and 47 do not perform any reads.

	index_id	Table	Index	Filtered	Unique	Rows	Seeks	Scans	Lookups	Reads	Updates
1	1	Table_1888	Index_1	0	1	38128199	6464388153	248501	1597518500	8062155154	2169976595
2	21	Table_1888	Index_21	0	0	38128205	4604192	0	0	4604192	153890418
3	40	Table_1888	Index_40	0	0	38128206	0	11	0	11	186522085
4	41	Table_1888	Index_41	0	0	38128206	2263209	40700	0	2303909	288356234
5	42	Table_1888	Index_42	0	0	38128206	561352904	3	0	561352907	186829746
6	43	Table_1888	Index_43	0	0	38128206	0	0	0	0	186526890
7	44	Table_1888	Index_44	0	0	38128206	1681656033	0	0	1681656033	389900596
8	47	Table_1888	Index_47	0	0	38128206	0	0	0	0	1248665902
9	53	Table_1888	Index_53	0	0	38128206	11859	3	0	11862	428364779
10	64	Table_1888	Index_64	1	1	298499	23565855	6193576	0	29759431	1922246283

Figure 14-3. Unused indexes

In most cases, these indexes are the easiest to deal with. You can disable and/or drop them with very little risk involved. Just remember to analyze a few things before you do this.

First, as I've mentioned, make sure the indexes are not used across all Availability Group nodes. It is very common to see unused indexes on a primary node being heavily utilized for reporting on readable secondaries.

Second, make sure the usage statistics are representative and that you don't overlook infrequent processes the index supports. This condition is tricky. You need to analyze the benefits and downsides of keeping the index. In some cases, you may consider removing the index and its overhead and running infrequent processes inefficiently. You can also consider disabling the index, reenabling it on schedule when needed.

Finally, pay extra attention to unique indexes. They may support unique constraints, and removing them may lead to data quality issues.

Nevertheless, in many cases unused indexes are low-hanging fruit, and removing them can immediately benefit the system.

Indexes with high maintenance costs

I'd consider indexes that have significantly higher numbers of updates over reads being the more complex case of unused indexes. You may benefit from removing them; however, you need to analyze their usage and estimate any negative impact when infrequently executed queries run without them.

I don't have a formal threshold after which indexes should be analyzed. Personally, I use several criteria. First, I check indexes with a low number of reads, especially those with a low number of seeks (see the index with index_id=40 in Figure 14-3). Next, I look at the indexes whose number of updates is significantly (i.e., an order or orders of magnitude) higher than the number of reads (index_id=53 in Figure 14-3).

You can see some of the queries that utilize the index using the code in Listing 14-11. This code analyzes plan cache data and may miss queries that don't have an execution plan cached. You can adjust the code to run against sys.query_store_plan and other Query Store catalog views (*https://oreil.ly/ub7Ej*) if you have Query Store enabled.

As a word of caution, the code is also slow. You may consider dumping the content of the plan cache into the table in a utility database and do the analysis in a nonproduction environment.

Listing 14-11. Detecting queries that use the index

```
DECLARE
    @IndexName SYSNAME = QUOTENAME('<INDEX NAME>');

;WITH XMLNAMESPACES
(DEFAULT 'http://schemas.microsoft.com/sqlserver/2004/07/showplan')
,CachedData
AS
(
    SELECT DISTINCT
        obj.value('@Database','SYSNAME') AS [Database]
        ,obj.value('@Schema','SYSNAME') + '.' + obj.value('@Table','SYSNAME')
            AS [Table]
```

```
            ,obj.value('@Index','SYSNAME') AS [Index]
            ,obj.value('@IndexKind','VARCHAR(64)') AS [Type]
            ,stmt.value('@StatementText', 'NVARCHAR(MAX)') AS [Statement]
            ,CONVERT(NVARCHAR(MAX),qp.query_plan) AS query_plan
            ,cp.plan_handle
        FROM
            sys.dm_exec_cached_plans cp WITH (NOLOCK)
                CROSS APPLY sys.dm_exec_query_plan(plan_handle) qp
                CROSS APPLY query_plan.nodes
                ('/ShowPlanXML/BatchSequence/Batch/Statements/StmtSimple') batch(stmt)
                CROSS APPLY stmt.nodes
                ('.//IndexScan/Object[@Index=sql:variable("@IndexName")]') idx(obj)
)
SELECT
    cd.[Database]
    ,cd.[Table]
    ,cd.[Index]
    ,cd.[Type]
    ,cd.[Statement]
    ,CONVERT(XML,cd.query_plan) AS query_plan
    ,qs.execution_count
    ,(qs.total_logical_reads + qs.total_logical_writes) / qs.execution_count
        AS [Avg IO]
    ,qs.total_logical_reads
    ,qs.total_logical_writes
    ,qs.total_worker_time
    ,qs.total_worker_time / qs.execution_count / 1000 AS [Avg Worker Time (ms)]
    ,qs.total_rows
    ,qs.creation_time
    ,qs.last_execution_time
FROM
    CachedData cd
        OUTER APPLY
        (
            SELECT
                SUM(qs.execution_count) AS execution_count
                ,SUM(qs.total_logical_reads) AS total_logical_reads
                ,SUM(qs.total_logical_writes) AS total_logical_writes
                ,SUM(qs.total_worker_time) AS total_worker_time
                ,SUM(qs.total_rows) AS total_rows
                ,MIN(qs.creation_time) AS creation_time
                ,MAX(qs.last_execution_time) AS last_execution_time
            FROM sys.dm_exec_query_stats qs WITH (NOLOCK)
            WHERE qs.plan_handle = cd.plan_handle
        ) qs
OPTION (RECOMPILE, MAXDOP 1);
```

Further actions would depend on the number of queries that utilize the index. In some cases, you can refactor them, switching to another index. In other cases, you may drop the index or leave it in the database.

Inefficient reads

Another target for analysis in OLTP environments are indexes with a large number of scans, especially when that number is significantly higher than the number of seeks. Figure 14-4 shows such an example.

	index_id	Table	Index	Filtered	Unique	Rows	Seeks	Scans	Lookups	Reads	Updates
1	1	Table_2887	Index_1	0	1	76707068	2616312067	157348	4961245333	7577714748	1398991251
2	3	Table_2887	Index_3	1	0	573442	231677400	0	0	231677400	1387934116
3	4	Table_2887	Index_4	0	0	76707068	21	59382702	0	59382723	854126441
4	5	Table_2887	Index_5	0	0	76707067	3393509	0	0	3393509	824102200
5	6	Table_2887	Index_6	0	0	76707068	1129131537	1	0	1129131538	868627246
6	8	Table_2887	Index_8	0	0	76707068	175291797	3	0	175291800	817555464
7	9	Table_2887	Index_9	0	0	76707068	0	3124770	0	3124770	857147269
8	35	Table_2887	Index_35	0	0	76707068	568834597	0	0	568834597	719062166

Figure 14-4. Indexes with inefficient reads

You can use an approach similar to what I discussed in the previous section and find queries that use those indexes. I usually start with indexes that have very little or no seeks at all. Queries that scan them usually need to be optimized, which may allow you to remove inefficient usage of the indexes.

Note whether the index is filtered. It is common to scan filtered indexes, and it may be completely normal when an index is small.

Inefficient clustered indexes and heaps

In tables with clustered indexes (index_id=1), a large user_lookup value indicates excessive Key Lookup operations. This is usually a sign of either inefficient clustered indexes or the presence of nonclustered indexes that do not cover frequently executed queries.

Figure 14-5 shows an example. The clustered index shows a large number of lookups with no seeks at all. This pattern is very common when a table has a synthetic CLUSTERED PRIMARY KEY defined on an IDENTITY column and queries use different columns and indexes to access the data.

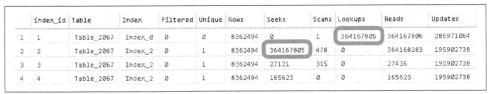

	index_id	Table	Index	Filtered	Unique	Rows	Seeks	Scans	Lookups	Reads	Updates
1	1	Table_2067	Index_0	0	0	8362494	0	1	364167805	364167806	286971064
2	2	Table_2067	Index_2	0	1	8362494	364167805	478	0	364168283	195902738
3	3	Table_2067	Index_2	0	1	8362494	27121	315	0	27436	195902738
4	4	Table_2067	Index_2	0	1	8362494	165623	0	0	165623	195902738

Figure 14-5. Inefficient clustered index

Some of these cases are very easy to analyze and address. For example, in the case shown in Figure 14-5, the index with `index_id=2` is clearly the one that does not cover frequently executed queries and leads to Key Lookup operations. You can consider making it a clustered index, especially if it is not very wide. Alternatively, you can include additional columns in the index to cover the queries.

Unfortunately, not all cases are easy and straightforward. For example, if you look at the statistics shown in Figure 14-4, you'll see that the clustered index is used for both index seek and key lookup operations. You'll also see that it does not clearly show nonclustered indexes that may be responsible for lookups. In this case, you'll likely want to keep the existing clustered index, analyze queries against nonclustered indexes, and potentially make those indexes covering.

Finally, the large number of lookups in heap tables (`index_id=0`) indicates excessive RID Lookup operations. The most common option to address this is to change one of the frequently used nonclustered indexes to become clustered.

Wrapping up

The `sys.dm_db_index_usage_stats` view is a great tool for detecting and removing inefficient indexes. However, as I've said many times already, make sure you are working with the data collected from all the servers in the Availability Group and over a representative period of time.

It is also very beneficial to include the data provided by the `sys.dm_db_opera tional_index_stats` view in your analysis. Let's look at this view in more details.

The sys.dm_db_index_operational_stats View

The `sys.dm_db_index_operational_stats` view provides low-level statistics on index access methods, locking, latching, I/O, and a few other areas. This data is incredibly useful for troubleshooting index performance and identifying locking and latching bottlenecks.

Listing 14-12 shows the simple code that utilizes this view. I show it for demo purposes here; you may benefit from combining the data with `sys.dm _db_index_usage_stats` and other views, as I'll discuss shortly.

Listing 14-12. Using the `sys.dm_db_index_operational_stats` view

```
SELECT
    t.object_id
    ,i.index_id
    ,s.name + '.' + t.name AS [Table]
    ,i.name AS [Index]
    ,i.type_desc
    ,i.has_filter AS [Filtered]
    ,i.is_unique AS [Unique]
    ,p.rows AS [Rows]
    ,ous.*
FROM
    sys.tables t WITH (NOLOCK)
        JOIN sys.indexes i WITH (NOLOCK) ON
            t.object_id = i.object_id
        JOIN sys.schemas s WITH (NOLOCK) ON
            t.schema_id = s.schema_id
        CROSS APPLY
        (
            SELECT SUM(p.rows) AS [rows]
            FROM sys.partitions p WITH (NOLOCK)
            WHERE
                i.object_id = p.object_id AND
                i.index_id = p.index_id
        ) p
        OUTER APPLY sys.dm_db_index_operational_stats
            (DB_ID(),i.object_id,i.index_id,NULL) ous
WHERE
    i.is_disabled = 0 AND
    i.is_hypothetical = 0 AND
    t.is_memory_optimized = 0 AND
    t.is_ms_shipped = 0
ORDER BY
    s.name, t.name, i.index_id
OPTION (RECOMPILE, MAXDOP 1);
```

Figure 14-6 shows the output of the code. You can look at the name of the columns in the output to get some sense of the information the view provides.

I am not going to cover all the columns in the output. Instead, I encourage you to read the Microsoft documentation (*https://oreil.ly/Ze2pc*).

Nevertheless, let's look at a few categories in the columns and discuss how to use them.

object_id	index_id	Table	Index	type_desc	Filtered	Unique	Rows	database_id	object_id	index_id	partition_number
1	1946490013	1	Table_0013	Index_1	CLUSTERED	0	1	0	11	1946490013	1	1
2	274100017	1	Table_0017	Index_1	CLUSTERED	0	1	134	11	274100017	1	1
3	1397580017	1	Table_0017	Index_1	CLUSTERED	0	1	0	NULL	NULL	NULL	NULL

hobt_id	leaf_insert_count	leaf_delete_count	leaf_update_count	leaf_ghost_count	nonleaf_insert_count	nonleaf_delete_count
72057597802774528	0	0	0	0	0	0
72057597681336320	61	0	234	0	3	0
NULL	NULL	NULL	NULL	NULL	NULL	NULL

nonleaf_update_count	leaf_allocation_count	nonleaf_allocation_count	leaf_page_merge_count	nonleaf_page_merge_count	range_scan_count
0	0	0	0	0	4214002
0	3	1	0	0	20302445
NULL	NULL	NULL	NULL	NULL	NULL

singleton_lookup_count	forwarded_fetch_count	lob_fetch_in_pages	lob_fetch_in_bytes	lob_orphan_create_count	lob_orphan_insert_count
0	0	0	0	0	0
3531733818	0	0	0	0	0
NULL	NULL	NULL	NULL	NULL	NULL

row_overflow_fetch_in_pages	row_overflow_fetch_in_bytes	column_value_push_off_row_count	column_value_pull_in_row_count	row_lock_count
0	0	0	0	0
0	0	0	0	594
NULL	NULL	NULL	NULL	NULL

row_lock_wait_count	row_lock_wait_in_ms	page_lock_count	page_lock_wait_count	page_lock_wait_in_ms	index_lock_promotion_attempt_count
0	0	0	0	0	0
0	0	377	0	0	4045
NULL	NULL	NULL	NULL	NULL	NULL

index_lock_promotion_count	page_latch_wait_count	page_latch_wait_in_ms	page_io_latch_wait_count	page_io_latch_wait_in_ms
0	0	0	1	1
0	1	27	1	1
NULL	NULL	NULL	NULL	NULL

tree_page_latch_wait_count	tree_page_latch_wait_in_ms	tree_page_io_latch_wait_count	tree_page_io_latch_wait_in_ms
0	0	0	0
0	0	0	0
NULL	NULL	NULL	NULL

page_compression_attempt_count	page_compression_success_count
0	0
0	0
NULL	NULL

Figure 14-6. Output from the sys.dm_db_index_operational_stats *view*

Data modification statistics

The leaf_insert_count, leaf_update_count, leaf_delete_count, leaf_ghost
_count, and leaf_allocation_count columns give you information about data modifications in the index. Unlike the sys.dm_db_index_usage_stats view, which counts the number of operations, the sys.dm_db_index_operational_stats view gives you the number of affected rows. You can correlate the information from both views to get a better understanding of index maintenance overhead.

In addition, the sys.dm_db_index_operational_stats view provides the same metrics for the intermittent and root levels of B-Tree Indexes through a set of nonleaf_* columns. You can use them for troubleshooting the ACCESS_METH ODS_HOBT_VIRTUAL_ROOT latch caused by root page splits and contention.

Data access statistics

The `singleton_lookup` and `range_scan_count` columns provide you with access method data. The first column counts seeks and lookup operations that return single rows. The second column counts index seek operations that perform a range scan of multiple rows along with index scans. You can use this data to estimate the efficiency of index seeks based on a `singleton_lookup` value. However, it is impossible to estimate how large the range scans are based on the `range_scan_count` value alone.

The `forwarded_fetch_count` column gives you the number of forwarding-pointer reads in the heap tables. Heap tables with a high value in this column are inefficient and need to be rebuilt. You can use this together with the `forwarded_record_count` data in the `sys.dm_db_index_physical_stats` view, as I discussed earlier in this chapter.

The `lob_fetch_in_pages`, `lob_fetch_in_bytes`, `row_overflow_fetch_in_pages`, and `row_overflow_fetch_in_bytes` columns give you statistics on off-row column access. The queries against these tables may select unnecessary columns, perhaps using the `SELECT *` anti-pattern.

Locking information

The `row_lock_count`, `row_lock_wait_count`, `row_lock_wait_in_ms`, `page_lock_count`, `page_lock_wait_count`, and `page_lock_wait_in_ms` columns give you row- and page-level locking statistics. You can use this information to detect the indexes and tables that suffer the most from the locking issues.

The `index_lock_promotion_attempt_count` and `index_lock_promotion_count` columns contain the number of lock escalation attempts and successful lock escalations on the index. The latter column is useful when you see a high percentage of intent lock waits (`LCK_M_I*`), which are often triggered by lock escalations.

Usually, I do not use the `sys.dm_db_index_operational_stats` view as the main tool for troubleshooting locking and blocking. Nevertheless, it is a useful tool to cross-check data collected from other venues, as I discussed in Chapter 8.

Latching information

The `page_latch_wait_count`, `page_latch_wait_in_ms`, `tree_page_latch_wait_count`, and `tree_page_latch_wait_in_ms` columns give you page-latch statistics for the index. The former two columns show the data for leaf-level index pages; the latter two for intermediate and root pages.

These metrics are extremely useful when you see a high percentage of PAGELATCH waits generated in users' databases. Indexes with the highest page latch waits are likely the ones that lead to hotspots and bottlenecks.

I/O information

Similarly, the `page_io_latch_wait_count`, `page_io_latch_wait_in_ms`, `tree_page_io_latch_wait_count`, and `tree_page_io_latch_wait_in_ms` columns point you to the indexes that experienced the most PAGEIOLATCH waits.

As with troubleshooting locking issues, you should not use `sys.dm_db_index_operational_stats` data as your main source for I/O performance troubleshooting. Nevertheless, it is useful to analyze indexes with the highest PAGEIOLATCH waits. You can drop them if they are not in use or compress them and get immediate relief by decreasing the I/O they introduce.

Wrapping up

The `sys.dm_db_index_operational_stats` view provides you with *a lot* of useful information for troubleshooting. The ability to look at low-level statistics on a per-index basis gives you another perspective to validate your assumptions and confirm potential root causes of issues. Do not use this view as your main source from which to drive conclusions, though.

Think about the situation when you troubleshoot disk subsystem performance. You may detect and drop nonclustered indexes with the highest `page_io_latch_wait_in_ms` values; however, nonoptimized queries will just start scanning other indexes. Moreover, it could lead to even higher I/O throughput if SQL Server starts to scan larger clustered indexes.

The proper approach during troubleshooting is to confirm nonoptimized queries as the source of the I/O bottleneck and then detect and optimize the most I/O-intensive queries. You may not even need `sys.dm_db_index_operational_stats` data during query optimization; however, in some cases, it may help to pinpoint I/O-intensive operators in the execution plan.

There is one exception, though: page latching. The `sys.dm_db_index_operational_stats` view can be the key tool for identifying hotspots in indexes. Obviously, you will need to analyze the schema and workload, and confirm the assumption. Nevertheless, the view usually points you in the right direction and speeds up troubleshooting.

As I have said multiple times, look at the system holistically and utilize all the tools available to you. The index usage and operational statistics views are great tools to have in your toolbox.

Holistic View: sp_Index_Analysis

The catalog and dynamic management views provide you with a lot of information for analysis. Unfortunately, there are quite a few of them, and you need to look at many different places to get the full picture. This becomes inconvenient and slows down the process.

In my workflow, I addressed this by writing the stored procedure sp_Index_Analysis, which combines the information from various views and returns it in a single output. You can download this code from this book's companion materials or from my blog (*https://aboutsqlserver.com*).

The stored procedure provides a large amount of information, including the following:

- Index definition and metadata
- Size of the index on disk and in the buffer pool
- Index usage statistics
- Index operational statistics
- Statistics information

You can see sample output in Figure 14-7.

The stored procedure collects the information from one or multiple databases and allows you to persist output in the table for further analysis. I usually consolidate collected data from all Availability Group nodes in a single table before I start researching it.

Obviously, you are not obligated to use this stored procedure. However, it will speed up the process and simplify your work.

	server	collected_on	database_id	database	guid	object_id	index_id	table	index
1	dbserver	2022-04-24 13:12:52.847	6	AppDB	1	1390627997	1	dbo.tbl_139062799	idx_1
2	dbserver	2022-04-24 13:12:52.847	6	AppDB	0	1348199853	1	dbo.tbl_134819985	idx_1
3	dbserver	2022-04-24 13:12:52.847	6	AppDB	0	93243387	1	dbo.tbl_93243387	idx_1

type	key_columns	included_columns	filter	max_key_length	rows	is_unique	is_disabled	lock_escalation
CLUSTERED	cntnr_name,sc	NULL	NULL	526	180173162	1	0	TABLE
CLUSTERED	delta_seq_nun	NULL	NULL	8	179977854	1	0	DISABLE
CLUSTERED	delta_seq_nun	NULL	NULL	8	116448546	1	0	TABLE

max_compression	total_pages	used_pages	data_pages	total_space_mb	used_space_mb	data_space_mb	buffer_pool_space_mb
NONE	1530884	1515056	1494061	11960.031	11836.375	11672.352	17.148
NONE	2422980	2422495	2411026	18929.531	18925.742	18836.141	NULL
NONE	3944236	3943575	3924964	30814.344	30809.180	30663.781	NULL

stats_date	user_seeks	user_scans	user_lookups	user_reads	user_updates	last_user_seek
2022-04-24 03:08:00	212675105	23	0	212675128	171501834	2022-04-24 13:02:00
2022-04-24 07:00:00	31833	8	0	31841	40149	2022-04-24 13:00:00
2022-04-24 07:04:00	31833	0	0	31833	4946	2022-04-24 13:00:00

last_user_scan	last_user_lookup	last_user_update	range_scan_count	singleton_lookup_count	forwarded_fetch_count
2022-03-18 09:58:0	NULL	2022-04-24 13:02	10932050	212675090	0
2022-03-18 15:27:0	NULL	2022-04-24 06:10	0	19877031	0
NULL	NULL	2022-04-24 06:19	0	13433214	0

lob_fetch_in_pages	row_overflow_fetch_in_pages	leaf_insert_count	leaf_update_count	leaf_delete_count	leaf_ghost_count
0	0	130328590	41173243	0	0
0	0	10329936	0	0	9547095
0	0	6671993	0	0	6761221

nonleaf_insert_cou	nonleaf_update_cou	nonleaf_delete_coun	leaf_allocation_count	nonleaf_allocation_count	row_lock_count
2882818	53525310	1804263	12961165	15147	305265513
414946	0	383109	414946	1957	21489764
673193	0	659906	673193	3175	299088

row_lock_wait_cou	row_lock_wait_in_	page_lock_cou	page_lock_wait_cou	page_lock_wait_in	index_lock_promotion_attempt_c
0	0	297383904	40	654	0
0	0	30222224	0	0	0
0	0	1680475	0	0	523

index_lock_promotion_cou	page_latch_wait_cou	page_latch_wait_in_ms	tree_page_latch_wait_cou	tree_page_latch_wait_in_ms
0	3216	4743	2396	4317
0	1	1	1	1
37	5	23	3	18

page_io_latch_wait_count	page_io_latch_wait_in_ms	page_compression_attempt_count	page_compression_success_count
5071739	8374927	0	0
48026	45560	0	0
21728	11558	0	0

Figure 14-7. sp_Index_Analysis output

Summary

SQL Server catalog and dynamic management views are gold mines for identifying inefficiencies in your database design and indexing strategy. You need to perform database schema and index usage analysis as part of system health checks.

You can use key system catalogs, such as `sys.tables`, `sys.indexes`, `sys.index_col umns`, `sys.foreign_keys`, and others, to identify database design inefficiencies. The possible issues include inefficient heap tables and clustered indexes, nonindexed foreign key constraints, and redundant indexes, among many others.

Always check whether the `IDENTITY` columns are reaching maximum data type capacity. Reaching data type capacity may lead to prolonged downtime.

You can use the `sys.dm_db_index_usage_stats` view to analyze and detect inefficient indexes in the database. This includes unused and suboptimal indexes, indexes with high maintenance costs, and inefficient clustered indexes, among other issues. Another view, `sys.dm_db_index_operational_stats`, provides low-level statistics on access, locking, latching, and I/O. It may help you detect hotspots during page latching and find indexes that contribute to other performance issues. Both views are cleared when SQL Server restarts and when the database goes offline. They do not represent index usage on secondary Availability Group replicas. Make sure you are dealing with representative information during your analysis.

Finally, the `sp_Index_Analysis` stored procedure provides holistic information about indexes, including their metadata, size on disk and in the buffer pool, and usage and operational metrics. You can download it from the book's companion materials.

Now it's time for us to discuss virtualizing, as well as troubleshooting SQL Server in a virtualized environment.

Troubleshooting Checklist

☐ Detect potential database schema inefficiencies with the catalog views.

☐ Review the current values and remaining capacity of the `IDENTITY` columns.

☐ Analyze index usage with the `sys.dm_db_index_usage_stats` and `sys.dm _db_index_operational_stats` views, and address possible issues.

CHAPTER 15

SQL Server in Virtualized Environments

Virtualization is now so common that, more often than not, the SQL Server instances we troubleshoot and tune run in virtual environments—which can add complexity.

I will start this chapter by outlining a few considerations regarding database virtualization in general. Next, I will talk about best practices for configuring SQL Server in virtual machines (VMs). Finally, I will provide a few troubleshooting tips for virtual SQL Server instances.

This chapter is by no means a comprehensive guide to SQL Server virtualization. My goal is to provide you with enough knowledge to detect inefficiencies in your SQL Server setup and troubleshoot common performance issues in virtual environments.

I'd also like to give you enough context to speak the virtualization infrastructure team's language. The best results are achieved when multiple teams work together, contributing to one another's expertise. Work with the virtualization team when you need to configure and maintain virtual SQL Server instances and troubleshoot problems they may have.

To Virtualize or Not to Virtualize, That Is the Question

The question of whether to virtualize SQL Server environments has always led to debates. Fifteen years ago, I was a fierce opponent of virtualization, but I've changed my mind. Still, our opinions are irrelevant: virtualization provides multiple benefits, it is widely used, and database engineers deal with virtualized SQL Server instances on a regular basis.

One benefit of virtualization is that it reduces infrastructure costs. You can deploy multiple VMs to the same physical hardware and use it in a much more cost-efficient manner.

Second, virtualization dramatically simplifies system maintenance. You can upsize or downsize VMs with simple configuration changes. You can upgrade hardware by moving VMs to a new, more powerful host with little effort. You can also migrate data to faster storage without any downtime by copying your virtual disks.

Finally, virtualization can provide another layer of High Availability (HA) by restarting or even moving VMs to other hosts in the event of hardware failure. While I do not recommend relying solely on virtualization when you design your HA strategy, it can work as another layer of protection when you combine it with the native SQL Server HA technologies.

Unfortunately, these benefits introduce performance overhead. The amount of overhead varies: it may be unnoticeable in small systems, but it grows with the size of the VMs. For example, in large VMs with dozens of cores and terabytes of memory, overhead may be closer to or even exceed 10%.

Virtualization also impacts licensing costs. In SQL Server Enterprise Edition, virtualization may save you a significant amount of money if you license SQL Server at the host level and overprovision the host (I will talk about overprovisioning shortly). On the other hand, if you are using core-based licensing and/or want to avoid overprovisioning, the performance overhead of virtualization may require you to add more CPUs to your VM, which will lead to the need to buy extra licenses.

In the end, you need to analyze the license cost implications and decide whether virtualization's benefits outweigh the performance overhead it introduces. It's a typical "it depends" situation, which, as a database engineer, you no doubt are very familiar with. In my opinion, virtualization is usually the right answer, except in rare edge cases and in critical systems where you need to get the most from the hardware.

There's one specific scenario when I consider virtualization especially helpful: database consolidation. It is much easier to maintain multiple SQL Server VMs consolidated on a host than multiple databases running on a single SQL Server instance.

In this scenario, virtualization isolates the systems. You can use different versions of SQL Server and OS, apply separate maintenance schedules, support system-specific security and compliance requirements, and reduce the performance impact of instance-level features such as transparent data encryption (which also encrypts tempdb) or auditing.

Pay attention to your SQL Server licensing model, though. The Standard Edition of SQL Server requires you to license *logical cores* in VMs, which can be more expensive than a single physical SQL Server instance. The Enterprise Edition, on the other hand, offers the option to license *physical cores* on the host, regardless of how many logical cores you allocate to database VMs.

Let's begin by discussing provisioning and troubleshooting, starting with configuring SQL Server VMs.

Configuring SQL Server in Virtualized Environments

While the overhead of virtualization is rather small, this is true only when the VMs are provisioned and configured correctly. Improperly implemented, virtualization can seriously hurt the performance of database servers.

There are several areas you need to pay attention to during implementation, including capacity planning, CPU configuration, memory, storage, and the network. I'll examine these one by one.

Capacity Planning

One of the main goals of virtualization is to reduce hardware costs. Infrastructure teams and virtualization administrators tend to put as many VMs on the hosts as possible, maximizing their use of physical hardware, but this strategy isn't always optimal for database deployments. The key to successful SQL Server virtualization is proper capacity planning on both the host and guest levels.

All guest VMs share and compete for the resources on the host. It is possible to allocate and reserve resources (most importantly, CPUs and RAM) for individual guests; however, virtualization administrators prefer to avoid doing so and often *overcommit* these resources. For example, a host with 32 physical cores and 512 GB of RAM may run two dozen VMs, allocating twice as many logical cores and RAM between them.

Overcommitment reduces the need for physical hardware and saves money. It may be acceptable for many noncritical databases that operate under light loads. On the other hand, overcommitment can seriously hurt the performance of critical databases as VMs compete for resources. It can introduce unnecessary delays while VMs wait for CPU availability, leading to memory pressure in VMs and other bottlenecks. It is better to reserve resources for critical VMs.

However, resource reservation also has some negative implications. For example, it may limit your ability to move a VM to another host online in some scenarios. Discuss this with your infrastructure team—they may have other options for prioritizing workload and resource utilization in critical VMs.

When you speak with your infrastructure team, though, be careful with your terminology. For example, the term *overcommitment* has different meanings for database and infrastructure engineers. The first time I discussed this with virtualization administrators, I used it to mean that the number of allocated logical resources exceeds the host's available physical resources. To my surprise, the virtualization administrators did not consider resources to be overallocated until they crossed the ratio of 3:1.

You will need to analyze databases based on their load, SLA, and business criticality. I usually classify them into three tiers:

Tier 1

Mission-critical databases operate under heavy load. VMs for these databases should not operate on overcommitted hosts or they should have resource reservation enabled. You will also need to pay attention to CPU configuration, which I will discuss shortly.

Tier 2

Production databases operate under medium load. They often work fine with some degree of resource overcommitment on the hosts. They may also use resource prioritization over less critical VMs when sharing the same host.

Tier 3

Non-mission–critical databases operate under light load and don't have performance SLAs. Resources on hosts with such databases are usually overcommitted.

When you classify your databases, work with your virtualization administrators to define the proper topology for VMs and their configuration. Obviously, critical tier-1 databases require the most attention and planning.

As a general rule, avoid guest overprovisioning in virtual environments. It is better and easier to provision VMs with enough resources to handle the current load, then add extra resources as the load grows. Make sure you have proper monitoring in place and proactively identify when you need to upgrade.

Fortunately, the price of mistakes and incorrect configurations in virtual environments is much lower than with physical hardware. It is easy to add extra resources to under-provisioned VMs and shuffle VMs around hosts as needed. Keep this in mind when you are doing capacity planning.

CPU Configuration

I'll start with a counterintuitive statement: in shared environments, adding CPUs to VMs can *decrease* their performance rather than *improve* it. In many cases, a VM with fewer cores will outperform a VM with more cores *if* the allocated cores have enough bandwidth to handle the load.

The reason this can occur has to do with how hypervisors handle scheduling. The algorithms are a bit different in Hyper-V and VMware.

A Few Words About Scheduling

Implementing efficient scheduling for multi-CPU VMs has always been difficult. Threads running on different CPUs need to be synchronized, and it is impossible to run a VM's workload on just a subset of CPUs.

The first version of VMware's hypervisor used the concept of *gang scheduling*. In this model, the hypervisor does not allow the VM to execute until it has enough physical CPUs to assign to all CPUs in the VM. For example, a VM with four allocated CPUs would stay suspended until the host has four available CPUs to assign to it.

While gang scheduling worked reasonably well with small VMs, it did not scale well with large, multi-CPU VMs, so VMware introduced another scheduling model. In *relaxed co-scheduling*, the hypervisor allows CPUs in large VMs to execute more independently, monitoring and throttling them when needed.

Relaxed co-scheduling isn't perfect. Performance is still limited by the slowest and most bottlenecked CPU, and there are still cases when a hypervisor needs to schedule all CPUs to run simultaneously, as with gang scheduling.

Hyper-V, on the other hand, uses a different model that relies on the guest OS. Modern versions of Windows and Linux understand when they are running inside a VM, and a kernel in the guest OS asks the hypervisor for CPU time. This model is optimized to reduce (but not eliminate) the need for cross-CPU scheduling synchronizations. It is more efficient with large VMs and CPU overcommitment.

Scheduling overhead and implementation lead us to a simple rule: *in shared and, especially, overcommitted environments, allocate just enough CPUs to handle the load.* Monitor performance after that, adding CPUs as the load grows. Both VMware and Hyper-V environments benefit from this, although the impact of overprovisioned VMs is higher in VMware.

It may still be OK to overprovision critical VMs if you are using resource reservation or running them on hosts that are not overcommitted. Just make sure the topology does not change over time. I've seen many virtualization administrators add other VMs to critical hosts without telling the database engineers.

A few components are involved in CPU configuration in virtualized environments. Following are the important components in the host:

Physical CPU (pCPU)
> This is a physical CPU chip installed on the server; sometimes called the *physical socket* (pSocket).

Physical Core (pCore)
> This is an independent processing core in the physical CPU.

Logical Core (`lCore`)
> Also known as the *logical CPU*, this is the logical processing unit on the physical core. With hyper-threading, each physical core has two logical cores. The total number of logical CPUs on the host can be calculated as (number of `pCPU`) * (number of `pCore` per `pCPU`) * (number of `lCore` in `pCore`).

> For example, a host with two Intel Xeon Gold 6346 CPUs with hyper-threading enabled will have 2 `pCPU` * 16 `pCore` * (2 `lCore` per `pCore`) = 64 total logical cores.

Following are the important components in a VM:

Virtual Socket (`vSocket`) and Virtual Core (`vCore`)
> A *virtual socket* is a virtualized CPU chip that can be configured with one or multiple virtual cores. In VMs, virtual sockets are treated like physical sockets and, in turn, like separate NUMA nodes. (More about this shortly.)

Virtual CPU (`vCPU`)
> This is a virtual processor assigned to a VM. As you might have guessed, the total number of `vCPUs` in a VM can be calculated as (total number of `vSocket`) * (number of `vCore` per `vSocket`).

There are a few elements to consider when you configure SQL Server VMs. The first is whether to enable or disable hyper-threading—a much more complicated decision in the virtual world.

Enabling hyper-threading may improve the host's throughput; however, it can also degrade the throughput of individual VMs. In theory, the host considers hyper-threading during scheduling, when assigning `vCPUs` to the physical cores. In practice, everything may depend on the host's workload.

As always, you need to test performance with and without hyper-threading enabled. Unfortunately, this is hard to measure in virtual environments, because the load on the host changes quickly. Hyper-threading is often a good option for noncritical workloads; however, it may be safer to keep it disabled in tier-1 SQL Server VMs.

The second important element is NUMA configuration. Windows and SQL Server Enterprise Edition are NUMA aware. Aligning the virtual NUMA configuration in guest VMs with the physical NUMA (`pNuma`) configuration may improve performance.

Obviously, it is better to test and tune configuration for your actual workload. For the initial configuration, my rule of thumb is to keep 8 to 12 `vCores` per `vSocket` aligned with the NUMA memory configuration. Remember during alignment that Enterprise Edition uses soft NUMA by default when a NUMA node has more than eight schedulers.

My approach may also change if the host is not overcommitted and the VM's CPU and RAM requirements would fit into a single NUMA node. I can keep the VM within a single pNuma boundary when this is the case.

Let's look at a few examples. I'll assume you have a server with two 16-core CPUs and 256 GB of RAM per NUMA node installed. Table 15-1 shows possible configurations of VMs depending on their requirements.

Table 15-1. Possible VM configurations

VM configuration	vCore and vSocket assignment	Comment
8 CPUs 128 GB of RAM	1 vSocket 8 vCores per vSocket	Everything fits into a single pNuma node.
12 CPUs 192 GB of RAM	1 vSocket, 12 vCores per vSocket or 2 vSockets, 6 vCores per vSocket	Test and choose the optimal configuration.
16 CPUs 256 GB of RAM	2 vSockets, 8 vCores per vSocket or 1 vSocket, 16 vCores per vSocket	Test and choose the optimal configuration. The first option allows more flexibility to the host and can lead to better performance in overcommitted hosts.
8 CPUs 384 GB of RAM	2 vSockets 4 vCores per vSocket	Requires memory from two NUMA nodes.
20 CPUs 256 GB of RAM	2 vSockets 10 vCores per vSocket	Requires cores from two NUMA nodes.

Make sure to check that all NUMA nodes in SQL Server have been correctly aligned and have the same number of CPUs. As I mentioned in Chapter 2, SQL Server assigns connections to NUMA nodes in a round-robin fashion. Uneven CPU distribution across nodes will lead to scheduling issues, since some schedulers in this configuration will handle more work and become busier than others. You can check for this condition by running the code in Listing 15-1.

Listing 15-1. Checking the distribution of schedulers in NUMA nodes

```
SELECT
    parent_node_id AS [NUMA Node]
    ,COUNT(*) AS [Schedulers]
    ,SUM(IIF(status = N'VISIBLE ONLINE',1,0))
        AS [Online Schedulers]
    ,SUM(IIF(status = N'VISIBLE OFFLINE',1,0))
        AS [Offline Schedulers]
    ,SUM(current_tasks_count)
        AS [Current Tasks]
    ,SUM(runnable_tasks_count)
        AS [Runnable Tasks]
FROM
    sys.dm_os_schedulers WITH (NOLOCK)
WHERE
```

```
    status IN (N'VISIBLE ONLINE',N'VISIBLE OFFLINE')
GROUP BY
    parent_node_id
OPTION (RECOMPILE, MAXDOP 1);
```

Some time ago, I had to troubleshoot performance issues in a VM running on a host with two 18-core CPUs. The VM had been provisioned with 17 vSockets and 2 vCores per vSocket. In this configuration, Windows saw 3 physical NUMA nodes, with 16, 16, and 2 vCPUs, respectively. SQL Server, in turn, used soft NUMA and split the first 2 nodes in half.

Figure 15-1 shows the output of Listing 15-1 in that configuration. The fifth NUMA node had two schedulers that were significantly busier than the others.

	Numa Node	Schedulers	Online Schedulers	Offline Schedulers	Current Tasks	Runnable Tasks
1	0	8	8	0	43	10
2	1	8	8	0	38	2
3	2	8	8	0	40	7
4	3	8	8	0	34	1
5	4	2	2	0	77	51

Figure 15-1. NUMA node and schedulers in an unbalanced configuration

Figure 15-2 shows the CPU load graph from the server. You can see that those two CPUs were maxed out, which led to intermittent performance issues and spikes in HADR_SYNC_COMMIT waits.

We reconfigured the VM with 2 vSockets and 17 vCores per vSocket, aligning it with the physical hardware configuration. In this mode, Windows saw two NUMA nodes; however, SQL Server split the CPUs into two 5-core and four 6-core nodes. Even though that would have led to an imperfect configuration, it would be more balanced than the original one.

In the end, we downgraded the VM to 32 vCPUs, which led to four 8-core soft NUMA nodes perfectly aligned with the hardware. We considered keeping 34 vCPUs and disabling the soft NUMA feature but decided against it, since the VM still had enough power to handle the workload.

The vSocket/vCore configuration is especially important in non-Enterprise editions of SQL Server, which can utilize a limited number of sockets. Incorrect configurations may prevent them from using all the vCPUs in the VM. You can detect this condition easily by observing the CPU load on the server: you'll see some CPUs busy and others idling. You can also get this information from the [Offline Schedulers] column in the output of Listing 15-1. Alternatively, you can check the status column in the `sys.dm_os_schedulers` view. Figure 15-3 illustrates the output from this view in the Standard Edition with several schedulers disabled.

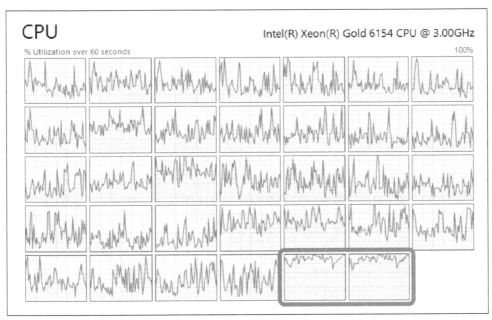

Figure 15-2. CPU load in an unbalanced configuration

	scheduler_address	parent_node_id	scheduler_id	cpu_id	status	is_online
1	0x00000200D9220040	0	0	0	VISIBLE ONLINE	1
2	0x00000200D9240040	0	0	1	VISIBLE ONLINE	1
3	0x00000200D9260040	0	0	2	VISIBLE ONLINE	1
4	0x00000200D9280040	0	0	3	VISIBLE ONLINE	1
5	0x00000200D92A0040	0	0	4	VISIBLE OFFLINE	0
6	0x00000200D92C0040	0	0	5	VISIBLE OFFLINE	0
7	0x00000200D9C20040	0	0	6	VISIBLE OFFLINE	0
8	0x00000200D9C40040	0	0	7	VISIBLE OFFLINE	0
9	0x00000200D9C60040	0	0	8	VISIBLE OFFLINE	0
10	0x00000200D9C80040	0	0	9	VISIBLE OFFLINE	0
11	0x00000200D9CA0040	0	0	10	VISIBLE OFFLINE	0

Figure 15-3. The status of schedulers

This problem with unbalanced NUMA/scheduler configurations can also occur with nonvirtualized SQL Server instances, if some schedulers have been disabled through an affinity mask or if the system is using a version of Enterprise Edition with Client Access Licenses that limit it to 20 physical cores. However, it is much more common in virtual environments that allow provisioning VM configurations that do not exist with physical hardware. Remember to validate this during your health check.

Memory

As with CPU configuration, it is possible to provision more memory to VMs than the amount of physical memory installed on the host; however, this may lead to serious performance issues on database servers.

Unless you use resource reservation, the host does not allocate memory for the VM immediately: allocation occurs only when applications in the VM request it. However, the host does not know when applications deallocate that memory and release it to the OS, so VMs continue to consume memory when this happens. As the amount of allocated memory on the host grows, the host starts to reclaim it from guests using the *balloon driver*. This driver is installed in the guest VM and it requests memory from its OS, releasing it to the host. This will lead to external memory pressure in SQL Server and, potentially, paging within the OS.

By default, SQL Server responds to memory pressure by trimming memory consumption and releasing memory to the operating system, but this still leads to a performance hit. The situation becomes worse if you have *lock pages in memory* (LPIM) enabled or have set the *minimum server memory* value incorrectly. Those conditions could prevent SQL Server from releasing memory and could lead to OS instability and failovers.

There is very little you can do about this besides conducting proper capacity planning. Do not overprovision memory in VMs unless you are using resource reservation or can guarantee that the host will not be overcommitted. SQL Server does a better job managing a smaller amount of available memory than handling regular memory pressure due to ballooning.

Be very careful with LPIM and other features that may prevent SQL Server from responding to memory pressure. Do not forget that the host may suddenly become overcommitted if other VMs migrate to it, which can happen with VM load balancing or during a disaster, when other hosts in the infrastructure go down.

Finally, do not forget that memory configuration can affect the CPU configuration in the VM. If your VM needs memory from multiple pNuma nodes, make sure the vSocket/vCore configuration matches that topology.

Storage

All virtualization platforms provide multiple options to configure storage. Most commonly, VMs use *virtual disks* (vmdk in VMware and vhdx in Hyper-V) presented as separate drives inside guest VMs. The host places virtual disks either in physical storage directly or, in VMware vSphere, in another data store optimized for virtual disks (see Figure 15-4).

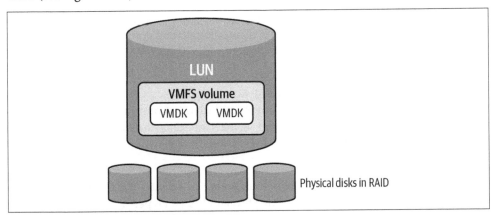

Figure 15-4. VMware vSphere storage stack

It is possible to map physical storage directly to VMs, bypassing virtual disks, but I rarely recommend this option. It does not result in a noticeable performance increase compared to properly configured virtual storage, and you lose the flexibility of virtualized storage and the ability to move data between storage arrays.

Most storage configuration will be specific to your system's infrastructure and done outside of the SQL Server VM, but in tier-1 systems, you should split the I/O workload between different SCSI controllers and data stores. This might sound a lot like the old recommendation to spread database objects across multiple drives, but it serves a different purpose: it helps balance I/O requests and reduces the saturation of disk queues during spikes in the I/O workload. One example is the checkpoint process, which can generate huge numbers of write requests and increase I/O latency (see Chapter 3).

 Keep all related data stores in the same storage protection group, to avoid data corruption in the event of a disaster.

There is a limit on the number of virtual SCSI controllers each VM can support. For example, in VMware, you can use only four PVSCSI controllers per VM. I generally put a transaction log drive on one of the controllers, combine the tempdb and OS drives on another one, and use the two remaining controllers for the data files. However, I sometimes change my approach based on the number of databases on the server, the number of data files in the database, and the I/O workload distribution between files. You can analyze the disk performance counters and sample data in the `sys.dm_io_virtual_file_stats` view while choosing the optimal configuration.

Increase and tune the queue depth in SCSI controllers and use the latest version of the drivers available. Make sure you are using the optimal controller type for storage configuration. For example, VMware vSphere offers the vNVMe controller, which is optimized for local flash storage.

As with CPU and memory, the host and storage infrastructure need to have enough throughput to handle I/O load. It is not a good idea to combine multiple I/O-heavy VMs on the same host or to place them in the same data stores, as they may impact each other. Remember that VM topology may change over time, and to monitor performance.

One risk mitigation option is to rely on a Quality of Service (QoS) solution, such as Virtual Volumes (VVols) in vSphere or Storage QoS in Hyper-V. These can mitigate the impact of noisy neighbors and make your I/O workload more predictable.

Most configuration problems occur when SQL Server VMs are provisioned using general practices that don't account for SQL Server behavior and I/O patterns. These problems are easy to address when you are working with and combining the knowledge of virtualization and storage administrators.

It is always a good idea to test I/O performance on the server when possible. The `DISKSPD` utility (*https://oreil.ly/r0M29*) can emulate a generic SQL Server workload for you.

Network

I am not going to spend a lot of time discussing network configuration in virtualized environments, since in most cases, it is dictated by the physical infrastructure and host-level configuration and you have little control over it. There is one aspect I'd like to mention, though.

It is very easy to create virtual network (vNIC) adapters in VMs, but this doesn't guarantee traffic separation on a physical level. Depending on the configuration, the host might route the traffic from multiple VMs and/or vNIC adapters through the same physical NIC on the host. The usual victim of this problem is the heartbeat network in a Windows Failover Cluster. The lack of physical traffic separation may lead to cluster stability issues and unexpected failovers on hosts with network-traffic–heavy VMs.

Virtual network configuration is another area where you need to work closely with colleagues from the virtualization and infrastructure teams. For example, don't just request new vNIC adapters for your cluster network; explain what you're trying to accomplish and ask them to build a QoS solution that prioritizes cluster heartbeat traffic.

Virtual Disk Management

As you know, virtualization abstracts storage configuration from VMs. Virtual disks appear as fully provisioned drives there, but on the host level, you need to configure them with one of the following methods:

Thin provisioning
> In this mode, the virtual disk does not take up any space on the host besides what is currently being used. This allows you to over-allocate storage space on the host and to run out of space if virtual disks in multiple VMs grow beyond the physical storage capacity. Dynamic disks in Hyper-V belong to this category, which VMware calls *thin* provisioning.

Thick provisioning without zeroing out
> Storage space for virtual disks on the host is pre-allocated, but disks are not zeroed out. The blocks on the disk are zeroed out when they are written for the first time. This allows you to expand the disk quickly, at the cost of first-write overhead. VMware calls this mode *zeroedthick* provisioning.

Thick provisioning with zeroing out
> Storage space for virtual disks on the host is pre-allocated and zeroed out at creation. There is no first-write overhead; however, disk expansion may take time and lead to I/O load. Fixed-size disks in Hyper-V belong to this category, which VMware calls *eagerzeroedthick* provisioning.

The decision of how to provision disks depends on many factors. For example, nothing is wrong with thin provisioning if first-write overhead is acceptable and there is proper storage capacity monitoring in place. However, virtual disk expansion may pause (stun) the VM. With thin provisioning this could take milliseconds, but if a large amount of space needs to be zeroed out, it could be seconds or even minutes—which can lead to issues or even failovers in production.

Remember this, and factor disk space management into your maintenance strategy. It is safer to expand the disks during planned system maintenance and to disable automatic failover when you expand the disks on primary nodes in the cluster.

Backup Strategy and Tools

Multiple tools are available for performing VM-level backups. Many of them claim they're SQL Server–friendly and can replace native SQL Server backups. Whether that's true, and whether to use them, is a common topic of debate between infrastructure and database teams. Infrastructure teams like them because they are snapshot based, which saves storage space. Database teams often don't trust them and don't like their limitations.

In the end, it is another "it depends" situation. These tools may be perfectly acceptable in some cases; however, you need to carefully test your tool to make sure it meets your requirements. In particular, you need to review a few areas:

- Ability to meet Recovery Point Objective (RPO) and Recovery Time Objective (RTO) goals.

- Ability to restore the database in a new system using a different storage configuration.

- Compatibility with database features such as FILESTREAM and In-Memory OLTP.

- Proper support for point-in-time restore (and page-level restore, as a "nice to have" feature, useful for dealing with database corruption).

- Automated backup validation process (which should be easy to implement and use).

- Operational impact: if the tool could stun the VM during the process, is that acceptable?

- Of course, don't forget to validate that the tool operates correctly and can survive a Disaster Recovery (DR) event in the middle of backup. Also check that the tool does not introduce database corruption. I usually implement a database consistency check and run a DBCC CHECKDB as part of the backup validation process.

Don't discount external backup tools immediately; understand their benefits and downsides. This will provide you with data points for meaningful and productive discussion and decision-making with other teams.

Troubleshooting in Virtual Environments

Troubleshooting and performance tuning of SQL Server instances running in virtual environments is not very different from what you'll do for instances running on bare metal hardware. Issues with instances, databases, and applications present the same way whether SQL Server is virtualized or not. You'll use the same approaches to detect and mitigate them in all environments.

Virtualization, however, adds another layer of complexity to troubleshooting. Validating that host-level configuration and performance are not contributing to the issue adds a step. To make matters worse, VMs' placement and workload are rarely static—so the analysis you complete today may not be relevant tomorrow. Unfortunately, very few metrics are visible inside guest VMs. You need to look at the host to detect the issues.

This is yet another reason to include virtualization administrators in troubleshooting, especially if unexplained performance issues appear suddenly without any changes in the workload. Host-level changes may trigger them, and your virtualization administrators have the tools and knowledge to analyze host-level metrics. (That said, remember that there may be other root causes—for example, in parameter-sensitive execution plans, regression due to parameter sniffing may lead to the same outcome.)

Let's discuss how to troubleshoot the most common issues related to virtualization.

Insufficient CPU Bandwidth

CPU-related bottlenecks are perhaps the trickiest area to troubleshoot in virtualized environments. They require you to analyze both the guest VM and the host load and to address potential issues on both sides.

CPU load information in a guest VM is incomplete. The guest VM will show vCPU utilization within the OS but does not take any host-level load into consideration. For example, the guest OS may show low CPU utilization; however, the system can still suffer from a CPU bottleneck if the host itself is overloaded.

There is a key metric that indicates how long the VM is waiting for available CPU to execute: it's called *CPU ready time* in VMware and *CPU wait time* in Hyper-V. Conceptually, it is similar to SOS_SCHEDULER_YIELD waits in SQL Server, which occur when a worker stays in a runnable queue waiting for an available scheduler.

A high CPU ready time indicates scheduling problems on the host. This occurs when the host does not have enough CPU bandwidth to handle the load. The problem may be exaggerated by overprovisioned VMs, since scheduling overhead increases with the number of vCPUs.

What is an acceptable threshold for CPU ready time? Well, that's another hotly debated question. It may vary based on the tier and criticality of the VMs. I like it to be less than 1% in tier-1 systems and less than 2% to 3% in tier 2 systems in VMware. It is a little harder to set the threshold in Hyper-V, as I'll show you in the next section.

When you see that the CPU ready time is high, review the VM configuration and the load on the host. (I'll show you how to monitor CPU ready time shortly.) Move some VMs to different hosts if needed. Do not overprovision VM resources: smaller VMs are likely to perform better than overprovisioned ones. Don't take this suggestion to extremes, though—assign enough vCPUs to handle the load.

Let's look at how you can get CPU-related metrics in Hyper-V and VMware.

Analyzing CPU metrics in Hyper-V

Several CPU-related performance counters are available on the host level. In Hyper-V, they include the following:

Hyper-V Hypervisor Logical Processor *performance object*

The performance counters in the Hyper-V Hypervisor Logical Processor object provide statistics about logical processors on the host. The `% Total Run Time` counter shows overall lCPU utilization on the host. High values (above 90%) may indicate that the host is overloaded. Consider moving some VMs to other hosts when you see this.

The `% Guest Run Time` and `% Hypervisor Run Time` counters show you how much time the lCPU spends handling the guest OS and hypervisor code, respectively.

Hyper-V Hypervisor Virtual Processor\% Total Run Time *performance counter*

This counter shows overall vCPU utilization in the guest OS. High values (above 85% or 90%) across all vCPUs indicate insufficient CPU bandwidth in the VM. If only some vCPUs are overloaded, this may indicate an unbalanced workload due to uneven scheduler distribution in the NUMA nodes, or an inefficient NUMA and/or I/O configuration in Windows. You can tune some NUMA I/O parameters (see the Microsoft documentation (*https://oreil.ly/omnUc*) for details).

There are also `% Guest Run Time` and `% Hypervisor Run Time` counters, which are similar to the Hyper-V Hypervisor Logical Processor performance object.

Hyper-V Hypervisor Virtual Processor\CPU Wait Time Per Dispatch *performance counter*

This performance counter provides the CPU wait time (CPU ready time) in Hyper-V. Unfortunately, it does not show you the percentage of time the vCPU spends in a waiting state, just the average wait time in nanoseconds.

It is hard to define what `CPU Wait Time Per Dispatch` value indicates a problem: the value will be lower with faster CPUs. It's safe to say that this value should not exceed the low microseconds range in critical systems. I also recommend baselining the counter and looking at trends over time.

Finally, analyze this counter when you see a high `Hyper-V Hypervisor Logical Processor\% Total Run Time` value. The virtualization expects the host to operate under a heavy load. That load may not always indicate the performance impact in VMs, and analyzing the `CPU Wait Time Per Dispatch` counter may help you estimate that impact. High values in both counters confirm that the host is overloaded. A high value for `% Total Run Time` and a low value for `CPU Wait Time Per Dispatch` may be acceptable.

Analyzing CPU metrics in VMware ESXi

There are two approaches to looking at performance metrics in VMware. Covering all the metrics available in VMware vSphere is beyond the scope of this book, so see the

VMware documentation (*https://oreil.ly/YlzzM*) for additional details. Here, we'll look at a few of the most important metrics.

First, you can use performance charts in the vSphere Client to analyze high-level resource utilization on the host. The values, however, are averaged over time intervals and do not show spikes and abnormalities in the load.

Second, vSphere provides the ESXTOP utility, which gives a real-time view of what is happening on the host. It provides extremely detailed information on resource utilization and allows you to troubleshoot performance issues in real time. You can run the ESXTOP utility from a console session or an SSH session on the host. It gives several views, which you can switch between by typing the character in parentheses: for example, CPU (c), memory (m), network (n), and VM disk statistics (v).

It is also useful to filter the output down to VMs only by typing a capital (V). By default, ESXTOP samples data every five seconds. You can change the interval by typing (s) and specifying the number of seconds to use.

Figure 15-5 shows the CPU view in ESXTOP, collected on one of the hosts.

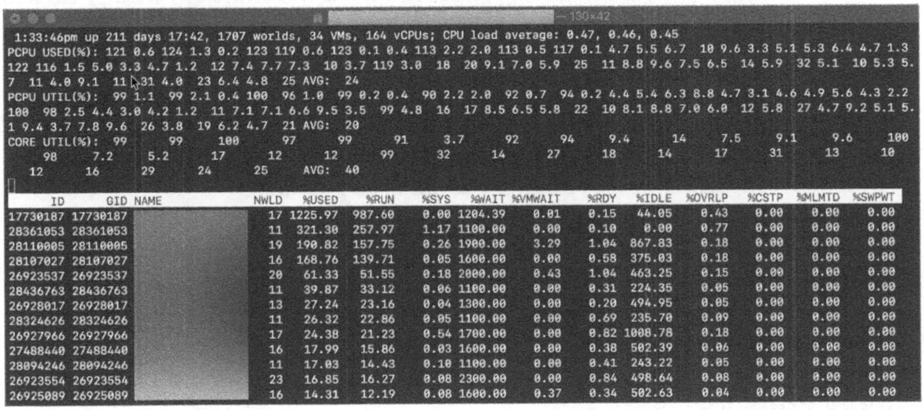

Figure 15-5. ESXTOP: CPU view

The top line on the screen shows the host statistics. Three CPU Load Average values give CPU utilization information for the last 1, 5, and 15 minutes, respectively. The value 1.0 means the physical CPUs on the host are fully utilized. The CPU Load Average being consistently above 1.0 means the host does not have enough CPU bandwidth to handle the load.

PCPU USED(%) and PCPU UTIL(%) provide utilization data on the logical core (lCore), while CORE UTIL(%) shows physical core (pCore) utilization metrics. You can use these to analyze the host CPU's load in real time.

Unfortunately, CPU usage metrics for individual VMs are harder to interpret. ESXTOP calculates them based on a percentage of the base CPU frequency on the host across multiple vCPUs assigned to the VM. Factors like hyper-threading and turbo boost may also impact its calculations.

Nevertheless, there are a few metrics to pay close attention to:

%MLMTD *column*

> This column indicates the percentage of time the VM was ready to run, but vCPUs had not been scheduled due to resource pool settings on the host. If you see values above 0, especially in critical VMs, discuss resource allocation and throttling with your virtualization administrators.

%RDY *column*

> This column shows the CPU ready time for VMs, which, as noted, should be less than 1% in critical VMs and should not exceed 2% to 3% in tier-2 and tier-3 VMs. A high CPU ready time may be a sign of an overloaded host, overprovisioned VMs, or both.
>
> The CPU ready time can also accumulate due to resource throttling, in which case you'll see non-zero %MLMTD values.

%CSTP *column*

> This column shows the VM's co-stop time. With relaxed co-scheduling, VMware may suspend the VM if there is an uneven work distribution between vCPUs. As with %RDY, the %CSTP value should be as small as possible.
>
> Co-stop time is usually not a problem in VMs with database servers, since the load among all the vCPUs is balanced. If you see high %CSTP values, check the schedulers and the NUMA configuration, and make sure you don't run any nonessential applications inside the VM.

Memory Pressure

You've learned that memory overcommitment on the host can force the balloon driver to introduce memory pressure, leading to performance and stability issues in SQL Server. This condition is a common cause for failovers in AlwaysOn Failover Clusters and Availability Groups, especially when the nodes have LPIM enabled. SQL Server does not release enough memory, so the OS becomes unresponsive, failing the IsAlive cluster check.

You can easily detect these conditions by analyzing SQL Server's Failover Cluster Error Logs and ballooned memory metrics on the host and guest levels. Unfortunately, there is no easy solution besides doing better capacity planning for the host and guest VMs. As with CPU configuration, do not overprovision VM memory if the host does not have enough resources.

You can troubleshoot memory issues in SQL Server VMs using the techniques described in Chapter 7. In Hyper-V, on the host level, you can look at the `Mem ory\Available Mbytes` and `Hyper-V Dynamic Memory Balancer\Available Memory` performance counters. Low values indicate insufficient memory on the host, which may lead to ballooning and other issues.

There are a few metrics to check in the `ESXTOP` utility. The first is related to VM memory swapping. Critical database servers' VMs should not do any swapping on the host level. The `%SWPWT` column in the CPU view (Figure 15-5) shows the time the host spent on swapping. Detailed metrics are available in the memory view (Figure 15-6), which you can switch to by typing `m`. There are multiple memory counters, some of which are not shown here. You can toggle between them by typing `f`.

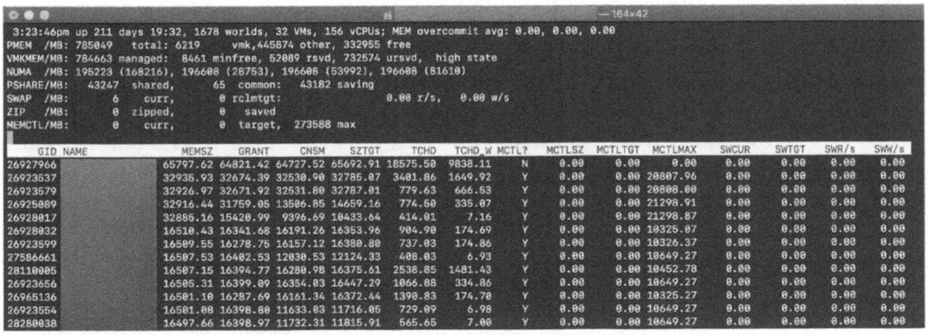

Figure 15-6. *ESXTOP: Memory view*

Let's look at the most important values for troubleshooting:

Swap-related columns
> The `SWR/s` and `SWW/s` columns show the VM's current swap activity. Non-zero values indicate that the VM is currently swapping. Swapping should not occur in database VMs, because it will impact their performance.
>
> The `SWCUR` column indicates the size of the currently swapped VM memory. This value should also be zero in database VMs; however, it is possible to see non-zero values if some unused VM memory was swapped some time ago and hasn't been used since. This condition—a low value in the `SWCUR` column and no swapping in the `SWR/s` and `SWW/s` columns—may be acceptable in noncritical systems.
>
> It is important to remember that these columns indicate host-level swapping and are invisible from within the VM.

Memory ballooning
> There are several `MCTL` columns related to ballooning. The `MCTL?` column indi-cates whether a balloon driver is installed within the OS. The `MCTLSZ` (`MB`)

and MCTLTGT (MB) columns provide the size of the reclaimed memory and the amount of memory the host wants to reclaim. Finally, the MCTLMAX (MB) column shows the maximum amount of memory the balloon driver can reclaim.

Again, ballooning is extremely dangerous in database VMs. Address it by properly configuring VMs and hosts and avoiding memory overcommitments.

Disk Subsystem Performance

As you may remember from Chapter 3, disk subsystem troubleshooting requires you to look at the entire storage stack, from SQL Server down to the physical storage array; analyze the metrics from each component; and pinpoint the bottlenecks.

Virtualization is just another layer in this stack, and you need to validate that it does not introduce noticeable overhead to I/O performance. In Hyper-V, you can compare disk performance counters from the host and guest OSes. In VMware, you can use the data from the ESXTOP utility.

Figure 15-7 shows the VM virtual disk view in the ESXTOP utility. The column names are self-explanatory and show statistics on I/O operations and latency for virtual disks.

```
3:52:47pm up 211 days 20:01, 1678 worlds, 32 VMs, 156 vCPUs; CPU load average: 0.46, 0.47, 0.47

    GID VMNAME          VDEVNAME NVDISK    CMDS/s  READS/s WRITES/s MBREAD/s MBWRTN/s LAT/rd LAT/wr
17730187                       -      2      2.38     0.00     2.38     0.00     0.02  0.000  0.352
26923537                       -      6     37.35     0.00    37.35     0.00     1.90  0.000  1.310
26923554                       -      8      2.70     0.00     2.70     0.00     0.03  0.000  0.349
26923579                       -      2      0.79     0.00     0.79     0.00     0.00  0.000  0.351
26923599                       -      4      0.00     0.00     0.00     0.00     0.00  0.000  0.000
26923656                       -     16      0.64     0.00     0.64     0.00     0.00  0.000  0.362
26925089                       -      5      1.43     0.00     1.43     0.00     0.01  0.000  0.386
26927966                       -      1    147.66    42.60   105.06     0.47     0.68  0.502  0.350
27172740                       -      3      0.64     0.00     0.64     0.00     0.00  0.000  0.433
27488440                       -     14      1.11     0.00     1.11     0.00     0.01  0.000  0.468
28107027                       -     17   2052.47  1976.81    75.66    83.00     0.58 15.176  8.404
```

Figure 15-7. ESXTOP: virtual disk view

You can also look at the disk adapter view (type **d**), shown in Figure 15-8, to see whether I/O activity is unbalanced across disk adapters and troubleshoot high virtual disk latency. The DAVG, KAVG, QAVG, and GAVG columns represent devices, the VMware kernel, the adapter queues, and the VM's OS latencies for I/O requests.

Check that guest VMs are using the latest versions of virtualization tools and that all host and guest drivers are up to date. Use multiple vSCSI adapters and split the workload among them. Increase their queue depth as needed.

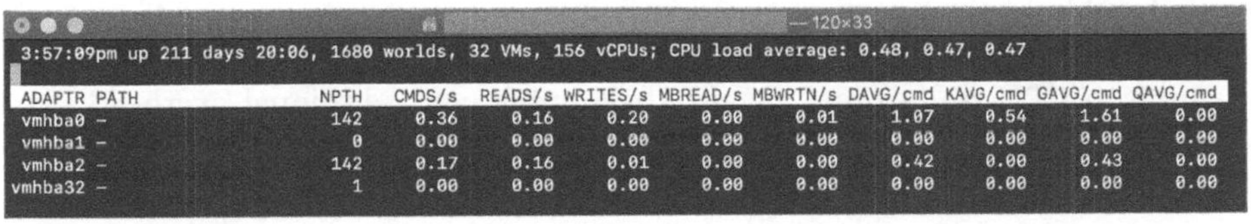

Figure 15-8. ESXTOP: disk adapter view

Make sure no VMs have snapshots present. Snapshots add significant I/O overhead that can affect busy systems. Likewise, some maintenance tasks, such as cloning VMs or migrating large virtual disks to different storage, can introduce sudden, hard-to-explain performance degradation to the VMs.

There is no doubt that virtualization adds additional complexity to troubleshooting and may introduce issues, but these challenges can be addressed. Most issues I encounter in virtual environments relate to an incorrect virtualization setup or an inefficient troubleshooting strategy that does not analyze the full ecosystem. Taking a holistic view and collaborating across multiple teams will solve these problems.

There are always times when you need to get the most from your hardware, and in such cases, virtualization is not the best choice. Overhead is the price you pay for the flexibility that virtualization provides. Remember this when making decisions.

Summary

Virtualization has become extremely common. It reduces hardware cost and simplifies many maintenance tasks. It adds overhead, which increases with the size of the VMs, but which may be acceptable in many cases.

Proper capacity planning is essential with virtualization. Do not overcommit resources on the hosts with critical tier-1 database VMs. Consider utilizing resource reservation when possible. Tier-2 and tier-3 VMs, on the other hand, can sustain some degree of overcommitment.

As a general rule, do not overprovision VMs, especially in overcommitted environments. It's easier to handle scheduling and resource management with smaller VMs, and they often achieve better performance than larger ones.

Pay attention to CPU, memory, and NUMA alignment in your VM configuration. Make sure schedulers are evenly distributed across NUMA nodes in SQL Server. Set up your vSocket/vCore configuration properly, especially if you are using non-Enterprise editions of SQL Server.

While troubleshooting performance issues in SQL Server isn't much different when the instance is virtualized, you still need to check the virtualization layer. Pay attention to CPU ready time, memory ballooning, and additional overhead (which improperly configured virtualization can introduce). Work together with virtualization administrators during troubleshooting.

In the next chapter, we'll look at SQL Server in cloud environments and the challenges cloud setups may introduce.

Troubleshooting Checklist

- ☐ Validate VM configuration, paying particular attention to CPU and memory configuration and NUMA alignment.
- ☐ Validate that the schedulers are evenly distributed across the NUMA nodes in SQL Server.
- ☐ Make sure guest OS tools and drivers are the latest version.
- ☐ Split the I/O workload across vSCSI controllers and increase queue depths if needed.
- ☐ Check the host configuration. Make sure the host is not overcommitted when you deal with critical tier-1 systems.
- ☐ Do not overprovision an SQL Server VM unless it uses resource reservation or has dedicated resources on the host.
- ☐ Adjust SQL Server's memory settings and LPIM based on your environment.
- ☐ Make sure there are no VM snapshots on production VMs.

CHAPTER 16

SQL Server in the Cloud

Cloud computing is the new norm. Businesses are reducing their datacenter footprints and either building hybrid solutions or migrating to the cloud completely. Troubleshooting and tuning cloud-based database systems has thus become a common task for database engineers.

Cloud database instances use the same SQL Server Engine internally, and you can use familiar tools and techniques when dealing with them. There are some minor differences between the technologies, however, and that's what this chapter will cover.

I will start with a high-level discussion of cloud applications, then move to SQL Server's cloud offerings: first, SQL Server instances running in cloud VMs; then, the managed database services available in Microsoft Azure, Amazon AWS, and Google Cloud Platform. I'll also give you an overview of the services architecture and platform monitoring tools, as well as the limitations of both.

Cloud Platforms: A 30,000-Foot View

A long time ago, when cloud computing was just beginning to emerge, I picked up a sticker at a conference (Figure 16-1). It read, "There is no cloud, it's just someone else's computer."

There was a time when this really was the best definition of cloud computing, though the situation has become more complex over time. clouds are still just *someone else's datacenters*; however, they've evolved and now provide many services to help you build applications, offering out-of-the-box solutions to complex problems and often significantly reducing project implementation time.

Figure 16-1. There is no cloud

All the major cloud providers offer managed database services, taking care of routine database administration tasks and providing High Availability for databases. They also allow you to provision and run regular virtual machines and "lift-and-shift" on-premises infrastructure to the cloud.

In my opinion, the lift-and-shift approach rarely leads to the best long-term results. There are some legitimate cases when it is beneficial, and it is often the fastest cloud migration path for complex on-premises systems. However, I am a true proponent of the idea that to get the most from the cloud, you need to architect your system to run in the cloud. You need to take advantage of cloud services and account for the behavior of cloud platforms.

There are a few key differences between cloud and on-premises infrastructure.

Platform Reliability

Every cloud operates on commodity hardware. Outages can and *will* happen, more often than with on-premises hardware, so applications and database servers need to be able to handle it.

Let me put things into perspective. Amazon AWS provides a SLA of 99.5% uptime for EC2 VMs, which translates to up to 3.6 hours of downtime per month. To make matters worse, in the event of an SLA breach, the only thing you'd get back is service credits, which would not cover the business impact of the outage.

The implications of platform reliability go beyond the database tier. Applications need to be resilient, and they should handle transient errors. They also need to be idempotent. For example, if the database or message queue becomes unavailable in the middle of a business transaction, the system should be able to reprocess the transaction after recovery.

Throttling

The second key factor is throttling. cloud services and resources have hard throttling in place. For example, if you pay for elastic block storage (EBS) volumes with provisioned IOPS in AWS, you will not get more IOPS than you pay for. This is different from on-premises virtualization, where critical VMs can be impacted by noisy neighbors and the overall host load, but rarely have Quality of Service (QoS) throttling applied to them.

That throttling means you'll need to do thorough capacity planning when you provision cloud systems. Fortunately, the consequences of mistakes and under-provisioned services are lower than with improperly sized on-premises hardware. In most cases you can scale services up quickly. It may be expensive, though.

Unfortunately, there are some *hard* limitations. For example, VMs have limits on the maximum I/O and network throughput they support, managed database services may have the transaction log generation rate capped, and so on. You need to take these limitations into consideration when you design cloud infrastructure. Almost every workload can be supported in the cloud; however, moving high-end workloads there may require you to rearchitect the system to succeed.

Topology

I am sure you are aware of cloud topology. Nevertheless, let me outline the key topology elements here:

Cloud region
> Each cloud region represents a separate datacenter in a specific geographic area. For example, Microsoft Azure's West US region datacenter is in California and West US 2 is in Washington State.
>
> Spreading services and databases across regions allows you to build geo-redundant systems. However, bear in mind the latency of cross-region communication when you design your system. In edge cases, when you spread servers across continents, the latency can get into the range of hundreds of milliseconds. Cross-region database calls may significantly increase the length of database transactions. It is better to implement asynchronous message-based communication when possible.

Availability zones
> Availability zones (AZs) represent isolated infrastructure within each cloud region. Think of them as separate buildings in the datacenters or even separate datacenters in the same town, independent from one another. They provide the required redundancy within each region: *theoretically*, at least, issues in one AZ should not affect other AZs.

Being physically separated, AZs have different network infrastructures, and communication between them will lead to some latency. This latency is usually very low—less than 1 to 2 milliseconds—but can still add overhead to synchronous Availability Group replication in busy OLTP systems.

Most managed cloud services provide multi-AZ redundancy out of the box or can be provisioned to run in multiple AZs. cloud VMs, on the other hand, live in a single AZ, so you need to build a proper HA solution when you use them.

Before we start looking at options for provisioning and troubleshooting SQL Server in the cloud, I'd like to briefly touch on the topic of connectivity to cloud database instances.

Connectivity Considerations and Transient Error Handling

Connection and connectivity issues are among the most common kinds of errors that arise during cloud deployments. Fortunately, in many cases they are also relatively easy to address. There are two different types of connectivity problems.

Accessing the Database Instance

The first is inability to access the database instance. When you provision a cloud resource, its connectivity is restricted by default. You cannot reach it externally, nor can other cloud services reach it unless the access rules are configured to allow that. This condition will show up as a general connectivity error when a client cannot connect to an SQL Server instance.

The solution greatly depends on the topology. If you need to access your database instance through the public internet, configure it to be publicly accessible and permit the client IP addresses. In more complex cases, such as connecting cloud resources with on-premises infrastructure, work with cloud and network engineers to ensure that the database instance is added to the right virtual network or virtual private cloud (VPC) and that security groups (network firewall rules) are properly configured.

Transient Errors

The second type of problem is related to transient errors. In addition to failover events, the database server may prevent you from connecting to it when you reach the service tier's resource limits. For example, it might terminate queries or even connections with high resource utilization if the session generates a large number of transaction log records.

Managed database services in Microsoft Azure will provide additional details when transient errors occur: you can see the error codes and conditions in the Microsoft

---

documentation (*https://oreil.ly/WMF71*). Managed services in Amazon AWS and Google GCP, on the other hand, are less specific, and issues may present as a lack of available workers (THREADPOOL waits) or overall performance problems.

Since an application should be resilient, it should implement retry logic to handle errors. When possible, it is better to reopen the connection before retrying, since some transient errors make the session unhealthy. Also, cloud services have measures to prevent denial-of-service (DoS) attacks, so don't flood the instance with connection requests when you reopen the connection. If you cannot reconnect immediately, wait a few seconds before another attempt.

A word of caution: avoid client/server setups with remote client applications talking to cloud database instances. These setups are prone to high latency, transient errors, and connectivity issues. They may work for noncritical applications; however, they are not resilient enough to be used in critical systems. In such setups, ASYNC_NET WORK_IO waits usually stay at the top of the list due to the latency between client and server. Unfortunately, the workers waiting in that state are unavailable to other sessions, which may lead to worker thread starvation and THREADPOOL waits. Correlate those waits when you troubleshoot cloud systems.

Finally, make sure to increase connection and command timeout settings when you connect to SQL Server remotely, especially if you expect to run client applications over slow networks.

Now let's look at options for provisioning SQL Server in the cloud.

SQL Server in Cloud VMs

Every cloud provider offers managed SQL Server services, but some teams decide to manage the instances themselves and host SQL Server in cloud VMs. This usually involves one of the following:

- Lift-and-shift migrations, when an entire infrastructure is moved to the cloud "as is," with minimal changes
- Complex SQL Server infrastructure requirements or workloads that are not supported by managed services
- Situations when database teams want to have full control over the environment
- Proprietary database-as-a-service implementations, which can be significantly less expensive than managed services with mature database teams

Troubleshooting and supporting SQL Server instances running in cloud VMs is very similar to doing the same for *virtualized* on-premises instances, as discussed in Chapter 15. After all, you are dealing with the same product and have the same set of tools. cloud portals provide resource utilization metrics from a hypervisor perspective, which is conceptually similar.

There are still a few differences in platform behavior you need to pay attention to. Let's look at them.

I/O Setup and Performance

Modern hardware allows you to build very powerful servers that can hide performance problems. For example, the impact of nonoptimized queries, excessive transaction log generation, and other issues may be offset by extra CPUs, lots of RAM to cache the data, and submillisecond storage latency. Sometimes, though, these problems resurface when you move SQL Server to the cloud.

During capacity planning, it is easy to estimate the compute (CPU and RAM) requirements of VMs, since the performance of similarly sized VMs is comparable on premises and in the cloud. Pay attention to VM instance classes and hardware generations in the cloud, though, since these dictate what the underlying hardware would be.

Storage is a different matter. On premises, your storage scalability usually depends on your storage hardware. Modern storage can sustain a load of hundreds of thousands of IOPS and multi-GB/s throughput and can scale with spikes in the SQL Server workload.

Cloud storage behaves differently. Each cloud provider supports multiple storage types and tiers and limits the number of IOPS and throughput in each. Some storage tiers handle bursting and allow you to exceed the limits covering load spikes, but storage becomes heavily throttled after it exhausts the bursting credit.

To make matters worse, fast storage and large VMs are expensive, so people tend to under-provision them compared to on-premises infrastructure. Slow I/O and insufficient VM sizes may lead to performance issues that were previously hidden by fast on-premises hardware.

Of course, it is better to address the root causes of problems and tune the system. However, when that is impossible or impractical, make sure your cloud infrastructure—and particularly your storage—is provisioned properly. It is impossible to give generic advice on how to do this in all systems, but here are a few tips:

- Analyze I/O throughput in your on-premises systems before the cloud migration. Use storage-level key performance indicators (KPIs) as a performance target for provisioning.

- Use disk types with guaranteed performance characteristics that will support the workload.

- Put data and log files on different disks to scale throughput as needed. The same applies to different filegroups and, in extreme cases, even data files.

- Consider building RAID arrays in your OS. For example, in Microsoft Azure, two 1 TB P30 premium disks in a RAID-0 array will provide you with more IOPS and better throughput than one 2 TB P40 disk.

- Remember that VMs limit the number of IOPS and the throughput they support.

You can troubleshoot disk performance using the approaches discussed in Chapter 3. You can also access I/O metrics and estimate whether you are close to reaching your cloud portal's resource utilization limits.

High Availability Setup

Proper HA implementation is a *must* for SQL Servers running in cloud VMs. Usually, database teams implement Availability Groups to achieve this, but you can also use Failover Clusters if needed.

It is crucial to provision VMs in different availability zones for redundancy. This requires creating and tuning a multisubnet Windows Server Failover Cluster (WSFC), and will introduce a small, usually acceptable amount of synchronous replication latency.

Never use cross-region synchronous replication when you provision multiregion SQL Server infrastructure. The network latency will lead to extremely high HADR_SYNC _COMMIT waits and may introduce significant blocking in the database.

If your organization's HA strategy requires that your system can survive a region-level disaster and operate in a secondary region after failover, you may need to provision multiple replicas in that secondary region. For this, Distributed Availability Groups are often a better choice than individual replicas. They allow you to reduce network traffic between regions and, in my opinion, are easier to manage from an HA stand-point. Keep in mind that Distributed Availability Groups will require a different post-failover recovery strategy than regular Availability Groups in the event of a region-level disaster.

Consider using a cloud DNS service (Azure DNS, Amazon Route53, Google cloud DNS) for application connectivity. This will simplify the cross-region failover process, especially if you have Distributed Availability Groups set up. You can also benefit from architecture that uses separate connection pools for primary and readable secondaries in active-active multiregion applications. Services in each region will connect to local SQL Server replicas and run read-only queries when asynchronous replication latency and access to slightly outdated data is acceptable.

Cross-Region Latency

The cloud infrastructure makes it very tempting to build geo-redundant systems, with applications serving customers' requests in multiple regions. However, this is not a trivial task if you are using a relational database that accepts writes on the single primary node due to the latency of cross-region calls.

That latency depends on the distance between the datacenters. If you spread servers between the East US and EastUS2 Azure regions, it's unlikely to exceed just a few milliseconds, but if you are using datacenters on the other side of the globe, latency can reach 200 to 300 milliseconds per call.

Architect your system to address the impact of latency. Applications that run multiple individual queries in business transactions do not handle it well. The duration of each call quickly adds up, leading to performance issues and bad user experience.

As an example, imagine that an application residing in the West US Azure region needs to insert 100 rows into the database residing in the West Europe datacenter. This implementation, with 100 individual INSERT calls, would take about 15 seconds to complete and might lead to significant blocking, since exclusive (X) locks would be held for prolonged periods. The alternative would be to pass all 100 rows in a single TVP batch to a stored procedure, leading to a single cross-region call, which is much more efficient.

You can solve some latency problems by utilizing local in-region readable secondary nodes for the read workload. Remember, however, that replication in the Availability Group is also subject to latency. Do not use readable secondaries if you need to read up-to-date data. More importantly, do not mix reads from secondaries and writes into a primary node in a single business transaction.

What if an application inserts data into the primary node and immediately reloads it from the replica, expecting it to be up to date? This would never work with the latency involved in cross-region replication. You should not use it in a single region either—even if it may work under normal circumstances, any spikes in transaction log generation or backlogs in the send/redo queues would break it.

Finally, don't forget about the latency of SQL Server authentication calls to the domain controller. You learned in Chapter 13 that these can affect the system if their latency is high enough. Consider provisioning domain controllers or using cloud services that integrate with Active Directory in each region if you need to use Windows authentication.

Still, overall, running SQL Server in cloud VMs is very similar to running virtualized SQL Server instances on premises. You manage, troubleshoot, and tune them using the same set of tools and techniques in both places. The processes stay the same with all cloud providers.

Let's look next at managed database services, which are different for each cloud provider.

Managed Microsoft Azure SQL Services

In addition to SQL Server running in Azure VMs, the Microsoft Azure SQL family includes Azure SQL Database, Azure SQL Managed Instance, and Azure SQL Edge (a version of SQL Server optimized for Internet of Things [IoT] use cases and running on ARM- and x86-based edge devices). In this section I will focus on Azure SQL Managed Instance and SQL Database.

All of these technologies internally use the same SQL Server Engine, share the same codebase, and behave in a similar way. The troubleshooting and tuning techniques I describe in this book will work with all of them. In some cases, however, you may have to use different methods to collect data. For example, managed cloud services abstract you from the underlying OS, so you must look at Azure Portal or query the dynamic management views to see resource utilization instead of using the `PerfMon` utility. Your analysis and mitigation approaches will remain the same regardless of what technology you are using.

Services Architecture and Design Considerations

Microsoft has offered Azure SQL Database since 2010. You can think of it as a database as a service (DBaaS) that provides a SQL Server database for you to use. The technology supports most database features and takes care of HA, backups, and underlying SQL Server and OS maintenance. It has quite a few limitations, however, especially on the instance scope. For example, you cannot run cross-database queries, use the CLR and Service Broker, or use SQL Agent.

In 2018, Microsoft added a new product, Azure SQL Managed Instance (SQL MI). SQL MI, in a nutshell, is a virtualized SQL Server instance that supports most standard SQL Server features. In many cases, you can lift-and-shift on-premises SQL Server instances to SQL MI with little effort.

Make sure you review your technologies' resource limitations. Some, such as I/O throughput and log generation rate limits, may be insufficient to support a high-end OLTP workload.

Like SQL Database, SQL MI is a managed cloud service that takes care of backups, HA, and underlying patching. You still need to perform in-database administration tasks, like index and statistics maintenance, in both technologies.

You can upgrade or downgrade the underlying hardware by specifying the number of logical CPUs (vCores) for a given instance. The number of vCores also controls the amount of provisioned memory. With SQL MI, for example, each vCore gives you either 5.1 GB, 7 GB, or 13.6 GB of RAM, depending on the instance type. (Keep in mind that those numbers may change as new hardware types become available.)

Both technologies come with multiple service tiers. The *General Purpose* and *Business Critical* tiers are supported in both SQL Database and SQL MI. The third tier, *Hyperscale*, is available only in SQL Database.

A service's tier level controls its uptime SLA and some feature availability: for example, In-Memory OLTP is available only in the Business Critical tier. The more important implications of the tier, however, are storage and HA implementation.

 Azure SQL Database supports another purchase model based on Database Throughput Units (DTUs), which comes with three other service tiers. The Basic and Standard tiers have similar architecture to the General Purpose tier, while the Premium tier is similar to the Business Critical tier.

Figure 16-2 shows the compute and storage configuration in the General Purpose tier. The compute layer with the SQL Server process is stateless. It persists only transient data, such as tempdb on the local SSD storage. Database files and backups are stored in redundant Azure Blob Storage.

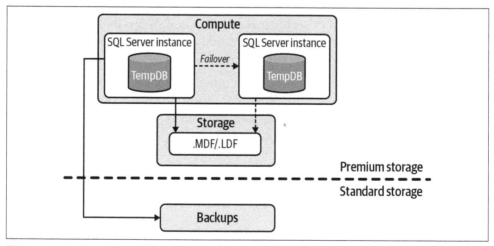

Figure 16-2. Compute and storage configuration in General Purpose service tier

In case of failover, another SQL Server instance attaches to the same database files and picks up the load. Conceptually, it behaves like an AlwaysOn SQL Server Failover Cluster; however, the internal implementation is different and uses Azure Service Fabric.

SQL Database can be provisioned with zone redundancy, with its storage replicated across multiple AZs. MI does not yet support this feature at the time of this writing.

In the Business Critical tier, implementation is based on AlwaysOn Availability Groups. In the configuration shown in Figure 16-3, the SQL Database or MI consists of multiple replicas that store database files in local SSDs. Failover in this configuration is just the regular AlwaysOn Availability Group failover.

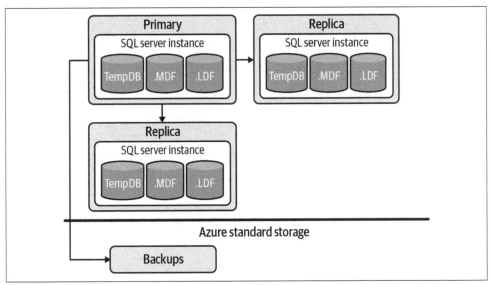

Figure 16-3. Compute and storage configuration in Business Critical service tier

As you can guess, the underlying topology dictates a few things. For example, disk performance in the General Purpose tier is slower, but allows you to work with larger databases because it is not limited by the size of local SSDs. The Business Critical tier, on the other hand, provides lower I/O latency and lets you scale the read workload with readable secondaries. However, you get the overhead of synchronous replication and potential issues with HADR_SYNC_COMMIT waits (discussed in Chapter 12).

Like the General Purpose tier, the Business Critical SQL Database can be zone redundant. The replicas, in this mode, are distributed across AZs. This option provides better HA at the cost of slight overhead during synchronous replication.

The Hyperscale service tier supports *very large databases* (VLDBs). The architecture (Figure 16-4) is more complex and includes the following:

- Page servers that manage data files stored in Azure Blob
- Availability Group–based compute nodes that handle requests
- Log Service transaction log management, which accepts the stream of log records from the primary node and distributes it to page servers and secondary compute nodes

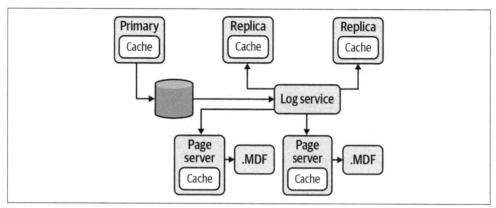

Figure 16-4. Architecture of the Hyperscale service tier

As of December 2021, the Hyperscale tier supports databases up to 100 TB in size. In theory, page servers allow databases to scale almost indefinitely, though their performance would greatly depend on the workload.

Each compute node has a local SSD-based cache for *hot* (active) data, which is built upon Buffer Pool Extension technology. When the active data fits into the cache, the nodes can access data very quickly. Getting data from remote page servers, however, would be much less efficient.

Test your workload to evaluate whether it would benefit from Hyperscale architecture. It may be a good choice for large OLTP databases that work with a relatively small amount of hot data and an undemanding workload. Large analytical workloads, on the other hand, usually process a lot of data that would not fit into the local cache, and page servers may introduce performance overhead.

The size of the data also matters. Though this is poorly documented, each page server handles up to 1 TB of data. This architecture is thus unnecessary for small databases, which would not be properly scaled on the storage level. Here is an interesting use case, though: because the data is not persisted on compute nodes, you can bring new nodes online and scale read workloads very quickly. This may reduce costs if your system workload is inconsistent.

In the end, all products and service tiers use SQL Server in the background. Let's talk about how you can troubleshoot them.

Troubleshooting Approaches

When troubleshooting managed SQL Server–based cloud services, you look at the same set of metrics as with regular SQL Server instances, although you may need to collect them slightly differently. Usually, you start troubleshooting a regular SQL Server instance by analyzing its ecosystem and resource utilization in the OS. You don't have access to OS metrics in managed cloud services, but you can review the service's resource utilization in the Azure portal or through DMVs.

Figure 16-5 shows a screenshot of SQL Database metrics from the Azure portal. (Please note that I have cut and enlarged the relevant parts, so don't be confused by the disconnected lines in the chart.)

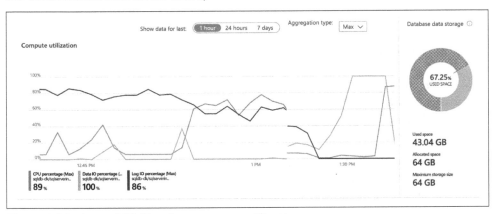

Figure 16-5. Azure SQL Database resource utilization

You can get similar information from the `sys.dm_db_resource_stats` view (*https://oreil.ly/wyaZN*), which collects data every 15 seconds and maintains it for approximately one hour. Figure 16-6 shows an example of its output.

	end_time	avg_cpu_percent	avg_data_io_percent	avg_log_write_percent	avg_memory_usage_percent	xtp_storage_percent	max_worker_percent
1	2021-11-24 18:38:09.600	76.89	0.00	0.00	32.22	0.00	1.25
2	2021-11-24 18:37:54.550	88.73	0.00	0.00	32.22	0.00	1.25
3	2021-11-24 18:37:39.553	88.59	0.00	0.00	32.22	0.00	1.25
4	2021-11-24 18:37:24.540	87.85	0.00	0.00	32.22	0.00	1.25
5	2021-11-24 18:37:09.517	88.66	0.00	0.00	32.22	0.00	1.25

max_session_percent	dtu_limit	avg_login_rate_percent	avg_instance_cpu_percent	avg_instance_memory_percent	cpu_limit	replica_role
0.04	NULL	NULL	76.05	81.78	4.00	0
0.04	NULL	NULL	76.05	81.78	4.00	0
0.04	NULL	NULL	75.37	81.78	4.00	0
0.04	NULL	NULL	75.37	81.78	4.00	0
0.04	NULL	NULL	75.37	81.78	4.00	0

Figure 16-6. Output from the `sys.dm_db_resource_stats` view

For longer but less granular retention, you can use the `sys.resource_stats` view (*https://oreil.ly/luAvK*) in SQL Database (Figure 16-7) or the `sys.server_resource_stats` view (*https://oreil.ly/koZ6j*) in SQL MI.

	start_time	end_time	database_name	sku	storage_in_megabytes
1	2021-11-24 18:28:53.9200000	2021-11-24 18:33:54.3166667	SQLServerInternals	GeneralPurpose	44072
2	2021-11-24 18:23:53.3233333	2021-11-24 18:28:53.9200000	SQLServerInternals	GeneralPurpose	65534
3	2021-11-24 18:18:52.8100000	2021-11-24 18:23:53.3233333	SQLServerInternals	GeneralPurpose	54863
4	2021-11-24 18:13:52.2333333	2021-11-24 18:18:52.8100000	SQLServerInternals	GeneralPurpose	46914
5	2021-11-24 18:08:51.7733333	2021-11-24 18:13:52.2333333	SQLServerInternals	GeneralPurpose	38389

avg_cpu_percent	avg_data_io_percent	avg_log_write_percent	max_worker_percent	max_session_percent	dtu_limit
32.19	65.06	0.00	1.25	0.04	NULL
2.65	19.16	7.64	2.75	0.04	NULL
7.10	8.99	32.46	2.75	0.04	NULL
8.95	6.46	46.39	2.75	0.04	NULL
18.92	11.53	37.61	2.75	0.04	NULL

xtp_storage_percent	avg_login_rate_percent	avg_instance_cpu_percent	avg_instance_memory_percent	cpu_limit	allocated_storage_in_megabytes
0.00	NULL	75.81	81.93	4.00	65536
0.00	NULL	17.85	81.92	4.00	65536
0.00	NULL	40.54	81.98	4.00	54864
0.00	NULL	41.29	81.94	4.00	48512
0.00	NULL	43.15	81.88	4.00	48512

Figure 16-7. Output from the `sys.resource_stats` view

The sustained maxed-out resource utilization in the output would indicate that SQL Database or MI does not have enough bandwidth to handle the workload and is being throttled. You can either upgrade the instance to get more bandwidth or tune the system to reduce the load.

As you learned in Chapter 6, in SQL Server 2017 and later you can enable automatic tuning and allow SQL Server to correct regressed parameter-sensitive plans. This feature is enabled by default in SQL Database and can be enabled in MI databases. You can also allow SQL Database to create indexes automatically to address inefficient queries. It will monitor their usefulness and keep or drop them based on the settings (Figure 16-8).

Wait statistics–based troubleshooting works with both managed services (in SQL Database, use the `sys.dm_db_wait_stats` view (*https://oreil.ly/AUZtj*) instead of the `sys.dm_os_wait_stats` view). You will see and deal with the same wait types as with regular SQL Server instances. Other dynamic management views discussed in this book will work. You can also use Query Store, which is enabled in SQL Database by default and can be enabled in MI.

To evaluate I/O latency, you can use the `sys.dm_io_virtual_file_stats` view, which can help you understand whether Azure Blob Storage is providing enough throughput at the General Purpose service tier. In the Hyperscale tier, page-server–related metrics are added to execution plans, to the `sys.dm_exec_requests` and execution statistics views, and to multiple Extended Events (xEvents).

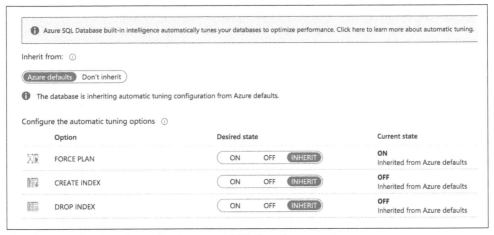

Figure 16-8. Automatic tuning in Azure SQL Database

You can use xEvents with both SQL Database and SQL MI. Keep in mind that SQL Database uses a slightly different T-SQL syntax for xEvent management. It also only supports `ring_buffer`, `event_counter`, and `event_file` targets. SQL MI supports all targets, as does regular SQL Server. With the `event_file` target, you need to place the file in Azure Blob Storage. This may introduce some latency, so be careful when you need to capture performance-critical events.

There is no access to the `PerfMon` utility in managed cloud services. However, you can use the `sys.dm_os_performance_counters` view to get SQL Server performance counters.

Finally, you can read about several other Azure-specific dynamic management views in the Microsoft documentation (*https://oreil.ly/ZG09I*). The `sys.event_log` view in SQL Database can replace the SQL Server Error Log to provide connection-related information and data about deadlocks.

Amazon SQL Server RDS

Amazon AWS offers several database technologies as part of its managed Relational Database Services (RDS) family. It supports multiple versions of SQL Server, starting with the soon-to-be-obsolete SQL Server 2012. You can choose any SQL Server edition, including SQL Server Express.

Conceptually, SQL Server RDS is similar to Azure SQL MI: you deal with virtualized SQL Server instances that may host multiple databases. There are some limitations: for example, SQL Server RDS does not support `FILESTREAM` or `UNSAFE CLR`. However, most SQL Server features are supported.

SQL Server RDS supports multi-AZ deployment for HA. In this mode, RDS creates another SQL Server instance in a different AZ, using either Availability Groups or Database Mirroring with synchronous replication. Because AZs are completely isolated from each other, this may lead to additional commit latency that can cause issues in highly transactional systems.

In Enterprise Edition, you can create in-region read replicas to scale the read workload. RDS uses asynchronous Availability Groups replication to support them internally. Unfortunately, multiregion replicas are not supported, so you can't use RDS if your system needs to survive a region-level outage.

Some SQL Server RDS administration tasks, including bringing databases online and offline, renaming databases, and enabling Change Data Capture (CDC), require specific stored procedures that are provided in the rdsadmin and msdb databases. One noteworthy procedure is rds_read_error_log, which replaces the xp_readerrorlog procedure. Read the AWS documentation (*https://oreil.ly/TnISI*) for a full list of tasks and stored procedures to cover them.

The AWS Console provides several tools for at-a-glance monitoring. Here we'll look at cloudWatch and Performance Insights. Another tool, Enhanced Monitoring, collects data on memory and storage utilization within the virtual instance. While it's important, the data is pretty basic, so this section will focus on the other two.

CloudWatch

CloudWatch provides data on overall resource utilization collected at the Hypervisor level, including CPU load, I/O and network throughput, and storage utilization (see Figure 16-9). High resource utilization indicates that the instance is overloaded and should be upgraded or tuned.

Pay attention to I/O metrics: storage performance often becomes the main bottleneck in the cloud. This is especially important if you provision your RDS instance using General Purpose disks. That storage type comes with burstable credits to offset spikes in I/O workload. However, disk performance will be heavily throttled when credits are exhausted, which presents as intermittent performance issues in SQL Server. Consider switching to provisioned IOPS disks, which are more expensive but offer predictable performance.

Figure 16-9. CloudWatch metrics

Performance Insights

Performance Insights is the most comprehensive monitoring tool, with several types of data. First, it gives you subsets of the OS and SQL Server performance counters (Figure 16-10), much like the PerfMon utility.

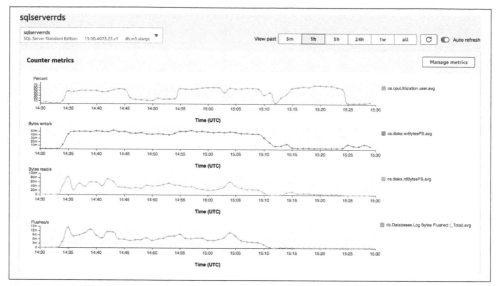

Figure 16-10. Performance Insights: performance counters

The second graph shows detailed information about the database load over time. You can group the data by wait type, SQL, and user and host information, as shown in Figure 16-11.

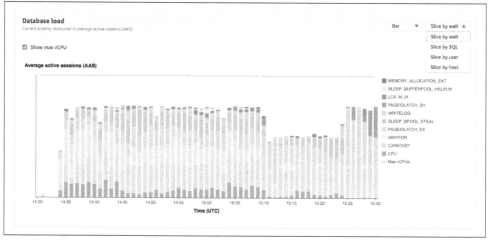

Figure 16-11. Performance Insights: database load information

The third graph, another projection of the database load, shows the most expensive database queries (Figure 16-12), top waits, and most active users.

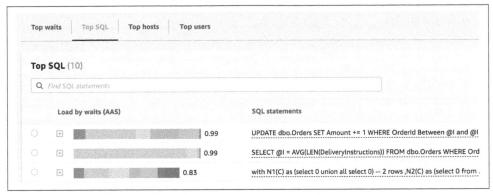

Figure 16-12. Performance Insights: most expensive queries

Overall, Performance Insight's capabilities are on par with SQL Server's basic performance monitoring utilities. It is useful for quick troubleshooting, when you need to evaluate general server health and pinpoint the worst-performing queries.

Standard SQL Server troubleshooting techniques work just fine in RDS. You can query DMVs, use Query Store, and utilize xEvents just as you would in regular SQL Server instances. With xEvents, you can use the event_file target to save data to the *D:\RDSDATA\LOG* folder.

Google Cloud SQL

Like Amazon AWS and Microsoft Azure, Google includes managed database services in its platform offering. Google SQL supports SQL Server much like Amazon RDS and Azure SQL MI do, providing a virtualized SQL Server instance where you can create multiple databases.

Google Cloud Platform provides HA support by maintaining a standby instance of SQL Server in another AZ by performing storage-level replication. There is no overhead from AlwaysOn Availability Group replication; however, storage is replicated synchronously, which may lead to commit latency similar to that of other technologies. With Enterprise Edition, you can also provision read replicas, which use AlwaysOn Availability Groups under the hood.

Google officially started to support SQL Server in its cloud SQL family in 2021, and its monitoring and troubleshooting toolset were not yet mature as of December 2021, when this was written. The Google Cloud Platform UI's monitoring tools are quite simple and limited to basic resource utilization metrics (see Figure 16-13). That said, I expect it to improve over time until it is on par with other database technologies the platform provides.

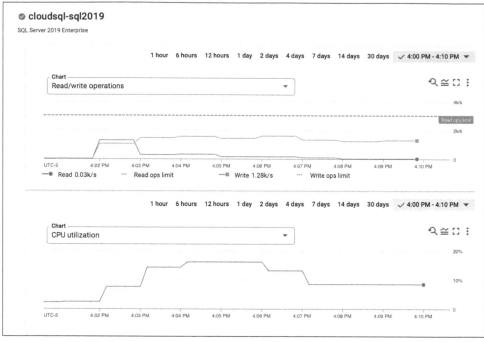

Figure 16-13. Google Cloud SQL resource utilization graphs

You can use third-party monitoring tools or troubleshoot using native SQL Server features, such as DMVs and Query Store. There is one critical limitation, however: the administrator login provided by the platform does *not* have permissions to create xEvents or SQL Traces.

Summary

All major cloud providers allow you to run SQL Server in cloud VMs and offer managed database services that take care of HA, backups, and SQL Server/OS maintenance. All of these offerings use the SQL Server Engine under the hood and allow you to use the same troubleshooting and tuning techniques you use with regular on-premises SQL Server instances.

Each provider gives you access to a cloud console to monitor resource utilization of SQL Server VM or managed database instances. High resource utilization will lead to performance throttling, which you can address by tuning the system or upgrading the instance.

Pay specific attention to storage subsystem performance. Use storage with guaranteed performance for database workloads. If you run SQL Server in a cloud VM, consider building RAID-0 arrays in the OS, which may give you a better cost/performance ratio than individual disks.

Regardless of what you choose, make sure your applications are resilient and can handle transient errors. Outages will happen, and applications should recover from them.

When you build a multiregion system, take cross-region communication latency into account. Do not use synchronous replication across the regions. Batch T-SQL operations to reduce the number of cross-region calls, and do not use readable secondaries if you need up-to-date data.

Troubleshooting Checklist

☐ Evaluate whether the database instance's HA setup can meet the required SLA if there is a disaster at the AZ or region level.

☐ Review your instance setup and resource utilization, paying particular attention to storage setup and performance.

☐ Validate your index/statistics maintenance strategies, even with managed services.

☐ Perform general SQL Server health checks just as you would with a regular on-premises instance.

Thank you again for reading this book! I hope you enjoyed it. SQL Server is a great technology, and troubleshooting and tuning it is one of the most exciting and rewarding parts of our job. It has been a pleasure and honor to write for you.

Wait Types

This appendix provides a list of the most common wait types you'll encounter during troubleshooting. It outlines conditions when the waits may occur and gives you some tips on high-level troubleshooting strategy.

Do not consider this appendix to be a replacement for the Microsoft documentation (*https://oreil.ly/6oto3*) or the SQLSkills Wait Types Library (*https://oreil.ly/Wt5Mx*). Nevertheless, it should work as good reference material within the book.

ASYNC_IO_COMPLETION

The `ASYNC_IO_COMPLETION` wait occurs during asynchronous I/O operations not related to the buffer pool. Common cases include:

- Regular checkpoint
- Internal checkpoint when you start a database backup or run `DBCC CHECKDB`
- Reading GAM pages from data files
- Reading data pages from the database during a database backup (unfortunately, this tends to skew the average wait time, making it harder to analyze)

A noticeable percentage of `ASYNC_IO_COMPLETION` waits may indicate an overloaded I/O subsystem, especially when it is present with other I/O-related waits. Perform I/O system troubleshooting (see `PAGEIOLATCH` waits later in this appendix).

See Chapter 3 for additional details.

ASYNC_NETWORK_IO

The ASYNC_NETWORK_IO wait occurs when SQL Server waits for a client to consume data. Three common cases may trigger this wait:

- A slow network, often when clients are connected to the database server in another datacenter or in the cloud

- Client applications running in under-provisioned virtual machines (VMs) or on overloaded servers

- Incorrect application design when the client processes data in row-by-row fashion

This wait does not always indicate issues on the server. Nevertheless, insufficient client communication consumes workers and other SQL Server resources. You may want to troubleshoot when you see a significant percentage of these waits in the system.

For the troubleshooting:

- Check network performance on the server, looking at network performance counters and other available key performance indicators (KPIs).

- Detect client applications that generate waits using the sys.dm _os_waiting_tasks, sys.dm_exec_requests, sys.dm_exec_sessions, and sys.dm_exec_connections views (you can use Listing 2-3). For short-time profiling, use the wait_completed xEvent capturing the sqlserver.client_host name and sqlserver.client_app_name actions.

- Review application code and the performance of application servers.

See Chapters 13 and 16 for additional details.

BACKUPBUFFER

See the BACKUPIO wait type.

BACKUPIO

The BACKUPIO and BACKUPBUFFER waits indicate insufficient backup/restore through-put. They may occur due to slow or overloaded network and/or disk subsystems. In the latter case, it is common to see them together with other I/O-related waits.

When you see backup-related waits, troubleshoot the performance of the backup process. Analyze disk and network subsystem performance. Consider implementing backup compression, stripe backups, and tune backup options.

See Chapter 13 for additional details.

BTREE_INSERT_FLOW_CONTROL

The BTREE_INSERT_FLOW_CONTROL wait indicates the existence of indexes with ever-increasing keys that introduce hotspots. This wait replaces some of the PAGELATCH waits when you enable the OPTIMIZE_FOR_SEQUENTIAL_KEY index option.

Check troubleshooting notes for PAGELATCH waits and see Chapter 10 for additional details.

CXCONSUMER

The CXPACKET, CXCONSUMER, and EXCHANGE waits occur during execution of the queries with parallel execution plans. See the CXPACKET wait for additional information and Chapter 6 for an in-depth discussion.

CXPACKET

The CXPACKET, CXCONSUMER, and EXCHANGE waits occur during execution of the queries with parallel execution plans. These waits are completely normal and are expected to be present, especially in systems with data warehouse/reporting workloads. In OLTP systems, however, an excessive number of parallelism waits may require investigation.

Parallelism waits do not present problems by themselves—they are just a sign of expensive queries that use parallel execution plans. In OLTP systems, detect (Chapter 4) and optimize (Chapter 5) queries. Tune parallelism settings. Do not set MAX DOP=1 as this just hides the problem.

See Chapter 6 for additional details.

DIRTY_PAGE_TABLE_LOCK

The DIRTY_PAGE_TABLE_LOCK, DPT_ENTRY_LOCK, PARALLEL_REDO_FLOW_CONTROL, and PARALLEL_REDO_TRAN_TURN waits may occur on readable secondary nodes in AlwaysOn Availability Groups.

A large number of these waits may be a sign of issues with the parallel redo process. When this happens, you could see the waits present in sys.dm_os_waiting_tasks and sys.dm_exec_requests views along with elevated CPU load and redo queue growth. As of now, the only mitigation options I am aware of are patching SQL Server and/or disabling parallel redo with the T3459 trace flag.

See Chapter 12 for additional details.

DPT_ENTRY_LOCK

See the `DIRTY_PAGE_TABLE_LOCK` wait type.

EXCHANGE

The `CXPACKET`, `CXCONSUMER`, and `EXCHANGE` waits occur during execution of the queries with parallel execution plans. See the `CXPACKET` wait for additional information and Chapter 6 for an in-depth discussion.

HADR_GROUP_COMMIT

The `HADR_GROUP_COMMIT` wait occurs when the primary AlwaysOn Availability Group node is trying to optimize replication performance by grouping multiple commit log records together before sending them to secondary nodes.

I rarely see this wait become problematic. If you see a high percentage of this wait type and notice some impact in system transaction throughput, troubleshoot the performance of AlwaysOn replication (see the `HADR_SYNC_COMMIT` wait). You can also disable group commit with the `T9546` trace flag.

See Chapter 12 for additional details.

HADR_SYNC_COMMIT

The `HADR_SYNC_COMMIT` wait occurs when the primary AlwaysOn Availability Group node is waiting for synchronous secondaries to harden transaction log records. These waits always present in Availability Groups that use synchronous replication.

Analyze the average wait time of these waits. It should be as small as possible and should not exceed a few milliseconds when synchronous replicas reside in the same datacenter with the primary node. If you see larger numbers, investigate the performance of the replication, paying attention to network latency and throughput, disk performance, and general load on synchronous replicas.

The transactions stay active with all locks held until the primary node receives the confirmation that the `COMMIT` t-log record is hardened on synchronous secondaries. Thus, high `HADR_SYNC_COMMIT` wait time may contribute to blocking in the system.

See Chapter 12 for additional details.

HTBUILD

The HTBUILD, HTDELETE, HTMEMO, HTREINIT, and HTREPARTITION waits occur during management of internal hash tables in batch-mode execution. In environments with columnstore indexes, these waits may indicate poorly maintained columnstore indexes with large delta stores and/or unevenly sized rowgroups. Analyze the rowgroups state with the sys.column_store_row_group view and rebuild the indexes as needed.

See Chapter 13 for additional details.

HTDELETE, HTMEMO, HTREINIT, and HTREPARTITION

See the HTBUILD wait type.

IO_COMPLETION

The IO_COMPLETION wait type occurs during synchronous reads from and writes to data files, and during some read operations in the transaction log. Here are a few examples:

- Reading allocation map pages from the database
- Reading the transaction log during database recovery
- Writing data to tempdb during sort spills

A noticeable percentage of IO_COMPLETION waits may indicate an overloaded I/O subsystem, especially when present with other I/O-related waits. Perform I/O system troubleshooting (see the PAGEIOLATCH wait). Pay specific attention to tempdb latency and throughput; bad tempdb performance is one of the most common reasons for this wait.

See Chapters 3 and 9 for additional details.

LATCH_*

The waits with a name starting with (LATCH_) are triggered by latches that are not related to the buffer pool. SQL Server generates different LATCH waits depending on the type of the latches (shared, exclusive, etc.).

You can use the sys.dm_os_latch_stats view to get latch statistics and details and to analyze possible bottlenecks.

See Chapter 10 for additional details.

LCK_M_*

The waits with a name starting with (LCK_M_) occur during blocking. Each lock type in SQL Server has a corresponding wait type.

Analyze when the lock type is used, and detect and address the root cause of the blocking.

This appendix provides additional details for the LCK_M_I*, LCK_M_R*, LCK_M_S, LCK_M_SCH_M, LCK_M_SCH_S, LCK_M_U, and LCK_M_X wait types.

See Chapter 8 for additional details.

LCK_M_I*

SQL Server acquires intent locks (LCK_M_I*) at the object (table) and page levels. At the table level, this usually occurs under two conditions:

- Incompatibility with schema modification locks. In this case, you'd usually also see schema lock waits (LCK_M_SCH_S and LCK_M_SCH_M) present. See the LCK_M_SCH_M wait for more details.
- A full incompatible table-level lock held by another session. This typically occurs due to lock escalations or a code that uses TABLOCK and TABLOCKX hints. You can use the Blocking Monitoring Framework and the sys.dm_index_opera tional_stats view (Chapter 14) for lock escalation troubleshooting.

Intent lock waits due to blocking on the page level usually indicate nonoptimized queries and scans. Analyze individual blocking cases to find the root cause of the blocking.

See Chapter 8 for additional details.

LCK_M_R*

The LCK_M_R wait type indicates waits for range locks. SQL Server acquires them in the SERIALIZABLE isolation level. Another possibility is the existence of nonclustered indexes that have the IGNORE_DUP_KEY=ON option set.

When you see these waits, identify and address the root cause of the blocking. Avoid using the IGNORE_DUP_KEY=ON option in nonclustered indexes. Do not use the SERIALIZABLE isolation level unless absolutely necessary.

See Chapter 8 for additional details.

LCK_M_S

The LCK_M_S wait type indicates waits for shared (S) locks. This lock type is acquired by SELECT queries in READ COMMITTED, REPEATABLE READ, and SERIALIZABLE isolation levels. Nonoptimized SELECT queries are the most common case for these waits.

When you see a large number of these waits, focus on query optimization (Chapter 5). When queries are running in the READ COMMITTED isolation level, consider enabling the READ_COMMITTED_SNAPSHOT database option and eliminate reader/writer blocking (this would hide rather than solve the problem with nonoptimized queries).

See Chapter 8 for additional details.

LCK_M_SCH_M

The LCK_M_SCH_M wait type indicates waits for the schema modification (Sch-M) locks when sessions cannot obtain exclusive locks for the objects.

When you see these waits, evaluate your deployment strategy for database changes. Also, look at index and partition maintenance strategies; they both require acquiring table locks during execution. Consider using low-priority locks during an index rebuild and a partition switch when the feature is supported. Finally, analyze individual blocking cases to identify the root cause.

Check how often these waits occur. They may be triggered by one-off events and mistakes during deployment.

See Chapter 8 for additional details.

LCK_M_SCH_S

The LCK_M_SCH_S wait type indicates waits for schema stability (Sch-S) locks. This type of blocking occurs during schema modifications when other sessions held schema modification (Sch-M) locks on the objects.

See the LCK_M_SCH_M wait type troubleshooting strategy and Chapter 8 for additional details.

LCK_M_U

The LCK_M_U wait type indicates a wait for update (U) locks. SQL Server acquires them during update scans usually caused by nonoptimized writer queries (UPDATE, DELETE, MERGE). In many cases, you'll see them alongside the PAGEIOLATCH* and CXPACKET wait types.

When you see a large number of these waits, focus on query optimization (Chapter 5).

See Chapter 8 for additional details.

LCK_M_X

The LCK_M_X wait type indicates waits for exclusive (X) locks. The most typical cases for these waits include artificial serialization points (counters table), excessive usage of the REPEATABLE READ and SERIALIZABLE isolation levels, inefficient transaction management and long-running transactions, and table-level locking hints such as (TABLOCKX).

When you see a large number of these waits, analyze individual blocking cases and find the root causes of the blocking.

See Chapter 8 for additional details.

LOGBUFFER

The LOGBUFFER wait occurs when SQL Server waits for an available log buffer to write log records. Usually, this wait is present together with the WRITELOG wait and indicates insufficient transaction log throughput. See the WRITELOG wait for troubleshooting steps.

See Chapters 3 and 11 for additional details.

OLEDB

The OLEDB waits occur when SQL Server waits for data from an OLE DB provider. Most often it happens in the following cases:

- Calls to linked servers
- Execution of some SQL Server Integration Services (SSIS) packages
- Operations during DBCC CHECKDB execution
- Queries against dynamic management views (DMVs)

These waits may not always represent the problem. However, detect what triggered them and evaluate their impact.

See Chapter 13 for additional details.

PAGEIOLATCH*

PAGEIOLATCH* waits occur when SQL Server reads data pages from disk. These waits are very common and are present in most systems. There are six PAGEIOLATCH wait types that belong to different kinds of operations with buffer pool pages. Analyze all of them together to estimate the cumulative impact of PAGEIOLATCH waits.

An excessive number of PAGEIOLATCH waits shows that SQL Server is constantly reading data from disk. This usually occurs under two circumstances:

- Under-provisioned SQL Server, when the active data does not fit into memory
- Presence of nonoptimized queries that scan unnecessary data, flushing the contents of the buffer pool

You can cross-check the data by looking at the Page Life Expectancy performance counter, which shows how long data pages stay in the buffer pool.

A substantial percentage of PAGEIOLATCH waits always requires troubleshooting. While it does not always introduce customer-facing problems, especially with low-latency flash-based drives, the data growth may push the disk subsystem over the limit, quickly becoming a problem that affects the entire system.

For troubleshooting:

- Review the performance and latency of the disk subsystem with the sys.dm_io_virtual_file_stats view (Listing 3-1).
- Check if the high latency is caused by bursts in I/O activity by analyzing the SQL Server and OS performance counters. Tune the checkpoint process if necessary.
- Analyze the entire I/O stack and detect bottlenecks.
- Detect and tune the most I/O-intensive queries (Chapters 4 and 5).
- Analyze index metrics (Chapter 14) if you need to detect indexes that trigger most of those waits and/or find the largest buffer pool consumers.

See Chapters 3 and 15 for additional details.

PAGELATCH

The PAGELATCH waits indicate latches related to the buffer pool, which occur when threads need to simultaneously access or modify data and allocation map pages in the buffer pool. There are two main cases for those waits: contention in the tempdb system pages and hotspots in ever-increasing indexes.

When you see these waits, identify what triggers them. Check if they occurred in tempdb by analyzing the `wait_resource` column in the `sys.dm_os_waiting_tasks` view. Alternatively, you can capture the `sqlserver.latch_suspend_end` xEvent. For tempdb latches, make sure tempdb is configured correctly, reduce tempdb load, and consider enabling memory-optimized tempdb metadata if this is supported.

You can identify indexes that have hotspots with the `sys.dm_db_index_opera tional_stats` function. In SQL Server 2019 and later, you can reduce contention by enabling the `OPTIMIZE_FOR_SEQUENTIAL_KEY` index setting. You can also refactor the schema, implement hash partitioning, or utilize In-Memory OLTP.

See Chapters 9 and 10 for additional details.

PARALLEL_REDO_FLOW_CONTROL

See the `DIRTY_PAGE_TABLE_LOCK` wait type.

PARALLEL_REDO_TRAN_TURN

See the `DIRTY_PAGE_TABLE_LOCK` wait type.

PREEMPTIVE_OS_ACCEPTSECURITYCONTEXT

See the `PREEMPTIVE_OS_AUTH*` waits.

PREEMPTIVE_OS_AUTH*

The waits with names starting with `PREEMPTIVE_OS_AUTH`, along with the `PRE EMPTIVE_OS_LOOKUPACCOUNTSID` and `PREEMPTIVE_OS_ACCEPTSECURITYCONTEXT` waits, occur during user authentication.

When you see a significant percentage of these waits, check the performance of Active Directory controllers. Make sure SQL Server does not authenticate against Active Directory controllers in remote datacenters.

Also, check if the code is using an `EXECUTE AS OWNER` or `EXECUTE AS USER` context, which triggers authentication calls.

See Chapter 13 for additional details.

PREEMPTIVE_OS_LOOKUPACCOUNTSID

See the `PREEMPTIVE_OS_AUTH*` waits.

PREEMPTIVE_OS_WRITEFILE

The `PREEMPTIVE_OS_WRITEFILE` waits may indicate a bottleneck during synchronous writes to the files. When you see these waits, check if the server runs multiple SQL Traces or SQL audits using files as the targets to save the data. Also, check for the existence of database snapshots; they are another reason for these waits to appear.

See Chapter 13 for additional details.

PREEMPTIVE_OS_WRITEFILEGATHER

The `PREEMPTIVE_OS_WRITEFILEGATHER` wait occurs during the zero-initializing process. When you see this wait in the system, check and enable instant file initialization by granting *Perform volume management tasks* (`SE_MANAGE_VOLUME_NAME`) permission to the SQL Server startup account.

Review the transaction log's auto-growth parameters and check that there are no processes that regularly shrink the transaction log.

See Chapter 13 for additional details.

QDS*

The family of wait types starting with `QDS` are Query Store related. They may be a sign of the overhead introduced by Query Store data collection. Ignore `QDS_PERSIST_TASK_MAIN_LOOP_SLEEP` and `QDS_ASYNC_QUEUE` waits; they are benign.

When you see other `QDS` waits, check Query Store settings. Do not use the `QUERY_CAPTURE_MODE=ALL` data collection mode. Reduce the Query Store size if it is large. Also, enable the T7745 and T7752 trace flags.

See Chapter 4 for additional details.

RESOURCE_SEMAPHORE

The `RESOURCE_SEMAPHORE` wait occurs when queries wait for memory grants to execute. This wait type is always worth investigating when you see it become noticeable in the system.

When you see this wait, analyze memory usage in SQL Server. Check memory usage of memory clerks looking for the signs of external and internal memory pressure. Check the behavior of the balloon driver in virtualized environments. Validate that the server has been properly provisioned and SQL Server is correctly configured to handle the load.

It is also possible that RESOURCE_SEMAPHORE waits are triggered by specific queries. Analyze memory grant sizes with the sys.dm_exec_query_memory_grants view and optimize queries if needed.

See Chapter 7 for additional details.

RESOURCE_SEMAPHORE_QUERY_COMPILE

The RESOURCE_SEMAPHORE_QUERY_COMPILE wait occurs when SQL Server does not have enough memory to compile the queries. As with the RESOURCE_SEMAPHORE wait, this requires investigation.

Check if SQL Server performs excessive compilations with the SQL Compilations/ sec and SQL Recompilations/sec performance counters. Reduce compilations by parameterizing queries (Chapter 6). Perform general memory usage troubleshooting as described in the RESOURCE_SEMAPHORE wait.

I've also seen RESOURCE_SEMAPHORE_QUERY_COMPILE occur when very a active table had a (Sch-M) lock held during a prolonged offline index rebuild process. In parallel, SQL Server tried to recompile the large number of queries that accessed that table. The compilations were blocked and eventually consumed a large amount of memory, leaving other compilation requests to wait with that wait type.

See Chapter 7 for additional details.

THREADPOOL

The THREADPOOL wait occurs when SQL Server does not have available workers to handle user requests. This is a dangerous wait that needs to be investigated.

The most common cases when this wait may occur are as follows:

- Incorrect *max worker threads* configuration setting
- Insufficient amount of SQL Server memory (check OS and SQL Server configuration)
- Long blocking chains
- Excessive memory pressure
- Large number of connected clients
- Workload with excessive number of queries with parallel execution plans

In cloud environments, these waits may indicate that a database is running on an under-provisioned cloud service that cannot handle the load.

See Chapters 13 and 16 for additional details.

WRITE_COMPLETION

The `WRITE_COMPLETION` wait occurs during synchronous write operations to data and log files. In my experience, it is most common with database snapshots.

When you see this wait in the system, check if there are database snapshots present. Remember that some internal processes, like `DBCC CHECKDB`, create internal database snapshots.

When the `IO_COMPLETION` wait is present with other I/O-related waits, perform I/O system troubleshooting (see the `PAGEIOLATCH` waits).

See Chapter 3 for additional details.

WRITELOG

The `WRITELOG` wait occurs when SQL Server writes log records to the transaction log. It is normal to see this wait in any system; however, a significant percentage of this wait and/or a long average wait time may indicate a transaction log bottleneck. You can often see this wait together with `LOGBUFFER` waits, which is another sign of a bottleneck.

For troubleshooting, analyze the average wait time and transaction log write latency with the `sys.dm_io_virtual_file_stats` view (Listing 3-1). High numbers are impactful and may affect throughput in the system. Troubleshoot the performance of the transaction log (Chapter 11) and perform I/O system troubleshooting (see the `PAGEIOLATCH` waits).

See Chapters 3 and 11 for additional details.

Index

Symbols

or # in temporary table names, 264

A

ACCESS_METHODS_HOBT_COUNT latch, 305

ACCESS_METHODS_HOBT_VIRTUAL_ROOT latch, 304

ACID (atomicity, consistency, isolation, durability), 220

Active Temp Tables performance counter, 282

ACTIVE_BACKUP_OR_RESTORE log reuse wait, 326

ACTIVE_TRANSACTION log reuse wait, 323

ADR (accelerated database recovery), transaction log, 326

affinity I/O mask, setting, 46

affinity mask, setting, 13

allocation maps, 18

allocation order scan, index, 111

allocation units, 107

ALLOW_BATCH_MODE query hint, 133

ALLOW_SNAPSHOT_ISOLATION database option, 245

ALTER DATABASE SCOPED CONFIGURATION SET MAXDOP command, 14

ALTER DATABASE SET ACCELERATED_DATABASE_RECOVERY database option, 327

ALTER DATABASE SET ALLOW_SNAPSHOT_ISOLATION ON command, 245

ALTER DATABASE SET AUTOMATIC_TUNING (FORCE_LAST_GOOD_PLAN = ON) statement, 168

ALTER DATABASE SET PARAMETERIZATION FORCED command, 177

ALTER DATABASE SET READ_COMMITTED_SNAPSHOT ON/OFF command, 245

ALTER DATABASE SET TARGET_RECOVERY_TIME command, 62

ALTER INDEX REBUILD command, 123

ALTER INDEX REORGANIZE command, 122

ALTER TABLE REBUILD statement, 374

ALTER TABLE SET LOCK_ESCALATION statement, 256

ALTER TABLE WITH CHECK CHECK CONSTRAINT command, 379

AlwaysOn Availability Groups, 331-356
   asynchronous replication, 345-349, 442
   Availability Group queues, 333-337
   compression, 344
   failover event troubleshooting, 351-355
   monitoring code, 334-337
   parallel redo process, 350-351
   readable secondaries, 346-349, 433
   separate network for, 4, 416
   synchronous replication, 337-345, 433, 445

AlwaysOn Failover Clusters, separate network for, 5

AlwaysOn_health xEvent session, failover troubleshooting, 353

Amazon SQL Server RDS, 441-445

antivirus software, 6

asynchronous replication, Availability Groups, 345-349, 442

ASYNC_IO_COMPLETION wait, 64, 449

ASYNC_NETWORK_IO wait, 357-359, 450
   cloud environment, 431

compatibility, 224, 232-234
deadlocks, 11, 238-245
escalation, 251-256
index operational statistics, 399
lock types, 221-224
locking-related waits, 256-259, 451, 454-456
low-priority locks, 250
OBJECTSTORE_LOCK_MANAGER memory clerk, 200
optimistic isolation levels, 226, 247-249
schema locks, 249-250
transaction isolation levels, 226-228
types, 249-250
log blocks, 308
log buffers, 308
Log Bytes Flushed/sec performance counter, 328
log file, tempdb, 287
Log Flush Waits/sec performance counter, 328
Log Flush Write Time(ms) performance counter, 328
Log Flushes/sec performance counter, 328
Log Reader agent, 325
log record, 46, 307, 339
LOGBUFFER wait, 312, 328, 456
logical Core (lCore), 409
logical read, 46
logs and logging (see transaction log)
LOG_BACKUP log reuse wait, 323
LOG_MANAGER latch, 304
Longest Transaction Running Time performance counter, 277
loop join, 144-145, 149
low-priority locks, 250
LPIM (Lock Pages In Memory) permission, 189, 414
LSN (Log Sequence Number), 307

M

manual checkpoints, 61
MAXDOP, 14, 181
Maximum Server Memory setting, 13, 188, 189
Maximum Workspace Memory performance counter, 204, 213
MAXTRANSFERSIZE option, 365
MAX_GRANT_PERCENT query hint, 212
memory, 185-217
  allocations, 190-202
  configuration, 188-190

DBCC MEMORYSTATUS command, 202
hardware and OS considerations, 2
In-Memory OLTP (see In-Memory OLTP)
memory clerks, 191-202
memory grants and query execution, 202-213
utilization of, 185-188, 190
virtualized environments, 414, 422-424
memory allocator, 190
memory broker, 191
memory grant feedback, 146, 211, 278
memory grants and query execution, 202-213
  controlling memory grant size, 212-213
  MEMORYCLERK_SQLQERESERVA-TIONS memory clerk, 200
  optimizing memory-intensive queries, 206-211
  properties, 203
Memory Grants Outstanding performance counter, 204
Memory Grants Pending performance counter, 204
Memory Management performance object, 204
Memory Manager, 186
memory nodes, 190
memory objects, 191
Memory Usage by Memory Optimized Objects report, 215
memory-optimized tables (see In-Memory OLTP)
memory-optimized tempdb metadata, 286
MEMORYCLERK_SQLBUFFERPOOL memory clerk, 193-193
MEMORYCLERK_SQLCLR memory clerk, 201
MEMORYCLERK_SQLCLRASSEMBLY memory clerk, 201
MEMORYCLERK_SQLCONNECTIONPOOL memory clerk, 201
MEMORYCLERK_SQLEXTENSIBILITY memory clerk, 201
MEMORYCLERK_SQLQERESERVATIONS memory clerk, 200, 204
MEMORYCLERK_XTP memory clerk, 201, 215
Memory\Available Mbytes performance counter, 423
merge join, 145, 149
Microsoft Azure SQL managed services, 435-441

About the Author

Dmitri Korotkevitch is a Microsoft Data Platform MVP and Microsoft Certified Master (SQL Server) with years of IT experience, including years of experience working with Microsoft SQL Server as an application and database developer, database administrator, and database architect.

Dmitri specializes in the design, development, and performance tuning of complex OLTP systems that handle thousands of transactions per second around the clock. Currently, he leads the Database Services team at Chewy.com and he provides SQL Server consulting services and trainings to clients around the world.

Dmitri regularly speaks at various SQL Server events. He blogs at *aboutsqlserver.com*, rarely tweets as @aboutsqlserver and he can be reached at *dk@aboutsqlserver.com*.

Colophon

The animal on the cover of *SQL Server Advanced Troubleshooting and Performance Tuning* is a western burrowing owl (*Athene cunicularia*). Owls in the *Athene* genus are known as the "little owls," and their name represents the little owl that was traditionally associated with the Greek goddess Athena. The burrowing owl is small, but has longer legs than most owls. It is found in North and South America, and, as its common name suggests, they live in burrows in open areas, rather than in trees like most owls.

There are 16 extant subspecies of the burrowing owl. There are slight differences in appearance among them, but most have brown heads and wings, with white spots, prominent white eyebrows, and a white chin patch. The chest and abdomen are white, with variable brown patterns depending on the subspecies. Juveniles look similar, but lack the white spotting. Males and females are similar in appearance, but males are lighter in color because they spend more time outside during the day and their feather color is faded by the sun.

The owls often nest in burrows made by ground squirrels. If they can't find a burrow, and the soil is suitable, they will dig their own. Pairs will usually mate for life. The female lays from 4 to 12 eggs per clutch and incubates them for 3 to 4 weeks. After the eggs hatch, both parents share in feeding the chicks. They eat mostly small rodents and large insects. They also eat fruit and seeds, unlike other owls.

The burrowing owl is endangered in Canada and threatened in Mexico and some US states. However, they are widespread in open regions of South America and therefore have a conservation status of least concern. Many of the animals on O'Reilly covers are endangered; all of them are important to the world.

The cover illustration is by Karen Montgomery, based on an antique line engraving from *Brehms Thierleben*. The cover fonts are Gilroy Semibold and Guardian Sans. The text font is Adobe Minion Pro; the heading font is Adobe Myriad Condensed; and the code font is Dalton Maag's Ubuntu Mono.